A

POLITICAL AND CIVIL HISTORY

OF THE

UNITED STATES OF AMERICA,

FROM THE YEAR 1763

TO THE CLOSE OF THE ADMINISTRATION

OF PRESIDENT WASHINGTON, IN MARCH, 1797:

INCLUDING

A SUMMARY VIEW OF THE

POLITICAL AND CIVIL STATE

OF THE

NORTH AMERICAN COLONIES, PRIOR TO THAT PERIOD.

BY TIMOTHY PITKIN.

IN TWO VOLUMES.

VOL. II.

NEW HAVEN:

PUBLISHED BY HEZEKIAH HOWE AND DURRIE & PECK.

1828.

DISTRICT OF CONNECTICUT, to wit:

L. S. Be it remembered, That on the twenty-third day of January, in the fifty-second year of the Independence of the United States of America, A. D. 1828, TIMOTHY PITKIN, of the said District, hath deposited in this Office the Title of a Book, the right whereof he claims as author ; in the words following—to wit :

" A Political and Civil History of the United States of America, from the year 1763 to the close of the administration of President Washington, in March, 1797 : including a summary view of the Political and Civil state of the North American Colonies, prior to that period. By TIMOTHY PITKIN. In two volumes."

In conformity to the act of the Congress of the United States, entitled " An act for the encouragement of learning, by securing the copies of maps, charts, and books, to the authors and proprietors of such copies, during the times therein mentioned"--and also to the act entitled " An act supplementary to an act entitled ' An act for the encouragement of learning, by securing the copies of maps, charts, and books, to the authors and proprietors of such copies, during the times therein mentioned,' and extending the benefits thereof to the arts of designing, engraving, and etching historical and other prints."

CHAS. A. INGERSOLL,
Clerk of the District of Connecticut.

CONTENTS.

CHAPTER XV.

* Inserted xvi. by mistake.

CHAPTER XIX.

CHAPTER XX.

CHAPTER XXI.

CHAPTER XXII.

CHAPTER XXIII.

APPENDIX.

CONTENTS.

ERRATA.

Page 36, in 12th line from the top read *Maryland* for "Delaware."
" 123, at the bottom, read *wild* for "western."
" 279, in the 8th line from the bottom, read 79 for "80," and in the 9th line, for "88" read 89.
" 323, in the 18th line from the top, before the word esteem, read *their* for "your."
" 330, in the second line from the top, insert "*in*" between the words " and its."
" 498, in the 8th line from the top, read *charter* for "charters."

☞The reader will observe that four or five notes referred to, are not in the appendix. We had originally intended to insert them, but from their length, they would make the second volume considerably larger than the first, and as the substance of them is contained in the body of the work, they have been omitted.

HISTORY, &c.

---◆---

CHAPTER XI.

Outlines of the plan of confederacy submitted to congress by Dr. Franklin, July, 1775
—Not acted upon—June 11th, 1776, congress appoint a committee of one from a
state to prepare a plan of confederation—Plan reported July following—Is debated
in congress at various times until the 15th of November, 1777, when it is adopted
—Outlines of the system—Congress divided as to terms of union—Particularly the
mode of voting in congress, the rule of apportioning expenses among the states,
and the disposition of the western lands—Articles sent to the several states with a
circular letter—Adopted by some states without amendment—Principal amendments
proposed by several states—All the states except New Jersey, Delaware and Maryland, instruct their delegates to ratify and sign the articles, if their amendments
should be rejected by congress—Objections of New Jersey—Congress nearly equally divided on the amendment proposed about the western lands—Articles ratified
by New Jersey and Delaware—Maryland gives special instructions to her delegates
not to ratify them, without an amendment securing the western lands for the benefit
of the union—These instructions laid before congress—States of Virginia and Connecticut empower their delegates to agree to the confederacy, exclusive of Maryland
—Other states unwilling to do this—Compromise about the western lands—New
York cedes for the benefit of the union her claim to lands west of a certain line—
Congress recommend to the other states to make liberal cessions for the same purpose—Virginia cedes her right to the country north west of the Ohio—Maryland
accedes to the union, and the articles signed by her delegates March first, 1781—
the union then completed.

It will be remembered, that in the summer of 1775, Dr. Franklin submitted to congress, articles of confederation and perpetual
union among the colonies, but which were not finally acted upon.
A majority in that body were not then prepared for so decisive
a step. The purport of his plan was, that the colonies entered
" into a firm league of friendship with each other, binding on
themselves and their posterity, for the common defense against
their enemies, for the security of their liberties and properties,

the safety of their persons and families, and their mutual and general welfare."

Each colony was to retain its own laws, customs, rights, privileges and peculiar jurisdiction; delegates to be chosen from each colony annually, to meet in congress; and their sessions were to be held in each colony by rotation; congress to have the power of determining on war and peace; sending and receiving ambassadors, and entering into alliances (the reconciliation with Great Britain;) settling disputes and differences between colony and colony about limits or any other cause; and the planting of new colonies, when proper. To have power "to make such general ordinances as, though necessary to the general welfare, particular assemblies cannot be competent to use; those that may relate to general commerce, or general currency; the establishment of posts; and the regulation of the common forces: And the appointment of all general officers, civil and military, appertaining to the general confederacy."

The charges of war, and all other general expenses incurred for the common welfare, to be defrayed out of a common treasury, to be supplied by each colony, in proportion to its number of male polls between sixteen and sixty years of age; the taxes for paying such proportion to be laid and levied by each colony.

The number of delegates from each colony was to be regulated, from time to time, by the number of such polls returned, one delegate to be allowed for every five thousand polls, and the number to be taken triennially. One half of the members, "inclusive of proxies," to be necessary for a quorum, and each delegate to have a vote in all cases, and if absent, might appoint any other delegate from the same colony, his proxy, to vote for him.

An executive council was to be appointed by congress out of their own body, to consist of twelve persons; of whom in the first appointment, one third, viz. "four shall be for one year, four for two years, and four for three years; and as the said terms expire, the vacancies shall be filled by appointments for three years; whereby one third of the members will be changed annually."

"This council, (two thirds to be a quorum in the recess of congress,) are to execute what shall have been enjoined by that body;

to manage the general continental business, and interests; to receive applications from foreign countries; to prepare matters for the consideration of congress; to fill up, pro tempore, continental offices that fall vacant; and to draw on the general treasurer for such moneys as may be necessary for general services, and appropriated by the congress to such services."

No colony to engage in offensive war with any nation of Indians without the consent of congress. A perpetual alliance, offensive and defensive, was to be entered into with the six nations of Indians; their limits to be ascertained and their lands secured to them, not encroached upon, nor any purchases made of them by any colony. The boundaries and lands of all the other Indians to be ascertained and secured in the same manner; and persons to be appointed to reside among them, and prevent injustice in the trade with them, and to relieve at the general expense, " by occasional and small supplies," their personal wants and distresses. And all purchases from them to be by congress, for the general advantage and benefit of the United States. Congress was empowered from time to time, to propose amendments, which, if approved by a majority of the colony assemblies, to be binding.

The other British colonies upon the continent of North America, were permitted to join the confederacy. These articles, if approved by the several provincial conventions or assemblies, were " to continue firm till the terms of reconciliation proposed in the petition of the last congress to the king are agreed to; till the acts since made, restraining the American commerce and fisheries are repealed; till reparation is made for the injury done to Boston, by shutting up its port; for the burning of Charlestown; and for the expense of this unjust war, and till all the British troops are withdrawn from America. On the arrival of these events, the colonies will return to their former connexion and friendship with Britain, but on failure thereof, this confederation to be perpetual."

The subject of a compact between the colonies, remained in this situation, until June, 1776. A majority of congress having then come to the resolution of declaring America independent, the necessity of such a compact, as well for mutual security and succor, as for obtaining foreign aid, was obvious.

On the 11th of June 1776, therefore, the day following that, in which the resolution in favor of independence passed in committee of the whole, congress determined to appoint a committee to prepare and digest the form of a confederation ; and the next day, the following gentlemen were selected for this important object.   Mr. Bartlet, from New Hampshire ; Samuel Adams, from Massachusetts ; Mr. Hopkins, from Rhode Island ; Mr. Sherman, from Connecticut ; R. Livingston, from New York ; Mr. Dickinson, from Pennsylvania ; Mr. McKean, from Delaware ; Mr. Stone, from Maryland ; Mr. Nelson, from Virginia ; Mr. Hewes, from North Carolina ; E. Rutledge, from South Carolina ; and Mr. Gwinnett, from Georgia.

This committee, on the 12th of July following, reported a plan of confederacy, consisting of twenty articles.   Eighty copies only were ordered to be printed, and the members, as well as the secretary and printer, were under an injunction not to disclose the contents of it, or furnish copies to any person.   On the 22d of the same month, it was discussed in committee of the whole, and was under consideration, until the 20th of August, when an amended draft was reported to the house.

The difficulty in agreeing upon the details of the system, as well as the gloomy aspect of American affairs at this period, prevented congress from resuming this subject, until April 1777 ; when they resolved, that two days in each week should be employed, " until it shall be wholly discussed."   The amended draft was considered and debated accordingly, until the 26th of June, when it was again postponed to the 2d of October, and was not finally adopted by congress, until the 15th of November, 1777.

The outlines of the system were, that the thirteen states formed a confederacy, under the style and name of " the United States of America ;" by which they entered, " into a firm league of friendship with each other, for their defense, the security of their liberties, and their mutual and general welfare, binding themselves to assist each other against all force offered to, or attacks made upon them, or any of them, on account of religion, sovereignty, trade, or any other pretence whatever."

Each state was to retain its sovereignty, freedom, and independence, and every power, jurisdiction, and right, not expressly delegated to the United States in congress assembled. Delegates were to be annually appointed by each state, not less than three, nor more than seven, to meet in congress, on the first Monday of November, every year ; and each state had a right to recall their delegates within the year, and to appoint others, in their stead. No person to be capable of being a delegate, for more than three years, in any term of six years, or of holding any office of emolument under the United States—each state to maintain its own delegates, and in determining questions, to have one vote.

No state was to enter into a treaty, agreement, or alliance with any foreign nation ; nor were any two or more states, to enter into any confederation or alliance whatever, between themselves, without the consent of congress.

The states were likewise prohibited from laying imposts, which should interfere with any stipulations in treaties entered into by congress with any nation, prince, or state, in pursuance of any treaties already proposed to France and Spain. Nor could they keep vessels of war, in time of peace, except such number only as congress should deem necessary, for the defense of the state, or its trade ; nor keep up any body of forces, except such number, as, in the judgment of congress, were requisite, to garrison their forts ; nor engage in any war, except actually invaded by enemies, or in such imminent danger of invasion, as not to admit of the delay of consulting congress.

All the charges of war and other expenses, to be incurred for the common defense, or general welfare, were to be defrayed out of a common treasury, to be supplied by the several states, in proportion to the value of all lands within each state granted to, or surveyed for any person, as such lands, buildings, and improvements thereon, should be estimated, according to such mode as congress might from time to time, direct and appoint ; the taxes for paying such proportion to be laid and levied by the legislatures of the several states, within the time agreed upon by congress.

The general legislature had the sole and exclusive power of peace and war, except in case of invasion, or imminent danger of invasion of any state—of sending and receiving ambassadors —entering into treaties and alliances, with a proviso, that no treaty of commerce should abridge the legislative power of the respective states, of imposing such imposts and duties on foreigners, as their people were subject to, or of prohibiting exportation or importation of any species of goods or commodities whatever —of deciding captures made on land or water—of granting letters of marque and reprisal, in time of peace—appointing courts for trial of piracies and felonies committed on the high seas, and for the trial of appeals, in all cases of captures. Congress were, also, invested with the power of finally determining all disputes and differences then subsisting, or which should arise, between two or more states, concerning boundary, jurisdiction, or any other cause whatever, and the manner of exercising this power, was particularly pointed out, in the articles—no state, however, was to be deprived of territory, for the *benefit* of the United States. They had, likewise, the sole right of regulating the alloy and value of coin struck by themselves, or by the states ; of fixing the standard of weights and measures, of regulating the trade, and managing all affairs with the Indians, not members of any of the states, establishing and regulating post-offices, appointing all officers of the land forces, in the service of the United States, excepting regimental officers ; appointing all naval officers, and making rules for the government of the land and naval forces.

They were authorized to appoint a committee, to sit, in the recess of congress, to be denominated a committee of the states, to consist of one delegate from each state—to appoint other committees and civil officers—to appoint a president of congress ; but no person was to serve in that office, more than one year, in any term of three years—to ascertain the necessary sums of money to be raised, and to appropriate and apply the same—to borrow money, or emit bills on the credit of the United States, transmitting to each state, every half year, the amount so borrowed or emitted—to build and equip a navy—to agree on the number of land forces, and to make requisitions from each state, for its quota, in proportion to the number of white inhabitants of such state, the legislature of each state to appoint the regimental officers, raise the men, and clothe, arm, and equip them, at the expense of the United States. Congress were never to engage in war, grant letters of marque and reprisal, enter into any treaties or alliances, coin money, or regulate its value, ascertain the sums and expenses necessary for the defense and welfare of the United States, emit bills of credit, borrow or appropriate money, agree upon the number of vessels of war, or the number of land and sea forces, or appoint a commander in chief of the army and navy, unless *nine states* should assent to the same—nor could a question, on any other point, except adjournment from day to day, be determined, unless by the votes of a majority of the United States in congress. A committee of the states, or any nine of them, were authorized to execute, in the recess of congress, such of the powers of that body, as by the consent of nine states, congress should think expedient to vest them with ; but no power was to be delegated to this committee, the exercise of which required the voice of nine states in congress. Every state was to abide by the determination of congress, on all questions submitted to them by the confederation ; the union was to be perpetual, nor was any alteration in the articles to be made, unless agreed to, in congress, and afterwards confirmed by the legislatures of *every state.* The articles provided, that Canada, acceding to the confederation, and joining in the measures of the United States, should be admitted into the union ; but no other colony, without the consent of nine states.

This plan of union, was to be proposed to the legislatures of all the states, and, if approved, they were advised to authorize their delegates in congress, to ratify the same ; this being done, it was to be conclusive.*

* Note 1.

In forming a plan of union, among thirteen states, differing in extent, wealth, and population, as well as in habits, education, and religious opinions, and between some of which serious disputes existed relative to boundaries, unanimity on all questions, was not to be expected.

In discussing its principles, a diversity of sentiment prevailed among the states, on three important points.

First, as to the *mode* of voting in congress, whether, by states, or according to wealth or population.

Second, as to the *rule*, by which the expenses of the union, should be apportioned among the states.

Third, relative to the *disposition* of the vacant and unpatented western lands.

With respect to the first, it was urged by Virginia, that the votes, should be in proportion to the population or wealth of each state, and not by states, as reported by the committee.

When this part was under the consideration of congress, in October 1777, it was first proposed, as an amendment, that the states of Rhode Island, Delaware, and Georgia, should each have one vote, and all the other states one vote, for every fifty thousand white inhabitants. The states of Virginia and Pennsylvania, (the latter then represented by one member only,) were in favor of this proposition—North Carolina divided, and the other states against it. It was then moved, that each state should send one delegate for every thirty thousand inhabitants, and that each delegate have a vote. On this question, Virginia was in the affirmative, North Carolina divided, and all the other states in the negative.

It was also proposed, that the representatives of each state, be computed by numbers, proportioned according to its *contribution* of money, or tax levied and paid. The state of Virginia alone, was in favor of this proposition ; and on the final question, that the votes should be by states, Virginia was against it, and North Carolina divided.

With respect to the expenses of the union, it was decided, in committee of the whole, that they should be paid by the states, in proportion to the number of inhabitants of every age, sex and quality, (except Indians not paying taxes,) in each state, the number to be taken every three years. As this included slaves, strong objections were made by the states having this species of population, and an alteration was proposed and finally carried, that the expenses of the union, should be borne by the states in proportion to the *value* of all lands granted to, or surveyed for any person, and the buildings and improvements thereon, to be estimated according to such mode as congress should direct.

The states of New Hampshire, Massachusetts, Rhode Island, and Connecticut were opposed to this alteration; the states of New York and Pennsylvania divided, and the states of New Jersey, Maryland, Virginia, North and South Carolina, in its favor.

Some of the states were of opinion, that congress should be invested with the power of settling and fixing the limits of such states, as claimed to the Mississippi, or south sea, by virtue of their original charters or grants, and that the lands beyond such *limits*, should enure to the benefit of the United States. An amendment was, therefore, proposed, that congress should have the sole and exclusive power, to ascertain and fix the western boundary of such states, as claimed to the south sea, and to dispose of all lands beyond such boundary, for the benefit of the union.

This being negatived, the proposition was varied, providing that congress should fix the western bounds of each state, and lay out the lands beyond such bounds into *new* states.

Maryland voted for this amendment, New Jersey was divided, and the other states were against it. The following circular letter to the states accompanied this system.

"Congress having agreed upon a plan of confederacy for securing the freedom, sovereignty, and independence of the United States, authentic copies are now transmitted for the consideration of the respective legislatures. The business, equally intricate and important, has in its progress been attended with uncommon embarrassments and delay, which the most anxious solicitude and persevering diligence could not prevent.

" To form a permanent union, accommodated to the opinion and wishes of the delegates of so many states, differing in habits, produce, commerce, and internal police, was found to be a work which nothing but time and reflection, conspiring with a disposition to conciliate, could mature and accomplish. Hardly is it to be expected that any plan, in the variety of provisions essential to our union, should exactly correspond with the maxims and political views of every particular state. Let it be remarked, that after the most careful inquiry, and the fullest information, this is proposed as the best which could be adapted to the circumstances of all, and as that alone which affords any tolerable prospect of general ratification. Permit us then earnestly to recommend these articles to the immediate and dispassionate attention of the legislatures of the respective states. Let them be candidly reviewed under a sense of the difficulty of combining in one general system the various sentiments and interests of a continent divided into so many sovereign and independent communities, under a conviction of the absolute necessity of uniting all our councils and all our strength to maintain and defend our common liberties. Let them be examined with a liberality becoming brethren and fellow citizens surrounded by the same imminent dangers, contending for the same illustrious prize, and deeply interested in being forever bound and connected together by ties the most intimate and indissoluble.

" And finally, let them be adjusted with the temper and magnanimity of wise and patriotic legislators, who, while they are concerned for the prosperity of their own more immediate circle, are capable of rising superior to local attachments when they may be incompatible with the safety, happiness and glory of the general confederacy.

" We have reason to regret the time which has elapsed in preparing this plan for consideration. With additional solicitude we look forward to that which must be necessarily spent before it can be ratified. Every motive loudly calls upon us to hasten its conclusion.

"More than any other consideration, it will confound our foreign enemies, defeat the flagitious practices of the disaffected, strengthen and confirm our friends, support our public credit, restore the value of our money, enable us to maintain our fleets and armies, and add weight and respect to our councils at home, and to our treaties abroad.

"In short, this salutary measure can no longer be deferred. It seems essential to our very existence as a free people; and without it, we may soon be constrained to bid adieu to independence, to liberty, and safety; blessings which, from the justice of our cause and the favor of our Almighty Creator, visibly manifested in our protection, we have reason to expect, if, in an humble dependence on his divine providence, we strenuously exert the means which are placed in our power. To conclude, if the legislature of any state shall not be assembled, congress recommend to the executive authority to convene it without delay; and to each respective legislature, it is recommended to invest its delegates with competent powers ultimately, in the name and behalf of the state, to subscribe articles of confederation and perpetual union of the United States, and to attend congress for that purpose, on or before the 10th day of March, 1778."

The plan was considered by the legislatures of the several states, in the winter of 1778, and by some was adopted without amendments, by others, various amendments were proposed.

In June 1778, the delegates from the several states, in congress, were called upon for their instructions, on this important subject. New Hampshire, New York, Virginia and North Carolina, had adopted the plan, without amendments; but some material alterations were proposed by the others; all the states however, except New Jersey, Delaware and Maryland, had instructed their delegates to ratify the articles, even if the amendments proposed by them, should be rejected by congress.

These various amendments shew the views of the states, at that period, on the new and important subject of a confederacy.

One of the principal objections of Maryland, as well as some of the other states, was, that the western lands were not secured for the benefit of the union.　In pursuance of their instructions, the 'Maryland delegates proposed an amendment, vesting congress with power " to appoint commissioners, who should be fully authorized and empowered to ascertain and restrict the boundaries of such of the confederated states which claim to extend to the river Mississippi or south sea."

On this interesting question the states were almost equally divided; Rhode Island, New Jersey, Pennsylvania, Delaware and Maryland, were in favor of the amendment, Massachusetts, Connecticut, Virginia, South Carolina and Georgia against it, and New York divided, the delegates from North Carolina not being present.

Massachusetts proposed that the rule for settling the proportion of taxes to be paid by each state, should be reconsidered, " so that the rule of apportionment might be varied from time to time, by congress, until experience shall have shown what rule of apportionment shall be most equal, and consequently most just."

This state also, recommended the reconsideration of the rule of apportioning the number of forces to be raised by each state on the requisition of congress.

These amendments were negatived; two states only voting for the first, and three for the second.

Rhode Island felt a strong interest in having a share in the western lands; she therefore proposed an amendment, providing " that all lands within those states, the property of which, before the present war, was vested in the crown of Great Britain, or out of which revenues from quit-rents arise payable to the said crown, shall be deemed, taken, and considered, as the property of these United States, and be disposed of and appropriated by congress, for the benefit of the whole confederacy, reserving, however, to the states within whose limits such crown lands may be, the entire and complete jurisdiction thereof."

Connecticut not only recommended that the taxes to be paid by each state, should be in proportion to its number of inhabitants, instead of the value of its lands, but also the following limitation of the powers of the general government, in relation to a standing army : " Provided that no land army shall be kept up by the United States in time of peace, nor any officers or pensioners kept in pay by them, who are not in actual service, except such as are, or may be rendered unable to support themselves by wounds received in battle in the service of the said states, agreeably to the provisions already made by a resolution of congress."

The most material amendment suggested by Pennsylvania, was, that the number of land forces to be furnished by each state, should be according to the whole number of inhabitants of every description, instead of the *white* inhabitants as provided in the articles.

South Carolina was jealous of the power conferred upon the general government, in relation to a military force. She proposed that " the troops to be raised should be deemed the troops of that state by which they are raised. The congress or grand council of the states may, when they think proper, make requisition of any state for two thirds of the troops to be raised, which requisition shall be binding upon the said states respectively ; but the remaining third shall not be liable to be drawn out of the state, in which they are raised, without the consent of the executive authority of the same. When any forces are raised, they shall be under the command of the executive authority of the state in which they are so raised, unless they be joined by troops from any other state, in which case the congress or grand council of the states may appoint a general officer to take the command of the whole ; and until the same can be done, the command shall be in the senior officer present, who shall be amenable for his conduct to the executive authority of the state in which the troops are, and shall be liable to be suspended thereby. The expenses of the troops so to be raised shall be defrayed by the state to which they belong ; but when called into service by the United States, they shall be fed and paid at the expense of the United States."

South Carolina also suggested, that the lands and improvements thereon, should be valued by persons to be appointed by the legislatures of the respective states, at least once in ten years, and oftener, if required by congress ; and that future alterations in the articles might be made, if agreed to by eleven states in congress, and afterwards confirmed by the legislatures of eleven states.

Georgia was desirous that the colonies of East and West Florida, as well as Canada, should have the privilege of acceding to the confederacy, and proposed an amendment to that effect. The delegates from New Jersey, presented a representation on the subject of the union, from the legislature of that state, addressed to congress. This representation contained more just and enlightened views in relation to a federal compact, particularly as to the powers of congress, in regard to the trade of the United States, than generally prevailed at that period.

One of the objections made by this state was, that the general government was not vested with the sole and exclusive power of regulating commerce with foreign nations.

The remarks in this representation, concerning several of the articles, contain much sound political wisdom, and cannot fail to gratify the reader.

" 1. In the fifth article," they say, " where, among other things, the qualifications of the delegates from the several states are described, there is no mention of any oath, test, or declaration, to be taken or made by them previous to their admission to seats in congress. It is indeed to be presumed the respective states will be careful that the delegates they send to assist in managing the the general interest of the union, take the oaths to the government from which they derive their authority, but as the United States, collectively considered, have interests, as well as each particular state, we are of opinion that some test or obligation binding upon each delegate while he continues in the trust, to consult and pursue the former as well as the latter, and particularly to assent to no vote or proceeding which may violate the general confederation, is necessary. The laws and usages of all civilized nations evince the propriety of an oath on such occasions ; and the more solemn and important the deposit, the more strong and explicit ought the obligation to be.

" 2. By the sixth and ninth articles, the regulation of trade seems to be committed to the several states within their separate jurisdictions, in such a degree as may involve many difficulties and embarrassments, and be attended with injustice to some states in the union. We are of opinion that the sole and exclusive power of regulating the trade of the United States with foreign nations ought to be clearly vested in the congress ; and that the revenue arising from all duties and customs imposed thereon, ought to be appropriated to the building, equipping, and manning a navy for the protection of the trade and defense of the coasts, and to such other public and general purposes as to the congress shall seem proper, and for the common benefit of the states. This principle appears to us to be just ; and it may be added, that a great security will by this means be derived to the union from the establishment of a common and mutual interest.

" 3. It is wisely provided in the sixth article, that no body of forces shall be kept up by any state in time of peace, except such number only as, in the judgment of the United States in congress assembled, shall be deemed requisite to garrison the forts necessary for the defense of such state. We think it ought also to be provided and clearly expressed, that no body of troops be kept up by the United States in time of peace, except such number only as shall be allowed by the assent of nine states. A standing army, a military establishment, and every appendage thereof, in time of peace, is totally abhorrent from the ideas and principles of this state. In the memorable act of congress declaring the united colonies free and independent states, it is emphatically mentioned, as one of the causes of separation from Great Britain, that the sovereign thereof had kept up among us, in time of peace, standing armies without the consent of the legislatures. It is to be wished the liberties and happiness of the people may by the confederation be carefully and explicitly guarded in this respect.

" 4. On the eighth article we observe, that as frequent settlements of the quotas for supplies and aids to be furnished by the several states in support of the general treasury, will be requisite, so they ought to be secured. It cannot be thought improper, or unnecessary, to have them struck once at least in every five years, or oftener if circumstances will allow. The quantity or value of real property in some states may increase much more rapidly than in others; and therefore the quota which is at one time just, will at another be disproportionate.

" 5. The boundaries and limits of each state ought to be fully and finally fixed and made known. This we apprehend would be attended with very salutary effects, by preventing jealousies, as well as controversies, and promoting harmony and confidence among the states. If the circumstances of the times would not admit of this, previous to the proposal of the confederation to the several states, the establishment of the principles upon which, and the rule and mode by which the determination might be conducted, at a time more convenient and favorable for despatching the same at an early period, not exceeding five years from the final ratification of the confederation, would be satisfactory.

" 6. The ninth article provides, that no state shall be deprived of territory for the benefit of the United States. Whether we are to understand that by territory is intended any land, the property of which was heretofore vested in the crown of Great Britain, or that no mention of such land is made in the confederation, we are constrained to observe, that the present war, as we always apprehended, was undertaken for the general defense and interest of the confederating colonies, now the United States. It was ever the confident expectation of this state, that the benefits derived from a successful contest were to be general and proportionate; and that the property of the common enemy, falling in consequence of a prosperous issue of the war, would belong to the United States, and be appropriated to their use. We are therefore greatly disappointed in finding no provision made in the confederation for empowering the congress to dispose of such property, but especially the vacant and impatented lands, commonly called the crown lands, for defraying the expenses of the war, and for such other public and general purposes. The jurisdiction ought in every instance to belong to the respective states within the charter or determined limits of which such lands may be seated; but reason and justice must decide, that the property which existed in the crown of Great Britain, previous to the present revolution, ought now to belong to the congress, in trust for the use and benefit of the United States. They have fought and bled for it in proportion to their respective abilities; and therefore the reward ought not to be predilectionally distributed. Shall such states as are shut out by situation from availing themselves of the least advantage from this quarter, be left to sink under an enormous debt, whilst others are enabled, in a short period, to replace all their expenditures from the hard earnings of the whole confederacy?

" 7. The ninth article also provides that requisitions for the land forces to be furnished by the several states shall be proportioned to the number of white inhabitants in each. In the act of independence we find the following declaration: ' We hold these truths to be self-evident, that all men are created equal; that they are endued by their creator with certain unalienable rights, among which are life, liberty, and the pursuit of happiness.' Of this doctrine, it is not a very remote consequence, that all the inhabitants of every society, be the color of their complexion what it may, are bound to promote the interest thereof, according to their respective abilities. They ought therefore to be brought into the account on this occasion. But admitting necessity or expediency to justify the refusal of liberty in certain circumstances to persons of a peculiar color, we think it unequal to reckon upon such in this case. Should it be improper, for special local reasons, to admit them in arms for the defense of the nation; yet we conceive the proportion of forces to be embodied ought to be fixed according to the whole number of inhabitants in the state, from whatever class they may be raised. If the whole number of inhabitants in a state, whose inhabitants are all whites, both those who are called into the field, and those who remain to till the ground and labor in the mechanical arts and otherwise, are reckoned in the estimate for striking the proportion of forces to be furnished by that state, ought even a part of the latter description to be left out in another? As it is of indispensable necessity in every war, that a part of the inhabitants be employed for the uses of husbandry and otherwise at home, while others are called into the field, there must be the same propriety that the owners of a different color who are employed for this purpose in one state, while whites are employed for the same purpose in another, be reckoned in the account of the inhabitants in the present instance.

" 8. In order that the quota of troops to be furnished in each state on occasion of a war may be equitably ascertained, we are of opinion that the inhabitants of the several states ought to be numbered as frequently as the nature of the case will admit, once at least every five years. The disproportioned increase in the population of different states may render such provision absolutely necessary.

" 9. It is provided in the ninth article, that the assent of nine states out of the thirteen shall be necessary to determine in sundry cases of the highest concern. If this proportion be proper and just, it ought to be kept up, should the states increase in number, and a declaration thereof be made for the satisfaction of the union.

" That we think it our indispensable duty to solicit the attention of congress to these considerations and remarks, and to request that the purport and meaning of them be adopted as part of the general confederation; by which means we apprehend the mutual interests of all the states will be better secured and promoted, and that the legislature of this state will then be justified in ratifying the same."

The question being taken in congress, whether the purport and meaning of the several amendments proposed by New Jersey should be admitted as part of the confederation, it was decided in the negative; three states in the affirmative, six in the negative, and one divided. The amendments of the other states were, also, negatived.

In July, 1778, a form of ratification was adopted, and the articles were soon after signed by the delegates from all the states, except New Jersey, Delaware and Maryland. A letter was immediately sent to these states, urging their immediate attention to the subject.

Sensible of the importance of completing the union, the legislature of New Jersey, in November 1778, authorized the delegates of that state to ratify the federal compact.

The same legislature declared that the articles were still considered " in divers respects unequal and disadvantageous to that state, and that the objections to such of them lately stated and sent to the general congress, on the part of that state, were still viewed as just and reasonable, and sundry of them as of the most essential moment to the welfare and happiness of the people thereof; yet, under the full conviction of the present necessity of acceding to the confederacy proposed, and that separate and detached state interests ought to be postponed to the general good of the union ; and moreover, in firm reliance that the candor and justice of the several states, would, in due time, remove as far as possible, the inequality which now subsists."

On the part of New Jersey, therefore, the articles were signed on the 25th of November, 1778. On the first of February 1779, Delaware followed the patriotic example of New Jersey. Her act of accession was accompanied with the following resolutions.

" *Resolved*, That this state think it necessary for the peace and safety of the state to be included in the union ; that a moderate extent of limits should be assigned for such of those states as claim to the Mississippi or South sea ; and that the United States in congress assembled, should and ought to have power of fixing their western limits.

" *Resolved also*, That this state consider themselves justly entitled to a right in common with the members of the union, to that extensive tract of country which lies to the westward of the frontiers of the United States, the property of which was not vested in, or granted to, individuals at the commencement of the present war: that the same hath been or may be gained from the king of Great Britain, or the native Indians, by the blood and treasure of all, and ought therefore to be a common estate, to be granted out on terms beneficial to the United States.

" *Resolved also*, That the courts of law established within this state, are competent for the purpose of determining all controversies concerning the private right of soil claimed within the same ; and they now, and at all times hereafter, ought to have cognizance of all such controversies ; that the indeterminate provision proposed in the ninth article of the confederation for deciding upon controversies that may arise about some of those private rights of soil, tends to take away such cognizance, and is contrary to the declaration of the rights of this state ; and therefore ought to receive an alteration."

These resolutions were permitted to be filed among the papers of congress, but with an express condition, " that they were not to be considered as admitting any claim thereby set up, or intended to be set up."

On the 22d of February, 1779, the articles were ratified on the part of Delaware.

The assent of Maryland, was now only wanting, to complete the union.   She, however, still persisted in her refusal, without an amendment, securing the western lands, for the benefit of all the states.   In December 1778, the delegates from that state received special instructions on the subject.   These were drawn with much ability, and evinced a determination to withhold the assent of that state to the confederacy, without the security required ; and as they contain the reasons for this determination, after the other states had acceded to this great national compact, we here insert them.

" Having conferred upon you," they say to their delegates, " a trust of the highest nature, it is evident we place great confidence in your integrity, abilities, and zeal to promote the general welfare of the United States, and the particular interest of this state, where the latter is not incompatible with the former ; but to add greater weight to your proceedings in congress, and take away all suspicion that the opinions you there deliver, and the votes you give may be the mere opinions of individuals, and not resulting from your knowledge of the sense and deliberate judgment of the state you represent, we think it our duty to instruct as followeth on the subject of the confederation, a subject in which, unfortunately, a supposed difference of interest has produced an almost equal division of sentiments among the several states composing the union. We say a supposed difference of interests ; for if local attachments and prejudices, and the avarice and ambition of individuals, would give way to the dictates of a sound policy, founded on the principles of justice, (and no other policy but what is founded on those immutable principles deserves to be called sound,) we flatter ourselves, this apparent diversity of interests would soon vanish, and all the states would confederate on terms mutually advantageous to all ; for they would then perceive that no other confederation than one so formed can be lasting. Although the pressure of immediate calamities, the dread of their continuance from the appearance of disunion, and some other peculiar circumstances, may have induced some states to accede to the present confederation, contrary to their own interests and judgments, it requires no great share of foresight to predict, that when those causes cease to operate, the states which have thus acceded to the confederation will consider it as no longer binding, and will eagerly embrace the first occasion of asserting their just rights, and securing their independence. Is it possible that those states who are ambitiously grasping at territories, to which in our judgment they have not the least shadow of exclusive right, will use with greater moderation the increase of wealth and power derived from those territories, when acquired, than what they have displayed in their endeavors to acquire them ? We think not. We are convinced the same spirit which hath prompted them to insist on a claim so extravagant, so repugnant to every principle of justice, so incompatible with the general welfare of all the states, will urge them on to add oppression to injustice. If they should not be incited by a superiority of wealth and strength to oppress by open force their less wealthy and less powerful neighbors ; yet depopulation and consequently the impoverishment of those states will necessarily follow, which, by an unfair construction of the confederation, may be stripped of a common interest, and the common benefits desirable from the western country. Suppose, for instance, Virginia indisputably possessed of the extensive and fertile country to which she has set up a claim, what would be the probable consequences to Maryland of such an undisturbed and undisputed possession? They cannot escape the least discerning.

" Virginia, by selling on the most moderate terms a small proportion of the lands in question, would draw into her treasury vast sums of money; and in proportion to the sums arising from such sales, would be enabled to lessen her taxes. Lands comparatively cheap, and taxes comparatively low, with the lands and taxes of an adjacent state, would quickly drain the state thus disadvantageously circumstanced of its most useful inhabitants; its wealth and its consequence in the scale of the confederated states would sink of course. A claim so injurious to more than one half, if not to the whole of the United States, ought to be supported by the clearest evidence of the right. Yet what evidences of that right have been produced? What arguments alleged in support either of the evidence or the right? None that we have heard of deserving a serious refutation.

" It has been said, that some of the delegates of a neighboring state have declared their opinion of the impracticability of governing the extensive dominion claimed by that state. Hence also the necessity was admitted of dividing its territory, and erecting a new state under the auspices and direction of the elder, from whom no doubt it would receive its form of government, to whom it would be bound by some alliance or confederacy, and by whose councils it would be influenced. Such a measure, if ever attempted, would certainly be opposed by the other states as inconsistent with the letter and spirit of the proposed confederation. Should it take place by establishing a sub-confederacy, imperium in imperio, the state possessed of this extensive dominion must then either submit to all the inconveniences of an overgrown and unwieldly government, or suffer the authority of congress to interpose at a future time, and to lop off a part of its territory to be erected into a new and free state, and admitted into a confederation on such conditions as shall be settled by nine states. If it is necessary for the happiness and tranquility of a state thus overgrown, that congress should hereafter interfere and divide its territory, why is the claim to that territory now made, and so pertinaciously insisted on? We can suggest to ourselves but two motives; either the declaration of relinquishing at some future period a proportion of the country now contended for, was made to lull suspicion asleep, and to cover the designs of a secret ambition, or, if the thought was seriously entertained, the lands are now claimed to reap an immediate profit from the sale. We are convinced, policy and justice require, that a country unsettled at the commencement of this war, claimed by the British crown; and ceded to it by the treaty of Paris, if wrested from the common enemy by the blood and treasure of the thirteen states, should be considered as a common property, subject to be parcelled out by congress into free, convenient and independent governments, in such manner and at such times as the wisdom of that assembly shall hereafter direct.

" Thus convinced, we should betray the trust reposed in us by our constituents, were we to authorize you to ratify on their behalf the confederation, unless it be farther explained. We have coolly and dispassionately considered the subject; we have weighed probable inconveniences and hardships against the sacrifice of just and essential rights; and do instruct you not to agree to the confederation, unless an article or articles be added thereto in conformity with our declaration. Should we succeed in obtaining such article or articles, then you are hereby fully empowered to accede to the confederation.

"That these our sentiments respecting our confederation may be more publicly known, and more explicitly and concisely declared, we have drawn up the annexed declaration, which we instruct you to lay before congress, to have it printed, and to deliver to each of the delegates of the other states in congress assembled, copies thereof signed by yourselves, or by such of you as may be present at the time of delivery; to the intent and purpose that the copies aforesaid may be communicated to our brethren of the United States, and the contents of the said declaration taken into their serious and candid consideration.

"Also we desire and instruct you to move, at a proper time, that these instructions be read to congress by their secretary, and entered on the journals of congress.

"We have spoken with freedom, as become free men ; and we sincerely wish that these our representations may make such an impression on that assembly as to induce them to make such addition to the articles of confederation as may bring about a permanent union."

Maryland was particularly opposed to the extensive territorial claim of Virginia ; and the declarations of the former on this subject, drew from the latter, a strong remonstrance and vindication of her claim.

The legislature of Virginia, in December 1778, empowered their delegates in congress, to ratify the plan of union, with such other states, as would unite with them ; and declared that the same should be binding, without the assent of Maryland and Delaware, allowing these states, however, either a given or an indefinite time, to join the confederacy.   The state of Connecticut, also, in April 1779, authorized their delegates, to complete the confederacy exclusive of Maryland.

In May 1779, the delegates from Virginia, in pursuance of their instructions, presented to congress a paper signed by them, declaring they were ready " to ratify the confederation with one or more states named therein, so that the same shall be forever binding upon the state of Virginia." The other states, however, were unwilling to consent to a partial union, and some of them, though they had joined the confederacy, were still dissatisfied, on the subject of the western lands.

The states who claimed these lands, under special grants from the crown, considered their titles valid ; and as between them and the crown, there could perhaps be little doubt of their validity.   Yet policy, and even justice seemed to demand, that, in case these extensive tracts of wild lands, promising to be of immense value in future, should be finally secured by the joint exertions of all, should enure to the benefit of all. A majority of the states, however, had claims to these lands, which they deemed valid; and no mode of settling this interesting question, and of completing the union, seemed to present, but a compromise among the states themselves.

New York led the way, in effecting this compromise. In February 1780, the legislature of that state passed an act, " to facilitate the completion of the articles of confederation and perpetual union among the United States of America ;" with a preamble declaring that, " whereas nothing under divine Providence can more effectually contribute to the tranquility and safety of the United States of America than a federal alliance, on such liberal principles as will give satisfaction to its respective members : and whereas the articles of confederation and perpetual union recommended by the honorable the congress of the United States of America have not proved acceptable to all the states, it having been conceived that a portion of the waste and uncultivated territory, within the limits or claims of certain states, ought to be appropriated as a common fund for the expenses of the war : and the people of the state of New York, being on all occasions disposed to manifest their regard for their sister states, and their earnest desire to promote the general interest and security ; and more especially to accelerate the federal alliance, by removing, so far as it depends upon them, the before mentioned impediment to its final conclusion." By this act the delegates of the people of New York in congress, were empowered, " to limit and restrict the western boundaries of that state, by such line or lines, and in such manner and form, as they shall judge to be expedient, either with respect to the jurisdiction as well as the pre-emption of soil, or reserving the jurisdiction in part, or in the whole, over the lands which may be ceded or relinquished, with respect only to the right or pre-emption of the soil." This act, also, declared, that the territory thus ceded, " should be and enure for the use and benefit of such of the United States, as should become members of the federal alliance of the said states, and for no other use or purpose whatever."

This act, together with the instructions of Maryland respecting the articles of confederation, and the remonstrance of Virginia abovementioned, all of which had been laid before congress, were referred to a committee of that body, and on the 6th of September, 1780, this committee reported and declared, that " they conceived it unnecessary to examine into the merits or policy of the instructions or declaration of the general assembly of Maryland, or of the remonstrance of the general assembly of Virginia, as they involved questions, a discussion of which was declined, when the articles of confederation were debated ; nor in the opinion of the committee, can such questions be now revived with any prospect of conciliation : that it appears more advisable to press upon the states which can remove the embarrassments respecting the western country, a liberal surrender of a portion of their territorial claims, since they cannot be preserved entire without endangering the stability of the general confederacy ; to remind them how indispensably necessary it is to establish the federal union on a fixed and permanent basis, and on principles acceptable to all its respective members ; how essential to public credit and confidence, to the support of our army, to the vigor of our councils, and success of our measures, to our tranquility at home, our reputation abroad, to our very existence as a free, sovereign, and independent people ; that we are fully persuaded the wisdom of the respective legislatures will lead them to a full and impartial consideration of a subject so interesting to the United States, and so necessary to the happy establishment of the federal union ; that they are confirmed in these expectations by a view of the beforementioned act of the legislature of New York, submitted to their consideration ; that this act is expressly calculated to accelerate the federal alliance by removing as far as depends on that state, the impediments arising from the western country, and for that purpose to yield up a portion of territorial claim for the general benefit." The committee, therefore, reported a resolution, which was adopted by congress, earnestly recommending to the several states, having claims to the western country, to pass such laws, and give their delegates such powers, as should effectually remove the only obstacle to a final ratification of the articles of confederation ; and that Maryland be requested to accede to the union.[*]

To induce the states to make liberal cessions, congress, on the 10th of October following, declared, that the territory which might be thus ceded, should be disposed of for the common benefit of the union and formed into republican states, with the same rights of sovereignty, freedom and independence as the other states ; to be of a suitable extent of territory, not less than one hundred, and no more than one hundred and fifty miles square ; and that the expense incurred by any state, since the commencement of the war, in subduing any British posts, or in maintaining and acquiring the territory, should be reimbursed. In compliance with this recommendation, the state of Virginia, on the second of January, 1781, ceded for the benefit of the United States, all her claim to lands north west of the Ohio.

Maryland, though she had refused formally to join the confederacy, had never relaxed in her exertions against the common enemy, but had cordially united with the other states, in supporting the war. Yielding, however, at last, to the earnest entreaties of congress, she authorized her delegates, in a formal manner to ratify the federal compact. This, however, was not done, without declaring in the preamble of the act giving this authority, that "Whereas it hath been said that the common enemy is encouraged, by this state not acceding to the confederation, to hope that the union of the sister states may be dissolved, and therefore prosecute the war in expectation of an event so disgraceful to America : And our friends and illustrious ally are impressed with an idea, that the common cause would be promoted by our formally acceding to the confederation ; this general assembly, conscious that this state hath from the commencement of the war strenuously exerted herself in the common cause, and fully satisfied that if no formal confederation was to take place, it is the fixed determination of this state to continue her exertions to the utmost, agreeable to the faith pledged in the union, from

* Secret Journals of Congress, vol. 1, pp. 243, 444.

an earnest desire to conciliate the affection of the sister states, to convince the world of our unalterable resolution to support the independence of the United States, and the alliance with his most christian majesty ; and to destroy forever any apprehensions of our friends, or hopes in our enemies, of this state being again united to Great Britain," &c.   And declaring at the same time, that by acceding to the confederation, she did not relinquish or intend to relinquish, any right or interest she had with the other confederated states to the western territory ; but claimed the same as fully as was done by the legislature of that state ; relying on the future justice of the several states relative to her claim. On the first of March, 1781, the delegates of Delaware, in behalf of that state signed the articles, and thereby completed the union.

This important event was, on the same day publicly announced at the seat of government, and immediately communicated to the executives of the several states, to the Amercan ministers in Europe, to the minister plenipotentiary of France, and to the commander in chief, to be announced to the army under his command.

CHAPTER XII.

British Ministry call upon the people of Great Britain for voluntary contributions—
Parliament meet January 20th, 1778—Ministers propose a plan of reconciliation on
the 17th of February—this plan contained in three bills—purport of the bills—sent
to America before they had passed—Governor Tryon, to whom they are entrusted,
sends them to general Washington and to the governors of some of the states—General Washington transmits them to congress—Are referred to a committee—Report
made against them—Answer of governor Trumbull to the letter of Tryon—Treaties
with France arrive in May, 1778—Are immediately ratified and published—Congress
prepare an address to the people of the United States—British commissioners arrive
in America to offer terms of reconciliation—Dr. Franklin secretly consulted as to
terms, before the commissioners left England—David Hartley and others go to
France to sound him on the subject of terms of reconciliation—Propose that America should yield certain advantages in trade, on condition of peace—British commissioners arrive in America—Propose to congress certain conciliatory propositions
—Congress refuse to listen to any terms short of independence and the withdrawing of the fleets and armies—Reply of the British commissioners—Governor Johnston, one of the commissioners, sends letters to several members of congress, and
through a lady makes certain offers to Mr. Reed—Congress declare this an attempt
to bribe one of their body and refuse all further intercourse with him—British commissioners present an address or manifesto to the people of the states making the
same offers they had sent to congress—The people refuse the offers—Congress issue a counter manifesto.

IT is now time to recur to the proceedings in Great Britain with
respect to America, in the winter of 1778. Parliament again
met, on the 20th of January, the time to which they had adjourned. During the recess, the ministry were engaged in devising
means to supply the loss of the army under general Burgoyne.
For this purpose, they appealed to the patriotism and loyalty of
the people in every part of Great Britain ; nor did they appeal in
vain. Large subscriptions in money were obtained from individuals, and some of the wealthy cities furnished a regiment of men,
at their own expense.

The ministry, at the same time, were preparing a plan of reconciliation and concession to be proposed to the people of the
United States, agreeably to the declaration of lord North, at the
time of adjournment.

Waiting, however, for the result of their appeal to the patriotism of individuals, this plan was not submitted to parliament, until the 17th of February, 1778, ten days after the American commissioners had completed their treaties with France.*

Three bills were presented by the ministry, which soon became
laws, containing their plan of reconciliation.   The first was, "An
act for removing all doubts and apprehensions concerning *taxation* by the parliament of Great Britain, in any of the colonies,
provinces and plantations in North America, and the West Indies," and for repealing the act for laying a duty on tea, imported into the colonies.   The second act restored the charter of
Massachusetts ; and the third authorized the king, "to appoint
commissioners, with sufficient power to treat, consult, and agree
upon the means of quieting the disorders now subsisting in certain
of the colonies, plantations and provinces in North America."

It was declared and enacted, by the first, that "the king
and parliament of Great Britain, would not impose any duty, tax,
or assessment whatever, payable in any of his majesty's colonies,
provinces, and plantations, in North America, or the West Indies,
except only such duties, as it might be expedient to impose for
the *regulation of commerce ;* the net produce of such duties to
be always paid and applied to, and for the use of the colony, province, or plantation, in which the same should be respectively levied, in such manner, as other duties collected by the authority of
the respective general courts or general assemblies of such colonies, provinces, or plantations, are ordinarily paid or applied." After restoring the ancient charter of Massachusetts, without which
the ministry well knew, no reconciliation was possible ; parliament authorized the commissioners to be appointed by the king,
"to treat, consult, and agree with such body or bodies politic and
corporate, or with such assembly or assemblies of men, or any
person or persons whatsoever, of and concerning any grievances,
or complaints of grievances existing or supposed to exist, in the
government of any of the said colonies, provinces, or plantations
respectively, or in the laws and statutes of this realm respecting

* David Hartley's Letters to his Constituents in England, October, 1778.

the same ; and of and concerning any *aid* or *contribution* to be furnished by all, or any of the colonies, provinces, or plantations respectively, for the common defense of this realm, and the dominions therewith belonging ; and of and concerning any other regulations, provisions, matters, and things, necessary or convenient for the honor of his majesty and his parliament, and for the common good of all his subjects." No agreement, however, made by these commissioners was to be ultimately binding, unless confirmed by parliament.

To enable the commissioners to carry these general powers into effect, the king might authorize them to proclaim a cessation of hostilities, on the part of his majesty, both by sea and land, for any time, and under any conditions or restrictions—to suspend the operation and effect of the act of parliament, passed in December, 1775, prohibiting all trade and intercourse with the colonies, and also, to suspend in any places and for any times, the operations and effects of any act or acts of parliament, or any clause of the same, passed since the 10th day of February, 1763, relating to any of the colonies. They, also, had power, on certain conditions, to grant pardons, and in case of a vacancy in the office of a governor in any colony, or in his absence, to nominate a successor. This act was to remain in force, until the first of June, 1779.

That the British ministry should have paid so little attention to the movements of France, during the winter of 1778, and should have placed such confidence in assurances of a pacific disposition, on the part of the courts both of France and Spain, has been a subject of no little surprise. When warned by their opponents in parliament, that unless a reconciliation with the colonists was soon effected, France would unite in supporting them ; they declared that France and Spain would be governed by their interest, and that this interest was manifestly opposed to the independence of such powerful colonies, in the neighborhood of their own. From this, or some other cause, the ministers had paid so little attention, to what was passing at the court of France, that even during the debates on their conciliatory bills, some of them, if their declarations are to receive credit, were ignorant of the completion of the treaties between France and America; though Mr. Fox, in the house of commons, and the duke of Grafton in the house of lords, openly declared their knowledge of the fact. The king and ministry, however, were soon officially informed of this important event by the French minister in England, de Noailles, who, on the 13th of March, presented the following declaration to the court of London:

" The United States of North America, who are in full possession of independence, as pronounced by them, on the 4th of July, 1776, having proposed to the king, to consolidate, by a formal convention, the connection begun to be established between the two nations, the respective plenipotentiaries have signed a treaty of friendship and commerce, designed to serve as a foundation for their mutual good correspondence." In making this communication, the French minister was persuaded, he said, that the court of London would find new proofs of a constant and sincere disposition for peace, on the part of the French court; and that his Britannic majesty would take effectual measures, to prevent any interruption of the commerce between France and the United States; and intimated, that for the purpose of affording effectual protection to such commerce, his master, in connection with the United States, had taken *eventual measures.*

On the receipt of this note, the king of Great Britain immediately recalled his minister from Paris; and on the 17th sent a message to parliament, with a copy of the above note, declaring the conduct of France, an unjust and unprovoked aggression on the honor of his crown, and the essential interests of his kingdom, contrary to the most solemn assurances, subversive of the law of nations, and injurious to the rights of every sovereign power in Europe; and that he was determined to be prepared, to exert all the force and resources of his kingdom, if necessary, to repel every insult and attack.

The answers of both houses gave assurances of the most zealous support and assistance, in measures necessary to vindicate the honor of the crown, and to protect the just rights and essential interests of the empire.

These answers did not pass without warm and animated debates. Those who were usually opposed to the ministry, were divided as to the course of policy proper to be pursued, in the critical situation in which the nation was placed. The duke of Richmond, the marquis of Rockingham, and others, were in favor of an immediate acknowledgment of the independence of America; while the earl of Chatham, the earl of Shelburne, and their friends, were strongly opposed to a dismemberment of the British empire.

France having now become a party in the war, for the support of American independence, the political affairs of the United States assumed a new aspect.

To counteract, and if possible, to prevent the effects of the new connection between the United States and the ancient enemy of Great Britain, was the first object of the British ministers, after being assured of this important event. They had sent to America copies of their conciliatory bills, even before they became laws, to be there distributed. Governor Tryon, to whom they were entrusted, received them about the middle of April, and immediately transmitted them to general Washington, and to the governors of some of the states. The general sent them to congress, and expressed his fears of their ill effects on the public mind, unless measures to counteract them were taken. Congress referred the subject to a committee, consisting of Governeur Morris, Mr. Drayton, and Mr. Dana. On the 22d of April, this committee made a report, which was, at once, unanimously accepted, and with the bills themselves, ordered to be published.

At that period of the contest, congress were not disposed to accept of terms, to which, in its commencement, they might have gladly listened. After severe animadversions on the bills themselves, the committee concluded their report by saying—"From all which, it appears evident, that the said bills are intended to operate on the hopes and fears of the good people of these states, so as to create divisions among them, and a defection from the common cause, now by the blessing of God, drawing near to a favorable issue; that they are the sequel of that insidious plan, which from the days of the stamp act, down to the present time, hath involved this country in contention and bloodshed, and that, as in other cases, so in this, although circumstances may force them to recede from their unjustifiable claims, there can be no doubt, but they will, as heretofore, upon the first favorable occasion, again display that lust of domination, which hath rent in twain the mighty empire of Britain.

"Upon the whole, the committee beg leave to report it, as their opinion, that, as the Americans united in this arduous contest, upon principles of common interest, for the defense of common rights and privileges; which union hath been cemented by common calamities and by mutual good offices and affection ; so the great cause, for which they contend, and in which all mankind are interested, must derive its success from the continuance of that union; wherefore, any men, or body of men, who should presume to make any separate or partial convention or agreement with commissioners under the crown of Great Britain, or any of them, ought to be considered and treated as open and avowed enemies of the United States."

The committee, also, reported, and congress declared, that the United States could not, with propriety, hold any conference or treaty, with any commissioners, on the part of Great Britain, unless they should, as a preliminary, either withdraw their fleets and armies, or in positive and express terms, acknowledge the *independence* of the states.

Conceiving the design of the enemy to be, to lull the people of America, into a fatal security, congress, called upon the states, to use the most strenuous exertions, to bring their quotas of troops into the field, as soon as possible, and to have their militia in readiness to act as occasion might require. Copies of the bills having been sent, by governor Tryon, to the governor of Connecticut, Jonathan Trumbull ; the answer of the latter, of the 23d of April, was as firm and decided, as the report of the committee of congress. "There was a day," says governor Trumbull, "when even this step, from our then acknowledged parent state, might have been accepted with joy and gratitude ; but that day is *past irrevocably.* The repeated rejection of our sincere and sufficiently humble petitions, the commencement of hostilities, the inhumanity which has marked the prosecution of the war on your part, in its several stages, the insolence, which displays itself, on every petty advantage, the cruelties, which have been exercised on those unhappy men, whom the fortune of war, has thrown into your hands, all these are insuperable bars to the very idea of concluding a peace with Great Britain, on any other conditions, than the most *absolute, perfect* independence."

This patriot and statesman, concluded his answer, by observing that, upon the restoration of union by a lasting and honorable peace, " the British nation may then, perhaps, find us, as affectionate and valuable friends, as we now are determined and fatal enemies, and will derive from that friendship more solid and real advantages, than the most sanguine can expect from conquest."

These proceedings took place before the treaties with France reached America. The treaties themselves were brought by Simeon Deane, who arrived at the seat of government at York, in Pennsylvania, on Saturday, the second of May, 1778. Congress not being in session, immediately assembled, and the treaties were laid before them ; and on the Monday following, were unanimously ratified and soon after published. The American people received them with mingled feelings of joy and gratitude. They had entered upon the mighty struggle for their liberties without stopping to count the cost or waiting for foreign aid—they had from the commencement come to the desperate resolution, " to die or be free." To this resolution they had constantly adhered, even in the darkest period of the contest, trusting in that God, in whom their fathers trusted. The alliance with France inspired new hopes, and increased their confidence in the final attainment of their object. They now saw their freedom and independence ultimately secured, by the guaranty of a powerful nation ; a nation whose interest and inclination united to induce a perseverance in support of the cause it had espoused. Their feelings of gratitude towards a monarch, who had thus interposed in their favor, knew no bounds. Congress unanimously expressed their highest sense of the magnanimity and wisdom of his most christian majesty, in forming this alliance.

On this interesting occasion, the national legislature again presented an address to the people of the United States, and recommended that the same be read by ministers of the gospel of all denominations, immediately after divine service, in their respective places of public worship.

After stating the calamities they had experienced, and the hardships they had suffered in a war, which had continued for three years, and which had been waged against them, in a manner without a parallel in the annals of the world, they say, " at length that God of battles, in whom was our trust, hath conducted us through the paths of danger and distress to the thresholds of security.   It hath now become morally certain, that, if we have courage to persevere, we shall establish our liberties and independence.   The haughty prince, who spurned us from his feet with contumely and disdain, and the parliament which proscribed us, now descend to offer terms of accommodation.   Whilst in the full career of victory, they pulled off the mask, and avowed their intended despotism.   But having lavished in vain the blood and treasure of their subjects in pursuit of this execrable purpose, they now endeavor to ensnare us with the insidious offers of peace.   They would seduce you into a dependence, which necessarily, inevitably lead to the most humiliating slavery.   And do they believe that you will accept these fatal terms ? because you have suffered the distresses of war, do they suppose that you will basely lick the dust before the feet of your destroyers ? can there be an American so lost to the feelings which adorn human nature ? to the generous pride, the elevation, the dignity of freedom ! is there a man who would not abhor a dependence upon those, who have deluged his country in the blood of its inhabitants ? we cannot suppose this ; neither is it possible that they themselves can expect to make many converts.

" What then is their intention ? is it not to lull you with the fallacious hopes of peace, until they can assemble new armies to prosecute nefarious designs ? if this is not the case, why do they

strain every nerve to levy men throughout their islands? why do
they meanly court every little tyrant of Europe to sell them his
unhappy slaves? why do they continue to embitter the minds of
the savages against you? surely this is not the way to conciliate
the affections of America. Be not, therefore, deceived. You
have still to expect one severe conflict. Your foreign alliances,
though they secure your independence, cannot secure your country from desolation, your habitations from plunder, your wives
from insult or violation, nor your children from butchery. Foil-
ed in their principal design, you must expect to feel the rage of
disappointed ambition. Arise then! to your tents! and gird
you for battle. It is time to turn the headlong current of vengeance upon the head of the destroyer. They have filled up the
measure of their abominations, and like ripe fruit must soon drop
from the tree. Although much is done, yet much remains to do.
Expect not peace, whilst any corner of America is in possession
of your foes. You must drive them away from this land of promise, a land flowing indeed with milk and honey. Your brethren
at the extremities of the continent, already implore your friendship and protection. It is your duty to grant their request. They
hunger and thirst after liberty. Be it yours to dispense to them
the heavenly gift. And what is there now to prevent it? After
the unremitted efforts of our enemies, we are stronger than before. Nor can the wicked emissaries, who so assiduously labor
to promote their cause, point out any one reason to suppose that
we shall not receive daily accessions of strength. They tell you,
it is true, that your money is of no value; and your debts so enormous they can never be paid, but we tell you, that if Britain pro-
secutes the war another campaign, that single campaign will cost
her more than we had hitherto expended. And yet these men
would prevail upon you to take up that immense load, and for it
to sacrifice your dearest rights. For, surely, there is no man so
absurd as to suppose, that the least shadow of liberty can be preserved in a dependent connection with Great Britain. From the
nature of the thing it is evident, that the only security you could
obtain, would be, the justice and moderation of a parliament,

who have sold the rights of their own constituents. And this slender security is still farther weakened, by the consideration that it was pledged to rebels, (as they unjustly call the good people of these states,) with whom they think they are not bound to keep faith by any law whatsoever. Thus would you be cast bound among men, whose minds, by your virtuous resistance, have been sharpened to the keenest edge of revenge. Thus would your children and your children's children, be by you forced to a participation of all their debts, their wars, their luxuries, and their crimes. And this mad, this impious system they would lead you to adopt, because of the derangement of your finances.

" It becomes you deeply to reflect on this subject. Is there a country upon earth, which hath such resources for the payment of her debts as America? such an extensive territory? so fertile, so blessed in its climate and productions? surely there is none. Neither is there any, to which the wise Europeans will sooner confide their property. What, then, are the reasons that your money hath depreciated? because no taxes have been imposed to carry on the war. Because your commerce hath been interrupted by your enemy's fleets. Because their armies have ravaged and desolated a part of your country. Because their agents have villainously counterfeited your bills. Because extortioners among you, inflamed with the lust of gain, have added to the price of every article of life. And because weak men have been artfully led to believe that it is of no value. How is this dangerous disease to be remedied? let those among you, who have leisure and opportunity, collect the monies which individuals in their neighbourhood are desirous of placing in the public funds. Let the several legislatures sink their respective emissions, that so, there being but one kind of bills, there may be less danger of counterfeits. Refrain a little while from purchasing those things which are not absolutely necessary, that so those who have engrossed commodities may suffer (as they deservedly will) the loss of their ill-begotten hoards, by reason of the commerce with foreign nations, which the fleets will protect. Above all, bring forward your armies into the field. Trust not to appearances of peace or safety. Be assured that, unless you persevere, you will be exposed to every species of barbarity. But if you exert the means of defense which God and nature have given you, the time will soon arrive, when every man shall sit under his own vine, and under his own fig-tree, and there shall be none to make him afraid.

" The sweets of a free commerce with every part of the earth will soon reimburse you for all the losses you have sustained. The full tide of wealth will flow in upon your shores, free from the arbitrary impositions of those whose interest and whose declared policy it was to check your growth. Your interests will be fostered and nourished by governments, that derive their power from your grant, and will therefore be obliged, by the influence of cogent necessity, to exert it in your favor. It is to obtain these things that we call your strenuous, unremitted exertions. Yet do not believe that you have been, or can be saved merely by your own strength. No! it is by the assistance of heaven, and this you must assiduously cultivate, by acts which heaven approves. Thus shall the power and the happiness of these sovereign, free and independent states, founded on the virtue of of their citizens, increase, extend and endure, until the Almighty shall blot out all the empires of the earth.'"*

In this state of political affairs, the British commissioners arrived in America, to propose terms of reconciliation, in pursuance of the late acts of parliament. The earl of Carlisle, governor Johnston, and Mr. Eden, landed at Philadelphia about the first of June.

Before noticing their proceedings in America, we would here state, that previous to leaving England, they as well as the British ministry deemed it important to ascertain the opinion of Dr. Franklin concerning the terms they were about to offer the Americans. For this purpose, William Pulteney, a member of parliament and brother in law to governor Johnston, went to Paris, about the last of March; and under a fictitious name, re-

---

* This was drawn by Samuel Chase. See Biography of Signers to the declaration of Independence, vol. ix. p. 207.

quested a conference with the American minister. In this conference Mr. Pulteney submitted to Dr. Franklin the terms of reconciliation, about to be proposed to the Americans, under a stipulation, that if disapproved by him, they were to remain a secret. Dr. Franklin expressed his opinion against them, and candidly told Mr. Pulteney they would never be accepted by his countrymen ; and that every proposition, implying a voluntary agreement to return to a state of dependence on Great Britain, would be rejected by them.* In April following, David Hartley, also, went to Paris, to sound the American minister as to terms which might probably restore harmony between the two countries. Mr. Hartley was a member of parliament, well acquainted with Dr. Franklin, and was himself very desirous of an accommodation. In a conference, he asked what terms would be accepted by the Americans, whether, in order to obtain peace, they would not grant some superior advantages in trade to Great Britain, and enter into an offensive and defensive bond of alliance with her. He also inquired, whether, if war should be declared against France, the Americans had bound themselves by treaty to join with her against Great Britain. Dr. Franklin informed him, that he was not authorized to propose any terms of reconciliation ; he told him, however, that, as to advantages in trade, Great Britain might think herself well off, if, after having injured the Americans, by commencing an unjust war, she could, on making reparation for those injuries, obtain advantages in commerce, equal with other nations. He, also, stated to him, that an offensive alliance with a nation so often engaged in war, could not be expected ; and that, in case Great Britain should declare war against France, America would make common cause with the latter.

Soon after this conference, Mr. Hartley, in a friendly note took leave of Dr. Franklin, and in a postscript, alluding to probable future events, added, " If tempestuous times should come, take care of yourself; events are uncertain, and *men* are capricious." To this the doctor returned the following characteristic answer,

* Franklin's Works, vol. 6, p. 395.

" I thank you for your kind caution ; but having nearly finished
a long life, I set but little value on what remains of it.   Like a
draper, when one chaffers with him for a remnant, I am ready
to say, " as it is only the fag-end, I will not differ with you about
it, take it for what you please.   Perhaps the best use an old fellow can be put to, is to make a martyr of him."   These notes
closed the conference with Mr. Hartley at that time.

A gentleman also by the name of Chapman, and a member of
the Irish parliament, about the same time visited Dr. Franklin, on
his way from Nice, on the pretence of paying his respects to a
man of such distinguished reputation.

In the course of conversation he urged Dr. Franklin to state
what terms would satisfy the Americans ; and whether they
would not, on obtaining peace and independence, submit to the
navigation acts, or give equivalent privileges in trade to Great
Britain.   To him the American minister made nearly the same
reply as to Mr. Hartley ; that peace was of equal value to the
English as to the Americans, that the latter were already in possession of independence, and that the grant of this therefore
would not be considered a favor, requiring as an equivalent, peculiar advantages in commerce.

· Dr. Franklin suspected he might have been requested by lord
Shelburne to sound him as to terms of peace.

The American minister at Paris, in the summer of 1778, also,
received an anonymous letter, requesting him to make some propositions which might be laid before the king ; and he was desired to drop a letter containing them, for a person who would be
in the church of Notre-Dame, at a certain time, to be known by
a rose in his hat.   Dr. Franklin, not choosing to negociate in this
way, paid no attention to the request, except to give information
to the police officers, who attended at the time and place designated, and saw a person arrive, having the proposed insignia.
Not finding the expected letter, the stranger soon retired and
took the road to Calais.*

* Franklin's Works, vol. 6, p. 396, and Histoire &c. de la Diplomtie Francaise, vol. 7.

The British commissioners soon after their arrival at Philadelphia applied to general Washington for a pasport for their secretary, Mr. Ferguson, as the bearer of despatches to congress. The general declined granting a pasport, without orders from that body.

The commissioners then sent their letter by the usual military posts, accompanied with their commission, the acts of parliament under which they acted, together with propositions of conciliation.

The propositions were, " To consent to a cessation of hostilities, both by sea and land."

" To restore free intercourse, to revive mutual affection, and renew the common benefits of naturalization, through the several parts of the empire.

" To extend every freedom to trade, that the respective interests of Britain and America could require.

" To agree, that no military force should be kept up in North America, without the consent of the general congress, or particular assemblies.

" To concur in measures calculated to discharge the debts of America, and to raise the credit and value of the paper circulation.

" To perpetuate the union, by a reciprocal deputation of an agent or agents, who shall have the privilege of a seat and voice, in the parliament of Great Britain, or, if sent from Great Britain, to have a seat and voice in the assemblies of the different colonies, to which they may be deputed respectively, in order to attend to the several interests of those by whom they may be deputed.

" In short, to establish the power of the respective legislatures in each particular colony, to settle its revenue, its civil and military establishments, and to exercise a perfect freedom in legislation and internal government, so that the British colonies throughout North America, acting with Great Britain, in peace and in war, under one common sovereign, may have the irrevocable enjoyment of every privilege, short of a total separation of interests, or consistent with that union of force, on which the safety of their common religion and liberty depends."

After stating these propositions, the commissioners referred to the connection lately formed with France. "In our anxiety," they observed, "for preserving these several and essential interests, we cannot help taking notice of the *insidious interposition* of a power, which has, from the first settlement of these colonies, been actuated with enmity to us both. And notwithstanding the pretended date or present form of the French offers to North America, yet it is notorious, that these were made in consequence of the plans of accommodation previously concerted in Great Britain, and with a view to prevent our reconciliation, and *to prolong this destructive war.*"*

Some of the members were indignant at the insinuations in the letter against the honor of their new ally, and when that part was read, which mentioned the "insidious interposition" of France, a motion was made, to proceed no farther, declaring that they could not hear language, reflecting "on the honor of his most christian majesty, the good and faithful ally of these states." This motion, however, was finally postponed, and the letter and papers were read and referred to a committee, consisting of Richard H. Lee, S. Adams, Mr. Drayton, G. Morriss, and Mr. Witherspoon.

Congress now considered the independence of the United States secured by their alliance with France, and that they could listen to no terms, short of an absolute and unconditional acknowledgment of it; they therefore, on the report of this committee, by an unanimous vote, directed their president to send the following answer to the commissioners.

"I have received the letter from your excellencies of the 9th instant, with the enclosures, and laid them before Congress. Nothing but an earnest desire to spare the effusion of human blood, could have induced them to read a paper containing expressions so disrespectful to his most christian majesty, the good

Note 2.

and great ally of these states, or to consider propositions so derogatory to the honor of an independent nation.

" The acts of the British parliament, the commission from your sovereign, and your letter, suppose the people of these states, to be subjects of the crown of Great Britain, and are founded on the idea of dependence, which is utterly inadmissible.

" I am further directed to inform your excellencies, that congress are inclined to peace, notwithstanding the unjust claims, from which this war originated, and the savage manner, in which it hath been conducted. They will, therefore, be ready to enter upon the consideration of a treaty of peace and commerce, not inconsistent with treaties, already subsisting, when the king of Great Britain shall demonstrate a sincere disposition for that purpose. The only solid proof of this disposition will be, an explicit acknowledgment of the independence of these states, or the withdrawing his fleets and armies."

The British commissioners after their arrival in New-York, sent a second letter to the national legislature, in which they say,— " You propose to us as a matter of choice one or other of two alternatives, which you state as preliminaries necessary even to the beginning of a negociation for peace to this empire.

" One is an explicit acknowledgment of the independence of these states. We are not inclined to dispute with you about the meaning of words : but so far as you mean the entire privilege of the people of North America to dispose of their property, and to govern themselves without any reference to Great Britain, beyond what is necessary to preserve that union of force, in which our mutual safety and advantage consist; we think that so far their independency is fully acknowledged in the terms of cur letter of the 10th of June. And we are willing to enter upon a fair discussion with you, of all the circumstances that may be necessary to ensure or even to enlarge that independency.

" In the other alternative you propose, that his majesty should withdraw his fleets and his armies.

" Although we have no doubt of his majesty's disposition to remove every subject of uneasiness from the colonies, yet there are circumstances of precaution against our ancient enemies, which joined to the regard that must be paid to the safety of many, who from affection to Great Britain, have exposed themselves to suffer in this contest, and to whom Great Britain owes support at every expense of blood and treasure, that will not allow us to begin with this measure. How soon it may follow the first advances to peace on your part, will depend on the favorable prospect you give of a reconciliation with your fellow citizens of this continent and with those in Britain. In the mean time, we assure you that no circumstance will give us more satisfaction, than to find that the extent of our future connection is to be determined on principles of mere reason and the considerations of mutual interest, on which we are willing likewise to rest the permanency of any arrangements we may form.

"In making these declarations, we do not wait for the decisions of any military events. Having determined our judgment by what we believe to be the interests of our country, we shall abide by the declarations we now make in every possible situation of our affairs.

"You refer to treaties already subsisting, but are pleased to withhold from us any particular information in respect to their nature or tendency.

"If they in any degree are to affect our deliberations, we think you cannot refuse a full communication of the particulars, in which they consist, both for our consideration and that of your own constituents, who are to judge between us, whether any alliance you may have contracted be a sufficient reason for continuing this unnatural war. We likewise think ourselves entitled to a full communication of the powers by which you conceive yourselves authorized to make treaties with foreign nations.

"And we are led to ask satisfaction on this point, because we have observed in your proposed articles of confederation, No. 6 and 9, it is stated that you have the power of entering into treaties and alliances under certain restrictions therein specified, yet we do not find promulgated any act or resolution of the assemblies of particular states conferring this power on you.

" As we have communicated our powers to you, we mean to proceed without reserve in this business ; we will not suppose that any objection can arise on your part to our communicating to the public so much of your correspondence as may be necessary to explain our own proceedings. At the same time we assure you, that in all such publications, the respect which we pay to the great body of people you are disposed to represent, shall be evidenced by us in every possible mark of consideration and regard."

On the receipt of this letter, congress declared, that as neither the independence of the United States was acknowledged, nor the British fleet and armies were withdrawn, no answer should be returned.

The letter itself was no doubt designed rather for the people of America, than the members of the national legislature. The British commissioners could not believe, that the Americans, when fully acquainted with the terms of reconciliation, would consent to an alliance with their ancient enemy. They, therefore, suggested, that as the articles of confederation were not fully ratified, the treaties with France could not be binding without the assent of the states themselves ; and this suggestion was made with an expectation, that the people would prefer British offers of peace to French alliance.

But the commissioners were unacquainted with the character either of the people of America, or their representatives in the national legislature. Governor Johnston addressed private letters to several members of congress, with some of whom he had formerly been acquainted, on the subject of his mission ; particularly to Mr. Reed, Robert Morris, Mr. Laurens, and Mr. Dana. These letters, in July, 1778, were directed to be laid before congress ; and disclosed the objects of the writer. To Mr. Reed, in a letter written before he left England, he said, " the man, who can be instrumental in bringing us all to act once more in harmony, and to unite together the various powers, which this contest has drawn forth, will deserve more from the king and the people, from patriotism, humanity, and all the tender ties, that are affected by the quarrel and reconciliation, than ever was bestowed on human kind." To Mr. Morris, he wrote, "I believe the men, who have conducted the affairs of America, incapable of being influenced by improper motives; but in all such transactions there is risk, and I think, that whoever ventures should be secured; at the same time, that honor and emolument should naturally follow the fortunes of those, who have steered the vessel in the storm and brought her safe to port. I think Washington and the president have a right to any favor, that grateful nations can bestow, if they could once more unite our interest and spare the miseries and devastations of war." To Mr. Dana, he declared, among other things, that Dr. Franklin, in March, was satisfied, that the articles which the commissioners wished to make the basis of a treaty, were beneficial to America, and such as he should accept.

Mr. Reed, also, at the same time stated, in his place in congress, that on the 21st of June, he received a written message from a lady of character, having connection with the British army, wishing to see him on business, which could not be committed to writing. That in a conference with this lady, he was given to understand, that it was particularly wished by governor Johnston, that his influence should be obtained, in bringing about a re-union between the two countries, if consistent with his principles and judgment; and in such case, he might have £10,000 sterling, and any office in the colonies, in the gift of the crown.

That an answer being expected, he replied, that "he was not worth purchasing, but such as he was, the king of Great Britain was not rich enough to do it."

These letters, connected with the offers made to Mr. Reed, were considered by congress, as an attempt to bribe the members of that body; and on the 11th of August, they declared it to be "incompatible with the honor of congress, to hold any manner of correspondence with Mr. Johnston, especially to negotiate with him, upon affairs in which the cause of liberty is interested."

This declaration was sent to the British commissioners at New York. It drew from Mr. Johnston, a very angry counter-declaration. The charges made against him were not absolutely denied or acknowledged; but congress were accused of malice and treachery, of making the declaration with an intent to influence the minds of their constituents, and to prevent the effects of the British mission. He, therefore, for the future, declined acting as one of the commissioners, in any business, in which congress should be concerned.

It may be proper in this place, to state, that governor Johnston, soon after this, returned to Great Britain, and in a speech delivered in parliament, November, 1778, denied the transaction with Mrs. Ferguson, as stated by Mr. Reed, and asserted that the offers, were made without any authority from him. This public declaration, drew from Mr. Reed in 1779, a vindication of himself, in a publication, containing a confirmation of his statement from Mrs. Ferguson herself.

This lady, in a written communication, declared that " Mr. Johnston conversed with her, on the subject of a settlement with the colonies, and spoke of Mr. Reed—But I should be particularly glad of Mr. Reed's influence in this affair ; Mrs. Ferguson, says he, and I think he looked a little confused, if this affair should be settled in the way we wish, we shall have many pretty things in our power ; and if Mr. Reed, after well considering the nature of the dispute, can, conformable to his conscience and view of things, exert his influence to settle the contest, he may command ten thousand guineas, and the best post in the government ; and if you should see him, I could wish you to convey that idea to him."

The colleagues of governor Johnston in a communication made to congress, denied any knowledge of his private letters to the members of that body, or of the transaction stated by Mr. Reed. They, at the same time, endeavored to prove, that in confirming the treaties with France, as well as in rejecting their pacific overtures, without consulting the assemblies of the states, congress had exceeded the powers committed to them. In the same communication, they attempted to persuade the American people, that their best interests forbid an adherence to the treaties, entered into, as they alleged, on the part of France, after a full knowledge of the concessions intended to be made by Great Britain, and with a view to prevent a reconciliation. To this communication congress made no reply ; but individuals of of that body, particularly Governeur Morriss and Mr. Drayton, in numerous publications controverted the facts stated by the commissioners, and endeavored to convince the Americans, that the concessions made on the part of Great Britain, were the *effect* and not the *cause* of the offers made on the part of France.

The British commissioners were still unwilling to believe, that congress, in rejecting their overtures, had acted in accordance with the wishes of their constituents. They could not imagine that the American people would cordially unite with their ancient enemies, and finally reject those terms, which they had heretofore been willing to accept.

On the third of October, therefore, they published a manifesto or declaration, addressed not only to congress, but to the members of the colonial assemblies or conventions, and all others, free inhabitants of the colonies, of every rank and denomination.

To congress they repeated the offers already made, and reminded them, " that they were responsible to their countrymen, to the world, and to God, for the continuance of this war, and for all the miseries with which it must be attended."

To the colonial assemblies, they separately made the offers presented to congress, and called upon them, by every motive, political as well as moral, to meet and embrace the occasion of cementing a free and firm coalition with Great Britain.

They next appealed to the various classes of the "free inhabitants of this once happy empire."

They called upon those in arms to recollect, that the grievances, whether real or pretended, which led them into rebellion, had been forever removed, and that the just occasion had arrived for their returning to the class of peaceful citizens.

To those, whose profession it was to exercise the functions of religion, they said, " it cannot be unknown, that the foreign power, with which congress were endeavoring to connect them, has ever been averse to toleration, and inveterately opposed to the interests and freedom of the places of worship, which they serve."

To all the lovers of peace, they observed, " that they were made, by their leaders, to continue involved in all the calamities of war, without having either a just object to pursue, or a subsisting grievance, which might not instantly be redressed."

The commissioners then added a declaration, as novel in its principles, as it was calamitous in its consequences. If any person should think it for " the benefit of the colonies, to separate themselves from Great Britain," they thought it right, they said, " to leave them aware of the change, which the maintaining such a position must make, in the whole nature and future conduct of the war, more especially, when to this position is added, the pretended alliance with the court of France.

" The policy, as well as benevolence of Great Britain," they subjoined, " have thus far checked the extremes of war, where they tended to distress a people still considered as our fellow-subjects, and to desolate a country, shortly to become a source of mutual advantage: but when that country professes the unnatural design, not only of estranging herself from us, but of mortgaging herself to our enemies, the whole contest is changed ; and the question is, how far Great Britain may, by every means in her power, destroy or render useless, a connection contrived for her ruin, and for the aggrandizement of France. Under such circumstances, the laws of self-preservation must direct the conduct of Great Britain ; and if the British colonies are to become an accession to France, will direct her to render that accession as of little avail to her as possible."

In conclusion, the commissioners offered pardon to all who should within forty days, withdraw from the civil or military service of the colonies, and continue good and peaceable subjects of the British king.

They directed copies of this manifesto to be circulated among the people of the United States, by means of flags of truce. Congress considered this as a violation of national law, and declared, that the agents so employed were not entitled to the protection of a flag; and recommended to the executives of the several states to seize and secure them.

The British commissioners seemed to imagine, that America was the absolute property of the British crown; and that as this property was *mortgaged* to France, the king had a right to *waste* and *destroy* it at pleasure. Viewing this part of the manifesto as a threat of more extensive devastation of the country in future, congress, on the 30th of October, issued a counter manifesto, declaring, "that if our enemies presume to execute their threats, or persist in their present career of barbarity, we will take such exemplary vengeance, as shall deter others from a like conduct. We appeal," they said, " to that God who searcheth the hearts of men, for the rectitude of our intentions; and in his holy presence declare, that as we are not moved by any light or hasty suggestions of anger and revenge, so through every possible change of fortune we will adhere to this our determination."

The commissioners found the American people as little disposed to accept the offers of reconciliation and pardon, as their representatives. The day of reconciliation had indeed passed. A re-union with Great Britain, on terms compatible with the permanent security of their essential rights, or with the political happiness and commercial prosperity of their country, the people of the United States were now convinced was impossible. Nor could they accede to any terms short of absolute independence, without violating their engagements with France.

The commissioners, therefore, at the expiration of the forty days, finding no applications for pardon, returned to Great Britain, and left the contest to be decided by the sword.

CHAPTER XIII.

French fleet and a French minister arrive in America in the summer of 1778—French minister received with great joy—Dr. Franklin appointed minister to France—His instructions—Plan of attacking Canada in conjunction with France adopted by congress—submitted to general Washington—Disapproved by him—his public and his private letters on this subject—Congress finally relinquish the scheme—Co-operation of Spain expected—Spain declines acceding to the treaties made with France—Reasons of this—Wishes security for her own American possessions—Offers her mediation between France and Great Britain—France accepts the mediation—Great Britain holds a correspondence on the subject for some months—Refuses to have her disputes with the Americans brought into the negociations—Rejects the final proposition of Spain—King of Spain joins France in the war, June, 1779—This in pursuance of a secret treaty made in April preceding—Manifestoes issued both by France and Spain—Answered by Great Britain—Pending this mediation the British minister through Mr. Hartley, again sounds Dr. Franklin at Paris, on the subject of reconciliation—Mr. Hartley with this view submits to him certain preliminary propositions---Not acceded to---Object of the British minister to break the alliance between the United States and France---Congress informed of the offered mediation of Spain by the French minister---Subject referred to a committee---Committee report instructions to be given to an American minister to negociate peace---These instructions create long debates and great divisions in congress---Particularly about the fisheries, the boundaries and the navigation of the Mississippi---Terms relative to peace ultimately settled in congress---The use of the fisheries and the navigation of the Mississippi not made ultimata---No treaty of commerce to be made with Great Britain, without a stipulation on her part not to disturb the Americans in taking fish on the banks of Newfoundland, &c.

THE French court, soon after the completion of the treaties with America, sent a minister plenipotentiary to the United States, accompanied with a powerful fleet. The immediate object of the naval force was, to shut up the British fleet in the Delaware. Aware of this, the British commissioners brought secret orders for the immediate evacuation of Philadelphia. In pursuance of these orders, the British army left that city on the 18th of June, and returned to New York, through New Jersey. On their way they were attacked by the Americans, and a severe engagement took place at Monmouth, in which both sides claimed the victory. Though the French fleet, consisting of twelve ships of the line and six frigates, sailed from Toulon on the 13th of April, yet in consequence of calms and head winds, it did not reach the American coast till the 6th of July, a few days after the British ships left the Delaware. With this fleet came Mr. Gerard, minister from the court of France. The first appearance of an envoy from one of the greatest powers in Europe, was highly gratifying to the people of America. He was received with every mark of attention, and his first audience was attended with much ceremony. As the executive as well as legislative power was vested in congress, communications between that body, and the minister, were either by select committees, or by the members themselves in a body. In the first mode, the substance of the conference was reported to congress, and in the second, the communications of the minister were taken down in writing in committee of the whole, and reported to the house. These modes of communication resulted from the organization of the general government, but were not well calculated for secrecy or despatch.

Soon after the arrival of the French plenipotentiary, congress determined to send a minister of a similar grade to represent the United States at the court of France; and on the 14th of September, Dr. Franklin, then at the advanced age of seventy one, was appointed. He was, among other things, instructed, "to assure the king and his minister, that neither the congress, nor any 'of the states they represent, have at all swerved from their determination to be independent, in July, 1776. But as the declaration was made in the face of the most powerful fleet and army, which could have been expected to operate against them, and without the slightest assurance of foreign aid, so, though in a defenseless situation, and harrassed by the secret machinations and designs of intestine foes, they have, under the exertions of that force, during those bloody campaigns persevered in their determination to be free : and that they have been inflexible in this determination, notwithstanding the interruption of their commerce, the great sufferings they have experienced from the want of those things which it procured, and the unexampled barbarity of their enemies.

" You are to give," they say, " the most pointed and positive assurances, that although the congress are earnestly desirous of peace, as well to arrange their finances, and recruit the exhausted state of their country, as to spare the further effusion of blood, yet they will faithfully perform their engagements, and afford every assistance in their power to prosecute the war for the great purpose of the alliance.

" You shall constantly inculcate the certainty of ruining the British fisheries, on the banks of Newfoundland, and consequently, the British marine, by reducing Halifax and Quebec; since by that means they would be exposed to alarm and plunder, and deprived of the necessary supplies formerly drawn from America.

" The plan proposed by congress for compassing these objects is herewith transmitted for your more particular instruction.

" You are to lay before the court the deranged state of the finances, together with the causes thereof; and show the necessity of placing them on a more respectable footing, in order to prosecute the war with vigor on the part of America.

" You are, by every means in your power, to promote a perfect harmony, concord, and good understanding, not only between the allied powers, but also between and among their subjects, that the connection so favorably begun may be perpetuated.

"You shall, in all things, take care, not to make any engagements or stipulations, on the part of America, without the consent of America previously obtained.*

The project of reducing Canada was brought before congress, soon after the arrival of the French minister, and was warmly supported, if not suggested by him. A detailed plan for effecting this object, was arranged by congress in October, and accompanied the instructions of the American minister to France. Large bodies of troops were to be collected at several points near the frontiers of that province, and in the ensuing campaign, the different posts of Detroit, Niagara, Oswego, and Montreal, were to be attacked at the same time; and in the reduction of Quebec and Halifax, a French fleet and army were to co-operate. The advantages to be derived from the execution of this measure, both to France and the United States, were stated in the plan itself.

* Note 8.

"The importance to France," congress say, "is derived from the following considerations:

" 1. The fishery of Newfoundland is justly considered as the basis of a good marine.

" 2. The possession of these two places (Quebec and Halifax) necessarily secures to the party and their friends, the island and fisheries.

" 3. It will strengthen her allies, and guarantee more strongly their freedom and independence.

" 4. It will have an influence in extending the commerce of France, and restoring her to a share of the fur trade, now monopolized by Great Britain.

" The importance to America results from the following considerations:

" 1. The peace of their frontiers.

" 2. The arrangement of their finances.

" 3. The accession of two states to the union.

" 4. The protection and security of their commerce.

" 5. That it will enable them to bend their whole attention and resources to the erection of a marine, which will at once serve and assist their allies.

" 6. That it will secure the fisheries to the United States and France their ally, to the total exclusion of Great Britain.*

The marquis de la Fayette was to go to France and urge the co-operation of the French court in the execution of this project. The plan itself was transmitted to general Washington for his observations. The general was of opinion, that it was too complicated and hazardous, as well as too extensive for the finances of the United States, and could not be undertaken with a reasonable, much less a certain prospect of success. His observations were communicated to congress on the 11th of November. The members of that body were not easily induced to relinquish a favorite measure; particularly if France should be disposed to carry it into effect. On a report of a committee, therefore, to whom the observations of the general were refer-

* Secret Journals of Congress, volume 2, pp. 114, 115—and Note 4.

red, they were still of opinion, that he "should be directed to
write to the marquis de la Fayette upon the subject; and also to
write to the minister of the states very fully, in order that eventual measures may be taken, in case an armament should be sent
from France to Quebec, to co-operate therewith to the utmost
degree which the finances of the states would admit." In reply
to the second communication on this subject, the general said,
"The earnest desire I have strictly to comply, in every instance
with the views and instructions of congress, cannot but make me
feel the greatest uneasiness, when I find myself in circumstances
of hesitation or doubt, with respect to directions. But the perfect
confidence I have in the justice and candor of that honorable
body, emboldens me to communicate without reserve, the difficulties which occur in the execution of their present order; and
the indulgence I have experienced on every former occasion, induces me to imagine that the liberty I now take will not meet
with disapprobation.

"I have attentively taken up the report of the committee of
the fifth (approved by congress) on the subject of my letter of the
11th ultimo, on the proposed expedition into Canada. I have
considered it in several lights, and sincerely regret that I should
feel myself under any embarrassment in carrying it into execution. I still remain of opinion, from a general review of things,
and the state of our resources, that no extensive system of co-operation with the French, for the complete emancipation of Canada, can be positively decided on, for the ensuing year. To propose a plan of perfect co-operation with a foreign power, without
a moral certainty in our supplies; and to have that plan actually
ratified with the court of Versailles, might be attended, in case of
failure in the condition on our part, with very fatal effects.

"If I should seem unwilling to transmit the plan as prepared
by congress, with my observations, it is because I find myself under a necessity (in order to give our minister sufficient ground to
form an application upon) to propose something more than a
vague and indecisive plan; which, even in the event of a total
evacuation of the states by the enemy, may be rendered imprac-

ticable in the execution by a variety of insurmountable obstacles ; or if I retain my present sentiments and act consistently, I must point out the difficulties, as they appear to me, which must embarrass his negociations, and may disappoint the views of congress.

"But proceeding on the idea of the enemy's leaving these states, before the active part of the ensuing campaign, I should fear to hazard a mistake, as to the precise aim and extent of the views of congress. The conduct I am to observe in writing to our minister at the court of France, does not appear sufficiently delineated. Were I to undertake it, I should be much afraid of erring through misconception. In this dilemma, I would esteem it a particular favor to be excused from writing at all on the subject, especially as it is the part of candor in me to acknowledge, that I do not see my way clear enough to point out such a plan for co-operation, as I conceive, to be consistent with the ideas of congress, and will be sufficiently explanatory, with respect to time and circumstances to give efficiency to the measure.

"But if congress still think it necessary for me to proceed in the business, I must request their more definite and explicit instructions, and that they will permit me, previous to transmitting the intended despatches, to submit them to their determination.

"I could wish to lay before congress more minutely the state of the army, the condition of our supplies, and the requisites necessary for carrying into execution an undertaking that may involve the most serious events. If congress think this can be done more satisfactorily in a personal conference, I hope to have the army in such a situation before I can receive their answer, as to afford me an opportunity of giving my attendance."*

A committee was appointed to confer with the commander in chief, agreeably to his suggestion, relative to the operations of the ensuing campaign, and particularly on the proposed plan for the emancipation of Canada, in co-operation with an armament from France. On the first of January, 1779, the committee in reporting the result of this important conference, say, " That im-

* Marshall's Life of Washington, vol. 3, pp. 577, 578, 579.

pressed with a strong sense of the injury and disgrace which must attend an infraction of the proposed stipulation on the part of these states, your committee have taken a general review of our finances ; of the circumstances of our army ; of the magazines of clothing, artillery, arms and ammunition ; and of the provisions in store, and which can be collected in season. Your committee have, also, attentively considered the intelligence and observations communicated to them by the commander in chief, respecting the number of troops and strong holds of the enemy in Canada, their naval force, and entire command of the water communication with that country ; the difficulties, while they possess such signal advantages, of penetrating it with an army by land ; the obstacles which are to be surmounted in acquiring a naval superiority ; the hostile temper of many of the surrounding Indian tribes towards these states ; and above all, the uncertainty whether the enemy will not persevere in their system of harrassing and distressing our sea-coast and frontiers by a predatory war. That upon the most mature deliberation, your committee cannot find room for a well grounded presumption, that these states will be able to perform their part of the proposed stipulations. That, in a measure of such moment, and calculated to call forth, and divert to a single object, a considerable proportion of the force of an ally, which may otherwise be essentially employed, nothing less than the highest probability of its success would justify congress in making the proposition.

 " Your committee are, therefore, of opinion, that the negociations in question however desirable and interesting, should be deferred till circumstances should render the co-operation of these states more certain, practicable and effectual."* Though the reasons of the commander in chief, publicly communicated to congress, were in themselves conclusive against the measure, yet other reasons of a delicate nature, had no little weight with him. He had serious apprehensions, that if Canada should be conquered by the aid of French troops, its inhabitants being mostly French, might wish to return to their former allegiance ;

* Secret Journals of Congress, vol. 2, pp. 127, 128.

and that the temptation to retain an old and favorite province, would be too great to be resisted on the part of France.

These apprehensions were communicated by general Washington, to a member of congress, in a private letter of the 14th of November.

" The question of the Canada expedition," says the general, " as it now stands, appears to me one of the most interesting that has ever agitated our national deliberations.

" I have one objection to it, untouched in my public letter, which is, in my estimation, unsurmountable, and claims all my feelings, for the true and permanent interest of my country. This is the introduction of a large body of French troops into Canada, and putting them into the possession of the capital of that province, attached to them by the ties of blood, habits, manners, religion and former connections of government, I fear this would be too great a temptation to be resisted, by any power actuated by the common maxims of national policy. Canada would be a solid acquisition to France, on all accounts ; and because of the numerous inhabitants, subjects to her by inclination, who would aid in preserving it under her power, against the attempt of any other, France, it is apprehended, would have it in her power to give law to these states.

" Let us suppose, that when the five thousand troops, (under the idea of that number, twice as many might be introduced) were entered into the city of Quebec, they should declare an intention to hold Canada as a pledge and surety for the debts due to France by the United States. It is a maxim founded on the universal experience of mankind, that no nation is to be trusted farther than it is bound by its interests ; and no prudent statesman or politician will venture to depart from it. If France should even engage in the scheme, in the first instance, with the purest intentions ; invited by circumstances, she could alter her views. As the marquis clothed his proposition, when he spake of it to me, it would seem to originate wholly from himself ; but it is not impossible, that it had its birth in the cabinet of France, and was put into this artful dress to give it a readier currency. I fancy I read in the countenance of some people, on this occasion, more than the interested zeal of allies. I hope I am mistaken, and that my fears of mischief make me refine too much and awaken jealousies, that have no sufficient foundation."*

Congress directed a letter to be written to the marquis de la Fayette, who had gone to France, apprizing him that on account of the exhausted state of the resources, and the deranged state of the finances of the United States, as well as from more extensive and accurate information concerning Canada, they did not judge it prudent or just, to enter into engagements with their allies, for the emancipation of that province.

It was natural that France should wish to see Canada, as well as the rest of America, separated from Great Britain, and that she should be willing to unite in measures to effect that object. Count de Estaing, the commander of the French fleet, had orders, to invite the Canadians to join the United States, and to renounce the domination of their new masters ; and even to promise them the protection of their former sovereign.

In pursuance of these orders, on the 28th of October, 1778, he published a declaration, addressed, in the name of the king of France, " to all the ancient French in Canada, and every other part of North America ;" calling upon them, not only in the name of the French king, but in the name of every thing dear to Frenchmen, to join the United States, and renounce the authority of Great Britain, promising them protection and support. After adverting to their former and present situation, the count thus concludes :

" I shall not ask the military companions of the marquis of Levi, those who shared his glory, who admired his talents and genius for war, who loved his cordiality and frankness, the principal characteristics of our nobility, whether there be other names in other nations, among which they would be better pleased to place their own.

" Can the Canadians who saw the brave Montcalm fall in their defense, can they become the enemies of his nephews ? Can

* Life of Washington by John Kingston and Gordon.

they fight against their former leaders, and arm themselves against their kinsmen? At the bare mention of their names, the weapons would fall out of their hands.

" I shall not observe to the ministers of the altars, that their evangelical efforts will require the special protection of providence, to prevent faith being diminished by example, by worldly interest, and by sovereigns whom force has imposed upon them, and whose political indulgence will be lessened proportionally as those sovereigns shall have less to fear. Shall not observe, that it is necessary for religion, that those who preach it, should form a body in the state, and that in Canada no other body would be more considered, or have more power to do good than that of the priests' taking a part in the government, since their respectable conduct has merited the confidence of the people.

" I shall not represent to that people, nor to all my countrymen in general, that a vast monarchy, having the same religion, the same manners, the same language, where they find kinsmen, old friends and brethren, must be an inexhaustable source of commerce and wealth, more easily acquired and secured by their union with powerful neighbors, than with strangers of another hemisphere, among whom every thing is different, and who, jealous and despotic governments, would sooner or later treat them as a conquered people, and doubtless much worse than their countrymen the Americans, who made them victorious. I shall not urge to a whole people, that to *join* with the United States is to secure their own happiness ; since a whole people when they acquire the right of acting and thinking for themselves, must know their own interest ; but I will declare and I now formally declare, in the name of his majesty, who has authorized and commanded me to do it, that all his former subjects in North America, who shall *no more acknowledge* the supremacy of Great Britain, may depend upon his protection and support.'"*

After the conclusion of the treaties with France, the aid and co-operation of Spain, was confidently expected by the Americans ; and her accession to the treaties, agreeably to the secret

* Annual Register for 1779, and Note 5.

article, was earnestly solicited. This was refused on the part of his catholic majesty. Though desirous of reducing the power of Great Britain, by the independence of her North American colonies, the king of Spain was unwilling to be instrumental in effecting this, without some security against the probable consequences to his own extensive possessions in American, bordering on those colonies.

The security required by the Spanish court was, an exclusive right to the navigation of the river Mississippi, and a relinquishment of all claim, on the part of the Americans, to the country west of the Alleghany mountains; and the king of Spain was highly displeased with his most christian majesty, for concluding treaties with the United States, without having insisted on this security.*

He, however, offered his mediation between France and Great Britain; and the United States were to be included in any negociations for peace, which might be the consequence. This mediation was readily accepted on the part of France, and was listened to by Great Britain. Neither party, however, could have entertained a serious thought that peace could result from the mediation of a power, so closely connected with France, by the ties of blood, as well as by feeling, interest, and by compact. In making the offer, Spain had two objects in view, the one, to prepare her maritime force, the other, and probably, not the least important, to draw from the Americans an explicit declaration concerning their claims to the western country, and the navigation of the Mississippi. Great Britain was willing to prevent an immediate junction of the house of Bourbon against her; and she did not yet relinquish the hope of breaking the alliance between France and the United States. A correspondence on the subject of the mediation was kept up, between the courts of London and Madrid, about eight months; in which each accused the other of a want of sincerity and good faith.

The final propositions made to the courts of Paris and London, by his catholic majesty, in his character of mediator, were, " that

* See Histoire de Diplomatie Francaise, &c. vol. 7.

there shall be a suspension of arms with France, without limitation, and under this condition—that neither of the belligerent powers shall break it without giving the other one year's previous notice. That with a view that this suspension of hostilities may re-establish reciprocal security and good faith between the two crowns, there shall be a general disarming within one month, in all the European; within four, in those of America; and within eight or one year, in the most remote parts of Africa and Asia. That in the space of one month a place shall be fixed upon, in which the plenipotentiaries of the two courts shall meet to treat of a definitive adjustment of peace, regulate the respective restitutions or compensations necessary in consequence of the reprisals that have been made without any declaration of war, and to settle such matters of complaint or pretensions, as the one crown may have against the other; to the accomplishment of which end, the king will continue his mediation; and does now, for the holding of this congress, make an offer of the city of Madrid. That a like suspension of hostilities shall be separately granted by the king of Great Britain to the American colonies, through the intercession and mediation of his catholic majesty, to whom the king of Great Britain shall promise the observance thereof, and with the condition not to break it, without giving his majesty one year's previous notice, in order that he may communicate the same to the said American provinces: and that there be a reciprocal disarming, the same as with France, in the same time and places, regulating the limits that shall not be passed by the one or the other party, with respect to the places they respectively occupy at the time of ratifying this arrangement. That for the purpose of settling these particulars and others relative to the stability of the said suspension, and the effects it may produce while it subsists, there shall be sent to Madrid one or more commissaries on behalf of the colonies; and his Britannic majesty shall also send his, under the mediation of the king, if necessary; and that in the mean time, the colonies shall be treated as *independent in fact*.

"Finally, in case all the belligerent powers, or any one of them, or if only the said colonies demand that the treaties or agreements, which shall be concluded, be guarantied by these powers and by Spain, the same shall be done. And the catholic king now makes an offer of his guarantee to these preliminaries."

The answer of the court of London, to this ultimatum, dated May 4th, 1779, was, that " the propositions of the catholic king tend directly to the end which Spain had proposed to form, from the pretensions of the colonies to independence, one common cause with them and with France. If the conditions which the court of Versailles had communicated to his catholic majesty, do not present a better aspect than this for the treaty, or do not offer less imperious and less unequal terms, the king of Great Britain has only to lament that he finds the hopes frustrated, which he had always conceived, of a happy restoration of peace, as well for his own subjects, as the world in general."*

As the court of London had previously informed his catholic majesty, that, in the proposed negociations, France would not be permitted to mingle, " the interests of those, she affected to call her allies ;" the answer to these final propositions must have been anticipated by the Spanish court. The receipt of this answer was, therefore, followed by a note bearing date the 16th of June, 1779, from the Spanish ambassador, to the British secretary of state, amounting to a declaration of war ; and in two days after, orders for reprisals were issued by the British king. This declaration of war by Spain, was in consequence of a secret treaty between his catholic majesty and the king of France, concluded on the 12th of April preceding.

This treaty has never been published, and its terms are not precisely known. There can be little doubt, that it was a renewal of the *family compact ;* and in all probability contained, also, assurances of aid, on the part of France, in securing to Spain her American possessions.

Manifestoes were soon issued by the courts of France and Spain, in vindication of their conduct, in relation to the Americans. These were soon followed by a justifying memorial, on

---

* Secret Journals of Congress, vol. 2, pp. 301, 302, 303.

the part of Great Britain.* Alluding to the *secret* manner, in
which France had encouraged the Americans, the British king
says—" as soon as the revolted colonies had completed their
criminal enterprize, by an open declaration of their pretended
independence, they thought to form secret connections with the
powers least favorable to the interests of their mother country ;
and to draw from Europe those military aids, without which it
would have been impossible for them to have supported the war
they had undertaken. Their agents endeavored to penetrate
into, and settle in the different states of Europe ; but it was only
in France, that they found an asylum, hopes, and assistance. It
is beneath the king's dignity to enquire into the *nature of the correspondence*, that they had the address to contract with the court
of Versailles, and of which the public effects were soon visible, in
the general liberty, or rather unbounded licence of an *illegitimate
commerce.* It is well known, that the vigilance of the laws cannot always prevent artful illicit traders, who appear under a thousand different forms, and whose avidity for gain makes them brave
every danger, and elude every precaution : but the conduct of
the French merchants, who furnished America not only with useful and necessary merchandize, but even with salt-petre, gun-
powder, ammunition, arms, and artillery, loudly declared, that
they were assured, not only of impunity, but even of the protection and favor of the ministers of the court of Versailles.

" An enterprise so vain and so difficult, as that of hiding from
the eyes of Great Britain, and of all Europe, the proceedings of a
commercial company, associated for furnishing the Americans
with whatever could nourish and maintain the fire of a revolt, was
not attempted. The informed public named the chief of the enterprise, whose house was established at Paris ; his correspondents at Dunkirk, Nanzt, and Bourdeaux, were equally known.
The immense magazines, which they formed, and which they re-
plenished every day, were laden in ships that they built or bought,
and they scarcely dissembled the objects, or the place of their

---

* This memorial was drawn by Gibbon, the historian, then one of the board of
trade.

destination. These vessels commonly took false clearances for the French islands in America, but the commodities which composed their cargoes were sufficient, before the time of their sailing, to discover the fraud and artifice."*   •

In the "observations" on this memorial, published by order of the French court, it is said, in answer to this part— " It is true, that the king of France hath promised to forbid arms to be exported to America, and they were actually forbidden ; and whatsoever the English ministry may say, that trade was hindered as much as possible, without attacking the liberty of citizens ; and without subjecting commerce to an inquisition, which is used in no corner of the globe, and with which the English themselves would have reproached us, as an act of unsufferable despotism."

While negociations, in consequence of the offered mediation, were pending, Great Britain attempted to detach the Americans from their alliance with France. For this purpose, Mr. Hartley, in the winter of 1779, with the privity of lord North, went to Paris, to confer with Dr. Franklin.

The great object of this conference, so far at least, as the British minister was concerned, was, to obtain from the Americans or from Dr. Franklin, some proposition, as the ground of reconciliation ; particularly an offer, on the part of the United States to abandon France, and make a separate treaty of peace.

With this view, on the 22d of April, 1779, Mr. Hartley, submitted to Dr. Franklin certain preliminary propositions, which might, as he said, lead to a permanent settlement of all differences.

These propositions were—

" 1. Five commissioners, (or any three of them,) to be appointed, on the part of his Britannic majesty, to treat, consult, and agree upon the final settlement and pacification of the present troubles, upon safe, honorable, and permanent terms, subject to ratification by parliament.

* Annual Register for 1779, p. 404.

•

" 2. That any one of the aforesaid commissioners may be empowered to agree, as a preliminary, to a suspension of hostilities by sea and land, for a certain term of five or seven years.

" 3. That any one of the aforesaid commissioners be empowered, as a second preliminary, to suspend the operation and effect of any and all acts of parliament respecting America, for a certain term of five or seven years.

" 4. That it is expected, as a third preliminary, that America should be *released*, *free*, and *unengaged*, from any *treaties* with *foreign powers*, which may tend to embarrass or defeat the present proposed negociation.

" 5. That a general treaty for negociation shall be set on foot, as soon as may be, after the agreement of the foregoing preliminaries."

A dissolution of the connection between America and France, a connection, which, as Mr. Hartley explicitly told Dr. Franklin, was " the great *stumbling block*, in the way of reconciliation," was the great object of these propositions. The British cabinet hoped, by an *offer*, on the part of America or her minister of treating separately, to create a jealousy and distrust on the part of France. Dr. Franklin, was too wise and circumspect, as well as too honest and honorable, to listen for a moment to a proposition of this kind.

In communicating these preliminaries, Mr. Hartley said to Dr. Franklin, " I think the interest of all parties coincides with the proposition of preliminaries. The proposed preliminaries appear to me to be just and equitable to all parties ; but the great object with me is to come to some preliminaries ; I could almost add whatever those preliminaries might be, provided a suspension of arms for an adequate term of years were one, I think it would be ten thousand to one against any future renewal of the war. It is not necessary to enter at large into the reasons which induce me to think, that the British ministry, as well as the American plenipotentiary, would consent to the tern.s of the proposed preliminaries ; for indeed I do not know that I am founded in that opinion with respect to either, but still I believe it of both. But what

can a private person do in such a case, wishing to be a mediator
for peace, having access to both parties, but equally uncertain of
the reception of his mediation on either side ? I must hesitate to
take any public step, as by a proposition in parliament, or by any
other means to drive the parties to an explanation upon any specific proposals : and yet I am very unwilling to let the session
pass without some proposition, upon which the parties may meet,
if they should be so inclined, as I suspect them to be. I have
been endeavoring to feel pulses for some months, but all is dumb
show. I cannot say that I meet with any thing discouraging, to
my apprehension, either as to equitableness or practicability of
the proposition for preliminaries. If I could but simply receive
sufficient encouragement that I should not run any hazard of ob-
structing any other practicable propositions, by obtruding mine,
I should be very much satisfied to come forward, in that case,
with mine to furnish a beginning at least which might lead to
peace. There is nothing that I wish so much as to have an opportunity of seeing and conversing with you, having many things
to say to you ; but if that cannot yet happen, I have only to say,
that whatever communication you may think proper to make to
me, which may lead to peace, you may be assured that I shall be
most strenuous in applying it to that end. In all cases of difficulty in human life, there must be confidence somewhere to enable
us to extricate nations from the evils attendant upon national
disputes, as they arise out of national passions, interests, jealousies,
and points of honor. I am not sure whether the extreme caution
and diffidence of persons in political life be not the cause almost
as frequently of the unnecessary protraction of the miseries of war,
as of the final production of any superior good to any state.
Peace *now* is better than peace a twelvemonth hence, at least by
all the lives that may be lost in the meanwhile, and by all the accumulated miseries that may intervene by that delay. When I
speak of the necessity of confidence, I would not have you to
think, that I trust to all professions, promiscuously, with confidence : my thoughts are free respecting all parties ; and for myself, if I thought it necessary for the end of attaining any addi-

tional confidence in your esteem, to enable me to co-operate the
more effectually towards the restoration of peace, there is nothing that I would wish you to be assured of but this ; that no fallacious offers of insincerity, nor any pretexts for covering secret designs, or for obtaining unfair advantages, shall ever pass through
my hands."

In answer to this communication, Dr. Franklin observed—
" I need not repeat, what we have each of us so often repeated, the wish for peace. I will begin by frankly assuring you,
that though I think a direct, immediate peace, the best mode
of present accommodation for Britain as well as for America, yet if that *is not* at this time practicable, and a truce is
practicable, I should not be against a truce ; but this is merely
on motives of *general humanity*, to obviate the evils men devil-
ishly inflict on men in time of war, and to lessen as much as possible, the similarity of earth and hell. For with regard to particular advantages, respecting the states I am connected with, I am
persuaded it is theirs to continue the war, till England shall be reduced to that perfect impotence of mischief, which alone can prevail with her to let other nations enjoy, ' *peace, liberty, and safety.*' I think, however, that a short truce, which must, therefore,
be an armed truce, and put all parties to an almost equal expense
with a continued war, is by no means desirable. But this proposition of a truce, if made at all, should be made to France, at
the same time it is made to America. They have each of them
too much honor, as well as too much sense, to listen separately
to any propositions which tend to separate them from each other. I will now give you my thoughts on your ideas of a negociation, in the order you have placed them. If you will number them
in your copy, you will readily see to which my observations refer,
and I may, therefore, be more concise.

" *To the first.* I do not see the necessity or use of five commissioners. A number of talkers lengthen discussions, and often embarrass instead of aiding a settlement. Their different particular
views, private interests and jealousies of each other, are likewise
so many rubs in the way, and it sometimes happens that a num-

ber cannot agree to what each privately thinks reasonable, and would have agreed to, or perhaps proposed if alone. But this as the parties please.

" *To the second.* The term of twenty one years, would be better for all sides. The suspension of hostilities should be expressed to be, between all parties at war : and that the British troops and ships of war now in any of the United States be withdrawn.

" *To the third.* This seems needless, and is a thing that may be done or omitted as you please. America has no concern about those acts of parliament.

" *To the fourth.* The reason of proposing this is not understood, nor the use of it, nor what inducement there can be for us to agree to it. When you come to treat with both your enemies, you may negociate away as much of these engagements as you can ; but powers who have made a firm solid league, evidently useful to both, can never be prevailed with to dissolve it, for the vague expectation of another *in nubibus ;* nor even on the certainty that another will be proposed, without knowing what are to be its articles. America has no desire of being free from her engagements to France. The chief is that of continuing the war in conjunction with her, and not making a separate peace ; and this is an obligation not in the power of America to dissolve, being an obligation of *gratitude and justice,* towards a nation which is engaged in a war on her account, and for her protection ; and would be forever binding, whether such an article existed or not in the treaty ; and though it did not exist, an honest American would cut off his right hand rather than sign an agreement with England contrary to the spirit of it.

" *To the fifth.* As soon as you please. If you had mentioned France in your proposed suspension of arms, I should immediately have shewn it to the minister, and have endeavored to support that idea. As it stands, I am in doubt whether I shall communicate your paper or not, though by your writing it is so fair, it seems as if you intended it. If I do, I shall acquaint you with the result.

" The bill of which you send me a copy was an excellent one at the time, and might have had great and good effects, if instead of telling us haughtily, that our humble petition should receive no answer, that the ministry had received and enacted that bill into a law. It might have erected a wall of brass round England, if such a measure had been adopted when friar Bacon's brazen head cried out, TIME IS! But the wisdom of it was not seen, till after the fatal cry of TIME IS PAST!"

France was not without apprehensions that the United States might consider themselves at liberty to make a separate peace. About the 1st of January, 1779, the French minister, in a communication to congress says, "It is pretended the United States have preserved the liberty of treating with Great Britain separately from their ally, as long as Great Britain shall not have declared war against the king his master." In consequence of this representation, congress, on the 14th of January, of the same year, unanimously declared, "that as neither France nor these United States may of right, so these United States will not conclude either truce or peace with the common enemy, without the formal consent of their ally first obtained; and that any matters and things which may be insinuated or asserted to the contrary thereof, tend to the injury and dishonor of the said states."*

The offer of mediation by his catholic majesty, was made known to congress by letters from Arthur Lee, and by the French minister, Mons. Gerard; and on the 17th of February, 1779, the subject was referred to a committee, consisting of G. Morris, Mr. Burke, Mr. Witherspoon, Samuel Adams, and M. Smith. This committee soon after reported as their opinion, "that his catholic majesty is disposed to enter into an alliance with the United States. That he hath manifested this disposition, in a decisive declaration made to the court of Great Britain. That, in consequence of such declaration, the independence of the United States must be finally acknowledged by Great Britain; and immediately thereon a negociation for peace will be set on foot, be-between the powers of France, Great Britain, and the United States, under the mediation of his catholic majesty; or that Spain will take part in the war, and his catholic majesty will unite his

* Secret Journals of Congress, vol. 2, p. 517.

force with the most christian king and the United States." In the event of a negociation, the committee were of opinion, that the United States should not treat of peace, but on the footing of an independent nation; and that, as a preliminary, their independence should be acknowledged on the part of Great Britain.

In case of such an acknowledgment, they recommended the appointment of ministers on the part of the United States, to assist at such negociation, and that such ministers should be instructed by congress.

" 1. What to insist on, as the ultimatum of the states.

" 2. What to yield, or require, on terms of mutual exchange or compensation."

Under the first head, the committee recommended six articles.

1. That the bounds of the United States, should be northerly by the ancient limits of Canada, as contended for by Great Britain, running from Nova Scotia, south westerly, west, and north westerly, to lake Nipissing, thence a west line to the Mississippi; easterly by the boundary settled between Massachusetts and Nova Scotia; southerly by the boundary between Georgia and Florida; and westerly by the Mississippi.

2. All the posts and places, within these limits, to be evacuated.

3. The right of fishing and curing fish, on the banks and coast of Newfoundland, equally with the subjects of France and Great Britain, to be reserved and ratified to the citizens of the United States.

· 4. The navigation of the Mississippi, as low down as the southern boundary of the United States, to be acknowledged and ratified free to the citizens of the states.

5. Free commerce to be allowed with some port or ports, below the southern boundary of the United States, on the river Mississippi, except for such articles as may be particularly enumerated.

6. In case the allies of the United States would agree to support them in such claim by continuing hostilities, to insist that Nova Scotia be ceded to the United States, or declared independent.

On the second head, the committee were of opinion,

1. That the claim to Nova Scotia be given up, in lieu of the equal share in the Newfoundland fishery, or such share of the fishery, in lieu of Nova Scotia, if both could not be obtained.

2. In case neither of these could be obtained in lieu of the other, then, if the Bermuda islands could be obtained, the claim to Nova Stotia be ceded in lieu thereof.

3. That it might be stipulated, that the United States should not trade to the East Indies, or engage in the slave trade, if adequate compensation could be obtained.

4. The United States not to establish any settlement or dominion, beyond the limits of the states, as settled at the conclusion of the treaty of peace.

5. The Floridas, if ceded to the United States by Great Britain, might be ceded to Spain, for an adequate compensation.

6. A reciprocal guarantee of American possessions, which should remain to the respective powers, at the conclusion of peace.

The committee were opposed to a truce, but were of opinion, that during the negociations, a cessation of hostilities might be admitted, in case the force of the enemy should be withdrawn from every post and place within the limits of the United States.

With respect to terms, to which the Americans should ultimately agree in a treaty of peace with Great Britain, rather than continue the war, the members of congress were much divided. It was, indeed, a subject of greater magnitude, than had come before that body, since the declaration of independence. It created long and warm debates in the national legislature, and was not finally settled, until the 14th of August, 1779 ; and not until two months after Spain had declared war against Great Britain.

While this important subject was before congress, the French minister declared to that body, in a conference held in July, that he was authorized to inform them, that Great Britain had rejected with haughtiness the formal acknowledgment of the independence of the United States. He suggested, therefore, whether under these circumstances, they ought not to be satisfied

with a *tacit*, instead of an *express* acknowledgment, agreeably to the alternative in the treaty.   He also urged " the
manifest and striking necessity of enabling Spain, by the determination of just and *moderate* terms, to press upon England with
her good offices, in order that we may know whether we are to
expect war or peace.   This step," he added, " is looked upon in
Europe, as immediately necessary.   It was the proper object of
the message I delivered in February last.   I established then the
strong reasons, which required, that, at *the same time* and without delay, *proper terms should be offered to his catholic majesty*,
in order to *reconcile* him perfectly to the American interest.   I
did not conceal, that it was to be feared, that any condition inconsistent with the established form of the alliance, which is the
binding and only law of the allies, and contrary to the line of
conduct which Spain pursued in the course of her mediation,
would lead her to drop the mediation, and prevent his catholic
majesty, by motives of honor and faithfulness, from joining in our
common cause, and from completing the intended triumvirate.
No loss, no unhappy event," he subjoined, " could be so heavy
on the alliance as this.   Indeed, although the British forces were
already kept in check by the combined efforts of France and
America, it is nevertheless evident, that the accession of Spain
can only give to the alliance a decided superiority adequate to
our purposes, and free us from the fatal chance that a single unlucky event may overturn the balance."*

The " moderate terms " mentioned by the French minister in
this communication, referred to the claim of the United States
to the western country and the navigation of the Mississippi.
While the subject of instructions to the American minister was
before congress, Mr. Gerard was strongly opposed to this claim, as
being unfounded, and took measures to have it relinquished.

The instructions in relation to the terms of peace, ultimately
adopted by congress, were,

" 1. The United States are sincerely desirous of peace, and
wish by every means, consistent with their dignity and safety, to

* Secret Journals of Congress, vol. 2, pp. 199, 200, and Note 6.

spare the further effusion of blood. They have, therefore, by your commission and these instructions, labored to remove the obstacles to that event, before the enemy have evidenced their disposition for it. But as the great object of the present defensive war on the part of the allies, is to establish the independence of the United States, and as any treaty whereby this end cannot be obtained must be only ostensible and illusory, you are, therefore, to make it a preliminary article to any negociation, that Great Britain shall agree to treat with the United States as sovereign, free and independent.

" 2. You shall take special care also, that the independence of the said states be effectually assured and confirmed by the treaty or treaties of peace, according to the form and effect of the treaty of alliance with his most christian majesty. And you shall not agree to such treaty or treaties, unless the same be thereby so assured and confirmed.

" 3. The boundaries of these states are as follows, viz :—These states are bounded north, by a line to be drawn from the north west angle of Nóva Scotia along the highlands which divide those rivers, which empty themselves into the river St. Lawrence, from those which fall into the Atlantic ocean, to the north western-most head of Connecticut river ; thence down along the middle of that river to the forty-fifth degree of north latitude ; thence due west in the latitude of forty-five degrees north, from the equator to the north western-most side of the river St. Lawrence or Cataraqui ; thence straight to the south end of Nipissing ; and thence straight to the source of the river Mississippi : west, by a line to be drawn along the middle of the river Mississippi, from its source to where the said line shall intersect the thirty-first degree of north latitude : south, by a line to be drawn due east from the termination of the line last mentioned in the latitude of thirty-one degrees north from the equator to the middle of the river Appalachicola, or Catahouchi ; thence along the middle thereof to its junction with the Flint river ; thence straight to the head of St. Mary's river ; and thence down along the middle of St. Mary's river to the Atlantic ocean: and east, by a line to be drawn along the middle of St. John's river from its source to its mouth in the bay of Fundy, comprehending all islands within twenty leagues of any part of the shores of the United States, and lying between lines to be drawn due east from the points where the aforesaid boundaries between Nova Scotia on the one part, and East Florida on the other part, shall respectively touch the bay of Fundy and Atlantic ocean. You are, therefore, strongly to contend that the whole of the said countries and islands lying within the boundaries aforesaid, and every citadel, fort, post, place, harbor, and road to them belonging, be absolutely evacuated by the land and sea forces of his Britannic majesty, and yielded to the powers of the states, to which they respectively belong, in such situation as they may be, at the termination of the war. But, notwithstanding the clear right of these states, and the importance of the object, yet they are so much influenced by the dictates of religion and humanity, and so desirous of complying with the *earnest request of their allies*, that if the line to be drawn from the mouth of the lake Nipissing to the head of the Mississippi cannot be obtained without continuing the war for that purpose, you are hereby empowered to agree to some other line between that point and the river Mississippi; provided the same shall in no part thereof be to the southward of latitude of forty-five degrees north. And in like manner, if the eastern boundary above described cannot be obtained, you are hereby empowered to agree, that the same shall be afterwards adjusted, by commissioners to be duly appointed for that purpose, according to such line as shall be by them settled and agreed on, as the boundary between that part of the state of Massachusetts Bay, formerly called the province of Maine, and the colony of Nova Scotia, agreeably to their respective rights. And you may also consent, that the enemy shall destroy such fortifications as they may have erected.

" 4. Although it is of the utmost importance to the peace and commerce of the United States that Canada and Nova Scotia should be ceded, and more particularly, that their equal common right to the fisheries should be guarantied to them, yet a desire of terminating the war has induced us not to make the acquisition of these objects an ultimatum on the present occasion.

" 5. You are empowered to agree to a cessation of hostilities during the negociation ; provided our ally shall consent to the same ; and provided it shall be stipulated that all the forces of the enemy shall be immediately withdrawn from the United States.

" 6. In all other matters not abovementioned, you are to govern yourself by the alliance between his most christian majesty and these states ; by the advice of your allies ; by your knowledge of our interests ; and by your own discretion, in which we repose the fullest confidence."[*]

In framing these instructions, the *fisheries*, the *navigation* of the Mississippi, and the *boundaries*, were the great subjects of division and debate in congress. On these questions, local feelings and interests had their influence. The states at the east, particularly Massachusetts, deemed it essential to their welfare, and almost to their existence, that a right to the fisheries, should at all events, be secured ; while Virginia, and some of the states at the south, were equally desirous of securing the free navigation of the Mississippi. After various propositions on these subjects, a majority of the states rejected both as ultimata.

As to boundaries, the principal question was respecting the north line ; and the ultimatum on this point, was finally limited to latitude forty-five.

Should peace be the result of the negociations under the mediation of Spain, it was deemed necessary, that the American minister should be prepared with instructions, on the subject of commercial arrangements with Great Britain. The state of Massachusetts here again pressed upon congress the importance of the fisheries, and urged, that no treaty of commerce, should be made with Great Britain, without some arrangement on her part, favorable to America, with ' respect to them. Though congress would not make this a *sine qua non* of peace ; yet a majority of the states, resolved, that no treaty of commerce with Great Britain should receive their assent, without an explicit stip-

* Secret Journals of Congress, vol. 2, pp. 225, 226, 227, and 228.

ulation on her part, not to molest or disturb the inhabitants of the
United States, in taking fish, on the banks of Newfoundland,
and other fisheries in the American seas, any where, excepting
within the distance of three leagues of the shores of the territories remaining to Great Britain at the close of the war, if a nearer
distance could not be obtained by negociation.   To ensure the
right of fishing, as well as the observance of such stipulation,
congress, also, by a solemn resolution, declared, that if, after a
treaty of peace, Great Britain should molest the citizens of the
United States, in taking fish in the places and limits above specified, the same would be a violation and breach of the peace,
that the states would make it a *common cause*, and that the force
of the union should be exerted to obtain redress ; and they also
pledged their faith to the several states, that, without *their unanimous consent*, no treaty of commerce should be entered into, nor
any trade or commerce carried on with Great Britain, without
the above stipulation on her part.*

On the question of making the fisheries a common cause, the
states of New Hampshire, Massachusetts, Rhode Island, Connéct-
icut, New York, New Jersey, Pennsylvania, and Delaware, were
in the affirmative, and the states of Maryland, Virginia, North
and South Carolina, in the negative.   Special instructions were
sent to Dr. Franklin, to procure from the French king an explanatory article as to the extent of his guarantee in the treaty of alliance ; declaring that in case, after the conclusion of the war,
Great Britain should molest the Americans in the fisheries, he
would make it a common cause.

Congress had now become satisfied, that the public interest
did not require that ministers should be continued at any of the
courts of Europe, except those of Versailles and Madrid.   They
were sensible, also, of the impolicy of having more than one
commissioner at any foreign court.   Serious divisions had arisen between the American commissioners in Europe, and which
had, also, produced divisions in congress.   In April, 1779, therefore, congress declared, that ministers plenipotentiary on the part

* Note 7.

of the United States, were for the present only necessary, at the courts of Versailles and Madrid. The American ministers at the other courts were, therefore, recalled. And they, also, not long after, very wisely decided, that the United States should be represented at a foreign court, by one minister only.—This policy has since been pursued by the general government, except on extraordinary occasions, and for important temporary objects.

CHAPTER XIV.

THOUGH Spain had joined in the war against Great Britain, she had not acceded to the treaties between France and America, and was, therefore, under no obligation to continue the war, for the purpose of securing the independence of the United States. To induce her to do this, congress, on the 17th of September, 1779, declared, " that if his catholic majesty should accede to the said treaties, and in concurrence with France and the United States, continue the present war with Great Britain, for the purposes expressed in the treaties, he shall not, thereby, be precluded from securing to himself the Floridas : On the contrary, if he should obtain the Floridas from Great Britain, the United States would *guaranty* the same to his catholic majesty; provided, that the United States should enjoy the free navigation of the river Mississippi into and from the sea."*

On the 26th of September, congress proceeded to the election of a minister to negociate peace with Great Britain.

The members were equally divided between John Adams and John Jay, both of whom had been nominated the day preceding; and after two unsuccessful ballots, the subject was postponed.

The divisions in congress between these two statesmen, who had borne so conspicuous a part in the political concerns of their country, and who possessed so large a share of the public confidence, arose, in no small degree, from local feelings and interests. The states at the north preferred Mr. Adams on account of the fisheries ; and those at the south were not, probably, without their fears, that his partiality for the fisheries, might induce him, to give up some other points deemed equally important to other parts of the union.

In the mean time, congress came to the resolution of sending a minister to Spain; and the next day Mr. Jay was appointed envoy to the court of Madrid, and Mr. Adams to negociate a treaty of peace with Great Britain. Mr. Jay was intrusted with the important business of procuring the accession of Spain, to the treaties the United States had made with France. In case his catholic majesty required additional stipulations, he was at liberty to propose such as should be " analogous to the principal aim of the alliance, and conformable to the rules of equity, reciprocity and friendship." If Spain should accede to the treaties,

* Secret Journals of Congress, vol. 2, p. 249.

and in concurrence with France and the United States, continue the war, for the purposes therein expressed, he was instructed to offer her the Floridas on the terms and conditions contained in the above-mentioned resolution.

For the beneficial enjoyment of the navigation of the Mississippi below latitude 31°, he was instructed to procure some convenient port on the Mississippi, below that latitude, for the use of the citizens of the states. He was, also, directed to obtain a loan of five millions of dollars ; before making any propositions for a loan, however, he was to solicit a subsidy, in consideration of the guarantee of the Floridas.*

Mr. Jay sailed for Spain the latter part of the year, but being driven by a storm to the West Indies, he did not arrive in that country until March, 1780.

Before noticing the transactions of the American minister at the court of Madrid, we would state, that in November, 1779, Mr. Gerard was succeeded by the chevalier de la Luzerne, as minister from the French court. The new minister was intrusted with important communications for congress.   •

He officially announced the failure of the negociations in Europe, under the mediation of Spain ; and informed the American government, " that he had it in command to impress upon the minds of congress, that the British cabinet had an almost insuperable reluctance to admit the idea of the independence of these United States, and would use every possible endeavor to prevent it.

" That they had filled several of the courts of Europe with negociations, in order to excite them to a war against France, or to obtain succors ; and were employing the most strenuous endeavors to persuade the several powers that the United States were disposed to enter into treaties of accommodation. That many persons in Europe were actively employed in bringing such treaties to perfection ; and that they had no doubt of their success. That the objects which the British cabinet hoped for, from these measures, was to destroy the superiority which France had at

* Secret Journals of Congress, vol. 2, pp. 261, 262, and Note 8.

sea, by diverting her power and resources from naval to land operations, and by engaging her in a land war, where she must risk very important interests, while England would risk nothing but money ; or to break or weaken the alliance, by destroying the confidence which the allies ought to have in each other. That his most christian majesty gave no credit to the suggestions of Britain, relative to the disposition of the United States ; and it was necessary, that measures be taken for preventing other powers from being deceived into a belief of them."

The French minister, also, stated the necessity of the greatest possible vigor in the operations of the ensuing campaign ; that France and Spain were prepared to make a very powerful diversion, and would exert themselves strenuously for preserving their naval superiority, and for employing the forces of the enemy in Europe and the West Indies. In answer to this communication, congress assured the French minister, that they entertained the most grateful sense of the unremitted attention of their illustrious ally to the interests of the United States. With respect to the suggestions of the British cabinet, that the United States were disposed to enter into treaties of accommodation with Great Britain ; they wished his most christian majesty, and all the powers of Europe, to be assured, that these suggestions were " insidious and without foundation." " It will appear," they said, " by the constitutions and other public acts of the several states, that the citizens of the United States, possessed of arms, possessed of freedom, possessed of political power to create and direct their magistrates as they think proper, are united in their determination to secure to themselves and their posterity the blessings of liberty, by supporting the independence of their government, and observing their treaties and public engagements with immovable firmness and fidelity."*

The new French minister was particularly intrusted with certain articles from the Spanish court, concerning the western country and the navigation of the Mississippi ; on which a precise explanation, on the part of the United States, was requested. On

* Secret Journals of Congress, vol. 2, pp. 304, 307.

this subject, in pursuance of his instructions, in January, 1780, in a second conference he made the following communication to congress. "That his most christian majesty, being uninformed of the appointment of a minister plenipotentiary to treat of an alliance between the United States and his catholic majesty, has signified to his minister plenipotentiary to the United States, that he wishes most earnestly for such an alliance; and in order *to make the way more easy*, has commanded him to communicate to the congress, *certain articles*, which his catholic majesty deems of great importance to the interests of his crown, and on which it is *highly necessary* that the United States explain themselves with *precision* and with such *moderation*, as may consist with their essential rights."

" That the articles are,

" 1. A precise and invariable western boundary to the United States.

" 2. The exclusive navigation of the river Mississippi.

" 3. The possession of the Floridas; and,

" 4. The land on the left or eastern side of the river Mississippi.

" That on the first article, it is the idea of the cabinet of Madrid, that the United States extend to the westward no farther than settlements were permitted by the royal proclamation bearing date the   day of   1763.

" On the second, that the United States do not consider themselves as having any right to navigate the river Mississippi, no territory belonging to them being situated thereon.

" On the third, that it is probable the king of Spain will conquer the Floridas, during the course of the present war; and in such an event, every cause of dispute relative thereto, between Spain and these United States, ought to be removed.

" On the fourth, that the lands lying on the east side of the Mississippi, whereon the settlements were prohibited by the aforesaid proclamation, are possessions of the crown of Great Britain, and proper *objects* against which the arms of Spain may be employed, for the purpose of making a *permanent conquest* for the

Spanish crown. That such conquest may, probably, be made during the present war. That, therefore, it would be advisable to *restrain* the *southern* states from making any settlements or conquests in these territories. That the council of Madrid consider the United States, as having no claim to those territories, either as not having had possession of them, before the present war, or not having any foundation for a claim in the right of the sovereignty of Great Britain, whose dominion they have abjured.

" That his most christian majesty, united to the catholic king, by blood and by the strictest alliances, and united with these states in treaties of alliance, and feeling towards them dispositions of the most perfect friendship, is exceedingly desirous of conciliating between his catholic majesty and these United States, the most happy and lasting friendship.

" That the United States may repose the utmost confidence in his good will to their interests, and in the justice and liberality of his catholic majesty ; and that he cannot deem the revolution, which has set up the independence of these United States, as past all danger of unfavorable events, until his catholic majesty and the United States, shall be established on those terms of confidence and amity, which are the objects of his most christian majesty's very earnest wishes."*

This communication disclosed the reasons why his catholic majesty had refused his assent to the French treaty of alliance, as well as the causes of his displeasure that the king of France had concluded a treaty without his concurrence ; and without insisting that the Americans should have purchased the aid of France, as well as Spain, in effecting their independence, by the sacrifice of all their western territory. The proclamation referred to, in this communication, was that of the 7th of October, 1763, by which, for the purpose of preventing improper settlements on lands reserved for the Indians, the governors of all the colonies were prohibited, during the pleasure of the crown, from granting lands, beyond the heads or sources of any of the rivers, which fall into the Atlantic ocean, from the west and north west, or of any

* Secret Journals of Congress, vol. 2, p. 809.

lands reserved for the Indians. The views of Spain, therefore, as disclosed by this communication of the French minister, were, that the United States could have no valid claim to lands lying west of the Alleghany mountains; thereby limiting their boundaries west, to the old line claimed by France, before the war of 1756.

This subject was extremely interesting to all the states, particularly to Virginia, who in fact had made settlements far west of these limits. Spain, it was evident, contemplated the conquest not merely of the Floridas, but of all the extensive country east of the Mississippi, watered by the rivers, which entered the parent stream from the north and east, as belonging to Great Britain, and to claim it by right of conquest. In her views on this subject, she was countenanced and supported by the court of France. To this, however, the United States could never assent. Many of the states claimed to the Mississippi, by virtue of their charters, as well as by the treaty of 1763. Congress, however, did not think proper, to explain themselves *directly* to the French minister, on these extraordinary views and pretensions of the Spanish court. The delegates of Virginia, were afterwards specially instructed by the legislature of that state on this subject; and on the 4th of October, 1780, congress directed the American minister at the Spanish court, to adhere to his first instructions respecting the right of the United States to the free navigation of the Mississippi, into and from the sea; which right, they said, if not attainable by an express acknowledgment, was not to be relinquished. As to boundaries, he is instructed to adhere strictly to those already fixed by congress; and in addition they said, " Spain having, by the treaty of Paris, ceded to Great Britain, all the country to the north-eastward of the Mississippi, the people inhabiting these states, while connected with Great Britain, and, also, since the revolution, have settled themselves at divers places, to the westward, near the Mississippi, are friendly to the revolution, and being citizens of these United States, and subject to the laws of that to which they respectively belong, congress cannot assign them over, as subjects to any other power."

To enforce these instructions, congress on the 17th of October, 1780, drew up and sent to their ministers, in France and Spain, a statement of their claim to the western country, as far as the Mississippi, explaining the reasons and principles on which it was founded. This was to be communicated to both courts, and was intended as an answer to the claim of the court of Madrid, as well as " to satify both those courts of the justice and equity of the intentions of congress."

This very able state paper was drawn by a committee, consisting of Mr. Madison, Mr. Sullivan, and Mr. Duane; and no doubt was from the pen of Mr. Madison. In support of the claim on the part of the United States, to extend west as far as the Mississippi, congress observed that it was unnecessary, " to take notice of any pretensions founded on a priority of discovery, of occupancy, or on conquest. It is sufficient that by the definitive treaty of Paris, of 1763, article seventh, all the territory now claimed by the United States, was expressly and irrevocably ceded to the king of Great Britain; and that the United States are, in consequence of the revolution in their government, entitled to the benefits of that cession."

" The first of these positions," they subjoined, " is proved by the treaty itself. To prove the last, it must be observed, that it is a fundamental principle in all lawful governments, and particularly in the constitution of the British empire, that all the rights of sovereignty are intended for the benefit of those from whom they are derived, and over whom they are exercised. It is known, also, to have been held for an inviolable principle by the United States, while they remained a part of the British empire, that the sovereignty of the king of England, with all the rights and powers included in it, did not extend to them in virtue of his being acknowledged and obeyed as king, by the people of England, or of any other part of the empire, but in virtue of his being acknowledged and obeyed as king of the people of America themselves; that this principle was the basis, first of their opposition to, and finally of their abolition of, his authority over them. From these principles it results, that all the territory lying within the limits of the states, as fixed by the sovereign himself, was held by him for their particular benefit, and must equally with his other rights and claims in quality of their sovereign, be considered as having devolved on them, in consequence of their resumption of the sovereignty to themselves.

" In support of this position it may be further observed, that all the territorial rights of the king of Great Britain, within the limits of the United States, accrued to him from the enterprises, the risks, the sacrifices, the expense in blood and treasure of the present inhabitants and their progenitors. If in latter times, expenses and exertions have been borne by any other part of the empire, in their immediate defense, it need only be recollected, that the ultimate object of them, was the general security and advantage of the empire ; that a proportional share was borne by the states themselves ; and that if this had not been the case, the benefits resulting from an exclusive enjoyment of their trade have been an abundant compensation. Equity and justice, therefore, perfectly coincide, in the present instance, with political and constitutional principles."*

In consequence of information communicated by the American minister appointed to negociate peace with Great Britain, congress, in October, 1780, gave him additional instructions. He was informed that a short truce, would be highly dangerous to the United States ; but if a truce should be proposed for so long a period, or an indefinite period, requiring so long notice, previous to a renewal of hostilities, as to evince on the part of Great Britain, a virtual relinquishment of the war, and an expedient only to avoid the mortification of an express acknowledgment of American independence, he might, with the concurrence of their ally, accede to it, on condition of the removal of the land and naval armaments from the United States : he was directed, however, in case of a truce, to hold up the United States to the world, " in a style and title not derogatory to the character of an independent and sovereign people."

With respect to those persons, who had either abandoned, or been banished from, any of the United States, he was instructed

* Secret Journals of Congress, vol. 2, pp. 327, 328. Note 9.

to ' make no stipulation whatever for their re-admittance; and as to an equivalent for their property, he might attend to propositions on that subject only on a reciprocal stipulation, that Great Britain would make full compensation for all the wanton destruction which the subjects of that nation had committed on the property of the citizens of the United States."

Congress, also, expressed a wish, that in a treaty of peace, the United States should not be bound by any public engagement, to admit British subjects to any of the rights or privileges of citizens of the United States ; but to be left at liberty to grant or refuse such favors, as the public interest and honor might dictate.*

In consequence of the success of the enemy at the south during the year 1780, the state of Virginia, in order to induce Spain to accede to the treaty of alliance, and to afford more effectual aid in the common cause, was willing to recede from insisting on the right of navigating the Mississippi, and of a free port below the thirty-first degree of north latitude ; and on these points, instructed their delegates in congress, to procure an alteration in Mr. Jay's instructions.

Congress therefore in February, 1781, directed Mr. Jay, no longer to insist on this part of his instructions, in case Spain, should unalterably persist in her refusal ; and provided, the free navigation of the Mississippi, above latitude thirty-one degrees, should be acknowledged and guarantied by the king of Spain, to the citizens of the United States, in common with his subjects.

This was done, as congress declared, because the Americans were desirous, " to manifest to all the world, and particularly to his catholic majesty, the moderation of their views, the high value they place on the friendship of his catholic majesty, and their disposition to remove every obstacle to his accession to the alliance subsisting between his most christian majesty and these United States, in order to unite the more closely in their measures and operations, three powers who have so great a unity of interests,

* Secret Journals of Congress, vol. 2, pp. 389, 340.

and thereby to compel the common enemy to a speedy, just, and honorable peace."

Soon after Mr. Jay's arrival at Cadiz, which, as we have before stated, was not until March, 1780, he sent his secretary, Mr. Carmichael from that place to Madrid, to sound the Spanish court, on the subject of his mission. As a preliminary, that court wished to obtain particular information, concerning the population, manufactures, commerce, military and naval power, and generally the wealth and resources of the United States, as well as the disposition of the Americans to persevere, in their struggle for independence.

The Spanish minister, therefore, requested of the American envoy answers to various questions on these subjects. To these Mr. Jay returned very long and able answers ; and afterwards went to Madrid, and had many conferences with the prime minister, count Florida Blanca. He was soon informed that the king of Spain, would not accede to the treaties made with France ; and indeed he was told in the most explicit terms, that his catholic majesty was displeased with the king of France, for concluding those treaties without his concurrence.

The letter of the king of Spain to the French king, of the 22d of March, 1778, in answer to one from the latter, announcing his determination to disclose to the court of London his connection with America, bears strong marks of dissatisfaction.*

The American minister found the Spanish court very slow in all their movements. Having refused to acknowledge the independence of the United States, the king would not formally receive Mr. Jay, as an American minister. This rendered his situation humiliating as well as embarrassing. His embarrassments were greatly increased, in consequence of bills drawn upon him by congress to a large amount, before any provision was made for their payment. Presuming on the good will of the Spanish court towards the cause of America, the national legislature ventured to draw these bills, making them payable at six months sight ; trusting their minister would be able be-

* This letter will be found, in vol. 7, of Histoire, &c. de le diplomatie Francaise.

fore they fell due, to procure money from the king of Spain, either by loan or subsidy, to pay them. The Spanish minister, when informed of this, expressed no little surprise, that a step of this kind should be taken by congress, without a previous arrangement with his master; and it was not without great difficulty, Mr. Jay obtained from him, an engagement to furnish part of the amount, for which the bills were drawn. When the American minister pressed the Spanish court on the subject of forming treaties with the United States, agreeably to his instructions, he was told that, as a preliminary, some definitive arrangement must be made respecting the navigation of the Mississippi; and he was informed, that his catholic majesty had determined to exclude all foreigners from entering the gulf of Mexico by the rivers from the north. The American minister was strongly pressed to yield on these points.

Though Mr. Jay had the promise of assistance in the payment of the bills drawn upon him, yet infinite delays and difficulties were constantly interposed in the fulfilment of this promise. In consequence of this, the credit of the American government was put in great jeopardy, the embarrassments of Mr. Jay increased, and his patience put to the severest trial. In order to meet the bills, he was obliged to apply to Dr. Franklin at Paris, and but for his assistance, the bills would have returned to America unpaid, and the credit of the American government greatly injured in Europe. While Mr. Jay was in this situation, and was pressing the Spanish minister to furnish the funds agreeably to his engagement in order to save the honor and credit of the United States, he was informed, that if he would yield to the terms of Spain, respecting the navigation of the Mississippi, the money would be furnished. This was resisted by Mr. Jay, with great firmness, not only as contrary to his instructions, and inconsistent with the rights and interest of his country, but as an unwarrantable attempt to take advantage of his peculiar situation. The firm and patriotic conduct of the American minister on this occasion, was afterwards highly approved by congress.

After Mr. Jay received his instructions to recede from insisting on the free navigation of the Mississippi, and a free port below the thirty-first degree of north latitude, he proposed to the Spanish court, a plan of a treaty, one article of which was that "the United States should relinquish to his catholic majesty, and in future forbear to use the navigation of the river Mississippi, from the point where it leaves the United States down to the ocean." This article was accompanied with a declaration, on the part of the American minister, that if the offer was not *then* accepted, but postponed to a general peace, the United States would not be bound by it in future. This offer fell far short of the views of the Spanish court—the proposed treaty was rejected, and the negociation remained in this state, until June, 1782, when Mr. Jay was called to Paris, and the negociation was transferred from Madrid to that place.

Soon after the appointment of Mr. Jay to Spain, Henry Laurens of South Carolina, was appointed minister to the states of Holland, not only for the purpose of obtaining loans, but forming treaties with that republic. Overtures for a commercial connection with the United States, had been made from Holland, in 1778. William Lee, the American minister to the court of Prussia, on his way to Berlin in August of that year, had an interview with John de Neufville, a principal merchant of Amsterdam, on the subject of a commercial treaty, between the states general of Holland, and the United States; and on the 4th of September following, Mr. de Neufville, by the order and direction of Van Berkel, pensionary of Amsterdam, proposed a plan of a treaty, between the two countries.

This plan was communicated to congress, and Mr. Laurens was appointed to carry it into effect, on the part of America. He did not sail for Europe, until the summer of 1780; and unfortunately, on the 3d of September, was taken by a British frigate on his passage, near Newfoundland. He threw his papers overboard, but by the activity of a British sailor, they were recovered. Among them was a copy of the above plan of a treaty with the states of Holland, and several letters from Mr. de Neufville, and from Mr. Stockton, the secretary of William Lee, concerning the same.

Mr. Laurens being carried to London, was examined before the privy council, and on the 6th of October committed a close prisoner to the tower, on a charge of high treason. The disclosure of his papers, greatly incensed the court of London against Holland, and the English minister at the Hague, Sir Joseph. Yorke, was istructed to present a memorial to the states general, on the subject. On the 10th of November, Sir Joseph Yorke, in pursuance of his instructions, demanded a disavowal of this conduct of Van Berkel, and also insisted "on speedy satisfaction, adequate to the offense, and the exemplary punishment of the pensionary and his accomplices, as disturbers of the public peace, and violaters of the rights of nations."

Satisfaction for the supposed offense not having been made by the states general, the British minister was ordered to withdraw from Holland; and this was soon followed by a declaration of hostilities against that country by the court of London.

In June, 1780, Mr. Adams, then in Europe, was appointed in the room of Mr. Laurens to obtain loans in Holland, and in December of the same year, was invested with full powers to negociate a treaty of amity and commerce with that country.

Mr. Adams, though not then acknowledged as a minister, was determined to sound the Dutch government on the subject of forming a commercial connection with the United States, and for that purpose to communicate to their high mightinesses his commission and credentials, and to present to them also a memorial on the subject. This intention he communicated to the French minister at the Hague, the duke de la Vauguion. The latter, however, was opposed to this proceeding, and endeavored to dissuade Mr. Adams from taking this step at so unfavorable a moment.

Mr. Adams, however, considered it a favorable time for the United States to press the subject; and he drew a memorial bearing date the 19th of April, 1781, which he presented to the president of their high mightinesses.

The states general of Holland were not yet prepared to acknowledge the United States, as a sovereign and independent
nation; nor could the president receive the memorial in form;
but he engaged to make a report of the substance of what Mr.
Adams had stated to him on this subject. This was done, and
the report was received, and referred to the several provinces for
their decision.

In this memorial, after stating the origin and causes of the war
in which the Americans were engaged, their determination to
maintain their independence, and that with this view, they had
established regular and permanent governments, he endeavored
to convince the people of Holland, that it was for their interest to
form a connection with the United States, and to support their
independence.

To induce them to do this, he appealed to their former situation, when struggling for their liberties against the mighty power
of Spain; observing, that the United States were now in the same
situation in respect to Great Britain; and that a similarity in
government, religion, liberality of sentiment, and freedom of inquiry in the two republics, evinced the propriety of a connection
between them. "If there was ever among nations," said Mr.
Adams, "a natural alliance, one may be formed between the
two republics. The planters of the four northern states found
in this country an asylum from persecution, and resided here
from the year one thousand six hundred and eight, to the year
one thousand six hundred and twenty, twelve years preceding
their migration. They ever entertained, and have transmitted
to posterity, a grateful remembrance of that protection and hos-
pitality, and especially of that religious liberty they found here,
having sought it in vain in England.

"The first inhabitants of the two other states, New York and
New Jersey, were immediate emigrants from this nation, and
have transmitted their religion, language, customs, manners and
character; and America in general, until her connection with
the house of Bourbon, has ever considered this nation as her
first friend in Europe, whose history, and the great character it

exhibits, in the various arts of peace, as well as achievements of war by sea and land, have been particularly studied, admired and imitated in every state.

" A similitude of religion, although it is not deemed so essential in this as in former ages to the alliance of nations, is still, as it ever will be thought, a desirable circumstance. Now it may be said with truth, that there are no two nations, whose worship, doctrine and discipline are more alike, than those of the two republics. In this particular, therefore, as far as it is of weight, an alliance would be perfectly natural.

" A similarity in the forms of government is usually considered as another circumstance which renders alliances natural; and although the constitutions of the two republics are not perfectly alike, there is yet analogy enough between them, to make a connection easy in this respect.

" In general usages and in the liberality of sentiments on those momentous points, the freedom of inquiry, the right of private judgment and the liberty of conscience, of so much importance to be supported in the world, and imparted to all mankind, and which to this hour are in more danger from Great Britain and that intolerant spirit which is secretly fermenting there than from any other quarter, the two nations resemble each other more than any others.

" The originals of the two republics are so much alike, that the history of the one seems but a transcript from the other : so that every Dutchman instructed in the subject, must pronounce the American revolution just and necessary, or pass a censure upon the greatest actions of his immortal ancestors; actions which have been approved and applauded by mankind, and justified by the decisions of heaven."

On the representation of the French court, on the 16th of August, 1781, Mr. Adams was instructed to propose a triple alliance between France, the united provinces of the Netherlands, and the United States of America, limited in its duration to the war then existing with Great Britain, and to be conformable to the treaties between France and America. The indispensable conditions of this alliance on the part of Holland, were an acknowledgment of American independence and sovereignty, and an agreement to make the war with Great Britain a common cause, neither party to conclude peace or truce, without the consent of the other, or to lay down their arms until the sovereignty and independence of America was assured by Great Britain. The United States, however, had now become more cautious of engagements of guarantee, and Mr. Adams was directed not to agree to any stipulations of offense, or guarantee of possessions.

The movements in Holland on American affairs were as slow as in Spain, and the patience of Mr. Adams, as well as that of Mr. Jay, was severely tried. At the commencement of the year 1782, no answer had been given to his memorial. Wearied with this delay, Mr. Adams, on the 9th of January of that year, waited upon the president of the states general, and after referring to his application, and stating that he had yet received no answer, said :—

" I now do myself the honor to wait on you, sir, and to demand, as I do, a categorical answer, that I may be able to transmit it to the United States of America." Mr. Adams was warmly supported by the merchants and manufacturers, who, desirous of sharing in the trade of America, presented petitions to the government in favor of a treaty. The states general, therefore, on the 19th of April, 1782, declared, " that Mr. Adams should be admitted and acknowledged, in the quality of an ambassador of the United States of North America to their high mightinesses ;" and in three days afterwards he was received as such.

Negociations then commenced, but a treaty of amity and commerce was not completed until the 8th of October following.

The American revolution had excited no small degree of interest in most of the courts of Europe. The effects of the war between Great Britain, and France and Spain, in the years 1779 and 1780, were felt not only by Holland, but by the northern European powers, in their commercial intercourse with the two latter nations. The right of searching neutral vessels for contraband of war, and enemy's property, as claimed and exercised by

Great Britain, as well as other interruptions of neutral commerce by that nation, had excited the resentment of those powers, and produced, in July, 1780, what was called, the armed neutrality; at the head of which was the celebrated empress of Russia. In February of that year, the empress Catherine presented to the courts of London, France and Spain, a spirited declaration, on the subject of neutral rights. She claimed, that neutral ships should enjoy a free navigation, even from port to port, on the coasts of the belligerents—that free ships should make free goods with the exception of contraband of war; and that no port should be deemed blockaded, but such as was invested by a number of enemy's ships so near as to render an entry dangerous.

The proceedings of Russia and of the other neutral powers connected with her, in an armed defense of these principles, were approved by congress; and in October of the same year, the commanders of American armed vessels were instructed to conform to the principles contained in the declaration of the empress. Soon after this, Francis Dana was appointed minister to the Russian court, with power to accede, in behalf of the United States, to a convention among the neutral and belligerent powers in Europe, for protecting the freedom of commerce and the rights of nations—he was also instructed to propose a treaty of amity and commerce between the United States and Russia. He was, however, directed to consult the American ministers in Europe, as well as the French court, respecting the objects of his mission.

In the mean time the empress of Russia offered herself to the court of London, as a mediatrix, between the belligerents in Europe; and at the desire of the British court, the emperor of Germany agreed to take part, in this mediation.

This offer was first made known to congress, in May, 1781, in a memorial presented to that body, by the chevalier de la Luzerne.

The French minister stated, that the mediation had been accepted by Great Britain, but that the court of France could not accept it, without the consent of its allies—that the king, at least, wished to have their assent before he formally agreed to it—that circumstances, joined to the confidence he had in the mediation, and in the justice of his cause and that of his allies, might induce him to enter upon the negociation, before the answer of congress could arrive. In either case, he said, it was of great importance that congress should give their plenipotentiary instructions proper to announce their disposition to peace, as well as their moderation, and to convince the powers of Europe, that the independence of the United States, and the engagements they had contracted with the king, were the sole motives which determined them to continue the war ; and that when they should have full and satisfactory assurances, on these *two capital points*, they were ready to conclude a peace.

" The manner of conducting the negociation," the minister said, " the *extent* of the powers of the American plenipotentiary, the *use* to be made of them, and the *confidence* to be reposed in the French plenipotentiaries and the king's ministers, are points which should be fully discussed with a committee."

To this committee the minister said he should communicate, " some circumstances relative to the sending Mr. Cumberland to Madrid ; to the use which Mr. Adams thought he was authorized to make of his plenipotentiary powers ; to the mission of Mr. Dana ; to the association of the neutral powers, and to the present state of affairs in the south."*

Agreeably to the suggestion of the minister, Mr. Carroll, Mr. Jones, Mr. Witherspoon, Mr. Sullivan, and Mr. Matthews, were appointed a committee to confer with him, on the subject of his memorial. In this conference, he informed the committee that the proceedings of congress in relation to the association of the neutral powers, were approved by the king ; and that they would, no doubt, be agreeable to the empress of Russia. The appointment of an American minister, however, to the court of St. Petersburg, was deemed premature, as the empress, in consequence of her offer of mediation, could take no step, which would show the least partiality in favor of the Americans.

* Note 10.

The views and wishes of the French court, in relation to the American negociator and his instructions, were fully disclosed in this conference.

" The minister communicated to them," the committee say in their report to congress, " several observations respecting the conduct of Mr. Adams ; and in doing justice to his patriotic character, he gave notice to the committee of several circumstances which proved it necessary that congress should draw a line of conduct to that minister, of which he might not be allowed to lose sight. The minister dwelt especially on a circumstance already known to congress, namely, the use which Mr. Adams thought he had a right to make of his powers to treat with Great Britain.

" The minister concluded on this subject," the committee say, " that if congress put any confidence in the king's friendship and benevolence ; if they were persuaded of his irrevocable attachment to the principle of the alliance, and of his firm resolution constantly to support the cause of the United States, they would be impressed with the necessity of prescribing to their plenipotentiary a perfect and open confidence in the French ministers, and a thorough reliance on the king ; and would *direct him to take no step without the approbation of his majesty ;* and after giving him, in his instructions, the principal and most important outlines of his conduct, they would order him, with respect to the manner of carrying them into execution, to receive his *directions* from the count de Vergennes, or from the person who might be charged with the negociation in the name of the king."

The minister urged the necessity of despatch, in preparing instructions, as the negociations might be soon opened, and as Great Britain, through Mr. Cumberland, was attempting to induce Spain to make a separate peace. He also stated, that the greatest difficulty in the negociation would arise, in the articles relating to America ; he therefore thought proper, to impress them, " with the necessity congress were under, of securing in their favor the benevolence and good will of the mediating powers, by presenting their demands with the greatest *moderation* and *reserve,* save independence, which will not admit of any modification."*

The result of this interesting conference, clearly evinced an intention on the part of the French court, to have the terms of peace, in respect to the United States, at the control of the French minister, with the exception of the question of independence. The appointment of Mr. Adams sole negociator, was highly displeasing to Vergennes, and the use he had made of his powers, had been a subject of complaint to congress. Mr. Adams possessed, no doubt, too unyielding and independent a spirit for the French prime minister, and was too little of a courtier to please the cabinet of Versailles.

In consequence of this representation on the part of the French government, congress resumed the important subject of instructions to their minister for negociating peace. After considerable debate on the question of boundaries, the fisheries, and the still more delicate subject suggested by the French minister, *of placing their plenipotentiary under the control of the French monarch ;* and after associating Dr. Franklin, Mr. Jay, Mr. Laurens, and Mr. Jefferson, with Mr. Adams, they finally, on the 15th day of June, 1781, gave them the following instructions :—

" You are hereby authorized and instructed to concur in behalf of the United States, with his most christian majesty, in accepting the mediation proposed by the empress of Russia and the emperor of Germany.

" You are to accede to no treaty of peace which shall not be such as may,

" 1st, Effectually secure the independence and sovereignty of the thirteen states, according to the form and effect of the trea-. ties subsisting between the said states and his most christian majesty,—and

" 2d, In which the said treaties shall not be left in their full force and validity.

" As to disputed boundaries and other particulars, we refer you to the instructions formerly given to Mr. Adams, dated August

* Note 11.

14th, 1779, and 18th of October, 1780, from which you will easily perceive the desires and expectations of congress; but we think it unsafe, at this distance, to tie you up by absolute and peremptory directions upon any other subject than the two essential articles abovementioned. You are, therefore, at liberty to secure the interest of the United States in such manner as circumstances may direct, and as the state of the belligerent, and the disposition of the mediating powers may require. For this purpose, you are to make the most candid and confidential communications upon all subjects, to the ministers of our generous ally, the king of France; to undertake nothing in the negociations for peace or truce without their knowledge and concurrence, *and ultimately to govern yourselves by their advice and opinion ;* endeavoring in your whole conduct to make them sensible how much we rely on his majesty's influence for effectual support, in every thing that may be necessary to the present security or future prosperity of the United States of America.

" If a difficulty should arise in the course of the negociation for peace, from the backwardness of Britain to make a formal acknowledgment of our independence, you are at liberty to agree to a truce, or to make such other concessions as may not affect the substance of what we contend for; and provided that Great Britain be not left in possession of any part of the thirteen United States."*

While the subject of boundaries was under discussion, the state of Virginia moved in the first place, that the American negociators should not recede from their former ultimatum, in any part, except with respect to so much thereof, as delineated the boundary from the intersection of the forty-fifth degree of north latitude, with the river St. Lawrence, to the mouth of the Illinois river, from which they might recede so far, as to agree that the boundary between these two points should run from the said intersection through the middle of said rivers, of lake Ontario, of the strait of Niagara, and of lake Erie, to the mouth of the Miami river, thence to a direct line to the source of the Illinois, and thence

* Secret Journals of Congress, volume 2, pp. 446, 447.

down the middle of that river to its confluence with the Mississippi. This being rejected by all the states except Virginia ; the latter then proposed that they should not in any case agree " to a cession of any part of the territory lying on the south east side of the Ohio ; nor admit any exclusive claim on the part of Great Britain to the territory lying between the said river, the rivers Mississippi and Illinois, and the lakes Erie and Ontario." This, also, was negatived by a large majority.

The states were, also, divided on the interesting and delicate question, respecting the power of France, in relation to the terms of peace. A majority were at first unwilling to place their ministers entirely under the control of the French court ; and their instructions were drawn without a clause to that effect. A committee was appointed to communicate them to the French minister, and to confer with him on the subject. This committee reported an amendment, adding the words " *ultimately to govern yourselves by their advice and opinion ;*" and this amendment was sanctioned by a majority of the states. Massachusetts, Rhode Island, Connecticut, and Delaware, however, retained independence enough to vote against it, and Pennsylvania was divided. Mr. Adams and Mr. Jay had strong objections to this part of their instructions. The latter stated his objections to congress, and he consented to act under them with very great reluctance.

The mediation having been accepted by the belligerents in Europe, the mediating powers transmitted to the courts of London, Paris, and Madrid, " articles to serve as a foundation of the negociations for the re-establishment of peace."

A congress was to be held at Vienna, where treaties were to be made, agreeably to the articles, under the care of the two imperial courts.

The articles relating to the United States were—

" Art. I. There shall be a treaty between Great Britain and the American colonies, concerning the re-establishment of peace in America ; *but without the intervention of any of the other belligerent parties,* nor even *that* of the two imperial courts, at least, unless their mediation shall be formally demanded, and granted upon this object.

"Art. II. This particular peace shall not, however, be signed, but conjointly and at the same time with that of the powers, whose interests shall have been treated by the mediating courts. The two peaces, by this means, although they may be treated separately, not being to be concluded the one without the other, they shall take care constantly to inform the mediators, of the progress of the state of that which regards Great Britain and the colonies, to the end that the mediation may be in a situation to regulate itself, in the prosecution of that which is confided to it, according to the state of the negociation relative to the colonies; and the one or the other of the, two pacifications which shall have been concluded, at the same time, although separately, shall be solemnly warranted by the mediating courts, and every other neutral power whose warranty the belligerent parties may judge proper to demand.

"Art. III. For rendering the pacific negociations independent of the events, always uncertain of war, which might stop or at least interrupt the progress of them, there shall be a general armistice between all the parties, during the term of one year, to be computed from the   day of the month of   of the present year, or of   years, to be computed from the   of the month of   , of the year 1782, if it should happen that the general peace should not be established in the course of the first term. And during the continuance of one or the other of these two terms, all things shall remain in the state in which they shall be found to have been, on the day of the signature of the present preliminary articles."*

Mr. Adams, soon after he was appointed minister, sailed for Europe. He remained in France, until August, 1780, when he went to Holland. In July, 1781, Vergennes invited him to Paris, to confer on the subject of peace, under the mediation abovementioned. Mr. Adams was opposed to the third article, relative

* Mr. Adams' Correspondence, pp. 109, 110.

to an armistice, and the *statu quo*; and stated his objections to the French minister.

He was indeed instructed to agree to no truce, unless it should be for so long a period, as to evince that it was on the part of Great Britain a virtual relinquishment of the war, and only an expedient to avoid an express acknowledgment of the independence of the United States. A question arose, in what character Mr. Adams was to appear at the proposed congress at Vienna, whether as the representative of an independent state, or otherwise.

The court of France was informed, that the king of Great Britain in accepting the mediation, declared, he was ready to make peace, " as soon as the league between France and his revolted colonies should be dissolved."

Without a variation of the haughty terms proposed by the court of London, it was evident nothing could be done at Vienna, so far as the United States were concerned.

Mr. Adams utterly refused to appear at the congress but as the representative of an independent nation. In a letter to Vergennes on this subject, among other things, he said :—

" It is impossible that there should be a treaty between Great Britain and the United States, at Vienna, unless both powers appear there, by representatives, who must be authorized by commissions or full powers, which must be mutually exchanged, and consequently admitted to be, what upon the face of them they purport to be. The commission from· the United States, for making peace, which has been in Europe almost two years, is that of a minister plenipotentiary ; and it authorizes him to treat only with ministers vested with equal powers. If he were to appear at Vienna, he would certainly assume the title and character of minister plenipotentiary ; and he could enter into no treaty or conference with any minister from Great Britain, until they had mutually exchanged authentic copies of their full powers.

" This, it is true, would be an acknowledgment of his character and title, and of those of the United States too ; but such an acknowledgment is indispensable, because, without it, there can be so treaty at all. In consequence, he would expect to enjoy all the prerogatives of that character, and the moment they should be denied him, he must quit the congress, let the consequences be what they might. And, I rely upon it, this is the intention of the two imperial courts, because otherwise they would have proposed the congress, upon the two preliminaries, a rupture of the treaty (with France) and the return of the Americans to their submission to Great Britain, insisted upon by her; and because I cannot suppose it possible that the imperial courts could believe the Americans capable of such infinite baseness, as to appear in such a posture; nor can I suppose that they mean to fix a mark of disgrace upon the Americans, or to pronounce judgment against them; and because, otherwise, all their propositions would be to no effect, for no congress at Vienna can make either one or the other of the two proposed peaces, without the United States.

"Upon looking over again the words of the first article, there seems to be room for dispute, which a British minister, in the present state of his country, would be capable of taking advantage of. The terms which are used are exceptionable. There are no American colonies at war with Great Britain. The power at war is the United States of America. No American colonies have any representative in Europe, unless Nova Scotia or Quebec may have an agent in London. The word colony implies a metropolis, a mother country, a superior political governor, ideas which the United States of America have long since renounced, forever.

"I am, therefore, clear, in my own opinion, that a more explicit declaration ought to be insisted on, and that no American representative ought to appear, without an express assurance, that while the congress lasts, and in going to it, and from it, he shall be considered as a minister plenipotentiary from the United States of America, and entitled to all the preprogatives of a minister plenipotentiary of a sovereign power. The congress might be to him and his country but a snare, unless the substance of this is intended, and if it is intended, there can be no sufficient reason for declining to express it in words. If there is a power upon earth which imagines that America will ever appear at a congress, before a minister of Great Britain or any other power, in the character of repenting subjects, supplicating an amnesty or a warranty of an amnesty, that power is infinitely deceived. There are very few Americans who would hold their lives upon such terms. And all such ideas ought forever to be laid aside by the British ministry before they propose mediations. The very mention of such a thing to the United States by Great Britain would be considered only as another repetition of injury and insult. It would be little less to France."

The answer of his most christian majesty to the mediators, on this question, was in accordance with the views of Mr. Adams.

"The two imperial courts cannot flatter themselves, that they can conduct the mediation to an happy conclusion, if they do not provide against the subterfuges, the subtleties, and the false interpretations, which any of the belligerent powers may employ, for understanding according to its views, the preliminary propositions. There is the difficulty which would infallibly occur, if we do not determine, beforehand, the sense of the expressions which relate to the Americans. The court of London, who will elude as much and as long as she can, any direct and indirect avowal of the independence of the United States, will take advantage of the general terms we employ in speaking of them, to maintain that she is not obliged to treat with her ancient colonies, as with a free and independent nation: That she is not, consequently, in a situation to admit a plenipotentiary on their part: That she is the mistress to see nothing in their representative but the deputy of a portion of her subjects, who appear to sue for pardon: From which it would result, when the mediation should be in activity, and the question should be to open and commence the negociations, that they would begin to contest concerning the character which the American plenipotentiary may display: That the king of England will not regard him, but as his subject, while the congress shall demand that he be admitted as the representative of a free people; by which means the mediation will find itself arrested in its first step.

" To prevent this inconvenience, it seems, that before all things, the *character* of the American agent ought to be determined in a manner the most precise and positive, and that the congress ought to be invited to confide its interests to the mediation. This invitation is so much the more indispensable, as the negociations relative to America, must march with an equal step with that which the court of Versailles and Madrid will pursue ; and by consequence, these two negociations, although separate, must be commenced at the same time."

The answer of the French court being communicated by one of the mediating powers, to the cabinet of London, his Britannic majesty, on the 15th of June, 1781, declared in reply, that he could not in any manner or form whatever, admit the interference of any foreign power, between him and his rebel subjects ; and therefore would not agree to the admission of any person as their minister at the proposed congress, as this would be totally incompatible with their situation as subjects. He would not, he said, consent to any measure, which might limit or suspend the exercise of the right every sovereign had, to employ the means in his power, to put an end to a rebellion in his own dominions ; and that the mediation of the two imperial courts must be limited to a peace between the European belligerents, and not to a peace with his revolted subjects.* He declared at the same time, " that in all points to be agitated in a future congress, England will behave with great equity and condesension ; but the dependence of her rebel subjects in America must be pre-established, and that this matter must be left entirely to the care of Great Britain."†

The views of the imperial courts on this point were in accordance with those of the British cabinet. They were unwilling indirectly to acknowledge the independence of the United States, without the consent of Great Britain. These views were made known to Mr. Dana, by a letter from the marquis de Verac, the French minister at St. Petersburgh, in September, 1781. Referring to the first preliminary article, he said, " the mediating powers

* Histoire &c. de la Diplomatie Francaise, vol. 7.

† Secret Journals of Congress, vol. 3, pp. 28, 29.

understand by this, that your deputies shall treat simply with the English ministers, as they have already treated in America, with the commissioners of Great Britain, in 1778.   That the conclusion of their negociations shall teach the other powers upon what footing they are to be regarded, and that their public character shall be acknowledged without difficulty, from the moment when the English themselves shall no longer oppose it."*   The reply of the court of London, put an end to all farther proceedings under the mediation of the imperial courts.

* Mr. Adams' Correspondence, p. 186.

CHAPTER XV.

France assists America with troops—6000 arrive at Newport in July, 1780—In the spring of 1781, join the American army near New York—Assist in the capture of lord Cornwallis in October of the same year—British ministry again attempt to make separate treaties with United States and France—Make advantageous offers to the latter—Both nations refuse to treat separately—Change of ministry in England —Pacific overtures made by the new administration—Mr. Oswald sent to Paris on the subject—His reception by Dr. Franklin and the French minister—Agree to treat of peace at Paris—Mr. Grenville sent as minister by the British—Commissioners of peace about the same time sent to America—Congress refuse to treat with them —Grenville declares to Dr. Franklin that the independence of the United States was to be acknowledged as a preliminary—New administration in England in consequence of the death of the marquis of Rockingham—Lord Shelburne placed at the head of it—Opposed to an express and open acknowledgment of American independence—Supposed to have sent Mr. Jones to Paris secretly to sound the American ministers on the subject—Mr. Jones arrives at Paris—Makes an extraordinary communication to Dr. Franklin—Great difficulties respecting the powers of the British negociators—Mr. Jay refuses to treat except as the representative of an independent nation—Views of the French minister on this subject—Grenville recalled—Oswald appointed to treat with America---His powers finally satisfactory---Negociations commence—American commissioners and Mr. Oswald agree on articles concerning boundaries and the fisheries to be inserted in a treaty if approved by the British cabinet---Sent to London---Mr. Jay resumes negociations with Spain at Paris— Views of the Spanish and French courts concerning the western bounds of the United States—Western line designated by the Spanish minister—Not approved by the American ministers---Extraordinary communication made to Mr. Jay on this subject by the secretary of Vergennes—Views of France on the subject of the fisheries---Articles sent to London not agreed to by the British court—Mr. Strachey sent to Paris to assist Mr. Oswald in further negociations---The subjects of boundaries, the fisheries, and compensation to the loyalists create great difficulties---Finally settled by a provisional treaty---This treaty concluded by the American minister without consulting the French court—Reasons of this---Correspondence between Dr. Franklin and Vergennes on this point---Delay in the negociations between Great Britain and France and Spain occasioned by the demand made by Spain, for the surrender of Gibraltar---Majority of the British cabinet agree to give up this fortress on certain conditions---The British monarch refuses to give it on any terms---Spanish minister obliged to relinquish the demand and treaties between those powers finally concluded---The treaties not approved by the house of commons---Change of administration---Provisional treaty ratified by the United States —The article about debts not satisfactory to some of the states---David Hartley sent by the new ministry to complete the definite treaty---Negociators not able to agree on any new terms, or to make any commercial arrangements.

FRANCE generously assisted the United States with men as well as money. In July, 1780, a French fleet with six thousand troops, arrived at Newport, in Rhode Island; and the next spring these troops joined the American army near New York. After making great preparations apparently with a view to attack that city, the allied army suddenly marched to the south to meet the British forces in that quarter. By their united efforts, with the assistance of a French fleet at the entrance of the Chesapeak, the British army, under lord Cornwallis, was compelled to surrender, on the 17th of October, 1781. This brilliant achievement put an end to military operations in America. Soon after this Mr. Hartley, with the knowledge of lord North, again applied to Dr. Franklin and to Mr. Adams, on the subject of a peace or truce. The object of the ministry was to enter into some arrangements with the United States, separate from France; this, the American ministers declined. At the same time, the British sent an emissary to the count de Vergennes, to sound him on the subject of a treaty separate from America. This emissary was a Mr. Forth, formerly secretary to lord Stormont; and through him very advantageous offers were made, to induce France to abandon her American allies. Among these offers, France was to retain all her conquests in the West Indies ; the British were to relinquish their right to have a commissary at Dunkirk, and to grant the French advantages in the East Indies ; and Dr. Franklin understood that the British ministry went so far, as to offer to restore Canada. France, however, refused to listen to these overtures, or to enter into negociations without the concurrence of her allies.*

Before inviting the attention of the reader to the change of the British administration, and the final overtures and negociations for peace, we would observe, that after the capture of the British army at Yorktown, the subject of the terms of peace again came before congress. The people of Massachusetts had not been inattentive to the important subject of the fisheries. On the 17th of November, 1781, the legislature of that state, instructed their delegates to " represent to congress the importance of the fisheries to that state, and to use their utmost influence, that instruc-

* Franklin's Works, vol. 6, and Secret Journals of Congress, vol. 3.

tions be given to the ministers appointed by congress for negociating peace, in the most pressing manner, to *insist*, that the
free and unmolested exercise of this right be continued and secured to the subjects of the United States of America, in a future
settlement of peace." This representation with other papers relating to the same subject, were referred to a committee, consisting of Mr. Lovell, Mr. Carroll, and Mr. Madison, who early in
January, 1782, made a report, in which they recommended that
the American ministers for negociating peace, be further instructed, not only with respect to the fisheries, but the boundaries and
the loyalists.

As the terms of peace had been placed under the control of
the French court, it was, no doubt, considered too late, to revoke
the authority thus given to their ally, or that this could not be
done, without hazarding too much; the committee, however, were
of opinion, that a representation should be made to his most
christian majesty, through the American ministers, showing the
views and expectations of the United States on these subjects.
They, therefore, recommended that the American negociators,
"be instructed to acquaint his most christian majesty, that notwithstanding the occasion presented to the United States, by the
signal advantages gained over the enemy, of enlarging their ultimatum for peace, the firm reliance which congress have on the
friendship and influence of his majesty has determined them not
to depart from their resolution, by which all the *objects* of their
desires and *expectations*, excepting only the independence of the
United States and their alliance with his majesty, are eventually
submitted to his councils. But that, in order to make him more
sensible of the *extent* and *foundation* of their desires and expectations, have thought it expedient that some observations should
be made to him relative to the several objects, which are most
likely to fall within the compass of negociation."

The committee then endeavored to prove by facts and reasoning, that the United States had good right to the boundaries, and
to the fisheries, as claimed in their original instructions to Mr.
Adams ; and that his most christian majesty, as well as the Amer-

ican ministers should insist on them. This report was recommitted to Mr. Carroll, Mr. Randolph, and Mr. Montgomery. The subject was before this committee until August following, when they reported " facts and observations in support of the several claims of the United States, not included in their ultimatum of the 15th of June, 1781."

These facts and observations were presented in detail, and as to boundaries, the claim on the part of the United States was founded on the various original grants made to the states themselves while colonies. This second report was recommitted and never finally acted upon by congress. The members were at that period, much divided on the subject of the claims of the individual states to the western territory, and this might be one reason why many were unwilling to give an indirect sanction to these claims, by accepting this report. The minister of France, afterwards, in a communication made to congress, on the subject of peace, declared, " that when negociations are entered into with sincerity, the king would most readily employ his good offices in support of the United States, in all *points* relating. to their *prosperity* ; that congress were themselves sensible of the distinction between the conditions of *justice* and *rigor*, and those of *convenience* and *compliance*, which depended on the good or bad situation of affairs ; that though the circumstances of the allies were very promising, such events might happen, as might make it advisable to adopt the part of *moderation*." Congress availed themselves of this opportunity to express their wishes to the French court, as to the terms of peace. In answer to this part of the French ministers communication, they declared, that they placed " the utmost confidence in his majesty's assurances, that he will readily employ his good offices in support of the United States, in all points relative to their prosperity ; and considering the territorial claims of these states as heretofore made, their participation of the fisheries, and of the free navigation of the Mississippi, not only as their indubitable rights, but as essential to their *prosperity*, they trust that his majesty's efforts will be successfully employed to obtain a sufficient provision and security for those rights. Nor can they refrain," they subjoined, "from making known to his majesty that any claim for restitution or compensation for property confiscated in the several states will meet with insuperable obstacles, not only on account of the sovereignty of the individual states, by which such confiscations have been made, but of the wanton devastations which the citizens of these states have experienced from the enemy, and in many instances from the very persons in whose favor such claims may be urged. That congress trust that the *circumstances of the allies* at the negociations for peace will be so prosperous, as to render these expectations consistent with the spirit of *moderation* recommended by his majesty."*

It must have been humiliating to the members of the national legislature, to be thus compelled, in consequence of former instructions, to become humble suppliants at the feet of a foreign power, for the attainment of objects all important to the future prosperity of their country.

With respect to peace itself, however, the arms of the allies were able to effect in America, what the mediation of the imperial courts could not accomplish in Europe.

The capture of lord Cornwallis and his army, convinced the British nation, that America could not be subdued by force ; and led to a change of administration and pacific overtures. Parliament met on the 27th of November, 1781, and though the speech from the throne, still breathed a spirit of hostility, and answers from both houses were procured, in accordance with it ; yet not long after the recess, the ministers found themselves in a minority in the house of commons. On the 22d of February, 1782, general Conway in the house, moved an address to the king, praying " that the war on the continent of North America, might no longer be pursued, for the impracticable purpose of reducing that country to obedience by force : and expressing their hope, that the earnest desire and diligent exertion to restore the public tranquillity, of which they had received his majesty's most gracious assurances, might, by a happy reconciliation with the revolted

* Secret Journals of Congress, vol. 3, pp. 222 and 248.

colonies, be forwarded and made effectual ; to which great end, his majesty's faithful commons would be ready to give their utmost assistance."

This motion being lost by a single vote only, was, five days after renewed, by the same gentleman, in a form somewhat different ; declaring, " that it was the opinion of that house, that the farther prosecution of offensive war, on the continent of North America, for the purpose of reducing the revolted colonies to obedience by force, would be the means of weakening the efforts of this country against her European enemies, and tend, under the present circumstances, dangerously to increase the mutual enmity, so fatal to the interests both of Great Britain and America ; and, by preventing a happy reconciliation with that country, to frustrate the earnest desire graciously expressed by his majesty, to restore the blessings of public tranquillity."

This motion was carried, and an address in pursuance of it, presented to the king ; who, in his answer on the first of March, assured the house, " that he should take such measures, as should appear to him to be most conducive to the restoration of harmony between Great Britain and her revolted colonies, so essential to the prosperity of both ; and that his efforts should be directed in the most effectual manner, against our European enemies, until such a peace could be obtained, as should consist with the interests and permanent welfare of his kingdom."

Not yet satisfied with the triumph obtained over the ministry, and considering the answer of the king not sufficiently explicit, the house of commons, on the 4th of March, on the motion of general Conway, declared, that all those who should advise or by any means, attempt the farther prosecution of offensive war in America, should be considered as enemies to their king and country. In this state of things, it was impossible for the ministry longer to continue in power ; and on the 19th, they relinquished their places. A new administration was soon after formed—the marquis of Rockingham, was placed at the head of the treasury, and the earl of Shelburne and Mr. Fox held the important places of secretaries of state.

The new ministers, soon after their appointment, sent a Mr. Oswald to France, to sound the French court, as well as Dr. Franklin, on the subject of peace. He was introduced to the latter, by lord Shelburne, and by Mr. Laurens who was then in London. In a conference with the count de Vergennes, Mr. Oswald was informed, that the French court were disposed to treat of peace ; but could do nothing without the consent of their allies ; and the count expressed a wish, that Paris might be the place of meeting, for entering upon this important business. About the 18th of April, the British agent went back to London, and on the 4th of May, returned to France with the assent of the British cabinet to treat of a general peace, and for that purpose, to meet at Paris. He also informed Dr. Franklin and the count de Vergennes, that Mr. Grenville was entrusted with the negociation, on the part of the court of London. This gentleman soon after came to Paris, and in company with Dr. Franklin, had an interview with the French minister. He intimated, that if England gave independence to America, France should restore the conquests she had made of the British Islands, receiving back those of Miquelon and St. Piere. The original object of the war being obtained, this he supposed would satisfy the court of France. The count de Vergennes smiled at the proposed exchange, and said, America does not ask you to give her independence ; Mr. Franklin will answer you, as to that point. Dr. Franklin then said, that the Americans considered themselves under no necessity of bargaining for a thing already their own, which they had acquired, at the expense of so much blood and treasure, and of which they were in possession.

In the conference between the French and English ministers, the feelings of the former, with respect to the terms of the treaty of peace in 1763, were strongly manifested. In answer to the intimation that France would be satisfied with the attainment of the original object of the war, Vergennes desired Mr. Grenville, to look back to the conduct of England, in former wars, and particularly the last, the object of which was, a disputed right to some western lands on the Ohio, and the frontiers of Nova Sco-

tia; and asked, " did you content yourselves with the recovery of
those lands ? No," said he, " you retained at the peace, all Canada, all Louisiana, all Florida, Grenada, and other West India
islands, the greater part of the northern fisheries, with all your
conquests in Africa, and the East Indies." He told the British
minister, it was not reasonable, " that a nation, after making
an unprovoked and unsuccessful war upon its neighbor, should
expect to sit down whole, and have every thing restored which
she had lost, in such a war."*

Mr. Grenville immediately despatched a messenger to London, and Mr. Oswald soon followed.

Not long after the first arrival of Mr. Oswald, doctor Franklin
wrote to Mr Jay, then in Spain, and requested his assistance, in the
negociations. In consequence of this communication Mr. Jay immediately set out for Paris, where he arrived the 23d of June.
A serious difficulty arose, in the commencement of a negociation
between so many parties, particularly in respect to America, as
to the powers of the British negociators. The first commission·
of Mr. Grenville confined him to treat with France, without nam-
ing her allies. As this was manifestly insufficient, a new one was
sent for, and arrived on the 15th of June. By this he was empowered to treat not only with the king of France, or his ministers, but
with the ministers of any other *prince* or *state* whom it might concern. Dr. Franklin doubted whether, by the word *state*, it was
intended to include America, the British government having never
yet acknowledged America as a state. Mr. Grenville, however,
explicitly informed him, that he was authorized to declare the independence of the United States, *previous to the treaty*, as a voluntary act, and to propose separately, as a basis, the treaty of
1763.†

It is proper here to state, that soon after the formation of the
new administration, Sir Guy Carlton was appointed commander
in chief in America, in the room of Sir Henry Clinton, and that
he, and admiral Digby, had powers to treat of peace. One ob-

* Franklin's Works, vol. 5.   † Franklin's Works, vol. 5, p. 265.

ject of conferring this power was to induce congress to agree to a separate treaty.

Sir Guy Carlton arrived in America the 5th of May, and two days after informed general Washington that he and admiral Digby were authorized to treat of peace, and requested a pasport for their secretary, as the bearer of despatches to congress, on the subject. A copy of this letter was forwarded by the general to that body. But the members being determined not to negociate without their allies, refused the pasport. The same commissioners on the 2d of August following, sent a second letter to the American commander, informing him that negociations for a general peace had commenced at Paris, and that Mr. Grenville had full powers to treat with all the parties at war, and that by his instructions, "the independency of the thirteen provinces was to be proposed by him, *in the first instance*, instead of being made *a condition of a general treaty.*" A majority of the new British cabinet, very early determined to " offer America unlimited, unconditional independence," as the basis of a negociation for peace, and so instructed their minister, Mr. Grenville.* This was a favorite measure with the marquis of Rockingham. On this point, the cabinet, however, was divided. The earl of Shelburne, though he acquiesced, was still opposed, and it was one of the last measures to which the king would assent.

The sickness of the marquis of Rockingham, and his death, which happened on the first of July, produced no little delay and difficulty in the negociations. The appointment of lord Shelburne first lord of the treasury, produced an open rupture in the cabinet. Lord John Cavendish, Mr. Fox, and some others, resigned their places. In consequence of this, William Pitt was made chancellor of the exchequer, and Thomas Townsend and lord Granthem, secretaries of state.

There can be little doubt, that the king, as well as lord Shelburne, still entertained a distant hope, that some arrangement might be made with the Americans, short of an *open* and *express* acknowledgment of their independence ; and the views of the

* Annual Register for 1782.

latter on this point, probably, had no little influence in placing him at the head of the administration.*

One of the reasons assigned by Mr. Fox for his resignation, was, that the cabinet, under the influence of lord Shelburne, had departed from the principles adopted by the preceding administration, on the great question of American independence. In vindication of himself, lord Shelburne, early in July, declared in parliament, that he had been, and yet was of opinion, that whenever parliament should acknowledge the independence of America, the sun of England's glory was set forever. Such, he said, were the sentiments, he possessed on a former day, and such were the sentiments he still held. That other noble lords thought differently ; and as the majority of the cabinet supported them, he acquiesced in the measure, dissenting from the idea ; and the point was settled to bring the matter before parliament. That if independence were to be granted, he foresaw in his own mind, that England was undone. He wished to God, he declared, that he had been deputed to the congress, that he might plead the cause of that country, as well as of this ; and that he might exercise whatever powers he possessed, as an orator, to save both from ruin, by bringing the congress to a conviction, that, if their independence was signed, their liberties were gone forever.† This declaration of the prime minister, after the statements made by Mr. Grenville and Sir Guy Carlton on the subject of American independence, as before mentioned, excited no little astonishment in France, as well as in America.

It was supposed, that, with a view of attempting some arrangement agreeably to his wishes, lord Shelburne contemplated sending Mr. Jones, afterwards Sir William Jones, to America. Certain it is that about the last of June, Mr. Jones, in company with

* Among the papers of Dr. Franklin was found the following memorandum. "Immediately after the death of lord Rockingham, the king said to lord Selburne, ' I will be plain with you, the point next my heart, and which I am determined, be the consequence what it may, never to relinquish but with my crown and life, is, to prevent a total unequivocal recognition of the independence of America. Promise to support me on this ground, and I will leave you unmolested on every other ground, and with full power as the prime minister of this kingdom.' The bargain was struck. The Hague, 1782."—*Franklin's Works, vol. 5, p. 326.*

† New Annual Register, 1782. History of England, vol. 7. Secret Journals of

a gentleman by the name of Paradise, went to Paris; and it was publicly given out, they were on their way to America, on business of a private nature; Mr. Paradise, to recover an estate belonging to him, and Mr. Jones as his counsel. While at Paris, the latter frequently saw and conversed with doctor Franklin and Mr. Jay, and as a matter of curiosity, presented to the former, with whom he had been acquainted in England, what he called " a fragment of Polybius, from his treatise on the Athenian government."* He took this singular mode, no doubt, of sounding the American commissioners, on the great question of peace: and no one can read this supposed fragment of a celebrated ancient historian, purporting to give a brief account of a contest between Athens and her colonies, without being satisfied as to its real object.

" Athens," says this fragment, " had long been an object of universal admiration, and consequently of envy; her navy was invincible, her commerce extensive; Europe and Asia supplied her with wealth; of her citizens, all were intrepid, many virtuous; but some too much infected with principles unfavorable to freedom. Hence an oligarchy was, in a great measure, established; crooked counsels were thought supreme wisdom; and the Athenians having lost their true relish for their own freedom, began to attack that of their colonies, and of the states which they had before protected! Their arrogant claims of unlimited dominion, had compelled the Chians, Coans, Rhodians, Lesbians, to join with *nine other* small communities in the *social war*, which they began with inconceivable ardor, and continued with industry surpassing all example and almost surpassing belief.

" They were openly assisted by Mausoleus, king of Caria, to whose metropolis the united islands had sent a *philosopher* named *Eleutherion*, eminent for the deepest knowledge of nature, the most solid judgment, most approved virtue, and most ardent zeal for the cause of *general liberty*. The war had been supported for three years with infinite exertions and valor on both sides, with deliberate firmness on the part of the allies, and with unabated violence on the part of the Athenians, who had, neverthe-

* Franklin's Works, vol. 1, p. 431.

less, despatched commissioners to Rhodes, with intent to propose
terms of accommodation ; but the states, (perhaps too pertinaciously) refused to hear any proposal whatever, without a previous recognition of their *total independence*, by the magistrates
and people of Athens.   It was not long after this that an *Athenian*, who had been a pupil of Isaeus together with Demosthenes,
and began to be known in his country as a pleader of causes, was
led by some *affair of his clients*, to the capital of Caria.   He was
a man, unauthorized, unemployed, unconnected, independent in
his circumstrnces as much as in his principles ; admitting no governor, under providence, but the laws ; and no laws, but which
justice and virtue had dictated, which wisdom approved, which
his country had freely enacted.   He had been known at Athens
to the sage Eleutherion, and their acquaintance being renewed,
he sometimes took occasion, in their conversations, to lament the
calamities of war, and to express his eager desire of making a
general peace on such terms, as *would produce the greatest good
from the greatest evil ;* for this," said he, " would be a work not
unworthy the divine attributes, and if mortals could effect it, they
would act like those beneficent beings, whom Socrates believed
to be the constant friends and attendants of our species."

The *Athenian*, in these conversations, is also represented, as
endeavoring to persuade Eleutherion, not to insist on such terms
of peace, as would wound the pride of Athens, without any substantial benefit to the colonies, and particularly not to insist on
an *express* acknowledgment of their independence.   " Let the
confederates," he said, " be contented with the *substance* of that
independence, which they have asserted, and the word will necessarily follow."

" Let them not hurt the natural, and, perhaps, not reprehensible pride of Athens, nor demand any concession, that may sink
in the eyes of Greece, a nation to whom they are and must be
united in language, in blood, in manners, in interest, in principles.   Glory is to a nation, what reputation is to an individual ;
it is not an empty sound, but important and essential.   It will be
glorious in Athens to acknowledge her error in attempting to re-

duce the islands, but an acknowledgment of her *inability* to reduce them, (if she be unable) will be too public a confession of weakness, and her rank among the states of Greece will instantly be lowered."

The Athenian declared, that whatever his own advice might be, he knew and positively pronounced, that Athens would never *expressly* recognize the independence of the islands; that an express acknowledgment of it was merely *formal* with respect to the allies; but the prejudices of mankind had made it *substantial* with respect to Athens.

" There is a *natural* union," he said, " between Athens and the islands which the gods had made, and which the powers of hell could not dissolve. Men, speaking the same idiom, educated in the same manner, perhaps in the same place; professing the same principles ; sprung from the same ancestors in no very remote degree ; and related to each other in a thousand modes of consanguinity, affinity and friendship, such men, (whatever they may say through a temporary resentment) can never in their hearts consider one another as aliens."

The Athenian then proposed " the general ground work and plan of a treaty," the substance of which was, that the *Carians* should be included in the pacification on advantagous terms, that the archon, senate, and magistrates of Athens should make a *complete recognition of rights* of all the Athenian citizens of all orders whatever, and all laws for that purpose be combined in one—" there should not be one *slave* in Attica." That there should be a perfect co-ordination between Athens and the *thirteen United Islands* ; they considering her not as a *parent*, whom they must *obey*, but as an *elder sister*, whom they could not help *loving*, and to whom they should give *pre-eminence of honor and co-equality of power*. The *new constitutions* of the confederate islands to remain. On every occasion requiring acts for the general good, there was to be an assembly of deputies from the senate of Athens and the *congress* of the islands, who should fairly adjust the whole business, and settle the ratio on both sides ; this committee to consist of fifty islanders and fifty Athenians, or of a

smaller number chosen by them. A proportionable number of
Athenian citizens, if thought necessary, were to have seats, and
the power of debating and voting on questions of common concern, in the great assembly of the islands, and a proportionable
number of the islanders to sit, with like power, in the assembly at
Athens. No obligation to make war, but for the common interest—commerce to flow in a free course, for the general advantages of the united powers, and an universal unlimited *amnesty* to be
proclaimed, in every part of Greece and Asia.

" This," said the ingenious Athenian, " is the rough sketch of
a treaty founded on virtue and liberty.

" The idea of it still fills and expands my soul ; and if it cannot be realized, I shall not think it less glorious, but shall only
grieve more and more at the perverseness of mankind.

" May the Eternal Being, whom the wise and virtuous adore,
and whose attribute it is to convert into good, that evil, which his
unsearchable wisdom permits, inspire all ranks of men to promote this or a similar plan! If this be impracticable, O human
nature ! But I am fully confident that if——more at large——
happiness of all.

" No more is extant," Mr. Jones added, "of this interesting
piece, upon which the commentary of the sage Polybius would
have been particularly valuable *in these times.*"*

The allusions in this singular and ingenious communication,
were too obvious to be misunderstood; and left little doubt on
the minds of the American commissioners, that the real object of
Mr. Jones in his visit at Paris, as well as his intended voyage to
America, was, if possible, to effect a reconciliation on terms short
of an *express* and *open* acknowledgment of the independence of
America. Mr. Jay was the more confirmed in this, by seeing in
a pamphlet put into his hands by Mr. Jones, containing an account of the proceedings of the " Society for constitutional information," a communication made to the society by Mr. Jones
himself, in which he announced his intention of leaving England
speedily, " on a mission connected with the interest and welfare
of his country."

These suspicions were communicated to congress both by Dr. Franklin and Mr. Jay. In a letter to the secretary of foreign affairs, the latter particularly stated his suspicions with respect to Mr. Jones; and on the 28th of June, Dr. Franklin, in a letter to the same, says, " It looks as if, since their late success in the West Indies, they a little repented of the advances they had made in their declarations respecting the *acknowledgment of our independence ;* and we have *good information*, that some of the ministry still flatter the king, with the hope of recovering his sovereignty over us, on the same terms as are now making with Ireland. However willing we might have been, at the commecement of this contest, to have accepted such conditions, be assured that we can have no safety in them at present.

" There are," he added," as reported, great divisions in the ministry on other points, as well as this; and those *who aim* at engrossing the power, flatter the king with this project of *re-union ;* and it is said, have much reliance on the operations of *private agents* sent into America to dispose minds in favor of it, and to bring about a separate treaty there, with general Carleton."

The noble biographer of sir William Jones, however, declares, that the object of his intended journey to America, was, " professional," and that the " surmises and insinuations " circulated to the contrary, were without foundation.

Yet the situation of the British cabinet at that time, the opinion of the earl of Shelburne on the question of American independence, as declared in parliament, the circumstance that Mr. Jones was his particular friend, and above all the internal evidence arising from the extraordinary communication made to Dr. Franklin; a communication, novel, indeed, in the annals of diplomacy, but certainly, in its style and manner, well calculated to disclose his supposed object, leave little doubt, but that this eminent scholar, was requested, by high authority, to sound Dr. Franklin, in a secret manner, as to terms of peace and reconciliation with America, the least wounding to British pride. Nor is it impossible, that Mr. Jones himself alluded to this transaction, in a familiar letter to lord Althrop, of the 5th of October,

1782, mentioned by his biographer, in which he says, " I know
not what * * * * * thinks ; but this I know, that the
sturdy trans-atlantic yeomanry will neither be *dragooned* or *bam-*
boozled out of their liberty." Whatever might have been the
real or ultimate views of Mr. Jones, he returned to England
without visiting America. The French court again apprehended,
that the Americans might be induced to make a separate peace,
and on terms short of absolute independence. These apprehensions being communicated to the members of congress, in October, 1782, they resolved, to adhere to the treaty of alliance, to
conclude neither a separate peace nor truce with Great Britain ;
and that they would prosecute the war with vigor, until by the
blessing of God on the united arms, a peace should be happily
accomplished ; by which the full and absolute sovereignty and
independence of the United States, having been duly assured,
their rights and interests, as well as those of their allies, should
be effectually provided for and secured ; and that they would not
enter upon the discussion of any overtures of pacification, but in
confidence and in concert with his most christian majesty.*

In the preamble to this resolve, after reciting the treaty of alliance, and the appointment of ministers to negociate and conclude
a general peace, in Europe, congress proceed to say, " Nevertheless it appears that the British court still flatters itself with the
vain hope of prevailing on the United States to agree to some
terms of *dependence* on Great Britain, or at least, to a separate
peace ; and there is reason to believe that commissioners may
be sent to America, to offer propositions of that nature to the
United States, or that several *emissaries* may be employed to
delude and deceive. In order to extinguish ill founded hopes,
to frustrate insidious attempts, and to manifest to the whole
world the purity of the intentions and the fixed and unalterable
determination of the United States," Resolved, &c.

Parliament adjourned on the 11th of July, having passed an
act, at the close of the session, authorizing the king " to conclude
a peace or truce," with the Americans.

* Secret Journals of Congress, vol. 3, p. 249.

Soon after this, Mr. Grenville, who was of the Fox party, was recalled from Paris, and Mr. Fitzherbert was on the 26th of July sent in his room, with powers to treat with France, Spain and Holland. About the same time, Mr. Oswald, then at Paris, received information that an order had been issued, for a commission to be made out to him, "to treat, consult, agree and conclude, with any commissioner or commissioners, named or to be named by the American colonies or plantations, or with any body or bodies corporate or politic, or any assembly or assemblies, or descriptions of men, or any persons whatsoever, a peace or truce with the said colonies or plantations, or any part or parts of them." A copy of this order being sent to Mr. Oswald, was shewn to the American commissioners and to the French minister. A question arose, as to the sufficiency of the powers to be given Mr. Oswald. The count de Vergennes thought a commission made in pursuance of them would be sufficient, and Dr. Franklin inclined to the same opinion ; Mr. Jay, however, thought it would be descending from the ground of independence, for them to treat, under the name of commissioners of *colonies* or *plantations*, when in fact, they were commissioners of *thirteen independent states*. Vergennes said names signified little, that the king of England styling himself king of France, was no obstacle to their treating with him. That an acknowledgment of American independence, instead of preceding, must, in the natural course of things, be the *effect* of the treaty; and that it would not be reasonable to expect the effect, before the cause ; that care must be taken, to insert proper articles in the treaty, to secure independence, as well as limits, against any future claims. A decision of the question was postponed, until the arrival of the commission. In the mean time, Mr. Jay, in a conference with Mr. Oswald, pressed the importance of his treating with them, on an equal footing, as the representatives of an independent state ; and explicitly told him, that he would have no concern in any negociation in which they should not be so considered. Mr. Oswald appeared satisfied with Mr. Jay's remarks, and expressed a wish that his commission had been otherwise ; Mr.

Jay suggested an alteration, and at the request of Mr. Oswald, reduced it to writing. The British negociator sent to his court for
this alteration, but before his despatches reached London, his
commission arrived.

The count de Vergennes, in a second conference with the
American commissioners, still thought the commission sufficient;
care must be taken, he said, to secure, *by treaty*, any future
claims from Great Britain. Mr. Jay, however, informed the
French minister, he did not consider American independence as
requiring any aid or validity from British acts; that, if Great Britain treated with them as with other nations, on a footing of
equality, that would be sufficient : That he did not consider an
explicit acknowledgment of American independence as necessary
to prevent farther claims from that country. Vergennes told the
American commissioners, that he delayed his negociation with
Mr. Fitzherbert until they were prepared to proceed with Mr.
Oswald. The day after this conversation, Mr. Fitzherbert sent
a courier to London.

Soon after this, Mr. Oswald received a letter from Mr. Townsend, on the subject of his commission, stating his majesty's intention to grant to America, full, complete, and unconditional independence, *by an article of treaty*.* This letter being shewn to
the American commissioners, they conjectured the proposition
of granting America, independence by an *article of treaty only*,
had been produced by the despatches of Mr. Fitzherbert. This
being suggested to Mr. Oswald, he admitted, that Vergennes had
gone so far as to tell that gentleman his opinion respecting the
commission. Mr. Jay took this opportunity to inform Mr. Oswald, what he supposed might be the policy of the French
court; and endeavored to convince him, that it was the interest
of his country to treat with them on an equal footing, and that
America should be placed in a situation, to be as independent of
France as of Great Britain.

Mr. Oswald desired Mr. Jay, to state his objections in writing;
and deliver them to him signed by the commissioners. Mr. Jay
drew a statement which was submitted to his colleague. Doctor

Franklin thought it imprudent to put their names to it, as in case Great Britain should remain firm, they could not retreat with a good grace. He, also, felt himself embarrassed by their instructions to be governed by the advice of the French court. Though the American commissioners did not choose to deliver this statement under their hands to the British negociator, yet at the earnest solicitation of Mr. Oswald, Mr. Jay gave him a copy, without their signatures; and at the same time furnished him with copies of the various resolutions of congress, relating to the independence of the United States.

Convinced of the propriety of his objections against treating with Mr. Oswald, under his commission, Mr. Jay proposed to Dr. Franklin, that these objections be stated in writing, and delivered to the French minister; and that an answer be requested, to enable them, hereafter, if necessary, to shew what was the advice of the French court on this question. Dr. Franklin approved of the proposal; and Mr. Jay drew a long memorial on the subject, which he submitted to the consideration of his colleague.

When Mr. Jay left Madrid, it will be remembered, further negociation with Spain, was transferred to Paris. This negociation on the part of the Spanish court, was entrusted to count de Aranda, its ambassador at the court of France.

As the proceedings with Spain, have an important connection with the negociations carried on at the same time, with Great Britain, it is proper here to state, that Mr. Jay, soon after his arrival at Paris, had a conference with the Spanish minister, in company with Dr. Franklin. In this conference, count de Aranda, at once, referred to the old subject of western limits; and asked Mr. Jay, what were the boundaries of the United States? He was informed that the river Mississippi was their boundary west, from its source, to latitude thirty one degrees north, and from thence east by a line, between Georgia and the Floridas.

The Spanish minister objected to the right of the United States to an extent so far west. He said, that the western country had never belonged, or claimed to belong to the ancient colonies; that before the war of 1756, it belonged to France, and after its

cession to Great Britain, remained a distinct part of her dominions, until by the conquest of West Florida, and certain posts on
the Mississippi and Illinois, it became vested in Spain;* or, if
Spain could not claim the whole, the residue was possessed and
claimed by the indians, and did not belong to the United States.
He, therefore, proposed to designate a line, on the east side of the
Mississippi, as a boundary between the two countries. He soon
after drew a line, on Mitchell's map of North America, beginning
at a lake, near the confines of Georgia, and east of Flint river, to
the confluence of the Kanaway with the Ohio; thence round the
western shores of lakes Erie and Huron, and thence round lake
Michigan to lake Superior; and sent the map to Mr. Jay. The
American commissioners soon after, shewed this map, with the
designated Spanish line, to count de Vergennes. Dr. Franklin pointed out to him the extravagance of this line, as a claim of
boundary, on the part of Spain; and insisted on the right of the
United States, to extend to the Mississippi. Vergennes, in reply,
said very little; but Mr. Rayneval, his principal secretary, who
was present, declared, that the United States had no right to extend their claim so far west.

The Spanish minister, afterwards, requested the American
commissioners to designate some line, east of the Mississippi, to
which they would agree. This they refused, and plainly told
him, that as the limits of the United States extended to that
river, they would never cede to Spain any part of the country
east of it.

Soon after this, Mr. Rayneval, requested an interview with
Mr. Jay, on the subject of limits with Spain. To this the latter
assented, and in a conference, Mr. Rayneval proposed what
he called, a *conciliatory line*, as a boundary between the United
States, and the Spanish American possessions. Being desired,
by Mr. Jay, to reduce his proposition to writing, Mr. Rayne-

* In the winter of 1781, a detachment of about sixty five Spanish militia men,
accompanied by sixty Indians, took possession of a small English fort, called St.
Joseph, situated near the source of the Illinois, hoisted the Spanish standard, and pretended to take possession of the post and its dependencies, and the river Illinois, in
the name of the Spanish king, and this is the conquest of the posts on the Mississippi
and Illinois, alluded to by the Spanish minister.—*Secret Journals of Congress, vol. 4,
p. 63.*

val, on the 6th of September, sent him what he called, his " idea on the manner of determining and fixing the limits between Spain and the United States, on the Ohio and Mississippi." This communication, no doubt, disclosed the real views of the French court, in relation to the important subject of the western country.

" It is evident," says Mr. Rayneval, " that the Americans can only borrow from England, the right they pretend to have to extend to the Mississippi; therefore, to determine this right, it is proper to examine what the court of London has thought and done on this head.

" It is known, that before the treaty of Paris, France possessed Louisiana and Canada ; and that she considered the savage people situated to the east of the Mississippi, either as independent, or as under her protection.

" This protection caused no dispute. England never thought of making any, except as to the lands situated towards the south of the Ohio, on that part, where she had given the name of Allegany to that river.

" A discussion about limits, at that time took place, between the courts of Versailles and London ; but it would be superfluous to follow the particulars. It will suffice to observe, that England proposed in 1755, the following boundary: It set out from the point where the river des Boeufs falls into the Ohio, at the place called Venango ; it went up this river towards lake Erie, as far as twenty leagues ; and setting off again from the same place, *Venango*, a right line was drawn as far as the last mountain of Virginia ; which descends towards the ocean. As to the savages situated between the aforesaid line and the Mississippi, the English minister considers them as independent ; from thence, it follows, that according to the very propositions of the court of London, almost the whole course of the Ohio belonged to France ; and that the countries situated to the westward of the mountains were considered as having nothing in common with the colonies.

" When peace was negociated, in 1761, France offered to make a cession of Canada to England. The regulation of the limits of this colony and Louisiana was in question. France pretended

that almost the whole course of the Ohio made a part of Louisiana ; and the court of London, to prove that this river belonged
to Canada, produced several authentic papers, among others, the
chart which Mon. Vaudreuil delivered to the English command-
ant,when he abandoned Canada. The minister of London maintained, at the same time, that a part of the savages situated to
the eastward of the Mississippi, were independent ; another part
under its protection ; and that she had purchased a part from the
five Iroquois nations. The misfortunes of France cut these discussions short. The treaty of Paris assigned the Mississippi for
the boundary between the possessions of France and Great Britain.

  " Let us see," adds Mr. Rayneval, " the dispositions which the
court of London has made, in consequence of the treaty of Paris.
If she had considered the vast territories situated to the eastward
of the Mississippi, as forming a part of her ancient colonies, she
would have declared so, and have made dispositions accordingly.
So far from any such thing, the king of England, in a proclamation of the month of October, 1763, declares, in a precise and
positive manner, that the lands in question are situated between
the Mississippi, and the ancient English establishments. It is,
therefore, clearly evident, that the court of London itself, when it
was yet sovereign of the thirteen colonies, did not consider the
aforementioned lands as forming part of those same colonies ; and
it results from this, in the most demonstrative manner, that they
have not at this time, any *right* over those lands. To maintain
the contrary, every principle of the laws of nature and nations
must be subverted.

  "The principles now established," Mr. Rayneval subjoins,
" are as applicable to *Spain*, as to the United States. This power cannot extend its claim *beyond the bounds of its conquests ;* she
cannot therefore pass beyond the Natchez, situated towards the
thirty-first degree of latitude : her rights are therefore confined to
this degree ; what is beyond, is either independent, or belonging
to England ; neither Spain nor the Americans can have any pretensions thereto. *The future treaty of peace can alone regulate
the respective rights.* The consequence of all that has been said,

is, that neither Spain nor the United States have the *least right*
to the sovereignty over the savages in question ; and that the
transactions they may carry on, as to this country, would be to
no purpose. But the *future* may bring forth new circumstances ;
and this reflection leads me to suppose, that it would be of use,
that the court of Madrid and the United States should make an
eventual arrangement.

"This arrangement may be made in the following manner. A
right line should be drawn from the eastern ahgle of the gulf of
Mexico, which makes the section between the two Floridas, to
fort Toulouse situated in the country of the Alibamas ; from
thence the river Louishatchi should be ascended, from the
mouth of which, a right line should be drawn to the fort or facto-
ry of Quenassie ; from this last place the course of the river Eu-
phasee is to be followed, till it joins the Cherokee ; the course of
this last river is to be pursued, to the place where it receives the
Pelissippi ; this last to be followed to its source ; from whence a
right line is to be drawn to Cumberland river, whose course is to
be followed until it falls into the Ohio. The savages to the west
of the line described should be free, and under the protection of
Spain ; those to the eastward should be free, and under the protection of the United States, or rather the Americans may make
such arrangements with them, as is most convenient to themselves. The trade should be free to both parties.

" By looking on the chart," says the French secretary, " we
will find, that Spain would lose almost the whole course of the
Ohio ; and that the establishments, which the Americans have
made on this river would remain untouched ; and that even a
very extensive space remains to form new ones.

" As to the course and navigation of the Mississippi, they follow
with the property, and they will belong, therefore, to the nation
to which the two banks belong. If then, by the future treaty of
peace, Spain preserves West Florida, she alone will be proprietor
of the course of the Mississippi, from the thirty-first degree of latitude, to the mouth of this river. Whatever may be the case with
that part, which is beyond this point to the north, the United

States *have no pretensions to it, not being masters of either border of the river.*

"As to what respects the *lands* situated to the northward of the Ohio, there is reason to presume that Spain can form no pretensions thereto. *Their fate must be regulated by the court of London.*"

This extraordinary communication, no doubt, developed the opinions of the French court on a question more interesting to the United States, than any that would probably occur in the course of the negociation; and placed the American negociators, who on this subject were at the mercy of the French cabinet, in a situation extremely embarrassing. France and Spain wished to induce the American ministers to agree on western limits, as a preliminary to negociations with Great Britain, and to leave the country west of such limits to be adjusted between them and the court of London. The line designated by Rayneval, though a little farther west than that pointed out by de Aranda, left not only the lands north of the Ohio, but a part of the country now constituting the state of Tennessee, and nearly the whole contained in the present states of Alabama and Mississippi, without the limits of the United States. The extensive country west, now inhabited by millions of American citizens, was "to be regulated by the court of London," in its arrangements with France and Spain.

Immediately after the receipt of this communication, Mr. Jay was informed, that Rayneval left Versailles for London, though it was given out he was gone into the country. He conjectured that one object of his mission was to interfere respecting Mr. Oswald's commission, and instructions concerning the fisheries and western limits; and he sent a messenger to London, to counteract any intended measures of this kind. Mr. Rayneval, soon after he returned from England, asked the American commissioners, what their demands were, as to the fisheries; and when informed, that they should insist on a right to them in common with Great Britain, he intimated, that their claims should be limited to the coast fishery. He was told by Dr. Franklin, that the right they claimed was essential to the interest of the United States, and particularly to New England ; Mr. Rayneval then said, it was natural for France, to favor the United States rather than England ; he supposed, however, Great Britain would be unwilling to relinquish a share in the fisheries, and that he wished as few obstacles to peace as possible.*

The suspicions of the American ministers, as to the views of the French court, concerning the fisheries and boundaries, were confirmed by a letter from Barbe de Marbois, chargè des affairs in America, a copy of which, (the original having been intercepted,) was, about this time, put into their hands. By this letter dated the 13th of March, 1782, (the authenticity of which, it is believed, has never been denied,) it appeared, that the ideas of Mr. Rayneval, relative to western limits, was not confined to himself alone. Mons. Barbois had been long in America, and well knew the deep interest felt, in one part of the union, in retaining the fisheries, and in the other, in securing the western country and the navigation of the Mississippi. He, also, well knew, the king of France was " master of the terms of the treaty of peace." The policy as well as intention of France, as disclosed by this letter, evidently was, that the *fisheries* and the *western country* should be relinquished by the United States, as the price of peace ; and Mons. Barbois, hints to Vergennes the propriety of taking early measures, to prevent any discontents in America, in consequence of such relinquishment.

After speaking of the different parties in the United States, on these subjects, he says, " there are some judicious persons, to whom one may speak of giving up the *fisheries*, and the *   *
* † of the west, for the sake of peace. But there are enthusiasts, who fly out at this idea, and their numbers cannot fail of increasing, when, after the English are expelled this continent, the burden of the war will scarce be felt."

On the subject of the fisheries, he suggested, that the king should " cause it to be intimated to congress, or to the ministers, his surprise, that the Newfoundland fisheries had been included

* Gordon, vol. 3, p. 349.   † Lands, no doubt.

in the additional instructions; that the United States set forth, therein, pretensions, *without paying regard to the king's rights*, and without considering the impossibility they are under, of making conquests, and keeping what belongs to Great Britain." In conclusion, he says, " but it is best to be prepared, for any discontent, although it should be temporary. It is remarked by some, that as England has other fisheries besides Newfoundland, she may, perhaps, endeavor that the Americans should partake in that of the grand bank, in order to conciliate their affections, or procure some compensation, or create a jealousy between them and us. But it does not seem likely, that she will act so contrary to her interest; and were she to do it, it will be better to have declared, at an early period to the Americans, *that their pretension is not founded, and that his majesty does not intend to support it.*"*

While the memorial drawn by Mr. Jay, to be presented to the French minister, was under the consideration of Dr. Franklin, the question about the powers of Mr. Oswald, was settled to the satisfaction of the American commissioners, by the arrival of a second commission, bearing date the 21st of September. A copy of the letter from the British secretary, Mr. Townshend, on this subject, was delivered to Dr. Franklin and Mr. Jay. Referring to the despatches of Mr. Oswald, requesting an alteration in his commission, the British secretary says, " a meeting of the king's confidential servants was held as soon as possible, to consider the contents of them, and it was at once agreed to make the alteration in the commission proposed by Dr. Franklin and Mr. Jay. I trust the readiness with which this proposal has been accepted, will be considered as an ample testimony of the openness and sincerity with which the government of this country is disposed to treat with the Americans."† The British negociator was now authorized to treat and conclude with any commissioners, vested with equal powers, " by and on the part of the thirteen *United States of America*, &c. a peace or truce with the United States." Under this commission, negoci-

* Franklin's Works, and Note 13.   † Franklin's Works, vol. 5, p. 174.

ations soon commenced between Dr. Franklin and Mr. Jay, (the other commissioners not having yet arrived at Paris,) and Mr. Oswald ; and on the 8th of October, certain articles were assented to, to be inserted in a future treaty, and sent by the latter to the court of London, for consideration. These articles embraced the subjects of boundaries and the fisheries. As to boundaries, they were nearly the same as claimed, in the first instructions to Mr. Adams; the north line running from latitude forty-five degrees on the St. Lawrence, to the south end of lake Nipissing, and from thence straight to the source of the Mississippi, and by that river to latitude thirty-one degrees north. By this line, the great lakes, with the exception of Superior, were included within the United States. The right to the fisheries, as formerly used, was confirmed and secured to the citizens of America.*

Mr. Oswald was particularly instructed to procure a restoration of the property of the American loyalists, confiscated during the revolution, or a compensation in money. The American commissioners informed him, that congress had no power to order a restitution of such property ; that the confiscations were made, under laws of the several states, over which they had no control. This subject was not then pressed further ; nor did these articles contain any provision, for the recovery of British debts in America.

The British ministry were dissatisfied with these articles ; and on the 23d of October, a Mr. Strachey, an under secretary, was sent to Paris, with new instructions to Mr. Oswald ; and the negociations were renewed. About the same time, Mr. Adams who had now completed a treaty with Holland, joined Dr. Franklin and Mr. Jay at Paris.

The great questions respecting boundaries, the fisheries, and the loyalists, again came under discussion.

The British negociators, insisted at first, that the river Ohio, should be the western limits of the United States.

To this proposition the American commissioners refused to listen for a moment, and at last, the great lakes were divided be-

... ... river Mississippi, from its source
... ... was made the western boun-
... series and the loyalists, produced
... difficulty. The British ministers were
... united States in the fisheries, to very
... was resisted with great firmness and perse-
... commissioners. They well knew their
... England, particularly to Massachusetts, and
... to yield them, at the suggestion either
... each court. Mr. Adams felt a peculiar inter-
... his countrymen the fisheries, as they had hither-
... he demanded them as a *right*, declaring that the
... first adventurers to America, first discovered
... that the inhabitants of New England had de-
... reserved them for the British empire, and had as
... them as the inhabitants of Canada or Nova Sco-
... in a division of the British empire, which was then
... a share in the fisheries should of course be allowed
... them.

... urged, that this would be advantageous to Great
... itself; as it would enable the people of the United
... more easily to pay for the manufactures, which they would
... from her; and would also prevent contention between
... and British seamen.

... some provision should be made for the loyalists, the Brit-
... had much at heart. This was strongly urged in two
... notes, from Mr. Oswald and Mr. Strachey. They in-
... stipulation either for the restitution of the property,
... compensation, before proceeding further in the negociation;
... insisted, that a refusal would be a great, if not an insuper-
... obstacle to peace, between the two countries. To these
... the American ministers replied, that they had no authority
... agree to a restoration of the property, if that were now
... and that no compensation would be made, or stipu-
... to be made, unless Great Britain on her part, would agree,
... a restitution to American citizens, for the heavy losses

they had sustained, by the unnecessary destruction of private property." " We have already agreed," they added, " to an amnesty more extensive than justice required, and full as extensive as humanity could demand : we can, therefore, only repeat, that it cannot be extended farther. We shall be sorry, if the absolute impossibility of our complying further with your propositions, should induce Great Britain to continue the war, for the sake of those, who caused and prolonged it : but, if that should be the case, we hope that the utmost latitude will not be again given to its rigours."*

A special messenger was sent to London, on this subject, and returned with an answer, still insisting on compensation to this class of people. The American commissioners still refused, but on the terms before stated ; and Dr. Franklin proposed as an offset to this claim, a new article, declaring, " that his Britannic majesty will recommend it to his parliament to provide for and make compensation to the merchants and shopkeepers of Boston, whose goods and merchandise were seized and taken out of the stores, warehouses, and shops, by order of general Gage, and others of his commanders or officers there ; and also to the inhabitants of Philadelphia for the goods taken away by his army there, and to make compensation also for the tobacco, rice, indigo, negroes, &c. seized and carried off by his armies under generals Arnold, Cornwallis, and others, from Virginia, North and South Carolina, and Georgia : and also for all vessels and cargoes belonging to the inhabitants of the said United States, which were stopt, seized, or taken, either in the ports or in the seas, by his governors, or by his ships of war, before the declaration of war against the said states. And that his Britannic majesty will also earnestly recommend it to his parliament to make compensation for all the *towns, villages,* and *farms,* burnt and destroyed by his troops or adherents in the United States."† As an ultimatum on this subject the American ministers proposed a stipulation, that congress should *recommend* to the several states, to provide for the restoration of the property of the loyalists. They

* American State Papers, vol. 1, p. 327.　† Do. p. 326.

at the same time, informed the British ministers, that such was the public feeling towards this class of people in America, that the recommendation would not, probably, be regarded by the States.*

This subject, as well as the fisheries, remained in suspense, therefore, until the 29th of November; when, after a long conference, the ultimatum of the American commissioners was finally agreed to, on the part of the British negociators. The latter, however, were very unwilling, by any expressions in the treaty, to acknowledge the *right* of the Americans to any part of the fisheries; but wished merely to allow them the *liberty* of fishing. But Mr. Adams insisted on their right, particularly on the grand bank, and in the open seas; and it was finally agreed, that the Americans should continue to enjoy unmolested the *right* to take fish on the grand bank, and on all the other banks of Newfoundland, also, in the gulf of St. Lawrence, and at all other places, in the sea, where the inhabitants of both countries had used, heretofore, to fish; and have *liberty* to take fish, on such part of the coast of Newfoundland, as British fishermen should use, and on the coast, bays, and creeks of all other the king's dominions, in America, with the *liberty* of drying fish on the unsettled parts of Nova Scotia, Magdalen Islands, and Labrador.

As large debts were due, from the Americans to the British merchants, at the commencement of the revolution, it was stipulated, that creditors, on either side, should meet with no lawful impediment to the recovery of the value of them, in sterling money.

The British king was, with all convenient speed, to withdraw all his armies, garrisons, and fleets from the United States, and from every post, place, and harbor within the same.

It was, also, stipulated that the navigation of the river Mississippi, from its source to the ocean, should be free to both parties; and that no negroes or other property belonging to the American inhabitants should be carried away on leaving America.

The articles were signed the next day, the 30th of November, but were not to take effect, until peace should be concluded between Great Britain and France. The limits between the United States and the Floridas, were fixed in latitude thirty one degrees, on the Mississippi, from thence to the middle of the river Apalachicola; thence along the middle thereof to its junction with the Flint river; thence straight to the head of St. Mary's river; and thence down the middle of St. Mary's to the Atlantic ocean. There was, however, a separate and secret article, providing "that in case Great Britain, at the conclusion of the present war, should recover, or be put in possession of West Florida, the line of north boundary between that province and the United States, should be a line drawn from the mouth of the river Yazous, where it unites with the Mississippi, due east to the river Apalachiola." Though the northern bounds of West Florida, by the British proclamation of October, 1763, were fixed at latitude thirty one degrees, yet afterwards, in the year 1774, by a commission and instructions given to governor Chester, the north bounds of that province were extended to the mouth of the river Yazous, and from thence east, to the river mentioned in the secret article.

In concluding this provisional treaty, as it was called, the American negociators did not consult the French court, or its ministers; and in this respect, violated their instructions. The count de Vergennes had at first suggested to them, that both negociations should proceed together, and the treaties be signed on the same day.

The American commissioners, however, were convinced, that the best interests of their country, demanded the course of proceeding adopted by them; and felt perfectly justified, in departing from their instructions.

They had strong reasons for believing, that on the great and interesting questions of boundaries, the fisheries, and even concerning the loyalists, the views of the French court were very different from theirs. Indeed it was not difficult to foresee, that in the adjustment of so many different claims, and counter claims, as must necessarily exist, between Great Britain, and the four powers, confederated against her, in such a war, great difficulties

at the same t
the public fe
the recomm
States.*
   This sub
therefore,
ference, t
ly agree
howeve:
acknow
ries; t
Mr.
and
can
the
al
s
t

...erates themselves,

...rant interests to settle,
.. u n Europe, the East and
art of the world; and each
advantagous for itself. If
..u o insist on terms less advan-
...ed, and even required of her,
...e beneficial to another. Nor was
Bourbon should wish to regain, at
... had lost by the humiliating terms of
... the last.

...val, the confidential secretary of the
...cerning western limits, had been com-
... before the commencement of negocia
...u, and it was impossible to believe, that this
... knowledge and approbation of the French
...s communication, and the claim made by the
...or, there could be no doubt, that France and
... either to secure the western country to them-
...u t to Great Britain for an equivalent elsewhere.
... less doubt, as to the real views of the French
... egard to the fisheries. With respect to the loyalists,
... he Vergennes himself, expressed an opinion to Mr.
... avor of some provision for them.*

... these circumstances, Mr. Adams and Mr. Jay determin-
... for themselves, and conclude the treaty, without con-
... the French court, or its ministers; and Dr. Franklin, in-
... d of their determination, agreed to proceed with them. Mr.
...ens did not join the other commissioners, until two days be-
...e the signing of the treaty, but he concurred in their proceed-
...s; and at his suggestion, a clause was inserted, prohibiting the
...ing away negroes, or other property belonging to American
inhabitants.

This negociation, so interesting to the United States, was fortunately intrusted to gentlemen distinguished for their firmness,

* American State Papers, Mr. Adams' Journal, vol. 1, p. 328.

As well as talents and integrity. They knew too well how much the future prosperity and happiness of their country depended, on securing the fisheries, the western country, and a part of the great lakes, to run the hazard of losing them, at the suggestion or advice of any power whatever.

Sensible, that without these advantages, independence itself, would be of comparatively little value, they had the firmness to declare, that without them, there should be no peace. Dr. Franklin, in August, 1782, speaking of the claim of Spain to the western country, says, " that my conjecture of that court's design, to coop up us within the Alleghany mountains, is now manifest. . I hope congress will insist on the Mississippi, as the boundary, and the free navigation of the river, from which they would exclude us."* Mr. Jay afterwards declared, " that he would never set his hand to a bad treaty, nor to one, which did not secure the fishery."

The American treaty (except the secret article) was communicated to the count de Vergennes, by Dr. Franklin, who, at the same time, informed him, that it was to be sent to America, by the Washington packet, under a passport from the king of England.

Vergennes made some objections to sending it under a British passport, as English letters might be transmitted by the same vessel, conveying improper information.

The passport, however, soon after arrived, and Dr. Franklin, in a note informed the French minister of this fact, and that the packet would sail immediately. He also inquired, what information he might give congress, as to the aids they had asked of the king. The answer of the French minister disclosed his own feelings as well as those of the French court, concerning the conduct of the American commissioners, in concluding a treaty, without their concurrence and advice.

"I cannot but be surprised, sir," he said, "that, after the explanation I have had with you, and the promise you gave, that you would not press the application for an English passport, for the sailing of the Washington packet, that you now inform me, you have received the passport, and that, at ten o'clock to-morrow morning, your courier will set out, to carry your dispatches. I am at a loss, sir, to explain your conduct, and that of your colleagues, on this occasion.

"You have concluded your preliminary articles, without any communication between us, although the instructions from congress, prescribe, that nothing shall be done, without the *participation of the king*.

"You are about to hold out a certain hope of peace to America, without ever informing yourself, on the state of the negociation on our part. You are wise and discreet, sir; you perfectly understand, what is due to propriety; you have, all you life, performed your duties. I pray you to consider how you propose to fulfil those, which are due to the king. I am not desirous of enlarging these reflections; I commit them to your integrity. When you shall be pleased to satisfy my uncertainty, I will entreat the king to enable me to answer your demands."

This note placed Dr. Franklin in a situation not less delicate than embarrassing. In his answer, after stating that the British had sent the passport, without being pressed to do it, he says, "nothing has been agreed in the preliminaries, contrary to the interest of France; and no peace is to take place between us and England, till you have concluded your's. Your observation is, however, just, that, in not consulting you, before they were signed, we have been guilty of neglecting *a point of bienseance*.

"But, as this was not from any want of respect for the king, whom we love and honor, we hope it will be excused; and that the great work which has hitherto been so happily brought to perfection, and is so glorious to his reign, will not be ruined by a *single indiscretion* of ours. And certainly the whole edifice sinks to the ground immediately, if you refuse, on that account, to give us any more assistance.

"We have not yet despatched the ship, and I beg leave to wait on you, on Friday, for your answer.

"It is not possible," he added, "for any one to be more sensible than I am, of what I, and every American owe to the king, for the many and great benefits and favors he has bestowed upon us. All my letters to America are proofs of this; all tending to make the same impression on the minds of my countrymen, that I felt in my own. And I believe no prince was ever more beloved and respected by his own subjects, or by the people of the United States. The English, I just now hear, flatter themselves, they have already divided us. I hope this *little misunderstanding* *will*, therefore be kept a secret, and that they will find themselves mistaken."[*]

At the time of the signature of the provisional treaty, the terms of peace, between Great Britain, and France and Spain, were not adjusted. Unable to obtain Gibraltar by force, Spain resolved to secure it by negociation, and her minister, count de Aranda, was instructed to make the acquisition of that fortress a *sine qua non*. This created great delay, as well as difficulty, in the negociations between those powers.

To effect this object, the aid of France was solicited; and Spain offered the French king her part of St. Domingo, if he would secure Gibraltar. Mr. Rayneval was intrusted with this delicate and important negociation, at the court of London. A majority of the British cabinet, after much debate, finally agreed to yield Gibraltar, on the two following conditions.

1st. The restitution of all the conquests made by Spain, viz. Minorca, West Florida and the Bahama Islands.

2d. The cession of the island of Porto Rico, or the restitution of Dominico, and the cession of Guadaloupe.

The king of France was willing to restore Dominico, and to cede Guadaloupe, and to take, in exchange, the Spanish part of St. Domingo; but the king of Spain was unwilling to restore West Florida.[†]

The king of England, however, at last put an end to this negociation, by declaring he would, *on no terms whatever, give up Gibraltar*. The ultimatum of the British court, in relation to territory, was the cession of both the Floridas, together with Mi-

* Franklin's Works, vol. 6, p. 510.   † Histoire &c. de Diplomatie Francaise, vol. 7.

area to Spain, on the restoration of the Bahamas : and this was finally accepted by de Aranda, though contrary to his instructions. Preliminary treaties between Great Britain, France and Spain, were finally settled and signed, on the 20th of January, 1783.

When these, with the provisional treaty with America, were laid before parliament, in February following, they became the subject of violent debates, and severe animadversion. The ministry were accused of sacrificing the interests of their country, by making unnecessary concessions to their enemies. One of the resolutions introduced into the house of commons, on the subject, by lord John Cavendish, was, that " the concessions made to the adversaries of Great Britain, by the provisional treaty, and preliminary articles, were greater than they were entitled to, either from the actual situation of their respective possessions, or from their comparative strength." This resolution was carried against the ministry, 207, to 190. The great object of the majority was, to compel lord Shelburne, and some of his adherents, to resign their places. This was effected by the extraordinary coalition of lord North and Mr. Fox, and their friends. On the 2d of April, a new administration was formed, at the head of which was placed the duke of Portland ; and lord North and Mr. Fox were made secretaries of state.

The provisional treaty having become effectual in consequence of the treaty between Great Britain and France, congress, on the 11th of April, 1783, proclaimed a cessation of hostilities, and on the 15th of the same month, formally ratified the treaty. The article concerning the recovery of debts contracted before the revolution, particularly its silence with respect to interest during the time of the war, produced dissatisfaction, in some of the states. In December, 1782, the legislature of Virginia instructed their delegates, to procure from congress a direction to their ministers, not to agree to the restitution of property confiscated by the states, " nor submit that the laws made by any independent state of the union, be subjected to the adjudication of any power on earth."

The executive council of Pennsylvania, in a letter to congress, stated the hardships to which the citizens of that state might be subjected by the article in the treaty relating to the recovery of debts, if taken strictly. This subject was considered by congress in May, 1782, and their commissioners were instructed to represent to the British negociators, the situation in which the citizens of the United States would be placed by an immediate collection of debts contracted before the war ; and to procure (if possible) an article, that no execution should issue, for any such debts, in less than three years after signing of the definite treaty. Congress, at the same time, declared that all demands for interest accruing during the war, would be highly inequitable and unjust ; and directed their negociators to procure a precise definition of the article relating to debts, expressly excluding all demand for interest, in order to prevent future disputes on that subject.

In April, 1783, after the formation of the new administration, David Hartley was sent to Paris, to complete the negociations between Great Britain and the United States. The negociators, however, were unable to agree on any alterations in the former articles ; nor were they able to agree on arrangements, for the future commercial intercourse between the two countries. On the 3d of September, 1783, a definitive treaty was signed, containing only the articles that were embraced in the provisional treaty of the preceding November. The definitive treaties, between Great Britain, France and Spain, were signed at the same time : and that between Great Britain and Holland, the day preceding.

The American definitive treaty was ratified by congress on the 14th of January, 1784, and on the same day a proclamation was issued, requiring all persons to carry the same into effect with good faith ; and it was also earnestly recommended to the legislatures of the respective states, to provide for the restoration of the property of the loyalists, agreably to the fifth article.

CHAPTER XVI.

The revolution not effected without great sacrifices and sufferings on the part of the Americans—Paper money issued—Depreciates—Taxes not called for by congress until November, 1777—Paper money made a tender in payment of debts—Prices of articles fixed by law—Congress attempt to call in the paper, but without success—States neglect to comply with the requisitions—Congress present an address to the states—Paper ceases to circulate in 1780—Distresses of the Americans for want of funds—Apply to France for aid—Special minister sent to the French court—King of France furnishes money—Loans obtained in Holland—New arrangements in the civil departments—Sufferings of the army—General Washington's letters on this subject—Revolt of the Pennsylvania line---Americans suffer from the burning of their towns--Discontents among the officers of the army---Half pay recommended by general Washington---Finally granted—Is unpopular in some of the states---Officers petition congress on this subject, and for a settlement of their accounts---Congress delay acting on their memorial---This creates great uneasiness among the officers---A meeting called by an anonymous notification to obtain redress---Prevented by general Washington---Congress grant five years full pay in lieu of the half pay for life---News of peace arrives---Arrangements made for disbanding the army---General Washington sends a circular letter to the states---Definitive treaty of peace arrives---Army finally disbanded---General Washington addresses the army for the last time---Takes leaves of his officers---Resigns his commission to congress.

AFTER a conflict of eight years, Great Britain was compelled to acknowledge the independence of the United States, and a complete separation took place between the two countries. This political revolution was not effected without immense sacrifices and sufferings on the part of the Americans.

Destitute of arms and ammunition, without a single ship of war, and without the means of procuring them, no resource was left, to enable them to resist the mighty force brought against them, but a paper medium.

During the year 1775, as we have before stated, bills of credit to the amount of three millions of dollars, were issued by congress, in addition to those issued by some of the individual states. By new emissions, at different times, this sum was increased at the close of the year 1778, to more than one hundred millions.

From the peculiar situation of the United States, without commerce, the union incomplete, the state governments imperfectly organized, congress deemed it imprudent to call for taxes, until November, 1777. At this time, they recommended to the several states, to raise by taxes, the sum of five millions of dollars, for the succeeding year. This sum was apportioned among the states, having reference generally, to the supposed number of inhabitants in each.* The sums so apportioned, however, were not to be considered as the final quota of any state; but the amount paid by each, was to be placed to its credit, bearing an interest of six per cent. from the time of payment, until the quotas should be finally adjusted, agreeably to the confederation, to be adopted and ratified by the states. If, on such adjustment, any state had paid more than its quota, it was to receive interest on the surplus; if less, then to pay interest on the deficiency, until, by a future tax, such surplus or deficiency should be adjusted.

Depreciation of this paper was the natural consequence of such large emissions. This was seriously felt, in the beginning of 1777; and to provide a remedy, congress in January of that year, made it a tender in payment of all public and private debts; and a refusal to receive it, was declared to be an extinguishment of the debt itself. And they thought proper to declare, that whoever should refuse to receive it, in exchange for any property, as gold and silver, should be deemed an enemy to his country. They, at the same time, resorted to the extraordinary expedient of regulating the prices of all articles necessary for the army; and if any persons refused to sell the surplus of what was wanted for the annual support of their families, the purchasing commissaries were authorized to take such surplus at the prices so fixed.

* To New Hampshire,	200,000	Delaware,	60,000
Massachusetts,	820,000	Maryland,	520,000
Rhode Island,	100,000	Virginia,	800,000
Connecticut,	600,000	North Carolina,	250,000
New York,	200,000	South Carolina,	500,000
New Jersey,	270,000	Georgia,	60,000
Pennsylvania,	620,000		

These extraordinary measures tended to increase rather than diminish the evil. The bills still continued to depreciate rapidly, and some more effectual remedy, than tender and regulating laws, was necessary. In 1779, congress attempted to establish a fund for sinking the bills then in circulation, by calling on the states to pay their quotas of fifteen millions of dollars for that year, and six millions annually for the eighteen succeeding years.

These calls upon the states were made in vain ; little was paid into the public treasury ; and new bills were issued, which swelled the amount in September, 1779, to one hundred and sixty millions. At this time, congress thought it necessary, to declare that the issues, on no account, should exceed two hundred millions. Nor did they then despair of their ultimate redemption at par. In a circular address to their constituents, they with apparent sincerity and zeal, endeavored to prove, that the United States had the ability, as well as disposition eventually to redeem their bills. After stating the probable future resources of the country, from an increase of population, a vast increase of agricultural productions, the avails of the western lands, &c., they say, " whoever examines the force of these and similar observations, must smile at the ignorance of those, who doubt the ability of the United States, to redeem the bills." They indignantly repelled the idea of a violation of the plighted faith of the nation.

" The pride of America," they observed, " revolts at the idea ; her citizens know for what purpose these emissions were made, and have repeatedly plighted their faith for the redemption of them ; they are to be found in every man's possession, and every man is interested in their being redeemed ; they must therefore entertain a high opinion of American credulity, who suppose the people capable of believing, on due reflection, that all America will, against the faith, the honor, and the interest of all America, be ever prevailed upon to countenance, support, or permit so ruinous, so disgraceful a measure."

While every one must applaud the spirit of these observations ; few, we believe, will not regret to find in the same address, remarks on the supposed advantages of paper money, calcula-

ed to make them doubt at least, whether congress were not trifling with the public, on so interesting and important a subject.

"Let it be remembered," they remarked, "that paper money
is the only kind of money, which cannot 'make unto itself wings
and fly away.' It remains with us, it will not forsake us, it is always ready and at hand for the purpose of commerce or taxes,
and every industrious man can find it."*

The continued failures of the states to comply with the requisitions made upon them, and the increasing wants of the country,
increased the issues, (notwithstanding the resolution of congress
to the contrary,) to more than three hundred millions ; and the
idea of redeeming the bills at their nominal value, was at length
abandoned. In March, 1780, the states were required to bring them
in at forty for one. The bills when brought in were to be cancelled, and new ones to issue in lieu of them, not exceeding one
twentieth part of their nominal amount. The new bills were to
be redeemable in six years, to bear an interest of five per cent.,
to be issued on the credit of the individual states, and their payment guarantied by the United States.

The new system of finance was equally unavailing. The old
bills were not brought in, and of course few new ones issued. The
general treasury was empty, the army without pay or clothing,
and often without provisions. The states were called upon for
supplies in specific articles. To keep the army together, congress were obliged to raise money, by drawing bills on their
ministers in Europe, without any assurance of their payment.

The continental bills, at last, became of so little value, that
they ceased to circulate ; and in the course of the year 1780, quietly died in the hands of the possessors.

In addition to this, the campaign of 1780, was unfortunate for
America. The cities of Charleston and Savannah were taken,
and the states of South Carolina and Georgia, were in possession
of the enemy. In this situation, congress had no other means of
providing for the next campaign, but foreign loans. To obtain
these, they, on the 22d of November, addressed a letter to their

* Journals of Congress, vol. 5, pp. 262, 266.

ally the king of France, stating their embarrassments, and declaring that a foreign loan of, at least, twenty-five millions of livres, was indispensably necessary, for a vigorous prosecution of the war.* Dr. Franklin was specially instructed, " to employ his unremitted and utmost abilities," to procure the aids required. At no time since the campaign of 1776, had the affairs of the United States worn so gloomy an aspect, as at the close of this year. General Washington, in a circular letter to the governors of the states, in October, says, " our finances are in an alarming state of derangement. The public credit is almost arrived at its last stage. The people begin to be dissatisfied with the feeble mode of conducting the war, and with the ineffectual burdens imposed on them, which, though light in comparison with what other nations feel, are from their novelty heavy to them. They lose their confidence in government apace."†

The absolute necessity of obtaining foreign loans, induced congress, in December, 1780, to send a special minister to France. Col. John Laurens, one of the aids of general Washington, and son of Henry Laurens, then a prisoner in the tower of London, was selected for this important mission.

He repaired to Paris, in the winter of 1781. Before his arrival, in consequence of the letter of congress and the solicitations of Dr. Franklin, promises of assistance had been made by the French court. The delay, however, in fulfilling these promises, ill accorded with the high and ardent feelings of the young American envoy. Knowing the pressing wants of his country, and the necessity of immediate aid, if afforded at all, after a delay of more than two months, he determined at the next levee day, to present in person, a memorial to the king, though directly contrary to the forms of court.

In conversation with Vergennes, on the morning of the day, on which he intended to present his memorial to the king, he expostulated with him, on delaying the promised aid, in such warm and bold language, that the minister replied. " Col. Lau-

* Note 15.   † Governor Trumbull's Papers.

rens, you are so recently from the head quarters of the American army, that you forget you are no longer delivering the orders of the commander in chief, but addressing the minister of a monarch, who has every disposition to favor your country." "Favor, Sir!" rejoined Laurens, "the respect which I owe my country will not admit the term—say the object of my mission is of mutual interest to our respective nations, and I subscribe the obligations; but as the most conclusive argument I can address to your excellency, the sword which I now carry, in defense of France, as well as of my own country, unless the succor I solicit is speedily accorded, I may be compelled to draw against France, as a British subject."

He presented his memorial to the king, on the same day. It was graciously received, and no doubt, was the means of hastening the promised succors.*

The king gave the United States, by way of subsidy, six millions of livres, and furnished a further sum, by way of loan.

Applications for loans in Holland had hitherto been unsuccessful. The Hollanders either distrusted the security, or were unwilling to incur the resentment of Great Britain, by lending the Americans money, to enable them to carry on the war.

His most christian majesty had, through his minister at the Hague, offered his assistance to the Americans in procuring loans in that country, but without effect. The king of France now engaged to become himself accountable for the sums which might be furnished. In consequence of this, and the exertions of Mr. Adams, a loan of ten millions of livres was obtained in Holland. The demands upon the French treasury from America, induced Vergennes to inform congress, that they must not expect future pecuniary aid from France. In a letter of the 11th of May, 1781, he said, he thought it his duty "freely and openly to declare, that the moment is come, not to spend the time in expectation, deliberation and useless exhortations: that though he would wish to avoid every disagreeable intimation, friendship

* See an account of this transaction given by Major Jackson, secretary to Laurens, in No. 2, of the American Quarterly Review, p. 426.

and common interest obliged France to speak without reserve
and with perfect sincerity: that the king has done, on this occasion, what he can do no more: that congress, if well informed
of the situation of his majesty's affairs, would be sensible that
an exertion like the present cannot be repeated; and that the
court would feel the deepest concern, if it was under the disagreeable but indispensable necessity of refusing the demands of
an ally whose case is now become his own."*

While congress were soliciting foreign aid, they felt the necessity of a more complete and efficient arrangement of their civil
departments at home. In January, 1781, they established an
office for the department of foreign affairs, at the head of
which was placed a person to be styled, "secretary of foreign affairs." In February following, they also determined to appoint a
superintendant of finance, and secretaries of war and marine.
The office of superintendant of finance was at that time, particularly necessary. This officer was directed to examine into the
public debts, the public expenditures and the public revenue—to
digest and report plans for improving and regulating the finances, and for establishing order and economy in the expenditures
of the public money—to direct the execution of all plans, which
should be adopted by congress respecting revenue and expenditures—to superintend and control the settlement of all public accounts—to direct and control all persons employed in procuring
supplies for the public service, and in the expenditures of public
money—to obtain accounts of all the specific supplies furnished
be the several states—to compel the payment of all monies due
to the United States, and in his official character, or in such
manner as the laws of the states might direct, to prosecute, in
behalf of the United States, for all delinquencies repecting the
public revenue and expenditures. Robert Morriss, an eminent
merchant of Philadelphia, was soon after appointed to this important office, and in the course of the year, Robert R. Livingston
was made secretary of foreign affairs, and Benjamin Lincoln secretary of war. To aid the finanical operations of the country.

* Secret Journals of Congress, vol. 3, p. 87.

Mr. Morriss, in May, submitted to congress a plan for a national bank, with a capital of 400,000 dollars. It was approved by congress, and they engaged that the subscribers should be incorporated by the name of " the president and directors of the bank of North America," as soon as the subscription should be filled. They, at the same time, made the bills of the bank receivable in payment of all taxes, duties and debts due the United States; and recommended to the individual states to punish those who should counterfeit the bills, and to provide that no other bank should be established during the war. In December, 1781, this bank, being the first in the United States, was incorporated, and went into successful operation. A considerable part of the money obtained in France, by Mr. Laurens, was brought into the United States in specie; and by these timely aids, and the united efforts of the allies, the military operations in America were brought to a close, in October of this year, by the capture of the British army at Yorktown.

The deranged situation of the American finances, added to the innumerable calamities necessarily incident to a state of war, produced unparalleled distress among all classes of citizens, but particularly those belonging to the army. The soldiers were not only paid in paper, worth little or nothing, but were often left entirely destitute of necessary clothing and provisions; and nothing but their unexampled patience and patriotism, with the influence of their beloved commander, could have so long kept them together.

A particular narrative of their sufferings, does not fall within our prescribed limits. Yet it ought never to be forgotten, that while general Howe and his army, in the winter of 1778, were enjoying ease and plenty, in the elegant and comfortable mansions of Philadelphia, general Washington and his troops, took up their winter quarters in a neighboring forest, in temporary log huts, built by themselves; the men half naked, and often without provisions. That their march to this place of cantonment could be traced by the blood from their naked feet. Their hardships and their patience under them, are thus described by general Washington, in one of his letters written at the time :—" Without arrogance, or the smallest deviation from truth, it may be said, that no history now extant, can furnish an instance of an army's suffering such uncommon hardships, as ours has done, and bearing them with the same patience and fortitude. To see men without clothes to cover their nakedness, without blankets to lie on, without shoes (so that their marches might be traced by the blood of their feet) and almost as often without provisions as with, marching through frost and snow, and at christmas, taking up their winter quarters, without a house or hut to cover them till they could be built, and submitting to it, without a murmur, is a mark of patience and obedience, which can scarcely be paralleled."*

In consequence of the deranged state of the quarter master's and commissary's departments, the commander in chief was compelled to procure provisions by military impressments; and this desperate resource sometimes failed, and he was obliged to make earnest calls upon the governors of the states. In a letter to governor Clinton of New York, in the winter of 1778, he says, " It is with great reluctance, I trouble you upon a subject which does not fall within your province; but it is a subject which occasions me more distress than I have felt since the commencement of the war, and which loudly demands the most zealous exertions of every man of weight and authority, who is interested in the success of our affairs—I mean the present dreadful situation of the army for want of provisions, and the miserable prospect for the future. It is more alarming than you will probably conceive, for to form a just idea, it were necessary to be on the spot. For some days past, there has been little less than a famine in camp; a part of the army has been a week without any kind of flesh, and the rest three or four days. Naked and starving as they are, we cannot enough admire the incomparable patience and fidelity of the soldiery, that they have not been, ere this time, excited by their sufferings, to a mutiny and dispersion. Strong symptoms, however, of discontent have appeared in particular instances, and nothing can long avert so shocking a catastrophe."

* Gordon, vol. 2, p. 311.

On the first of February, 1778, nearly four thousand men were returned as unfit for duty, for want of clothes; and of this number, scarcely a man had a pair of shoes.*

In consequence of the failure of the states to comply with the requisitions of congress, and other causes, the distresses of the American army, for want of clothing and provisions, in the subsequent years of the war, were also at times extreme. No one more keenly felt, or more deeply lamented this, or made greater exertions to prevent it, than the commander in chief. The condition of the troops at Morristown, in New Jersey, in January, 1780, is thus depicted in his letter to the governor of Connecticut: "The army have been near three months on a short allowance of bread; within a fortnight past almost perishing. They have been sometimes without bread, sometimes without meat, and oftener without both. They have borne this distress, in which the officers have shared a common lot with the men, with as much fortitude as human nature is capable of; but they have been at last, brought to such a dreadful extremity, that no authority or influence of the officers, no virtue or patience in the men themselves, could any longer restrain them from obeying the dictates of their feelings. The soldiers, have, in several instances, plundered the neighboring inhabitants even of their necessary subsistence. Without an immediate remedy, this evil will soon become intolerable, and unhappily for us, we have no prospect of relief through the ordinary channels. We are reduced to this alternative, either to let the army disband, or to call upon the counties of this state to furnish a proportion of cattle and grain for the supply of our wants. If the magistrates refuse their aid, we shall be obliged to have recourse to a military impress."†

At the close of the year 1780, the patience of the army, particularly that part composed of the Pennsylvania line, was exhausted. In addition to their distresses, in common with the rest of the army, some difficulties arose in the line of that state, as to the terms of their enlistment. On the first of January, 1781,

* Marshall's Life of Washington, vol. 3, pp. 368, 369, and 375
† Governor Trumbull's papers.

about thirteen hundred revolted and marched to Princeton. The commander in chief, and the other officers, endeavored to induce them to return to their duty, but without success. The soldiers said, "We neither can nor will be any longer amused. We are determined, at every hazard, to march in a body to congress and obtain redress." Some lives were lost, in attempting to prevent this revolt; and when general Wayne, to whom the soldiers were much attached, presented his pistol to their breasts, they turned their bayonets, and told him if he fired he was a dead man; they at the same time added, "We love you, we respect you; do not mistake us; we are not going to the enemy; on the contrary, were they now to come out, you would see us fight under your orders, with as much resolution and alacrity as ever."[*]

As soon as the British commander heard of this revolt, he secretly sent messengers, offering them the following terms, "to be taken under the protection of the British government, to have a free pardon for all past offenses, to have the pay due to them from congress faithfully paid, without any expectation of military service (except it might be voluntary) upon condition of laying down their arms, and returning to their allegiance."[†]

These offers were indignantly rejected, and two of the messengers delivered up to general Wayne as spies, and afterwards executed as such. Committees from congress, and from the assembly of Pennsylvania, met the insurgents at Trenton, and a compromise was effected, a part discharged, and the rest returned to their duty.

Congress, as well as the commander in chief, had serious apprehensions, that the revolt of the Pennsylvania line, would extend to every part of the army. A messenger was despatched to the New England states, urging immediate relief to the troops of their respective lines. "It is in vain," says general Washington, in his letter by this messenger, "to think an army can be kept together much longer, under such a variety of sufferings as ours have experienced; and unless some immediate and speedy measures are adopted to furnish, at least, three months pay to the

* Gordon, vol. 8, p. 151.   † New Annual Register for 1780.

troops in money, which will be of some value to them, and at the same time, ways and means are devised to clothe and feed them better (more regularly I mean) the worst that can befall us may be expected."

The Americans experienced calamities and sufferings peculiar to this war. Thousands were greatly injured and many ruined by placing confidence in the paper issued by congress.

The mode of warfare practised by the enemy, a mode unprecedented among civilized nations, also brought distress and ruin, upon almost every class of American citizens. Hundreds of dwelling houses, with all their furniture, were burned and destroyed in the most wanton manner. This was not confined to solitary instances, where the individual owner was particularly obnoxious, but whole towns and villages, inhabited by peaceful and unoffending citizens, were reduced to ashes.

In June, 1775, three hundred and eighty dwelling houses, and other buildings, were burnt at Charlestown, in Massachusetts. These were valued by a committee appointed for that purpose, at £159,960, 18, 8, lawful money, and 2000 persons were thereby reduced to poverty.

The value of houses and other buildings, including furniture, thus destroyed in Connecticut, was estimated at more than six hundred and thirty three thousand dollars, in addition to goods and merchandize, to the amount of nearly four hundred thousand dollars more.

The distresses and discontents in the army were not confined to the soldiers, but extended to the officers. Without pay, and often without comfortable subsistence, and sometimes entirely destitute, many of the officers, resigned their commissions, and others threatened to follow their example, unless assured of more adequate provision for their future support.

This gave no little alarm to the commander in chief; and to secure the services of the officers who remained, then so important to the country, he, in January, 1778, earnestly recommended a half pay establishment. In urging the propriety and necessity of this measure to the consideration of the national legislature, he, among other things, said, " a small knowledge of human nature will convince us, that with far the greatest part of mankind, interest is the governing principle; and that, almost every man is more or less under its influence. Motives of public virtue may for a time, or in particular instances, actuate men to the observance of a conduct purely disinterested ; but they are not of themselves sufficient to produce a persevering conformity to the refined dictates and obligations of social duty.

" Few men are capable of making a continual sacrifice of all views of private interest or advantage, to common good. It is in vain to exclaim against the depravity of human nature on this account—the fact is so, the experience of every age and nation has proved it ; and we must, in a great measure, change the constitution of man, before we can make it otherwise. No institution, not built on the presumptive truth of these maxims, can succeed.

" We find them exemplified in the American officers, as well as in all other men. At the commencement of the dispute, in the first effusion of their zeal, and looking upon the service to be only temporary, they entered into it, without paying any regard to pecuniary or selfish considerations. But finding its duration to be much longer than they at first suspected, and that instead of deriving any advantage from the hardships and dangers to which they were exposed, they, on the contrary, were losers, by their patriotism, and fell far short even of a competency to supply their wants, they have gradually abated in their ardor ; and with many, an entire disinclination to the service, under its present circumstances, has taken place. To this, in an eminent degree, must be ascribed the frequent resignations daily happening, and the more frequent importunities for permission to resign, and from some officers of the greatest merit. To this also may be ascribed the apathy, inattention and neglect of duty, which pervade all ranks, and which will necessarily continue and increase, while an officer, instead of gaining any thing, is impoverished by his commission ; and considers he is conferring, not receiving a favor by holding it. There can be no sufficient tie upon men possessing such sentiments. Nor can any method be adopted to oblige those, to a punctual discharge of duty, who are indifferent about their continuance in the service, and are often seeking a pretext to discharge themselves from it. Punishment in this case will be unavailing ; but when an officer's commission is made valuable to him, and he fears to lose it, you may then exact obedience from him. It is not indeed consistent with reason, or justice, to expect, that one set of men should make a sacrifice of property, domestic ease and happiness—encounter the rigors of the field—the perils aud vicissitudes of war, to obtain those blessings, which every citizen will enjoy, in common with them, without some adequate compensation. It must also be a comfortless reflection to any man, that after he may have contributed to securing the rights of his country, at the risk of his life, and the ruin of his fortune, there would be no provision made to prevent himself and family from sinking into indigence and wretchedness. Besides adopting some method to make the provision for officers, equal to their present exigencies, a due regard should be paid to futurity. Nothing, in my opinion, could serve more powerfully to reanimate their languishing zeal, and interest them thoroughly in the service, than a half pay establishment. This would not only dispel the apprehension of personal distress, at the termination of the war, from having thrown themselves out of professions and employments, they might not have it in their power to resume ; but would in a great degree, relieve the painful anticipation of leaving their widows and orphans a burden on the charity of their country, should it be their lot to fall in its defense."

In consequence of this representation, congress, in May following, unanimously granted to all officers commissioned by them, who should continue in service during the war, half-pay for seven years; and soon after extended it to the widows or orphans of such, as had, or should die in the service.

In the latter part of the year 1780, a new arrangement of the army, by a reduction of the number of regiments was deemed ne-

cessary ; and congress declared, that the officers who might be
reduced, should still be entitled to the seven years half-pay. The
commander in chief was, of course consulted on the subject of
the new arrangement. Satisfied that it would be difficult, if not
impossible to retain the best officers, without a more adequate
provision for them at the close of the war, general Washington
again pressed upon congress, the necessity of securing to them
half-pay for life. " In reasoning upon the measure of a future
provision," says the general, " I have heard gentlemen object, the
want of it in some foreign armies, without adverting to the difference of circumstances. The military state holds the first rank in
most of the countries of Europe, and is the road to honor and
emolument. The establishment is permanent, and whatever be
an officer's provision, it is for life—and he has a profession for
life. He has future, as well as present motives of military honor
and preferment ; he is attached to the service, by the spirit of government, by education, and in most cases, by early habit ; his
present condition, though not splendid, is comfortable ; pensions
and distinctions and particular privileges, are commonly his reward in retirement. In the case of the American officers, the
military character has been suddenly taken up, and is to end with
the war."

Convinced of the propriety as well as the necessity of the measure, congress, in October, 1780, complied with the wishes of the
general, and half-pay for life was granted to all the officers,
including those who might be reduced. This was satisfactory,
and the new arrangement of the army was effected without difficulty. This grant, however, was extremely unpopular in some
of the states ; and at the close of the year 1782, it was reported,
that congress did not intend to comply with their engagement.

This created no little alarm in the army ; and there was too
much reason to fear, that a majority of the national legislature
might be disposed to refer the officers to their respective states,
for a fulfilment of this engagement. In December of that year,
therefore, the officers presented a memorial to congress, not only
on the subject of the half-pay, but of the arrearages of pay still

" We have struggled," they say to congress, " with our difficulties year after year, under the hopes that each would be the last, but we have been disappointed. We find our embarrassments thicken so fast, and have become so complex, that many of us are unable to go further. We complain that *shadows* have been offered to us, while the *substance* has been gleaned by every person bearing the mark of civil authority throughout the United States. Our situation compels us to search for the cause of our extreme poverty. The citizens murmur at the greatness of their taxes, and are astonished that no part reaches the army. The numerous demands which are between the first collectors and the soldiers swallow up the whole. Our distresses are now brought to a point. We have borne all that we can bear—our property is expended—our private resources are at an end, and our friends are wearied out and disgusted with our constant applications."

With respect to the half-pay, in consequence of the odious point of view, in which it was considered by some of the states, they offered to commute it for full pay, for a certain number of years, or for a sum in gross. A committee, consisting of general McDougal, Col. Ogden, and Col. Brooks, was appointed to present this memorial. It was proposed in congress, to allow five years full pay, in lieu of the half-pay ; but after much debate and delay, the assent of nine states, (that number being required by the articles of confederation,) could not be obtained in favor of it ; and the subject was postponed.

Of these proceedings on their memorial, the committee made a report to the officers. Conscious of the merit of their long services and sufferings, as well as of the justice of their claims, their minds were ill prepared to brook this delay ; and many of them were disposed to construe a delay of justice into a denial of it. In this state of their feelings, on the 10th of March, a meeting of the officers was called, by an anonymous notification, " to consider, the late letter of our representatives in Philadelphia, and what measures (if any) should be adopted, to obtain that redress of grievances, which they seem to have solicited in vain."

This was accompanied, by an address from one, who called himself their fellow soldier, calculated by its peculiar style and manner, to inflame their passions, by bringing to their recollection, all their toils and all their sufferings; to induce a belief, in the injustice and ingratitude of their country, and to drive them to the last extremity, in order to obtain redress. The author told them, that he had shared in their toils and mingled in their dangers, that he had felt the cold hand of poverty, without a murmur, and had seen the insolence of wealth, without a sigh; and that till lately, very lately, he had believed in the justice of his country."

"After a pursuit of seven long years," he said, "the object for which we set out, is at length brought within our reach. Yes, my friends, that suffering courage of your's was active once—it has conducted the United States of America, through a doubtful and a bloody war. It has placed her in the chair of independency, and peace returns again to bless—whom? A country willing to redress your wrongs, cherish your worth, and reward your services, a country courting your return to private life, with tears of gratitude and smiles of admiration, longing to divide with you that independency, which your gallantry has given, and those riches, which your wounds have preserved? Is this the case? or is it rather a country, that tramples on your rights, disdains your cries, and insults your distresses? Have you not more than once suggested your wishes, and made known your wants to congress? Wants and wishes, which gratitude and policy should have anticipated, rather than evaded. And have you not lately, in the meek language of entreating memorials, begged from their justice, what you could no longer expect from their favor? How have you been answered? Let the letter, which you are called to consider to-morrow make reply. If this, then, be your treatment, while the swords you wear are necessary for the defense of America, what have you to expect from peace, when your voice shall sink, and your strength is dissipated by divisions? When those very swords, the instruments and companions of your glory, shall be taken from your sides, and no remaining mark of military distinction left, but your wants, infirmities, and scars?

Can you then consent to be the only sufferers by this revolution, and retiring from the field, grow old in poverty, wretchedness, asd contempt ? Can you consent to wade through the vile mire of dependency, and owe the miserable remnant of that life to charity, which has hitherto been spent in honor! If you can, go, and carry with you, the jest of tories and the scorn of whigs, the ridicule, and what is worse, the pity of the world. Go starve and be forgotten !"

He advises them to change the milk and water style of their last memorial, to carry their appeal from the *justice* to the *fears* of government ; and to suspect the man, who should advise to more moderation and longer forbearance.*

It required all the firmness and influence of general Washington, to allay the ferment created by the proceedings of congress, and this inflammatory address.

He immediately issued an order requiring a meeting of the officers, and expressing his disapprobation of any irregular meeting, in consequence of an anonymous notification.

In the mean time, the influence of the general was exerted, in private conversation with individual officers, to induce them to proceed with becoming moderation, and in a manner consistent with their high character and honor.

A meeting was held, agreeably to the order of general Washington, and was opened by an address from him, in which, alluding to the anonymous publication, he gave the author much more credit for the goodness of his pen, than the rectitude of his heart. After stating the great difficulties congress had to encounter in procuring funds from so many different states, declaring his opinion, that complete justice would be done, and assuring them, that all his influence should be exerted in their behalf, he thus concludes: "While I give you these assurances, and pledge myself, in the most unequivocal manner, to exert whatever ability I am possessed of, in your favor, let me entreat you, gentlemen, on your part, not to take any measure, which reviewed

* No doubt now remains, that general James Armstrong, then a major, was the author of this address.

in the calm light of reason, will lessen the dignity and sully the
glory you have hitherto maintained.   Let me request you to rely
on the plighted faith of your country, and place full confidence in
the purity of the intentions of congress, that previous to your dissolution as an army, they will cause all your accounts to be fairly
liquidated, as directed in the resolutions which were published to
you two days ago ; and that they will adopt the most effectual
measures in their power, to render ample justice to you for your
faithful and meritorious services.   And let me conjure you in the
name of our common country, as you value your own sacred hon-
or, as you respect the rights of humanity, and as you regard the
military and national character of America, to express your utmost horror and detestation of the man, who wishes, under any
specious pretences, to overturn the liberties of our country ; and
who wickedly attempts to open the flood gates of civil discord,
and deluge our rising empire in blood.

   " By thus determining and acting, you will pursue the plain and
direct road to the attainment of your wishes ; you will defeat the
insidious designs of our enemies, who are compelled to resort,
from open force to secret artifice.   You will give one more distinguished proof of unexampled patriotism and patient virtue, rising superior to the pressure of the most complicated sufferings ;
and you will, by the dignity of your conduct afford occasion for
posterity to say, when speaking of the glorious example you have
exhibited to mankind, had this day been wanting, the world had
never seen the last stage of perfection, to which human nature is
capable of attaining."

   The nature of this appeal was not to be resisted.   After general
Washington retired, the officers not only voted him their thanks for
his address, but unanimously resolved, that as they engaged in the
service of their country from the purest love and attachment to the
rights and liberties of human nature, no circumstances of distress
or danger should induce a conduct tending to sully their reputation
and honor, acquired at the price of their blood, and eight years
faithful service—that they still had unshaken confidence in the justice of congress and their country ; and that they viewed with ab-

horrence and rejected with disdain, the infamous propositions contained in the anonymous address. They also requested the commander in chief, to entreat congress for a speedy decision on their memorial; an event, they said, which, in the alternative of peace or war, would be highly satisfactory, produce immediate tranquillity in the minds of the army, and prevent any further machinations of designing men, to sow discord between the civil and military powers of the United States.

Thus ended an affair, which did indeed threaten discord between the civil and military powers. And had the commander of this victorious but suffering army, been governed by that love of power so natural to man, he might probably have triumphed over the civil institutions of his country.

In communicating these proceedings of the officers to congress, on the 18th of March, general Washington, in the most earnest manner, urged a compliance with the prayer of their memorial. " If," says the general, " besides the simple payment of their wages, a further compensation is not due to the sufferings and sacrifices of the officers, then I have been mistaken indeed; if the whole army have not merited whatever a grateful country can bestow, then I have been beguiled by prejudice, and built opinion on the basis of error. If this country should not, in the event, perform every thing which has been requested in the late memorial to congress, then will my belief become vain, and the hope, that has been excited, void of foundation.

" And, if (as has been suggested, for the purpose of inflaming their passions) the officers of the army ' are to be the only sufferers by this revolution; if retiring from the field, they are to grow old in poverty, wretchedness and contempt; if they are to wade through the vile mire of dependency, and owe the miserable remnant of that life to charity, which has, hitherto, been spent in honor,' then I have learned what ingratitude is, then shall I have realized a tale, which will embitter every moment of my future life."

On the 22d of March, congress granted to the officers five years full pay, in lieu of the half pay, to be paid in money, or securities on interest, provided it be at the option of the lines of the respective states, not officers individually, to accept or refuse the same. This grant was accepted by the officers in the manner directed.

The news of peace soon after arrived, and arrangements for disbanding the army were made ; but as the definitive treaty was not completed, those who were engaged during the war, were dismissed on furlough.

This was attended with some difficulty and delay, for want of funds, even to pay a small sum, to enable the soldiers to return to their homes ; and it was not until about the middle of June, that the army left the camp.

General Washington, on the 8th of June addressed a circular letter to the several states, giving them notice of his intended resignation, and congratulating them on the happy termination of the war, and on the numerous advantages and blessings, which, as a free and independent nation, they had now a right to expect. Having in the course of the war experienced, and at times too fatally experienced the evils arising from a failure, on the part of the states, to comply with the requisitions of congress, he reminded them, that, whether these advantages and blessings would be realized, depended, in a great measure, on themselves, on their prompt and mutual co-operation, in promoting the great interests of the union. He considered four things as essentially necessary, to the existence of the United States, as an independent power.

1. An indissoluble union of the states, under one federal head.

2. A sacred regard to justice.

3. The adoption of a proper peace establishment.

4. The prevalence of that 'pacific and friendly disposition, among the people of the United States, which would induce them to forget their local prejudices and policies, to make those mutual concessions, which were requisite to the general prosperity ; and, in some instances, to sacrifice their individual advantages, to the interest of the community.

The importance and necessity of these, he enforced with all that practical good sense, and sound political wisdom, for which he was so eminently distinguished.*

On the news of the signature of the definitive treaty, congress, by a general proclamation, finally discharged the army, from and after the 3d of November. They presented them the thanks of the United States for their long and faithful services, and bestowed on them that applause, they so justly merited, for their fortitude and magnanimity, in the most trying scenes of distress, and for a series of the most heroic and illustrious achievements, which exalted them to a high rank among the most zealous and successful defenders of the rights and liberties of mankind. The day previous to their final discharge, general Washington issued to the armies of the United States, his farewell orders.

After alluding to the proclamation of congress, he says, " It only remains for the commander in chief, to address himself once more, and that for the last time, to the armies of the United States, (however widely dispersed the individuals who composed them may be) and to bid them an affectionate—a long farewell.

" And being now to conclude these his last public orders, to take his ultimate leave, in a short time, of the military character, and to bid a final adieu to the armies he has so long had the honor to command, he can only again offer, in their behalf, his recommendations to their grateful country, and his prayers to the God of armies. May ample justice be done them here, and may the choicest of heaven's favors, both here and hereafter, attend those, who, under the divine auspices, have secured innumerable blessings for others. With these wishes, and this benediction, the commander in chief is about to retire from service. The curtain of separation will soon be drawn, and the military scene to him, be closed forever."

The British army did not finally leave the city of New York, until the 25th of November. On the same day general Washington, with some of his principal officers, and the remaining

* Note 16

part of the American troops, accompanied by the governor, lieutenant governor, some members of the council, and many of the citizens of the state of New York, marched in, and took possession of that city.

The joyful event of peace, was here celebrated, on the first of December. Here also four days after, the commander in chief took leave of his officers. Having met them at a place appointed, the general taking a glass of wine, thus addressed them —" With a heart full of love and gratitude, I now take leave of you. I most devoutly wish, that your latter days may be as prosperous and happy, as your former ones have been glorious and honorable." After a short pause, each one received the hand and embrace of their beloved general. Being then on his way to congress, to resign his commission, his officers, in a procession accompanied him to the boat in which he was to embark, and as it put from the shore, an alternate waving of hats, gave the last silent adieu.*

After remaining a few days at Philadelphia, for the purpose of settling his accounts, (the whole of which was only nineteen thousand three hundred pounds eleven shillings and nine pence, Virginia money,) he repaired to the seat of the general government, at Annapolis ; and on the 23d of December, at a public audience, and in the presence of a great concourse of his fellow citizens, he resigned into the hands of congress, that commission, which more than eight years before, he had, with so much diffidence, and in far other circumstances, received from them. In doing this, he made the following address.

" *Mr. President*—The great events, on which my resignation depended, having at length taken place, I have now the honor of offering my sincere congratulations to congress, and of presenting myself before them, to surrender into their hands the trust committed to me, and to claim the indulgence of retiring from the service of my country.

"Happy in the confirmation of our independence and sovereignty, and pleased with the opportunity afforded the United

* Gordon p. 377.

States, of becoming a respectable nation, I resign with satisfaction the appointment I accepted with diffidence,—a diffidence in
my abilities to accomplish so arduous a task; which, however,
was superseded by a confidence in the rectitude of our cause, the
support of the supreme power of the union, and the patronage of
heaven.

  "The successful termination of the war verified the most sanguine expectations; and my gratitude for the interposition of
Providence, and the assistance I have received from my countrymen, increases with every review of the momentous contest.

  "While I repeat my obligations to the army in general, I should
do injustice to my own feelings, not to acknowledge in this place,
the peculiar services and distinguished merits of the gentlemen,
who have been attached to my person, during the war. It was
impossible the choice of confidential officers, to compose my family, should have been more fortunate.

  "Permit me, sir, to recommend, in particular, those who have
continued in the service to the present moment, as worthy of the
favorable notice and patronage of congress.

  "I consider it an indispensable duty to close this last act of my
official life, by commending the interests of our dearest country to
the protection of Almighty God, and those, who have the super-
intendence of them, to his holy keeping.

  "Having now finished the work assigned me, I retire from the
great theatre of action, and bidding an affectionate farewell to
this august body, under whose orders I have so long acted, I here
offer my commission, and take my leave of all the employments
of public life."

The following answer was returned by the president.

  "Sir—The United States in congress assembled, receive with
emotions too affecting for utterance, the solemn resignation of
the authorities, under which you have led their troops with success, through a perilous and a doubtful war. Called upon by
your country to defend its invaded rights, you accepted the sacred
charge, before it formed alliances, and whilst it was without funds

or a government to support you. You have conducted the great
military contest with wisdom and fortitude, invariably regarding
the rights of the civil power, through all disasters and changes.
You have, by the love and confidence of your fellow citizens, enabled them to display their martial genius, and transmit their fame
to posterity. You have persevered, till these United States, aid-
ed by a magnanimous king and nation, have been enabled, under a just Providence, to close the war in freedom, safety, and
independence ; on which happy event we sincerely join you in
congratulations.   .

" Having defended the standard of liberty in this new world :
having taught a lesson useful to those who inflict, and to those
who feel oppression, you retire from the great theatre of action,
with the blessings of your fellow citizens ; but the glory of your
virtues will not terminate with your military command, it will continue to animate remotest ages.

" We feel with you our obligations to the army in general, and
will particularly charge ourselves, with the interests of those confidential officers, who have attended your person to this affecting
moment.

" We join you, in commending the interests of our dearest
country to the protection of Almighty God, beseeching him to
dispose the hearts and minds of its citizens to improve the opportunity afforded them, of becoming a happy and respectable nation. And for you, we address to him our earnest prayers, that
a life so beloved, may be fostered with all his care ; and that your
days may be as happy as they have been illustrious ; and that he
will finally give you that reward, which this world cannot give."*

This was the closing military scene of the American revolution.
This scene, with the declaration of independence, the surrender
of general Burgoyne, and the capture of lord Cornwallis, in pursuance of a late order of congress, have been selected, to be
commemorated by appropriate paintings, for national use. These
have been executed by John Trumbull, a celebrated American
artist, and placed in the capitol at the seat of the general government.

CHAPTER XVI.

After the peace of 1783, congress take measures to restore public credit—Amount of the debt of the United States—States requested to vest congress with power to levy duties on imports, and to establish funds for the payment of the interest of the debt —Address to the states on the subject—All the states grant the impost, except New York—Congress propose to enter into commercial treaties with most of the powers of Europe—Establish certain principles respecting treaties—Appoint ministers to form commercial arrangements with foreign nations—Pitt's bill respecting commercial intercourse with the United States—Not approved by the new ministry and the navigating interest—Lord Sheffield's observations upon it—King and council authorized to regulate the commerce with the United States—Americans excluded from the West India trade—Disputes with Great Britain about the inexecution of the treaty of peace—Mr. Adams sent minister to England—His instructions—His reception at the court of London—Presents a memorial to the British ministers— British complain of infractions of the treaty on the part of the United States—Congress recommend the repeal of all laws contrary to the treaty—Disputes with Spain renewed about limits and the navigation of the Mississippi—Gardoqui, minister from Spain arrives—Mr. Jay appointed to negociate with him—His instructions, and course of negociation with the Spanish minister—Cessions of lands by the states— Territory of the United States formed into a district—Ordinance of congress for the government of the territory—Inefficiency of the general government—Depressed state of American commerce—Insurrection in Massachusetts—Alarms congress— Troops ordered to be raised to assist Massachusetts—Meeting of commissioners from several states at Annapolis, to amend the articles of confederation—General convention recommended by these commissioners and by congress—Delegates to this convention appointed by all the states except Rhode Island.

One of the first objects which claimed the attention of congress, after the signature of the provisional articles of peace, was the restoration of public credit, and the establishment of funds for the payment of the debts incurred by the war. It was obvious, that duties on imports, must constitute no inconsiderable portion of these funds. Congress, however, had no power to levy these duties, without the assent of all the states.

The whole expense of the war, has been estimated at the sum of one hundred and thirty-five millions of dollars. In this is included the specie value of all the bills advanced from the treasury of the United States, reduced according to a scale of depreciation, established by congress. The whole amount of the debt of the United States, as ascertained in 1783, was about forty-two millions of dollars ; eight millions of which arose, from loans obtained in France and Holland, and the remainder was due to American citizens. The annual interest of this debt, was, two millions four hundred and fifteen thousand nine hundred and fifty-six dollars.

On the 12th of February, 1783, congress, with great unanimity, declared, " that the establishment of permanent and adequate funds on taxes or duties, which shall operate generally, and on the whole, in just proportion, throughout the United States, are indispensably necessary towards doing complete justice to the public creditors, for restoring public credit, and for providing for the future exigencies of the war."

It was much easier to agree, in this general resolution, than to provide the means for carrying it into effect. After much debate, congress, on the 18th of April, recommended to the states, as being " indispensably necessary, to the restoration of public credit, and to the punctual discharge of the public debts," to vest congress with power to levy certain specified duties on spirits, wines, teas, pepper, sugar, molasses, cocoa, and coffee, and a duty of five per cent. *ad valorem*, on all other imported goods. These duties were to be applied solely to the payment of the interest and principal of the public debt, and for that purpose, to continue twenty-five years : the collectors to be chosen by the states, but removeable by congress.

The states were also required, to establish for the same time, and for the same object, substantial and effectual revenues of such nature, as they should judge convenient, for supplying their proportion of one million five hundred thousand dollars, annually, exclusive of duties on imports ; the proportion of each state to be fixed, according to the articles of confederation.*

This system was not to take effect, until acceded to by every state, and when adopted by all, to be a mutual compact among the states, and irrevocable by any one, without the consent of the whole, or of a majority of the United States in congress.

The taxes and expenses of the union, had never yet been apportioned among the states, according to the rule prescribed by the confederation. A satisfactory valuation of houses and lands had never yet been completed ; and the difficulties in making such a valuation, seemed nearly insuperable. The proportions had been generally regulated by the supposed number of inhabitants. Congress now proposed to the consideration of the states, an alteration in the articles, providing, that the proportion should be governed by the number of white and other free citizens, including those bound to servitude for a term of years, and three fifths of all other persons.

To enforce the importance and necessity of adopting and carrying into effect, this system of finance, congress presented an address to the states. This was prepared by a committee consisting of Mr. Ellsworth, Mr. Madison, and Mr. Hamilton, who, then and afterwards, held a high rank among American statesmen.

After explaining the system itself, congress appealed to the gratitude and pride, as well as justice and plighted faith of the nation. They urged particularly, the propriety of the provision recommended for the payment of the national debt. " If other motives than that of justice," they said, " could be requisite, on this occasion, no nation could ever feel stronger ; for, to whom are the debts to be paid ?

* This sum of 1,500,000 dollars, was apportioned among the states, as follows :—

State	Amount	State	Amount
New Hampshire,	52,708	Delaware,	22,443
Massachusetts,	224,427	Maryland,	141,517
Rhode Island,	32,318	Virginia,	256,487
Connecticut,	132,091	North Carolina,	109,006
New York,	128,242	South Carolina,	96,183
New Jersey,	83,358	Georgia,	16,030
Pennsylvania,	205,189		

" To *an ally*, in the first place, who, to the exertion of his armies in support of our cause, has added the succors of his treasure; who, to his important loans, has added liberal donations; and whose loans themselves, carry the impression of his magnanimity and friendship.

" To individuals in a foreign country, in the next place, who were the first to give so precious a token of their confidence in our justice, and of their friendship for our cause, and who are members of a republic, which was second in espousing our rank among nations.

" Another class of creditors is, that illustrious and patriotic band of fellow citizens, whose blood and whose bravery have defended the liberties of their country, who have patiently borne, among other distresses, the privation of their stipends, whilst the distresses of their country disabled it from bestowing them; and who even now, ask for no more than such a portion of their dues, as will enable them to retire from the field of glory, into the bosom of peace and private citizenship, and for such effectual security for the residue of their claims, as their country is now unquestionably able to provide.

" The remaining class of creditors is composed partly of such of our fellow citizens as originally lent to the public the use of their funds, or have since manifested most confidence in their country, by receiving transfers from the lenders; and partly of those, whose property has been either advanced or assumed for the public service. To discriminate the merits of these several descriptions of creditors, would be a task equally unnecessary and invidious. If the voice of humanity plead more loudly in favor of some, than of others, the voice of policy, no less than justice, pleads in favor of all. A wise nation will never permit those, who relieve the wants of their country, or who rely most on its faith, its firmness, and its resources, when either of them is distrusted, to suffer by the event.

" Let it be remembered, finally, that it has ever been the pride and boast of America, that the rights, for which she contended, were the rights of human nature. By the blessing of the author of these rights, or the means exerted for their defense, they have prevailed against all opposition, and form the basis of thirteen independent states. No instance has heretofore occurred, nor can any instance be expected hereafter to occur, in which the unadulterated forms of republican government can pretend to so fair an opportunity of justifying themselves by their fruits. In this view, the citizens of the United States are responsible for the greatest trust ever confided to a political society.

" If justice, good faith, honor, gratitude, and all other qualities, which enoble the character of a nation, and fulfil the ends of government, be the fruits of our establishments, the cause of liberty will acquire a dignity and lustre, which it has never yet enjoyed ; and an example will be set, which cannot but have the most favorable influence on the rights of mankind.

" If on the other side, our government should be unfortunately blotted with the reverse of these cardinal and essential virtues, the great cause which we have engaged to vindicate, will be dishonored and betrayed ; the last and fairest experiment in favor of the rights of human nature will be turned against them, and their patrons and friends exposed to be insulted and silenced by the votaries of tyranny and usurpation."[*]

The propriety and necessity of adopting this system, was strongly pressed upon the states, by general Washington, in his address of the 8th of June. Alluding to it, he says, " no real friend to the honor and independency of America, can hesitate a single moment respecting the propriety of complying with the just and honorable measure proposed."

This plan, however, though thus ably supported and recommended, was never accepted by the states, in such a manner, as to go into operation. The pressure of common danger being removed, the bond of federal union became weak and feeble, and the inefficiency of the national government more apparent. A jealousy between the state and general governments, began to exist; and state interests predominated. The importing states levied contributions on their neighbors for their own benefit, and some of them would not relinquish the advantages of their local situation. Congress, indeed, had power to make treaties with foreign nations, but none to enforce the observance of them; they had power to contract debts, but were unable to enforce the collection of money for the payment of them. For this, they were dependent on the will of thirteen distinct legislative bodies.

That part of the financial plan, which required from the states a pledge of internal revenues for twenty five years, met with the greatest opposition. Congress, were at length, satisfied, that a general compliance with this part of the system was not to be expected, and confined their requests to that relating to duties on imports. In 1786, all the states, except New York, had complied with this part of the system. The operation of the acts, passed by some of the states, however, depended on similar acts from the others. The state of New York, instead of vesting congress with the power of levying the duties, reserved this right to itself agreeably to a law passed in 1784; and also refused to make the collectors amenable to, and removable by congress.

As the assent of New York was now only wanting, on this part of the plan, congress earnestly requested the executive of that state to convene the legislature, for the purpose of making their law conformable to those of other states. The governor of New York, however, declined complying with this request, alleging, that by the constitution of that state, he could only convene the legislature on *extraordinary occasions*; and as the subject had recently been before that body, and received their determination, such an occasion did not exist. To a second and more earnest application, he made the same reply. While this system of revenue was under the consideration of the states, congress could do nothing more than make requisitions, and these were not complied with. The requisitions for the payment of the interest of the domestic debt, from 1782 to 1786, amounted to more than six millions of dollars; yet, of this sum, up to March 31st, 1787, about one million only was paid.* The

* Report of the Board of Treasury.

interest of the domestic debt, therefore, was unpaid ; and the money borrowed in Europe, was applied to the payment of interest on foreign loans. In this situation, the domestic debt was deemed of little value, and was sold for about one tenth of its nominal amount.

Soon after the ratification of the definitive treaty, congress, turned their attention to the subject of commercial intercourse with foreign nations. Liberated from the commercial shackles of their colonial state, the Americans were now disposed to form commercial arrangements with most of the powers of Europe. With these views, congress declared, that it would be advantageous to conclude treaties with Russia, the court of Vienna, Prussia, Spain, Portugal, Genoa, Tuscany, Rome, Naples, Venice, Sardinia, and the Ottoman Porte.

Certain principles, by which the American negociators were to be governed, in the formation of these treaties, were at the same time, settled. Among the stipulations to be proposed on the part of America, some were of a novel character, and calculated to lessen the calamities of war. In case of hostilities between the contracting parties, fishermen, cultivators of the earth, artisans or manufacturers unarmed and inhabiting unfortified towns, villages, or places, who labored for the common subsistence of and benefit of mankind, and peaceably followed their respective employments, were to be allowed to continue the same, and not be molested by the armed force of the enemy, in whose power, by the events of war, they might happen to fall; but if it should be necessary to take any thing from them for the use of such armed force, it should be paid for, at a reasonable price. All merchants and traders, also, exchanging the products of different places, were to be allowed to pass free and unmolested ; and neither of the contracting parties was to grant or issue any commission to any private armed vessels, empowering them to take or destroy such trading ships, or interrupt such commerce.*

* Secret Journals of Congress, vol. 3, p. 484, and Note 17.

The first stipulation was inserted in a treaty between the United States and Prussia, concluded in the year 1785, with an addition, extending the same privileges and exemptions to all women and children, and to scholars. The duration of all the treaties was to be limited to ten years, except in particular cases, but in no case, to exceed fifteen. This was a very wise provision for a new and growing country. The American ministers were, also, particularly instructed in any negociations with Spain, not to relinquish or cede, in any event whatever, the right of freely navigating the river Mississippi from its source to the ocean. John Adams, Dr. Franklin, and Mr. Jefferson, were authorized to make and receive propositions for such treaties, for the term of two years.

The American commissioners at Paris, in 1783, as before stated, were unable to agree with the British negociator, in any commercial arrangement between their respective countries. Each nation, was, therefore, left to make its own regulations. In March, 1783, William Pitt, then chancellor of the exchequer, brought into the house of commons, a bill for the temporary regulation of commerce between Great Britain and the United States, founded upon very liberal principles. This bill, after stating the new situation in which the people of the United States were placed, declared, " And, whereas, it is highly expedient, that the intercourse between Great Britain, and the said United States, should be established on the most enlarged principles of reciprocal benefit to both countries, but from the distance between Great Britain and America, it must be a considerable time before any convention or treaty for establishing and regulating the trade and intercourse between Great Britain and the said United States of America, upon a permanent foundation, can be concluded :—

" Now for the purpose of making a temporary regulation of the commerce and intercourse between Great Britain and the said United States of America, and in order to evince the disposition of Great Britain, to be on terms of the most perfect amity with the said United States of America, and in confidence of a like friendy diposition on the part of the United States towards Great Britain, be it further enacted, that from and after the * * * * the ships and vessels of the subjects and citizens of the said United States of America, with the merchandize and goods on board the same, shall be admitted into all the ports of Great Britain, in the same manner as the ships and vessels of the subjects of other independent sovereign states ; but the merchandizes and goods on board such ships or vessels of the subjects or citizens of the said United States, being of the growth, produce, or manufacture of the said United States, shall be liable to the same duties and charges only, as the same merchandizes and goods would be subject to, if they were the property of British subjects, and imported in British built ships or vessels, navigated by British natural born subjects."

This bill, also, placed the intercourse between the United States and the British American colonies, on a footing equally liberal.

" And be it further enacted, that during the time aforesaid, the ships and vessels of the subjects and citizens of the said United States shall be admitted into the ports of his majesty's islands, colonies and plantations in America, with any merchandizes or goods, of the growth, produce or manufactures of the territories of the aforesaid United States, with liberty to export from his said majesty's islands in America, to the said territories of the said United States, any merchandizes or goods whatsoever ; and such merchandizes or goods, which shall be so imported into, or exported from the said British islands, colonies or plantations in America, shall be liable to the same duties and charges only, as the same merchandizes and goods would be subject to, if they were the property of British natural born subjects, and imported or exported in British built ships or vessels, navigated by British seamen.

" And be it further enacted, that during all the time herein before limited, there shall be the same draw-backs, exemptions and bounties on merchandizes and goods exported from Great Brit-

ain into the territories of the said United States of America, as
are allowed in the case of exportation to the islands, plantations,
or colonies, now remaining or belonging to the crown of Great
Britain in America."

This bill, had it been adopted, would have laid the foundation
of peace and harmony between the two countries. But the mover of it, with lord Shelburne, were soon after obliged to retire
from office, and their successors in April, 1783, procured an act
of parliament authorizing the king and council to regulate the
commercial intercourse between the United States and Great
Britain and her dependencies. The bill of Mr. Pitt was violently
opposed by the navigating interest, as calculated to encourage
the American marine, by securing the colonial trade to the people of the United States. "The navigation act," says lord Sheffield
in his well known observations on the commerce of the American
states, " prevented the Dutch from being the carriers of our trade.
The violation or relaxation of that act in favor of the West
India islands, or of the American states, will give that advantage
to the New Englanders, and encourage, to the greatest degree,
the marine of America, to the ruin of our own. The bill in its
present state, allowing an open trade between the American
states and our islands, relinquished the only use and advantage
of American colonies, or West India islands, *the monopoly of
their consumption, and the carriage of their produce;* for that
object alone we could be tempted to support the vast expense of
their maintenance and protection. Our *late wars* have been for
the *exclusive trade* of America, and our enormous debt has been
incurred for that object. Our remaining colonies on the continent and islands and the favorable state of English manufactures,
may still give us, almost exclusively, the trade of America. But
the bill grants the West India trade to the American states on
better terms than we can have it ourselves, and these advantages
are bestowed, while local circumstances insure many others,
which it is our duty to guard against, rather than promote. It
makes it the interest of our merchants to trade under the American flag. Shipping may be had in America at a much less ori-

ginal expense than is required here, but the quality is greatly inferior. It also makes it the interest of our remaining colonies in North America (for whom no advantages are reserved by the bill in question) to be as independent as the American states, in order to have their trade as open."*

British statesmen could not be persuaded, that the Americans would ever be united among themselves, or be able to form any lasting or beneficial engagements with other nations, not only for want of union, but from opposing interests, and from the imperfect powers of their general government. These views had no little influence with the British cabinet, in their conduct towards the United States. On this subject, lord Sheffield no doubt spoke the language of Englishmen in general, when he said, in the volume before alluded to, " It will not be an easy matter to bring the American states to act as a nation; *they are not to be feared as such by us.* It must be a long time before they can engage, or will concur, in any material expenses. A stamp act, a tea act, or such act that can never again occur, would alone unite them. Their climate, their staples, their manners are different; their interests opposite; and that which is beneficial to one, is destructive to the other. We might as reasonably dread the effects of combinations among the German, as among the American states, and deprecate the resolves of the Diet, as those of congress. In short, every circumstance proves that it will be extreme folly to enter into any engagements, *by which we may not wish to be bound hereafter.* It is impossible to name any material advantage the American states will or can give us in return, more than what we of course shall have. No treaty can be made with the American states that can be binding on the whole of them. The act of confederation does not enable congress to form more than *general treaties*—at the moment of the highest authority of congress, the power in question was withheld by the several states. No treaty that could be made, could suit the different interests. When treaties are necessary, they must be made with the states respectively. Each state has

* Lord Sheffield, pp. 136, 137, 138.

reserved every power relative to imports, exports, prohibitions, duties, &c. to itself. But no treaty at present is necessary. We trade with several very considerable nations, without commercial treaties."

The concluding remarks of lord Sheffield, in his celebrated observations on American commerce, tend not only to shew English views of the weakness and inefficiency of the American government, but also to elucidate the policy pursued by the British cabinet, with respect to the United States. " Some," says his lordship, " may doubt what turn the American states will take, and with many it may reasonably be a question, whether the trade will be again in so prosperous a state for America. *Confusion* and *anarchy* are likely to prevail for some time. Our descendants, the New Englanders, apt to be troublesome to themselves as well as to others, and encouraged by a party among us in the habit of bullying our ministers, may assume a tone, which, however, will now avail them little in Europe. Their natural disposition will be heightened by finding they have lost the principal market for their shipping, lumber, the produce of the whale fishery, and much of the carrying trade. They will machinate, and must attempt to manage. The weakness of the southern states has not a little to fear from their interference. It remains to be seen whether the southern will become the puppets of the northern, whether the middle colonies will be the dupes to the northern, or a barrier to the southern states ; we shall, however, see New Englanders emigrate from the government of their own forming, even to Nova Scotia and Canada, putting themselves under that British government of which they so loudly complained. Nothing is more uncertain than political speculations. The existence of one man, the merest accident, gives a turn to the affairs of the greatest countries, more especially of a country, in a state in which America now is ; but it is certain, that the confusion of the American states can now only hurt themselves. They must pay Europe in the best manner they can for clothing and many articles, for which they are not likely to have the credit they had while in more settled circumstances. If one or more states should prohibit the manufactures of any particular country, they will find their way to them through other states, and by various means. The difficulty will only raise the price on the consumers in the states where the articles are prohibited. The British manufactures found their way to every part of the country during a most rancorous war, and the most strenuous Americans acknowledge that no imposts or *excise laws* will, for a long time, be regarded in America. In the mean time, and at all times, Britain will have nothing to apprehend. The American states will hardly enter into real hostilities with Britain. Britain need not quarrel with them all; but should either happen, some stout frigates, cruising between Halifax and Bermuda, and between Halifax and the Bahamas, would completely command the commerce of this mighty continent, concerning which our prophets have so much amused themselves, deluding the unthinking—a strangely conducted war, is no proof to the contrary ; and a land war would not be necessary—but in some of the states, and possibly even in the New England provinces, when the animosity ceases, and the interested opposition to the return of the loyalists on the part of those who are in the possession of their lands, is no longer kept alive by apprehensions, the natural good wishes that we have to the Americans, which they will gradually allow themselves to see, their interest, our interest, and many circumstances may bring us close together.

" At present the only part Britain should take is most simple, and perfectly sure. If the American states choose to send consuls, receive them, and send a consul to each state. Each state will soon enter into all necessary regulations with the consul, and this is the whole that is necessary."

Orders in council were issued, in July, 1783, for regulating the trade between the United States and the British dominions. American vessels thereby were entirely excluded from the British West Indies ; and certain articles, such as fish, beef, pork, &c. were not allowed to be carried there, even in British bottoms. This prohibition was continued by temporary acts until 1788, when it was permanently established by act of parliament. From these and other regulations, congress perceived the necessity of a general power, to regulate the trade of the United States, by navigation acts, or acts countervailing the commercial regulations of foreign nations. On the 30th of April, 1784, therefore, they recommended to the states, to vest the general government, for the term of fifteen years, with power to prohibit any goods being imported into, or exported from the United States, in vessels belonging to, or navigated by, the subjects of any power, with whom the United States had not formed commercial treaties ; and, also, with the power of prohibiting, for the same term, the subjects of any foreign nation, unless authorized by treaty, from importing into the United States any goods or merchandize, not the produce or manufacture of the dominions of the sovereign, whose subjects they were. Though congress declared to the states, that unless vested with powers competent to the protection of commerce, they could never command reciprocal advantages, and that the trade of the United States must go into the hands of foreigners ; yet, obvious as these truths were, the states could not be induced to grant the powers asked for, in such a manner, that the same could be exercised by the general government. Some of the states themselves passed laws countervailing the regulations respecting the West India trade, by imposing higher tonnage duties, on *British vessels*, than on their own or those of other nations, as well as higher duties on goods imported in British bottoms. Massachusetts, indeed, prohibited the transportation of any goods, wares, or merchandize, the growth or produce of the United States, *in British ships.* But as these acts were neither uniform nor permanent, little benefit was derived, or could be expected from them ; and the Massachusetts act was soon repealed.

Difficulties with Great Britain were not confined to regulations respecting commerce. Serious disputes soon arose, concerning the execution of the treaty of peace ; and each nation complained of infractions by the other. On the part of the United States, it was alleged, that negroes had been carried away, contrary to the treaty; and as early as May, 1783, congress instructed their ministers for negociating peace, to remonstrate to the British court, against this conduct of their commander in America, and to take measures to obtain reparation. The United States, also, complained that the western posts had not been surrendered, agreeably to treaty stipulations. Great Britain, on her part, alleged, that legal impediments had been interposed, to prevent the collection of British debts in America ; and that the fifth and sixth articles, relating to the property of the loyalists, had not been complied with.

In June, 1784, the legislature of Virginia, not only declared, that there had been an infraction on the part of Great Britain, of the 7th article, in detaining the slaves and other property of the citizens of the United States, but instructed their delegates in congress, to request, that a remonstrance be presented to the British court, against such infraction, and to require reparation. They also directed them to inform congress, that the state of Virginia conceived, a just regard to the national honor and interest obliged her assembly, to withhold their co-operation in the complete fulfilment of the treaty until the success of such remonstrance was known, or they should have further directions from congress. They at the same time, declared, that as soon as reparation for such infraction should be made, or congress should judge it indispensably necessary, such acts as inhibited the recovery of British debts, should be repealed, and payment made, in such time and manner, as should consist with the exhausted situation of the state.*

In consequence of these difficulties and disputes, congress, early in the year 1785, determined to send a minister plenipotentiary to Great Britain ; and on the 24th of February, John Adams was appointed to represent the United States at the court of London. He was instructed " in a respectful but firm manner to insist, that the United States be put, without further delay, into possession of all the posts and territories within their limits which are now held

---

* State Papers, vol. 1, pp. 355, 356.

by British garrisons; and you will take the earliest opportunity of transmitting the answer you may receive to this requisition.

" You will remonstrate against the infraction of the treaty of peace by the exportation of negroes and other American property, contrary to the stipulations on that subject in the seventh article of it. Upon this head you will be supplied with various authentic papers and documents, particularly the correspondence between general Washington and others on the one part, and Sir Guy Carlton on the other.

" You will represent to the British ministry the strong and necessary tendency of their restrictions on our trade to incapacitate our merchants in a certain degree to make remittances to them.

" You will represent in strong terms the losses which many of our, and also of their merchants will sustain, if the former be unreasonably and immoderately pressed for the payment of debts contracted before the war. On this subject you will be furnished with papers, in which it is amply discussed."*

Mr. Jefferson was soon after appointed to represent the United States, at the court of Versailles, in the room of Dr. Franklin, who had leave to return home, after an absence of nine years. Mr. Livingston having resigned the office of secretary of foreign affairs, Mr. Jay, in March, 1784, and before his return from Europe, was appointed in his place.

Mr. Adams repaired to the British court, and was received as the first minister from the United States since their independence was acknowledged. The appearance of an ambassador from a country heretofore in colonial subjection to the British crown, was a novel spectacle throughout Europe, as well as in England. Nor could the circumstance fail to wound the pride of the British nation.

Mr. Adams, however, was received by the king in his first audience, with great politeness; and the address of the American minister as well as the answer of his majesty on this occasion from the novelty of the scene, possess a peculiar interest. The

* Secret Journals of Congress, vol. 3, pp. 535, 536.

ceremony of an address on his first introduction, was found to be indispensable. After the usual salutations, Mr. Adams thus addressed the king, "Sir, the United States of America have appointed me their minister plenipotentiary to your majesty, and have directed me to deliver to your majesty this letter, which contains the evidence of it. It is in obedience to their express commands, that I have the honor to assure your majesty of their unanimous disposition and design to cultivate the most friendly and liberal intercourse between your majesty's subjects and their citizens, and of their best wishes for your majesty's health and happiness, and for that of your royal family.

"The appointment of a minister from the United States to your majesty's court, will form an epoch in the history of England and America. I think myself more fortunate than all my fellow citizens, in having the distinguished honor to be the first to stand in your majesty's royal presence in a diplomatic character; and I shall esteem myself the happiest of men, if I can be instrumental in recommending my country more and more to your majesty's royal benevolence, and of restoring an entire esteem, confidence, and affection, or in better words, 'the old good nature, and the old good humor,' between people, who though separated by an ocean, and under different governments, have the same language, a similar religion, and kindred blood. I beg your majesty's permission to add, that, although I have sometimes before been entrusted by my country, it was never in my whole life in a manner so agreeable to myself."

To this the king replied:—

"Sir—The circumstances of this audience are so extraordinary, the language you have now held is so extremely proper, and the feelings you have discovered so justly adapted to the occasion, that I must say, that I not only receive with pleasure the assurances of the friendly disposition of the people of the United States, but that I am very glad the choice has fallen upon you to be their minister. I wish you, sir, to believe, and that it may be understood in America, that I have done nothing in the late contest but what I thought myself indispensably bound to do by the duty which I owed to my people. I will be very frank with you,

I was the last to conform to the separation : but the separation having been made, and having become inevitable, I have always said as I say now, that I would be the first to meet the friendship of the United States as an independent power. The moment I see such sentiments and language as your's prevail, and a disposition to give this country the preference, that moment I shall say, let the circumstances of language, religion, and blood, have their natural effect."

After this answer the king inquired of Mr. Adams, whether he came last from France ? and being answered in the affirmative, with his characteristic familiarity, he with a smile said to him, " there is an opinion among some people that you are not the most attached of all your countrymen to the manners of France."

Mr. Adams, surprised at the remark, and not less so at the air of familiarity with which it was made, in reply, observed— " that opinion, sir, is not mistaken ; I must avow to your majesty, I have no attachment but to my own country." To this the king immediately said, " an honest man will never have any other."*

In December, 1785, Mr. Adams presented a memorial to the British secretary of state, in which, after stating the detention of the western posts, contrary to the stipulations in the treaty of peace, he in the name and in behalf of the United States, required, " that all his majesty's armies and garrisons be forthwith withdrawn from the said United States, from all and every of the posts and fortresses before enumerated, and from every port, place and harbor, within the territory of the said United States, according to the true intention of the treaties."

To this memorial the British secretary, lord Carmarthen, returned an answer, on the 28th of February, 1786, in which he acknowledges the detention of the posts, but alleges a breach of the fourth article of the treaty of peace on the part of the United States, by interposing impediments to the recovery of British debts in America. " The little attention," says the secretary, " to the fulfilling this engagement on the part of the subjects

* Life of John Adams. Biography of the signers to the declaration of independence, vol. 8, pp. 311, 312, 313.

of the United States in general, and the direct breach of it in many particular instances, have already reduced many of the king's subjects to the utmost degree of difficulty and distress; nor have their applications for redress, to those whose situation in America naturally pointed them out as the guardians of public faith, been as yet successful in attaining them that justice, to which, on every principle of law as well as humanity, they were clearly and indispensably entitled.

" The engagements entered into by treaty ought to be mutual and equally binding on the respective contracting parties. It would be the height of folly as well as injustice, to suppose one party alone obliged to a strict observance of the public faith, while the other might remain free to deviate from its own engagements, as often as convenience might render such deviation necessary, though at the expense of its own national credit and importance.

" I flatter myself, however, sir, that justice will speedily be done to British creditors ; and I can assure you, that whenever America shall manifest a real determination to fulfil her part of the treaty, Great Britain will not hesitate to prove her sincerity to co-operate in whatever points depend upon her, for carrying every article of it into real and complete effect."

This answer was accompanied with a statement of the various instances, in which the fourth article had been violated by acts of the states. The complaints of Great Britain also extended to breaches of the fifth and sixth articles of the treaty, relating to the recovery of certain property and to confiscations.

The answer of the British secretary was submitted to congress; and in order to remove the difficulties complained of, that body, in March, 1787, unanimously declared, that all the acts, or parts of acts, existing in any of the states, repugnant to the treaty of peace, ought to be repealed ; and they recommended to the states, to make such repeal by a general law. They at the same time unanimously resolved, " that the legislatures of the several states cannot of right pass any act or acts, for interpreting, explaining, or construing a national treaty or any part or clause of it ; nor for restraining, limiting, or in any manner impeding, retarding, or contracting the operation and execution of the same ; for that on being constitutionally made, ratified and published, they become, in virtue of the confederation, part of the law of the land, and are not only independent of the will and power of such legislatures, but also binding and obligatory on them."

A circular letter to the states, accompanied these declarations, in which congress say, " we have deliberately and dispassionately examined and considered the several facts and matters urged by Great Britain, as infractions of the treaty of peace, on the part of America, and we regret, that, in some of the states, too little attention has been paid to the public faith pledged by that treaty."[*]

In consequence of this letter, the states of New Hampshire, Massachusetts, Rhode Island, Connecticut, Delaware, Maryland, Virginia and North Carolina, passed acts complying with the recommendations contained in it. The operation of the act of Virginia, however, which repealed all acts preventing the recovery of debts due to British subjects, was suspended, until the governor of that state should issue a proclamation, giving notice, that Great Britain had delivered up the western posts ; and was also taking measures, for the further fulfilment of the treaty of peace, by delivering up the negroes belonging to the citizens of that state, carried away, contrary to the seventh article of the treaty, or by making compensation for the same. Some of the states passed a general law, repealing all laws contrary to the treaty, merely in compliance with the recommendation of congress, and not because any law was supposed to be in existence, contrary to the treaty. The states of New Jersey, Pennsylvania and Georgia had no laws, as they declared, against the treaty. South Carolina observed, that the subjects of Great Britain had encountered no other difficulties, or impediments, in the recovery of their debts, than the citizens of America ; that such was the situation of the state, the legislature had conceived it necessary to pass laws, tantamount to shutting the courts.[†]

Mr. Adams was unable to obtain any explanation relative to interest on British debts during the war ; and the question was left to

---

* Journals of Congress, vol. 12.   † American State Papers, vol. 12.

be decided by the American courts; and in most instances, the interest for that period, was by the courts and juries disallowed. The secretary of foreign affairs was of opinion, that by the *strict construction* of the fourth article, interest was to be allowed— " The fourth article of the treaty," he observed, " must be understood not as reviving or restoring those debts, but as considering them to be and remain exactly and precisely in their pristine and original state, both with respect to extent and obligation. If this conclusion be just, your secretary can perceive no ground for the singular reasons and questions that have prevailed. respecting the payment of interest claimed by British creditors in virtue of express contracts between them and their American debtors. However harsh and severe," he subjoined, " the exaction of this interest, considering the war and its effects, may be and appear, yet the treaty must be taken and fulfilled with its bitter as well as sweets; and although we were not obliged to accept peace on those terms, yet having so accepted it, we cannot now invalidate those terms and stipulations, nor with honor or justice refuse to comply with them." The secretary, however, was of opinion, that interest could be demanded as a matter of strict right, in those cases only, when there was an express stipulation to pay interest ; that in other cases, the equity of allowing it, during the war, must be left with juries.*

It was a question of new impression, and it seemed unjust, as well as inequitable, to compel a debtor to pay interest, during the time, when all intercourse between him and his creditor was, by the laws of war, criminal. The British secretary, in conversation with the American minister, allowed that even a British creditor, by the laws of England, could not have received a remittance from his debtor in America during the war, without being guilty of high treason.†

The British court was not yet disposed to enter into any commercial treaty with the United States. The ministers were, no doubt, satisfied, that the advantages they enjoyed under

* Secret Journals of Congress, vol. 4, pp, 212, 213·
† American State Papers, vol. 1, p. 384.

their own regulations, were greater than could be obtained by any treaty they could make with America. And this was, probably, one of the principal reasons of their refusal to enter into any such treaty.

As the British court declined sending a minister to the United States, Mr. Adams, in October, 1787, at his request, had leave to return home. Congress, at the same time,*passed a resolution expressing their high sense of the services which Mr. Adams had rendered to the United States, in the execution of the various and important trusts from time to time committed to him, and presenting their thanks to him for the patriotism, perseverance, integrity and diligence with which he had ably and faithfully served his country.

The United States had also at this period to encounter difficulties with Spain as well as Great Britain. The two Floridas having been ceded to his catholic majesty, serious disputes soon arose, not only on the old subject of the navigation of the Mississippi, but with respect to the boundaries of Louisiana, and the ceded territory. The Spanish court still persisted in its determination to exclude the Americans from the navigation of the Mississippi.

This determination was made known in a letter from the Spanish minister for the department of the Indies, to an agent in America, Mr. Rendon ; and which, in November, 1784, was communicated to congress, by Marbois, the French chargè des affaires.

The Spanish agent in America, was commanded to give the states and congress to understand, that " until the limits of *Louisiana* and the two *Floridas* shall be settled, they are not to expose to process and confiscation the vessels which they destine to carry on commerce, on the river Mississippi, inasmuch as a treaty, concluded between the United States and England, on which the former ground their pretensions to the navigation of that river, could not fix limits in a territory, which that power did not possess, the two borders of the river being already conquered and possessed by our arms, the day the treaty was made, namely, the 30th of November, 1782.* As this letter refers to the limits of *Louisiana* as well as of the Floridas, it would seem that Spain had not yet relinquished her extensive claims, on the east side of the Mississippi.

In consequence of this communication, in December, 1784, congress declared it necessary to send a minister to Spain, for the purpose of adjusting the interfering claims of the two nations, respecting the navigation of the Mississippi, and other matters highly interesting to the peace and good understanding, which ought to subsist between them. This was prevented by the appointment of Don Diego Gardoqui, a minister from Spain, who arrived in the United States, and was acknowledged by congress in the summer of 1785. Soon after his arrival, Mr. Jay, then secretary of foreign affairs, was appointed to treat with the Spanish minister, on the part of the United States.

Mr. Jay was at first instructed, neither to make nor receive any propositions, or enter into a compact with the Spanish minister, without previously communicating the same to congress.

Afterwards, however, on the 25th of August, 1785, he was specially instructed, to insist on the right of the United States to their territorial bounds, and the free navigation of the Mississippi from its source to the ocean, as established in their treaty with Great Britain ; and directed neither to conclude, nor sign a treaty, until the same had been communicated to congress, and received their approbation. Negociations soon commenced between Mr. Jay and the Spanish minister. These were confined principally to the navigation of the Mississippi, and the northern limits of West Florida. It will be recollected, that by the provisional treaty of November 30th, 1782, the southern bounds of the United States, were fixed against West Florida, in latitude thirty-one degrees; but no treaty at that time having been concluded between Great Britain and Spain, a secret article provided, that

* Secret Journals of Congress, vol. 3, p. 517.

if the Floridas should be restored to Great Britain, the north line
of West Florida, should extend to the mouth of the river Yazoo,
where it united with the Mississippi, and from thence due east, to
the river Apalachicola.

In the course of the negociation, it was evident, the Spanish
minister was acquainted with the secret article ; and this created
no little difficulty, in the negociation concerning limits.

He insisted, that the bounds settled by the provisional treaty,
could not affect Spain, then in possession of the country by conquest ; and that her territorial rights must have been considered
as reserved, until a final settlement by a general peace.

He claimed, therefore, that as by the final treaty of peace,
Great Britain ceded the Floridas to Spain, the bounds of West
Florida, extended at least, as far north as when under the English government. With respect to the navigation of the Mississippi, Gardoqui declared, that the king his master, would not
permit any nation to navigate any part of that river, between the
banks claimed by him. Mr. Jay, insisted on the right of the United States to the free navigation of that river, and on the north
boundary of West Florida, as settled by the proclamation of
October 7th, 1763.

To induce the United States to yield on these points, the Spanish minister made certain propositions relative to commercial intercourse between the two countries ; the substance of which
was—

" 1. That all commercial regulations affecting each other, shall
be founded in perfect reciprocity. Spanish merchants shall enjoy all the commercial privileges of native merchants in the United States, and American merchants shall enjoy all the commercial privileges of native merchants in the kingdom of Spain and
in the Canaries and other islands belonging and adjacent thereto. The same privileges shall extend to their respective vessels
and merchandise consisting of the manufactures and productions
of their respective countries.

" 2. Each party may establish consuls in the countries of the
other, (excepting such provinces in Spain, into which none have

heretofore been admitted, viz., Bilboa and Guipusca,) with such powers and privileges as shall be ascertained by a particular convention.

" 3. That the *bona fide* manufactures and productions of the United States, (tobacco only excepted, which shall continue under its present regulations,) may be imported in American or Spanish vessels, into any parts of his majesty's European dominions and islands aforesaid, in like manner as if they were the productions of Spain. And on the other hand, that the *bona fide* manufactures and productions of his majesty's dominions may be imported into the United States, in Spanish or American vessels, in like manner as if they were the manufactures and productions of the said states. And further, that all such duties and imposts as may mutually be thought necessary to lay on them by either party, shall be ascertained and regulated on principles of exact reciprocity, by a tariff to be formed by a convention for that purpose, to be negociated and made within *one* year after the exchange of the ratification of the treaty ; and in the mean time, that no other duties or imposts shall be exacted from each others merchants and ships, than such as may be payable by natives in such cases.

" 4. That inasmuch as the United States, from not having mines of gold and silver, may often want supplies of specie for a circulating medium, his catholic majesty, as a proof of his good will, agrees to order the masts and timber which may from time to time be wanted for his royal navy, to be purchased and paid for in specie, in the United States ; provided the said masts and timber shall be of equal quality, and when brought to Spain, shall not cost more than the like may there be had from other countries.

" 5. It is agreed that the articles commonly inserted in other treaties of commerce for mutual and reciprocal convenience, shall be inserted in this, and that this treaty and every article therein, shall continue in full force for —— years, to be computed from the day of the date thereof."

As Mr. Jay, by his instructions, was not to conclude a treaty, until the same was communicated to congress and approved by them, and was also, specially directed to obtain a stipulation, acknowledging the right of the United States to their territorial claims and the free navigation of the Mississippi, as established in their treaty with Great Britain, he, on the 3d of August, 1786, submitted to congress the above plan of a commercial treaty, and stated the difficulties in obtaining the stipulation required. The nature of the difficulties on these important points, will best appear from the statement made to congress by Mr. Jay himself.

" My attention," said he, " is chiefly fixed on two obstacles, which at present divide us, viz., the navigation of the Mississippi, and the territorial limits between them and us.

" My letters written from Spain, when our affairs were the least promising, evince my opinion respecting the Mississippi, and oppose every idea of our relinquishing our right to navigate it. I entertain the same sentiments of that right, and of the importance of retaining it, which I then did.

" Mr. Gardoqui strongly insists on our relinquishing it. We have had many conferences and much reasoning on the subject, not necessary now to detail. His concluding answer to all my arguments has steadily been, that the king will never yield that point, nor consent to any compromise about it ; for that it always has been and continues to be, one of their maxims of policy, to exclude all mankind from their American shores.

" I have often reminded him that the adjacent country was filling fast with people ; and that the time must and would come, when they would not submit to seeing a fine river flow before their doors, without using it as a highway to the sea for the transportation of their productions ; that it would therefore be wise to look forward to that event, and take care not to sow in the treaty any seeds of future discord. He said that the time alluded to was far distant ; and that treaties were not to provide for contingences so remote and future. For his part, he considered the rapid settlement of that country as injurious to the states, and that they would find it necessary to check it. Many fruitless arguments passed between us; and though he would admit that the only way to make treaties and friendship permanent, was for neither party to leave the other any thing to complain of; yet he would still insist that the Mississippi must be shut against us. The truth is, that courts never admit the force of any reasoning or arguments but such as apply in their favor; and it is equally true, that even if our right to that navigation or to any thing else, was expressly declared in holy writ, we should be able to provide for it no otherwise, than by being in a capacity to repel force by force.

" Circumstanced as we are," Mr. Jay added, " I think it would be expedient to agree that the treaty should be limited to twenty five or thirty years, and that one of the articles should stipulate that the United States would forbear to use the navigation of that river below their territories to the ocean. Thus the duration of the treaty and of the forbearance in qusetion should be limited to the same period.

" Whether Mr. Gardoqui," Mr. Jay subjoined, " would be content with such an article, I cannot determine; my instructions restraining me from ever sounding him respecting it. I nevertheless think the experiment worth trying, for several reasons."

Among other reasons Mr. Jay stated, that the navigation of the Mississippi was not at that time very important, and would not probably become so, in less than twenty five or thirty years, and that a forbearance to use it, while it was not wanted, was no great sacrifice—that Spain then excluded the people of the United States from that navigation, and that it could only be acquired by war, for which the United States were not then prepared; and that in case of war, France would no doubt join Spain.

Congress were much divided on this interesting subject. The seven states at the north, including Pennsylvania, were disposed, in case a treaty could not otherwise be made, to forbear the use of the navigation of the Mississippi below the southern boundary of the United States, for a limited time, and a resolution was sub-

mitted to congress repealing Mr. Jay's instructions of the 25th of
August, 1785, and which was carried, seven states against five.

An additional resolution was also proposed, directing Mr. Jay
" that if in the course of his negociations with the minister of his
catholic majesty, it shall be found indispensable for the conclusion of the same, that the United States and their citizens, for
a limited time, should forbear to use so much of the river Mississippi, as is south of the southern boundary of the United States,
the said secretary be and hereby is authorized and directed, in
behalf of the United States, to consent to an article or articles,
stipulating on their part and that of their citizens, a forbearance
of the use of the said river Mississippi for a period not exceeding twenty years, from the point where the southern boundary of
the United States intersects the said river, to its mouth or the
ocean." This, however, was to be on the express condition, that
a stipulation of forbearance, should not be construed to *extinguish* the right of the United States, independent of such stipulation, to use and navigate said river from its source to the ocean ;
and that such stipulation was not to be made, unless it should be
agreed in the same treaty that the navigation and use of the said
river above such intersection to its source should be common to
both nations—and Mr. Jay was to make no treaty unless the
terrtiorial limits of the United States, were acknowledged and
secured according to the terms ageed between the United States
and Great Britain.

The members from the states of New Hampshire, Massachusetts,
Rhode Island, Connecticut, New York, New Jersey and Pennsylvania, unanimously voted for this resolution, and the members
from Maryland, Virginia, North Carolina, South Carolina and
Georgia, with equal unanimity against it. As by the confederation the assent of nine states was necessary in making a treaty
the same number was considered requisite in giving specific instructions in relation to it, and of course the resolution was
negatived ; and it was questioned whether the previous instructions given to Mr. Jay could be rescinded without the assent of
nine states. These proceedings in congress, though, with clos-

ed doors, soon became partially known, and excited great alarm in Virginia, and in the western settlements. In November, 1786, in consequence of a memorial from the western inhabitants, the Virginia assembly declared, unanimously, that the common right of navigating the Mississippi, and of communicating with other nations through that channel, was considered as the bountiful gift of nature to the United States, as proprietors of the territories watered by the said rivers and its eastern branches—that the confederacy having been formed on the broad basis of equal rights in every part thereof, and confided to the protection and gardianship of the whole, a sacrifice of the rights of any one part, would be a flagrant violation of justice, and a direct contravention of the end for which the federal government was instituted, and an alarming innovation on the system of the union. They therefore unanimously instructed their delegates in congress, " to oppose any attempt that may be made in congress, to barter or surrender to any nation whatever, the right of the United States to the free and common use of the river Mississippi; and to protest against the same as a dishonorable departure from that comprehensive and benevolent feeling which constitutes the vital principle of the confederation; as provoking the just resentment and reproaches of our western brethren, whose essential rights and interests, would be thereby sacrificed and sold; as destroying that confidence in the wisdom, justice and liberality, of the federal councils, which is so necessary at this crisis, to a proper enlargement of their authority; and finally as tending to undermine our repose, our prosperity, and our union itself: and also that said delegates be further instructed to urge the proper negociations with Spain, for obtaining her concurrence in such regulations touching the mutual and common use of the said river, as may secure the harmony and affection of the two nations, and such as the wise and generous policy of his catholic majesty will perceive to be no less due to the interests of his own subjects, than to the just and friendly views of the United States."*

After Mr. Jay's instructions of the 25th of August, 1785, were rescinded, negociations were renewed, but without effect. The

* H. Marshall's History of Kentucky, vol. 1, p. 262.

Spanish minister still refused to admit the United States to any share in the navigation of the river below the boundaries claimed by Spain, on any terms and conditions whatever. With respect to limits Mr. Jay could only obtain from him an intimation, that if all other matters were adjusted, he might give up all claim to the territory not comprehended within the Floridas as ascertained by the *separate and secret* article in the British treaty.*

While these negociations were pending, the fertile country at the west was settling with a rapidity beyond the most sanguine calculations; and it is not surprising, that the news of an actual or intended abandonment of the navigation of the Mississippi, the only outlet for their productions, should have excited great alarm among its inhabitants. They were much exasperated by the seizure and confiscation of American property by the Spaniards, on its way down the river, which took place about the same time. The *proposition* made in congress was magnified into an *actual treaty*, and called from the western people most bitter complaints and reproaches.

In December, 1786, a settler at the falls of Ohio, in a letter to the governor and legislature of Georgia says, " *The commercial treaty* with Spain is considered to be cruel, oppressive and unjust. The prohibition of the navigation of the Mississippi has astonished the whole western country. To sell us and make us vassals to the merciless Spaniards, is a grievance not to be borne. Should our country submit to such manacles, we should be unworthy the name of Americans, and a scandal to the annals of its history. It is very surprising to every rational person that the legislature of the United States, which has been so applauded for their assertion and defense of its rights and privileges, should so soon endeavor to subjugate the greatest part of their dominions even to a worse slavery than ever Great Britain presumed to subjugate any of hers. Ireland is a free country to what this will be, when its navigation is entirely shut ; we may as well be sold for bondmen as to have the Spaniards share all the benefits of

---

* Secret Journals of Congress, vol. 4, p. 300.

our toils. They will receive all the fruits, the produce of this large and fertile country at their own price (which you may be assured will be very low) and therefore will be able to supply their own markets and all the markets of Europe on much lower terms than what the Americans possibly can."

A copy of this letter and others of a similar character, were laid before congress. To quiet the apprehensions of the western inhabitants, the delegates from North Carolina, in September, 1788, submitted to congress a resolution, declaring that, " whereas many citizens of the United States, who possess lands on the western waters, have expressed much uneasiness from a report that *congress are disposed to treat with Spain for the surrender of their claim to the navigation of the river Mississippi ;* in order therefore to quiet the minds of our fellow citizens by removing such ill founded apprehensions, resolved, that the United States have a clear, absolute, and unalienable claim to the free navigation of the river Mississippi, which claim is not only supported by the express stipulations of treaties, but by the great law of nature."

The secretary of foreign affairs, to whom this resolution was referred, reported, that as the rumor mentioned in the resolution was not warranted by the negociations between the United States and Spain, the members be permitted to contradict it, in the most explicit terms. Mr. Jay also stated, there could be no objection to declaring the right of the United States to the navigation of the river clear and absolute—that this had always been his opinion ; and that the only question had been, whether a modification of that right for equivalent advantages, was advisable ; and though he formerly thought such a modification might be proper, yet that circumstances and discontents had since interposed to render it questionable. He, also, advised that further negociations with Spain, be transferred to the new general government. On this report, congress, on the 16th of September, 1788, in order to remove the apprehensions of the western settlers, declared that the members be permitted to contradict the report referred to by the delegates from North Carolina ; and at the same time resolved, " that the free navigation of the river Mississippi, is a clear and essential right of the United States, and that the same ought to be considered and supported as such."

All further negociations with Spain, were also, referred to the new federal government.*

The people of the United States had viewed the western lands as a fund to aid in the payment of the national debt. Congress, therefore, in April, 1783, called upon those states, who had not yet complied with their former requests on this subject, to make liberal cessions of their territorial claims ; and also requested those who had only complied in part, " to revise and complete such compliance, as a further means," they said, " as well as of hastening the extinguishment of the debt, as establishing the harmony of the United States."

Virginia, as we have before stated, ceded her right to all lands northwest of the river Ohio ; but one of the conditions of the cession was, that congress should guaranty all the other lands she claimed between the Atlantic ocean and the south east side of the river Ohio, and the Maryland, Pennsylvania, and North Carolina boundaries. Some of the states did not consider the cession sufficiently liberal, and a great majority in congress refused to accept it, with the condition of guaranty annexed. Virginia afterwards, gave up this condition, and the cession from that state was accepted. By the cession of New York, the western bounds of that state were limited by " a line from the north east corner of the state of Pennsylvania, along the north bounds thereof, to its north west corner, continued due west until it shall be intersected by a meridian line, to be drawn from the forty-fifth degree of north latitude, through a point twenty miles due west from the most westerly bent or inclination of the river or strait of Niagara ; thence by the said meridian line, to the forty-fifth degree of north latitude, thence by the said forty-fifth degree of north latitude." Massachusetts, by her deed of cession, made in April, 1785, surrendered her right to all lands west of the line, fixed by

* Secret Journals of Congress, vol. 4, pp. 452, 453.

New York. Connecticut, in September, 1784, ceded all lands in their charter limits, lying one hundred and twenty miles west of the western boundary of Pennsylvania. South Carolina, in August, 1787, granted to the United States, all her right to the country west of the ridge or chain of mountains, which divides the eastern from the western waters.

In consequence of these cessions, the United States became possessed of all the lands north west of the Ohio; and the establishment of a government for the inhabitants already settled, as well as those who might remove there, became necessary.

Congress, therefore, in July, 1787, established an ordinance for the government of this territory. This ordinance is the basis of the governments established by congress, in all the territories of the United States; and may be considered an anomaly, in American legislation. The whole territory was made one district, subject to be divided into two, at the pleasure of congress.

With respect to the mode of governing the settlers in this territory or colony, the ordinance provided, that until the number of free male inhabitants of full age, in the district, should amount to five thousand, the legislative, executive and judicial power, should be vested in a governor and three judges, who, together with a secretary, were to be appointed by congress. The governor was to remain in office three years, and the judges during good behavior. The governor with the judges were empowered to adopt and publish, such laws of the *original states* criminal and civil, as might be necessary and best suited to the circumstances of the district, and report them to congress; such laws to be in force, until disapproved by that body. The governor was empowered to divide the district into counties or townships, and to appoint all civil officers. As soon as the free male inhabitants of full age, should amount to five thousand, a general assembly was to be constituted, to consist of the governor, a legislative council, and house of representatives. The representatives to be chosen from the counties or townships, one for every five hundred free male inhabitants, until the number should amount to twenty-five; after that, the number to be

regulated by the legislature.   A representative must have been a
citizen of one of the United States for three years, and be a resident in the district, or have resided three years in the district ;
in either case, to have the fee-simple of two hundred acres of
land in the district.   An elector was to reside in the district, have
a freehold in fifty acres of land therein, and be a citizen of one
of the states, or a like freehold, and two years residence.   The
representatives to be chosen for two years.

The legislative council was to consist of five persons, to continue in office five years, unless sooner removed by congress, chosen in the following manner—the house of representatives to nominate ten persons, each possessed of a freehold in five hundred
acres of land—out of this number, congress were to appoint five
to constitute the council.   The general assembly had power to
make laws, for the government of the district, not repugnant to
the ordinance.   All laws to have the sanction of a majority of
both houses, and also the assent of the governor.   The legislative assembly, were authorized by joint ballot, to elect a delegate
who was to have a seat in congress, with the right of debating,
but not of voting.

It was necessary, also, to establish certain principles, as the
basis of the laws, constitutions, and governments, which might
be formed in the territory, as well as to provide for its future political connection with the American confederacy.
Congress, therefore, at the same time, established certain articles, which were to be considered as articles of *compact*,
between the original states and the people in the territory, and
which were to remain unalterable, unless by common consent.
By these, no person in the territory was ever to be molested, on account of his mode of worship, or religious sentiments ;
and every person was entitled to the benefits of the writ of habeas corpus, trial by jury, and all those other fundamental rights,
usually inserted in American bills of rights.   Schools and the
means of education were forever to be encouraged, and the utmost good faith to be observed towards the Indians ; particularly
their lands and property were never to be taken from them, with-

out their consent. The territory, and the states that might be formed therein, were forever to remain a part of the American confederacy ; but not less than three, nor more than five states were to be established.

The bounds of these states were fixed, with liberty for congress to alter them by forming one or two new states in that part of the territory lying north of an east and west line drawn through the southern bend, or extreme of lake Michigan. It was also provided, that whenever in any of those states, there should be sixty thousand free inhabitants, such state was to be admitted into the union, on the same footing with the original states in all respects whatever ; and be at liberty to form a permanent constitution and state government ; such constitution and government, however, was to be republican, and conformable to the principles of the articles. If consistent with the general interest of the confederation, such state, however, might be admitted as a member of the union, with a less number than sixty thousand free inhabitants.

By the sixth and last article it was provided, there should be neither slavery or involuntary servitude in the territory, otherwise than in the punishment of crimes, of which the party should have been duly convicted.* In consequence of this last wise and salutary provision, the evil of slavery has been prevented in all the new states formed out of this territory north and west of the river Ohio.†

While congress were thus forming a government for the territory, and laying the foundation of future new states at the west, they had lost all authority over the old states at the east. Many causes combined, at this period, to produce great distress, discontent and disaffection in different parts of the union. The general government, as before stated, was totally inefficient, and the authority of the state governments greatly weakened, and in some instances almost destroyed.

In addition to the debts of the union, the states individually had also incurred large debts during the war, for the payment of which

* Mr. Dane, of Massachusetts, it is said was the author of this article. † Note 18.

they were called upon by their creditors. Immediately after peace, in consequence of large importations of foreign goods, particularly from Great Britain, large debts were contracted by individuals, and which, from the want of internal as well as external resources, they were unable to pay. The people were pressed at the same time for the payment of the debts of the union, of the individual states, and of their own private debts. The courts of justice, which had been shut during the war, were filled with private suits. Under these circumstances, some of the states had recourse to the desperate expedient of paper money ; others made personal property a tender, at an appraised value, in satisfaction of debts ; and in Massachusetts, not only were the judges in several counties prevented from holding courts, but the government itself, in other respects, set at defiance, by an open and formidable insurrection of the people.

The enemies of the revolution, who had predicted that the Americans, when separated from their parent country, would be unable to govern themselves, but fall into confusion, now secretly rejoiced at the verification of their predictions. Its friends began almost to despair of the commonwealth, and at times were led to doubt, whether the people of America were indeed capable of self-government.

The only remedy that promised relief, was an essential alteration in the national compact. No amendments, however, could be made to the confederation, without the assent of every state in the union. Experience had proved that no relief could be expected from this quarter.

The state of American affairs at this period, is depicted in gloomy colors, by some of the great actors in the revolution, in their communications with each other; and the views and feelings of such men as have been styled " the guide-posts and landmarks in a state," at such a crisis, become extremely interesting.

As early as 1784, general Washington in a letter to the governor of Virginia, referring to the want of power in the federal government, says, " the disinclination of the individual states to yield competent powers to congress for the federal government, their unreasonable jealousy of that body, and of one another, and the disposition which seems to pervade each, of being all-wise and all-powerful within itself, will, if there is not a change in the system, be our downfall as a nation. This is as clear to me, as A, B, C, and I think we have opposed Great Britain, and have arrived at the present state of peace and independency to very little purpose, if we cannot conquer our own prejudices. The powers of Europe begin to see this, and our newly acquired friends, the British, are already acting upon this ground ; and wisely too, if we are determined in our folly. They know that individual opposition to their measures is futile, and *boast* that we are not sufficiently united as a nation to give a general one ! Is not the indignity alone of this declaration, while we are in the act of peacemaking and reconciliation, sufficient to stimulate us to vest more extensive and adequate powers in the sovereigns of of these United States ? "*

Mr. Jay, in a letter to general Washington, in March, 1786, observed, " you have wisely retired from public employments, and view, from the temple of fame, the various exertions of that sovereignty and independence, which providence has enabled you to be so greatly and gloriously instrumental, in securing to your country ; yet I am persuaded, you cannot view them with the eye of an unconcerned spectator. Experience has pointed out errors in our national government, which call for correction, and which threaten to blast the fruit we expected from our tree of liberty. The convention proposed by Virginia, may do some good, and would, perhaps, do more, if it comprehended more objects. An opinion begins to prevail, that a general convention for revising the articles of confederation, would be expedient. Whether the people are yet ripe for such a measure, or whether the system proposed to be obtained by it, is only to be expected from calamity and commotion, is difficult to ascertain.

" I think we are in a delicate situation, and a variety of considerations and circumstances, give me uneasiness. It is in contemplation to take measures for forming a general convention.

* North American Review for October, 1827, p. 289.

The plan is not matured. If it should be well concerted and take effect, I am fervent in wishes, that it may comport with the line of life you have marked out for yourself, to favor your country with your councils, on such an important and single occasion. I suggest this, merely as a hint for your consideration."

In a second letter to general Washington, in June of the same year, his feelings and views are thus expressed. "Our affairs seem to lead to some crisis, some revolution, something that I cannot foresee or conjecture. I am uneasy and apprehensive, more so than during the war. Then we had a fixed object, and though the means and time of obtaining it, were often problematical, yet I did firmly believe, that justice was with us. The case is now altered. We are going and doing wrong, and, therefore, I look forward to evils and calamities, but without being able to guess at the instrument, nature or measure of them. That we shall again recover, and things again go well, I have no doubt. Such a variety of circumstances would not, almost miraculously, have combined to liberate and make us a nation, for transient and unimportant purposes. I, therefore, believe, we are yet to become a great and respectable people—but *when* and *how*, only the spirit of prophecy can discern.

" What I most fear," he added, " is, that the better kind of people (by which I mean the people, who are orderly and industrious, who are content with their situation, and not uneasy in their circumstances) will be led, by the insecurity of property, the loss of confidence in their rulers, and the want of public faith and rectitude, to consider the claims of liberty as imaginary and delusive. This state of uncertainty and fluctuation must disgust and alarm such men, and prepare their minds for almost any change that may promise them quiet and security."

" Your statements," said general Washington, in reply to these communications, " that our affairs are drawing rapidly to a crisis, accord with my own. What the event will be, is also beyond my foresight. We have errors to correct ; we have, probably, had too good an opinion of human nature, in forming our confederation. Experience has taught us, that men will not adopt and carry into execution measures the best calculated for their own good, without the intervention of coercive power.

" I do not conceive, we can exist long as a nation, without lodging somewhere, a power, which will pervade the whole union, in as energetic a manner, as the authority of the state governments extend over the several states. To be fearful of investing congress, constituted as that body is, with ample authority for national purposes, appears to me, the climax of popular absurdity and madness. Could congress exert this, for the detriment of the people, without injuring themselves, in an equal, or greater proportion? Are not their interests inseparably connected with those of their constituents?

" By the rotation of appointment, must they not mingle frequently with the mass of citizens? Is it not rather to be apprehended, if they were possessed of the powers before described, that the individual members would be induced to use them, on many occasions, very timidly and inefficiently, for fear of losing their popularity and future election? We must take human nature as we find it; perfection falls not to the share of mortals. Many are of opinion, that congress have too frequently made use of the suppliant humble tone of requisition in their applications to the states, when they had a right to assert their imperial dignity, and command obedience. Be this as it may, requisitions are a perfect nullity, when thirteen sovereign, independent and disunited states, are in the habit of discussing and refusing them, at their option. Requisitions are actually little better than a jest and a bye-word throughout the land. If you tell the legislatures they have violated the treaty of peace, and invaded the prerogatives of the confederacy, they will laugh in your face. What then is to be done? It is much to be feared, as you observe, that the better kind of people, being disgusted with these circumstances, will have their minds prepared for any revolution whatever.

" We are apt to run from one extreme into another. To anticipate and prevent disastrous contingences, would be the part of wisdom and patriotism.

" What astonishing changes, a few years are capable of producing? I am told that even respectible characters speak of a
monarchial form of government, without horror. From thinking
proceeds speaking, thence to acting is often but a single step.
But how irrevocable and tremendous! What a triumph for our
enemies to verify their predictions! what a triumph for the advocates of despotism, to find that we are incapable of governing
ourselves, and that systems founded on the basis of equal liberty,
are merely ideal and fallacious? Would to God, that wise measures may be taken in time to avert the consequences, we have but
too much reason to apprehend."* The convention alluded to by
Mr. Jay, originated in Virginia.

In January, 1786, the legislature of that state appointed a number of gentlemen, "to meet such commissioners as were, or might
be appointed by the other states in the union, at such time and
place as should be agreed upon by said commissioners, to take
into consideration the *trade* and *commerce* of the United States;
to consider how far an uniform system, in their commercial intercourse and regulations, might be necessary to their common
interest and permanent harmony; and to report to the several
states such an act relative to this great object, as when unanimously ratified by them, would enable the United States in congress assembled, effectually to provide for the same." It was afterwards agreed, that this meeting should be held at Annapolis,
in Maryland, in September of the same year. Commissioners
from the states of Virginia, Delaware, Pennsylvania, New Jersey,
and New York, only attended. Delegates were appointed
by New Hampshire, Massachusetts, Rhode Island, and North
Carolina, but did not attend. In consequence of such a partial
representation of the states, the commissioners present, thought
it improper to proceed on the important business, with which
they were intrusted. They were now, more than ever, sensible
of the necessity of a general convention of all the states, and
were also satisfied, that the powers of this convention should ex-

* Marshall's Life of Washington, vol. 5.

tend to other objects, than merely the regulation of trade and commerce. They, therefore, drew up a report and address to the states, in which, after stating the defects of the federal government and that the situation of the United States " was delicate and critical, calling for an exertion of the virtue and wisdom of all the members of the confederacy," they recommended to all the states, to concur " in the appointment of commissioners, to meet at Philadelphia, on the second Monday in May, 1787, to take into consideration the situation of the United States, to devise such further provisions as should appear to them necessary, to render the constitution of the federal government adequate to the exigences of the union." This address was also sent to congress, as well as to the several states.

Virginia first appointed delegates, according to the recommendation of the meeting at Annapolis. The general assembly of that state, which commenced their session in October, 1786, selected seven of her most distinguished citizens, to meet delegates from the other states, at Philadelphia, in May following, and " to join with them, in devising and discussing all such alterations and further provisions, as may be necessary to render the federal constitution adequate to the exigences of the union." Other states soon after followed the example of Virginia. In February, 1787, the subject claimed the attention of congress, and they passed the following resolution—"Whereas there is provision, in the articles of confederation and perpetual union, for making alterations therein, by the assent of a congress of the United States, and of the legislatures of the several states ; and whereas experience hath evinced, that there are defects in the present confederation, as a means to remedy which, several of the states and particularly the state of New York, by express instructions to their delegates in congress, have suggested a convention for the purposes expressed in the following resolution; and such convention appearing to be the most probable means of establishing in these states a firm national government—*Resolved*, that in the opinion of congress, it is expedient, that on the second Monday in May next, a convention of delegates, who shall have been appointed by the several states, be held at Philadelphia, for the sole and express purpose of revising the articles of confederation, and reporting to congress and the several legislatures, such alterations and provisions therein, as shall, when agreed to in congress, and confirmed by the states, render the federal constitution adequate to the exigences of government, and the preservation of the union."

In consequence of this, delegates to the convention were appointed from all the states, except Rhode Island.

Many causes combined to convince congress and the American people, of the necessity of this measure; none, perhaps, had greater influence, than the insurrection in Massachusetts, in the year 1786. This open and formidable opposition to the laws, threatened not only the destruction of the government of that state, but of the union. So numerous were the insurgents in the western counties, and so confident of success, and even of support from their fellow citizens, that they refused all terms of accommodation offered by the legislature. They completely obstructed judicial proceedings in several counties, and for a time, it was extremely doubtful, whether a sufficient force could be found in Massachusetts, to reduce them to obedience.

The public arsenal at Springfield, containing arms and ammunition belonging to the United States, was threatened; and the secretary of war communicated his fears to congress on this subject. This communication, as well as a letter from the same officer, concerning some hostile movements of the Indians in the western country, was referred to a committee. In October, 1786, this committee made a *secret* report to congress, in which they stated, " that a dangerous insurrection has taken place, in divers parts of the state of Massachusetts, which was rapidly extending its influence; that the insurgents had already, by force of arms, suppressed the administration of justice in several counties; that though the legislature of said state was in session, yet from the circumstances attending it, it would undoubtedly defeat the object of the federal interposition, should a formal application for the same be made." The committee then added, that it ap-

peared to them, " that the aid of the federal government is necessary, to stop the progress of the insurgents, that there is the greatest reason to believe, that unless speedy and effectual measures
shall be taken to defeat their designs, they will possess themselves of the arsenal at Springfield, subvert the government, and
not only reduce the commonwealth to a state of anarchy and confusion, but probably involve the United States in the calamities
of a civil war." Under these circumstances, the committee were
of opinion, that the United States were bound by the confederation and good faith, as well as by principles of friendship and
sound policy, to be prepared to extend such aid as should be necessary to restore constitutional authority in Massachusetts, and
to afford protection to the public stores there deposited. For
these purposes, the committee recommended that a body of
troops be immediately raised.* The same committee made a
public report, in which they recommended the raising of thirteen hundred and forty men,† ostensibly for the purpose of protecting the frontiers against the hostile movements of the Indians,
but really, to aid in quelling the insurrection in Massachusetts.
These reports were accepted by congress, and the troops were
to be inlisted principally in the four New England states.

For the support and payment of these troops, the states were
called upon to pay into the public treasury, by the first of June,
1787, their proportion of five hundred thirty thousand dollars in
specie, and a loan of half a million of dollars, was authorized to
be opened immediately.‡ It was expected the money might
be obtained from individuals in Boston. Fortunately the state
of Massachusetts, by the firmness of its governor and legislature, and the patriotism of individuals, with four thousand militia, under the command and direction of general Lincoln, was

---

* Secret Journals of Congress, vol. 1, p. 268.

† These troops were apportioned among the states as follows :—

New Hampshire, 260,
Massachusetts, 660,
Rhode Island, 120, Infantry and Artillery.
Connecticut, 181,
Maryland and Virginia, each sixty Cavalry.

‡ Public Journal, vol 11, p. 180.

able to suppress the insurrection, without the aid of the federal arm.

The spirit of insurrection was not confined to Massachusetts alone, but was manifested, by partial risings, in New Hampshire and Connecticut ; but an immediate and firm interposition of the governments of those states, arrested its progress.

These scenes in Massachusetts were deeply felt throughout the union. By no one, however, more than by general Washington. In a reply to one of his correspondents on this subject, his feelings are thus expressed—" It is with the deepest and most heartfelt concern, I perceive, by some late paragraphs, extracted from the Boston papers, that the insurgents of Massachusetts, far from being satisfied with the redress offered by the general court, are still acting in open violation of law and government, and have obliged the chief magistrate, in a decided tone, to call upon the militia to support the constitution. What, gracious God, is man! that there should be such inconsistency and perfidiousness in his conduct. It is but the other day that we were shedding our blood to obtain the constitutions under which we live—constitutions of our own choice and making. And now we are unsheathing the sword to overturn them. The thing is so unaccountable, that I hardly know how to realize it ; or to persuade myself, that I am not under the illusion of a dream." In this alarming and almost desperate state of public affairs, the proposition of conferring upon congress the power of levying duties on imports, came again before the legislature of New York, and though supported by the talents and eloquence of Mr. Hamilton, was again rejected by a majority of fifteen. The final decision of New York, on this important question, in addition to the insurrection in Massachusetts and the distressed state of the country in general, rendered the necessity of a convention of the states, for the purpose of enlarging the powers of the general government, more apparent. New York, though she refused the impost, still appointed delegates, to meet the other states in convention at Philadelphia. They were appointed, however, " for the sole and express purpose of revising the articles of confederation and reporting to congress and to the several legislatures, such alterations and provisions therein, as shall, when agreed to in congress, and confirmed by the several states, render the federal constitution adequate to the exigences of government, and the preservation of the union."

The meeting of this convention, the formation and final adoption of a new system of general government, will be the subject of the succeeding chapter.

CHAPTER XVIII.

General convention meet at Philadelphia---Form rules for their proceedings---Propositions of Mr. Randolph for a new system of government---Amendments of the articles of confederation proposed by Mr. Patterson---Both debated---The amendments of Mr. Patterson rejected---Large majority agree to form a new system of government---To be divided into three great departments, legislative, executive and judicial---Legislative divided into two branches, house of representatives and senate--- Convention divided on the subject of the representation of the states in the senate--- Sketch of the debate on this question---States equally divided upon it---The subject referred to a large committee---Committee report a compromise between the large and small states---This finally adopted by a majority of the convention---Sketch of the powers granted to congress---General government prohibited from doing certain acts---The powers of the states restricted---The organization of an executive attended with great difficulty---Outlines of the first plan adopted by the convention---This afterwards rejected and a new plan formed and eventually adopted---Powers given to the executive---Judicial department to consist of a supreme court and inferior courts---In what cases they have jurisdiction---Constitution eventually different, in many respects, from what the members first contemplated---Difference between the articles of confederation and the constitution--- States divided on the subject of importing slaves, and on the subject of the powers of congress, relative to navigation acts---These differences settled by mutual concessions---General Washington's influence in the convention---Constitution considered by state conventions---People greatly divided in some of the states---Adopted by three states unanimously---By large majorities in four states---Rhode Island refuses to call a convention---The other five states much divided---Doubtful for a time whether they would ratify it without previous amendments---Massachusetts adopts it, and recommends certain amendments---Convention of New Hampshire meet and adjourn---The system strongly opposed in New York, Virginia and North Carolina, without previous amendments---Is warmly debated in the conventions of those states---New Hampshire follows the example of Massachusetts---Virginia and New York adopt it in the same manner by small majorities---North Carolina refuses her assent unless amended.

THE delegates appointed by the states to convene at Philadelphia, agreeably to the recommendation of the commissioners at Annapolis, and the resolve of congress, met at the time and place designated, (with the exception of those from New Hampshire, who did not join the convention until the 23d of July,) and proceeded on the important business of their appointment.

George Washington, one of the delegates from Virginia, was unanimously elected to preside in their deliberations. One rule adopted by the convention was, that " a house to do business should consist of the deputies of not less than seven states, and that all questions should be decided, by the greater number of those, which should be fully represented"—another, " that nothing spoken in the house be printed, or otherwise published or communicated, without leave."

The meeting of this august assembly, marks a new era in the political annals of the United States. Men most eminent for talents and wisdom, had been selected and were met to form a system of government for a vast empire. Such an assemblage for such an object, the world had never before witnessed. The result of their deliberations, on which the happiness of so many millions depended, was looked for with extreme solicitude.

From the peculiar situation of the states, the difficulties in forming a new system of general government, were, indeed, of no ordinary magnitude. Since the peace of 1783, political and commercial jealousies had arisen among the states ; and to these was added a difference in their extent, wealth, and population, as well as in the habits, religion, and education of their inhabitants. These together, presented obstacles apparently insurmountable. Nothing, indeed, but a spirit of mutual concession and compromise, could have overcome these obstacles and effected so fortunate a result.

The first great question among the members of this assembly, was, whether they should amend the old, or form a new system. By the resolve of congress, as well as the instructions of some of the states, they were met " for the sole and express purpose of revising the articles of confederation." Such, however, were the radical defects of the old government, that a majority determined to form an entire new one.

On the 29th of May, Edmund Randolph of Virginia, submitted to the convention, fifteen resolutions, as the basis of a new constitution.

These resolutions were—

" 1. *Resolved,* That the articles of the confederation ought to be so corrected and enlarged, as to accomplish the objects proposed by their institution, namely, common defense, security of liberty, and general welfare.

" 2. *Resolved,* Therefore, that the right of suffrage, in the national legislature, ought to be proportioned to the quotas of contribution, or to the number of free inhabitants, as the one or the other may seem best, in different cases.

" 3. *Resolved,* That the national legislature ought to consist of two branches.

" 4. *Resolved,* That the members of the first branch of the national legislature ought to be elected by the people of the several states, every   for the term of   , to be of the age of   years at least ; to receive liberal stipends, by which they may be compensated for the devotion of their time to public service ; to be ineligible to any office established by a particular state, or under the authority of the United States, (except those peculiarly belonging to the functions of the first branch,) during the term of service, and for the space of   after its expiration ; to be incapable of re-election for the space of   after the expiration of their term of service ; and to be subject to recall.

" 5. *Resolved,* That the members of the second branch of the national legislature ought to be elected by those of the first, out of a proper number of persons nominated by the individual legislatures ; to be of the age of   years, at least ; to hold their offices for a term sufficient to ensure their independency ; to receive liberal stipends, by which they may be compensated for the devotion of their time to the public service ; and to be ineligible to any office established by a particular state, or under the authority of the United States, (except those peculiarly belonging to the functions of the second branch,) during the term of service ; and for the space of   after the expiration thereof.

" 6. *Resolved,* That each branch ought to possess the right of originating acts ; that the national legislature ought to be empowered to enjoy the legislative right vested in congress, by the confederation; and moreover to legislate in all cases to which the separate states are incompetent, or in which the harmony of the United States may be interrupted by the exercise of individual legislation; to negative all laws passed by the several states, contravening in the opinion of the national legislature, the articles of union, or any treaty subsisting under the authority of the union; and to call forth the force of the union against any member of the union failing to fulfil its duty under the articles thereof.

"7. *Resolved*, That a national executive be institued, to be chosen by the national legislature for the term of   years, to receive punctually, at stated times, a fixed compensation for the services rendered, in which no increase or diminution shall be made, so as to affect the magistracy existing at the time of the increase or diminution; to be ineligible a second time; and that, besides a general authority to execute the national laws, it ought to enjoy the executive rights vested in congress by the confederation.

"8. *Resolved*, That the executive, and a convenient number of the national judiciary, ought to compose a council of revision, with authority to examine every act of the national legislature, before it shall operate, and every act of a particular legislature before a negative thereon shall be final; and that the dissent of the said council shall amount to a rejection, unless the act of the national legislature be again passed, or that of a particular legislature be again negatived by   of the members of each branch.

"9. *Resolved*, That a national judiciary be established to hold their offices during good behavior, and to receive punctually, at stated times, fixed compensation for their services, in which no increase or diminution shall be made, so as to affect the persons actually in office at the time of such increase or diminution. That the jurisdiction of the inferior tribunals, shall be, to hear and determine, in the first instance, and of the supreme tribunal to hear and determine, in the dernier resort, all piracies and felonies on the high seas ; captures from an enemy ; cases in which foreigners, or citizens of other states, applying to such jurisdictions, may be interested, or which respect the collection of the national revenue ; impeachments of any national officer ; and questions which involve the national peace or harmony.

" 10. *Resolved*, That provision ought to be made for the admission of states, lawfully arising within the limits of the United States, whether from a voluntary junction of government and territory, or otherwise, with the consent of a number of voices in the national legislature less than the whole.

" 11. *Resolved*, That a republican government, and the territory of each state, (except in the instance of a voluntary junction of government and territory,) ought to be guarantied by the United States to each state.

" 12. *Resolved*, That provision ought to be made for the continuance of a congress, and their authorities and privileges, until a given day, after the reform of the articles of union shall be adopted, and for the completion of all their engagements.

" 13. *Resolved*, That provision ought to be made for the amendment of the articles of union, whensoever it shall seem necessary ; and that the assent of the national legislature ought not to be required thereto.

" 14. *Resolved*, That the legislative, executive, and judiciary powers within the several states ought to be bound by oath to support the articles of union.

" 15. *Resolved*, That the amendments, which shall be offered to the confederation by the convention, ought, at a proper time or times, after the approbation of congress, to be submitted to an assembly or assemblies of representatives, recommended by the several legislatures, to be expressly chosen by the people to consider and decide thereon."

These resolutions of Mr. Randolph, called the Virginia plan, were debated and amended, until the 15th of June, when Mr. Patterson of New Jersey, offered to the convention the following propositions as amendments to the articles of confederation.

" 1. *Resolved*, That the articles of confederation ought to be revised, corrected, and enlarged, as to render the federal constitution adequate to the exigencies of government, and the preservation of the union.

" 2. *Resolved*, That in addition to the powers vested in the United States in congress, by the present existing articles of confederation, they be authorized to pass acts for raising a revenue, by levying a duty or duties on all goods and merchandize of foreign growth or manufacture, imported into any part of the United States—by stamps on paper, vellum, or parchment, and by a postage on all letters and packages passing through the general post office—to be applied to such federal purposes as they shall deem proper and expedient ; to make rules and regulations for the collection thereof ; and the same from time to time to alter and amend, in such manner as they shall think proper. To pass acts for the regulation of trade and commerce, as well with foreign nations as with each other ; provided, that all punishments, fines, forfeitures, and penalties, to be incurred for contravening such rules and regulations, shall be adjudged by the common law judiciary of the states in which any offense contrary to the true intent and meaning of such rules and regulations shall be committed or perpetrated ; with liberty of commencing, in the first instance, all suits or prosecutions for that purpose, in the superior common law judiciary of such state ; subject, nevertheless, to an appeal for the correction of all errors, both in law and fact, in rendering judgment, to the judiciary of the United States.

" 3. *Resolved*, That whenever requisitions shall be necessary, instead of the present rule, the United States in congress be authorized to make such requisitions in proportion to the whole number of white and other free citizens and inhabitants of every age, sex, and condition, including those bound to servitude for a term of years, and three fifths of all other persons not comprehended in the foregoing description, except Indians not paying taxes ; that if such requisitions be not complied with in the time to be specified therein, to direct the collection thereof in the non-complying states ; and for that purpose to devise and pass acts directing and authorizing the same ; provided, that none of the powers hereby vested in the United States in congress, shall be exercised without the consent of at least   states ; and in that proportion, if the number of confederated states should be hereafter increased or diminished.

" 4. *Resolved*, That the United States in congress, be authorized to elect a federal executive to consist of   persons, to continue in office for the term of   years ; to receive punctually at stated times, a fixed compensation for the services by them rendered, in which no increase or diminution shall be made, so as to affect the persons composing the executive at the time of such increase or diminution ; to be paid out of the federal treasury ; to be incapable of holding any other office or appointment during their time of service, and for   years thereafter ; to be ineligible a second time, and removeable on impeachment and conviction for malpractices or neglect of duty, by congress, on application by a majority of the executives of the several states.   That the executive, besides a general authority to execute the federal acts, ought to appoint all federal officers not otherwise provided for, and to direct all military operations ; provided, that none of the persons composing the federal executive shall, on any occasion, take command of any troops, so as personally to conduct any military enterprise as general or in any other capacity.

" 5. *Resolved*, That a federal judiciary be established, to consist of a supreme tribunal, the judges of which to be appointed by the executive, and to hold their offices during good behavior ; to receive punctually, at stated times, a fixed compensation for their services, in which no increase or diminution shall be made, so as to affect the persons actually in office at the time of such increase or diminution.   That the judiciary, so established, shall have authority to hear and determine, in the first instance, on all impeachments of federal officers ; and by way of appeal, in the dernier resort, in all cases touching the rights and privileges of ambassadors ; in all cases of captures from an enemy ; in all cases of piracies and felonies on the high seas ; in all cases in which foreigners may be interested, in the construction of any treaty or treaties, or which may arise on any act or ordinance of congress for the regulation of trade, or the collection of the federal revenue. That none of the judiciary officers shall, during the time they remain in office, be capable of receiving or holding any other office or appointment during their term of service, or for thereafter.

"6. *Resolved*, That the legislative, executive, and judiciary powers within the several states, ought to be bound, by oath, to support the articles of union.

"7. *Resolved*, That all acts of the United States, in congress assembled, made by virtue and in pursuance of the powers hereby vested in them, and by the articles of the confederation, and all treaties made and ratified under the authority of the United States, shall be the supreme law of the respective states, as far as those acts and treaties shall relate to the said states, or their citizens; and that the judiciaries of the several states shall be bound thereby in their decisions, any thing in the respective laws of the individual states to the contrary notwithstanding. And if any state, or any body of men in any state, shall oppose or prevent the carrying into execution such acts or treaties, the federal executive shall be authorized to call forth the powers of the confederated states, or so much thereof as may be necessary to enforce and compel obedience to such acts, or an observance of such treaties.

"8. *Resolved*, That provision ought to be made for the admission of new states into the union.

"9. *Resolved*, That provision ought to be made for hearing and deciding upon all disputes arising between the United States and an individual state, respecting territory.

"10. *Resolved*, That the rule for naturalizations ought to be the same in every state.

"11. *Resolved*, That a citizen of one state, committing an offense in another state, shall be deemed guilty of the same offense as if it had been committed by a citizen of the state in which the offense was committed."

These propositions, called the Jersey plan, no doubt embra
the general views of those in the convention, who wished me
to amend the articles of confederation.   They were deb
until the 19th of June, and were rejected by seven states ags
three, and one divided.   New York, New Jersey and Delav
were in favor of them, and all the other states against th
except Maryland, whose members were equally divided.

The question being thus definitely settled against amen
the articles of confederation, the convention resumed the res
tions of Mr. Randolph, and they were the subject of debate
amendment until the 4th of July, when, with the exceptio
those relating to the executive, they were referred to a com
tee consisting of Mr. Rutledge, Mr. Randolph, Mr. Gorham,
Ellsworth, and Mr. Wilson, for the purpose of reducing then
the form of a constitution.   On the 26th of the same mo
those relating to the executive having been adopted, they
various other propositions submitted by individuals, were refe
to the same committee, and the convention adjourned to the
of August, when the committee reported a draft of a constitut
This was under debate until the 8th of September, and un
went many material alterations.   A committee, consisting of
Johnson, Mr. Hamilton, G. Morriss, Mr. Madison, and Mr. K
was then selected, " to revise the style and arrange the articl
The manner in which these eminent scholars, and statesn
performed the duty assigned them, appears, from the great
cision and accuracy of the language of the constitution, as
as the happy arrangement of its various articles.

The report of this committee was made on the 12th and on
17th of September, after a session of about four months, the c
stitution was finally adopted and signed by all the members t
present.

Having determined to form a new system of government,
states were nearly unanimous, that it should consist of " a
preme legislative, executive and judiciary."   Equal unanim
however, did not prevail as to the mode of forming those th

great co-ordinate departments, the relative weight of the states in these departments, and the powers with which each should be invested. All the states, with the exception of Pennsylvania, were in favor of dividing the legislature into two branches, to be styled a house of representatives and senate. A question then arose, as to the votes of the states in these branches. This was a question between the great and small states ; and it created long and violent debates, particularly with respect to the representation or vote of the states in the senate, or second legislative branch. The small states, after some debate, consented that the right of suffrage in the house, should be in proportion to the whole number of white or other free citizens in each, including those bound to service for a term of years, and three fifths of all other persons. While they yielded this point, they insisted on an equal vote in the senate.

To this the large states were unwilling to assent ; and on this question the states remained, for a time, about equally divided. On the first trial, in committee of the whole, six states against five, decided that the right of suffrage in the senate should be the same as in the house ; the states of Massachusetts, Pennsylvania, Virginia, North Carolina, South Carolina, and Georgia being in the affirmative, and Connecticut, New York, New Jersey, Delaware and Maryland in the negative.

This question was again brought up, on a motion of Mr. Ellsworth, on the 29th of June, " *that in the second branch, each state should have an equal vote.*" This produced a long and warm debate. In support of his motion Mr. Ellsworth said, " I confess that the effect of this motion is, to make the general government *partly federal and partly national.* This will secure tranquillity, and still make it effectual ; and it will meet the objections of the larger states. In taxes they will have a proportional weight in the first branch of the general legislature. If the great states refuse this plan, we shall be forever separated. Even in the executive the larger states have ever had great influence. The provinces of Holland ever had it. If all the states are to exist, they must necessarily have an equal vote in the general government. Small communities, when associating with greater, can only be supported by an equality of votes. I have always found in my reading and experience, that in all societies the governors are ever rising into power. The large states, though they may not have a common interest for combination, yet they may be partially attached to each other for mutual support and advancement. This can be more easily effected than the union of the remaining small states to check it ; and ought we not to regard antecedent plighted faith to the confederation already entered into, and by the terms of it declared to be perpetual? And it is not obvious to me that the states will depart from this ground. When in the hour of common danger we united as equals, shall it now be urged by some that we must depart from this principle when danger is over? Will the world say that this is just ? We then associated as free and independent states, and were well satisfied. To perpetuate that independence, I wish to establish a national legislative, executive and judiciary ; for under these we shall, I doubt not, preserve peace and harmony—nor should I be surprised (although we made the general government the most perfect in our opinion) that it should hereafter require amendment. But at present, this is as far as I possibly can go. If this convention only chalks out lines of a good government, we shall do well."

Mr. Baldwin of Georgia said, " it appears to be agreed that the government we should adopt ought to be energetic and formidable, yet I would guard against the danger of becoming too formidable. The second branch ought not to be elected as the first. Suppose we take the example of the constitution of Massachusetts, as it is commended for its goodness : There the first branch represents the people, and the second its property."

" I would always exclude," said Mr. Madison, " inconsistent principles in framing a system of government. The difficulty of getting its defects amended are great and sometimes insurmountable. The Virginia government was the first which was made, and though its defects are evident to every person, we cannot get it amended. The Dutch have made four attempts to amend their system without success. The few alterations made in it were by tumult and faction, and for the worse. If there were real danger, I would give the small states the defensive weapon. But there is none from that quarter. The great danger to our general government is the great southern and northern interests of this continent, being opposed to each other. Look to the votes in congress, and most of them stand divided by the geography of the country, not according to the size of the states.

" Suppose the first branch granted money, may not the second branch, from state views, counteract the first? In congress, the single state of Delaware prevented an embargo, at the time all the other states thought it absolutely necessary for the support of the army. Other powers, and those very essential, besides the legislative, will be given to the second branch—such as the negativing all state laws. I would compromise on this question, if I could do it on correct principles, but otherwise not—if the old fabric of the confederation must be the ground-work of the new, we must fail."

The debate on this motion was renewed the next day, by Mr. Wilson of Pennsylvania, who commenced by saying— " The question now before us is of so much consequence, that I cannot give it a silent vote—gentlemen have said, that if this amendment is not agreed to, a separation to the north of Pennsylvania may be the consequence. This neither staggers me in my sentiments or my duty. If a minority should refuse their assent to the new plan of a general government, and if they will have their own will, and without it, separate the union, let it be done ; but we shall stand supported by stronger and better principles. The opposition to this plan is as twenty two to ninety, in the general scale—not quite a fourth part of the union. Shall three fourths of the union surrender their rights for the support of that artificial being, called state interest? If we must join issue I am willing, I cannot consent that one fourth shall controul the power of three fourths.

" If the motion is adopted, seven states will controul the whole, and the lesser seven compose twenty four out of ninety. One

third must controul two thirds—twenty four overrule sixty six.
For whom do we form a constitution, for meh, or for imaginary
beings called states, a mere metaphysical distinction? Will a
regard to state rights justify the sacrifice of the rights of men?
If we proceed on any other foundation than the last, our building
will neither be solid nor lasting. Weight and numbers is the
only true principle—every other is local, confined or imaginary.
Much has been said of the danger of the three larger states combining together to give rise to a monarchy, or an aristocracy.
Let the probability of this combination be explained, and it will
be found that a rivalship rather than a confederacy will exist
among them. Is there a single point in which this interest coincides? Supposing that the executive should be selected from
one of the large states, can the other two be gratified? Will not
this be a source of jealousy among them, and will they not separately court the interest of the smaller states, to counteract the
views of a favorite rival? How can an aristocracy arise from
this combination more than among the smaller states? On the
contrary, the present claims of the smaller states lead directly to
the establishment of an aristocracy, which is the few over the
many, and the Connecticut proposal removes only a small part
of the objection. There are only two kinds of bad government,
the one which does too much, and therefore oppressive, and the
other which does too little, and therefore weak. Congress par-
takes of the latter, and the motion will leave us in the same situation, and as much fettered as ever we were. The people see its
weakness, and would be mortified in seeing our inability to correct it.

The gentleman from Georgia has his doubts how to vote on
this question, and wishes some qualification of it to be made. I admit there ought to be some difference as to the numbers in the
second branch; and perhaps there are other distinctions which
could with propriety be introduced—such for example as the
qualifications of the elected, &c. However, if there are leading
principles in the system we adopt, much may be done in the detail. We all aim at giving the general government more energy.

The state governments are necessary and valuable—no liberty can be obtained without them. On this question depends the essential rights of the general government and of the people."

Mr. Ellsworth in reply observed, that he had the greatest respect for the gentleman (Mr. Wilson) who spoke last. " I respect his abilities," said he, " though I differ from him in many points. He asserts that the general government must depend on the equal suffrage of the people. But will not this put it in the power of few states to control the rest? It is a novel thing in politics that the few control the many. In the British government, the few, as a guard, have an equal share in the government. The house of lords, though few in number, and sitting in their own right, have an equal share in their legislature. They cannot give away the property of the community, but they can prevent the commons from being too lavish of their gifts. Where is or was a confederation ever formed, where equality of voice was not a fundamental principle? Mankind are apt to go from one extreme to another, and because we have found defects in the confederation, must we therefore pull down the whole fabric, foundation and all, in order to erect a new building totally different from it, without retaining any of its materials? What are its defects? It is said equality of votes has embarrassed us; but how? Would the real evils of our situation have been cured, had not this been the case? Would the proposed amendments in the Virginia plan as to representation, relieve us? I fancy not. Rhode Island has been often quoted as a small state, and by its refusal once defeated the grant of the impost. Whether she was right in doing so is not the question; but was it a federal requisition? And if it was not, she did not in this instance, defeat a federal measure.

" If the larger states seek security, they have it fully in the first branch of the general government. But can we turn the tables and say that the lesser states are equally secure? In commercial regulations they will unite. If policy should require free ports, they would be found at Boston, Philadelphia, and Alexandria. In the disposition of *lucrative offices* they would unite. But

I ask no surrender of any of the rights of the great states, nor do I plead duress in the makers of the old confederation, nor suppose they soothed the danger, in order to resume their rights when the danger was over. No ; *small states must possess the power of self-defense or be ruined.* Will any one say, there is no diversity of interests in the states ? and if there is, should not these interests be guarded and secured ? But if there is none, then the larger states have nothing to apprehend from an equality of rights. And let it be remembered, that these remarks are not the result of partial or local views. The state I represent is respectable, and in importance holds a middle rank."

Mr. Madison immediately replied, by saying that "notwithstanding the admirable and close reasoning of the gentleman," he was not yet convinced that his former remarks were not well founded. "I apprehend," said Mr. Madison, " he is mistaken as to the fact on which he builds one of his arguments. He supposes that equality of votes is the principle on which all confederacies are formed—that of Lycia, so justly applauded by the celebrated Montesquieu, was different. He also appeals to our good faith for the observance of the confederacy. We know we have formed one inadequate to the purposes for which it was made. Why then adhere to a system which is proved to be so remarkably defective ? I have impeached a number of states for the infraction of the confederation, and I have not even spared my own state, nor can I justly spare his. Did not Connecticut refuse her compliance to a federal requisition ? Has she paid for the two last years, any money into the continental treasury ? and does this look like government, or the observance of a solemn compact ? Experience shows that the confederation is radically defective, and we must, in a new national government, guard against those defects. Though the larger states in the first branch have a weight proportional to their population, yet as the smaller states have an equal vote in the second branch, such as negativing state laws, &c., unless the large states have a proportional weight in the representation, they cannot be more secure."

To the remarks made by Mr. Madison relative to Connecticut, Mr. Ellsworth replied that the state he represented had been strictly federal, and he appealed with confidence, to his excellency (the president,) for the truth of it during the war. " The muster rolls will show," he said, " that she had more troops in the field than even the state of Virginia. We strained every nerve to raise them ; and we neither spared money nor exertions to complete our quotas. This extraordinary exertion has greatly distressed and impoverished us, and it has accumulated our state debts—we feel the effects of it even to this day. But we defy any gentleman to show that we ever *refused* a federal requisition. We are constantly exerting ourselves to draw money from the pockets of our citizens as fast at it comes in ; and it is the ardent wish of the state to strengthen the federal government. If she has proved delinquent through inability only, it is not more than others have been, without the same excuse."

Mr. Bradford of Delaware, expressed himself with great warmth and even asperity, on this question.

" That all the states," he observed, " at present are equally sovereign and independent, has been asserted from every quarter of the house. Our deliberations here are a confirmation of the position ; and I may add to it, that each of them act from interested, and many from ambitious motives. Look at the votes which have been given on the floor of this house, and it will be found that their numbers, wealth, and local views, have actuated their determinations ; and that the larger states proceed as if our eyes were already perfectly blinded. Impartiality with them is already out of the question—the reported plan is their creed, and they support it right or wrong. Even the diminutive state of Georgia has an eye to her future wealth and greatness—South Carolina puffed up with the possession of her wealth and negroes, and North Carolina are all, from different views, united with the great states. And these latter, though it is said they can never, from interested views, form a coalition, we find closely united in one scheme of interest and ambition, notwithstanding they endeavor to amuse us with the purity of their principles and the rectitude of their intentions, in asserting that the general government must be drawn from an equal representation of the people. Pretences to support ambition are never wanting. Their cry is, where is the danger? And they insist that though the powers of the general government will be increased, yet it will be for the good of the whole ; and though the three great states form nearly a majority of the people of America, they never will hurt or injure the lesser states. I do not, gentlemen, trust you. If you possess the power, the abuse of it could not be checked ; and what then would prevent you from exercising it to our destruction? You gravely allege that there is no danger of combination, and triumphantly ask, how could combinations be effected? 'The larger states,' you say, 'all differ in productions and commerce ; and experience shows, that instead of combinations, they would be rivals, and counteract the views of one another.' This, I repeat, is language calculated only to amuse us. Yes, sir, the larger states will be rivals, but not against each other—they will be rivals against the rest of the states. But it is urged that such a government would suit the people, and that its principles are equitable and just. How often has this argument been refuted when applied to a *federal* government. The small states never can agree to the Virginia plan ; and why then is it still urged? But it is said that it is not expected that the state governments will approve the proposed system, and that this house must directly carry it to the people for their approbation ! Is it come to this then, that the sword must decide this controversy, and that the horrors of war must be added to the rest of our misfortunes ? But what have the people already said? 'We find the confederation defective—go and give additional powers to the confederation—give to it the imposts, regulation of trade, power to collect the taxes, and the means to discharge our foreign and domestic debts.' Can we not then, as their delegates agree upon these points ? As their ambassadors, can we not clearly grant these powers ? Why then, when we are met, must entire, distinct, and new grounds be taken, and a government, of which the people had no idea be instituted? And are we to be told, if we wont agree to it, it is the last moment of our deliberations? I say, it is indeed the last moment, if we do agree to this assumption of power. The states will never again be entrapped into a measure like this. The people will say the small states would confederate, and grant further powers to congress, the large states would not. Then the fault will be yours, and all the nations of the earth will justify us. But what is to become of our public debts if we dissolve the union? Will you crush the smaller states, or must they be left unmolested? Sooner than be ruined, there are foreign powers who will take us by the hand. I say not this to threaten or intimidate, but that we should reflect seriously before we act. If we once leave this place, and solemnly renounce your new project, what will be the consequence? You will annihilate your federal government, and ruin must stare you in the face. Let us then do what is in our power—amend and enlarge the confederation, but not alter the federal system. The people expect this and no more. We all agree in the necessity of a more efficient government—and cannot this be done? Though my state is small, I know and respect its rights, as much at least, as those who have the honor to represent any of the larger states."

Mr. King concurred in sentiment with those, who wished the preservation of state governments; but the general government, he said, " might be so constituted as to effect it. Let the constitution we are about forming be considered as a commission under which the general government should act, and as such it will be the guardian of the state rights. The rights of Scotland are secure from all danger and encroachments, though in the parliament she has a small representation. May not this be done in our general government? Since I am up," said Mr. King, " I am concerned for what fell from the gentleman from Delaware—'take a foreign power by the hand!' I am sorry he mentioned it, and I hope he is able to excuse it to himself on the score of passion. Whatever may be my distress, I never will court a foreign power to assist in relieving myself from it.

Towards the close of this interesting debate, Dr. Franklin, then at the advanced age of about eighty-two, arose and addressing himself to the chair, said, " it has given me great pleasure to observe that till this point, the *proportion of representation* came before us, our debates were carried on with great coolness and temper. If any thing of a contrary kind has on this occasion appeared, I hope it will not be repeated ; for we are sent hither to *consult*, not to *contend* with each other ; and declarations of a fixed opinion and of determined resolutions never to change it, neither enlighten nor convince us : positiveness and warmth on one side naturally beget their like on the other ; and tend to create and augment discord and division in a great concern, wherein harmony and union are extremely necessary, to give weight to our councils, and render them effectual in promoting and securing the common good.

" I must own that I was originally of opinion it would be better if every member of congress, or our national council, were to consider himself rather as a representative of the whole, than as an agent for the interests of a particular state, in which case the proportion of members for each state would be of less consequence, and it would not be very material whether they voted by states or individually. But as I find this is not to be expected, I now think the number of representatives should bear some proportion to the number of the represented, and that the decisions should be by the majority of members, not by the majority of states. This is objected to from an apprehension that the greater states would then swallow up the smaller. I do not at present clearly see what advantage the greater states could propose to themselves, by swallowing the smaller, and therefore do not apprehend they would attempt it. I recollect that in the beginning of this century, when the union was proposed of the two kingdoms, England and Scotland, the Scotch patriots were full of fears, that unless they had an equal number of representatives in parliament, they should be ruined by the superiority of the English. They finally agreed, however, that the different proportions of importance in the union, of the two nations, should be attended to ; whereby they were to have only forty members in the house of commons, and only sixteen of their peers were to sit in the house of lords; a very great inferiority of numbers! And yet to this day I do not recollect that any thing has been done in the parliament of Great Britain to the prejudice of Scotland ; and whoever looks over the lists of public officers, civil and military of that nation, will find, I believe, that the North Britons enjoy at least their full proportion of emolument. But, sir, in the present mode of voting by states, it is equally in the power of the lesser states to swallow up the greater ; and this is mathematically demonstrable. Suppose, for example, that seven smaller states had each three members in the house, and the six larger to have, one with another, six members. And that upon a question, two members of each smaller state should be in the affirmative, and one in the negative, they will make—

Affirmatives, 14   Negatives, 7

And that all the larger states should be unanimously in the negative, they would make Negatives, 36

In all, 43

" It is then apparent, that the 14 carry the question against the 43, and the minority overpowers the majority, contrary to the common practice of all assemblies in all countries and ages.

" The greater states, sir, are naturally as unwilling to have their property left in the disposition of the smaller, as the smaller are to leave theirs in the disposition of the greater. An honorable gentleman has, to avoid this difficulty, hinted a proposition of equalizing the states. It appears to me an equitable one ; and I should, for my own part, not be against such a measure, if it might be found practicable. Formerly, indeed, when almost every province had a different constitution, some with greater, others with fewer privileges, it was of importance to the borderers, when their boundaries were contested, whether by running the division lines they were placed on one side or the other. At present, when such differences are done away, it is less material. The interest of a state is made up of the interests of its individual

members.   If they are not-injured, the state is not injured. Small
states are more easily, well, and happily governed than large
ones.   If, therefore, in such an equal division, it should be found
necessary to diminish Pennsylvania, I should not be averse to the
giving a part of it to New Jersey, and another to Delaware ; but
as there would probably be considerable difficulties in adjusting
such a division ; and however equally made at first, it would be
continually varying by the augmentation of inhabitants in some
states, and their more fixed proportion in others ; and thence frequent occasion for new divisions ; I beg leave to propose for the
consideration of the committee another mode, which appears to
me to be as equitable, more easily carried into practice, and more
permanent in its nature.

" Let the weakest state say what proportion of money or force
it is able and willing to furnish for the general purposes of the
union.

" Let all the others oblige themselves to furnish an equal proportion.

" The whole of these joint supplies to be absolutely in the disposition of congress.   The congress in this case to be composed
of an equal number of delegates from each state : and their decisions to be by the majority of individual members voting.

" If these joint and equal supplies should on particular occasions not be sufficient, let congress make requisitions on the richer
and more powerful states for further aids, to be voluntarily afforded ; so leaving each state the right of considering the necessity and utility of the aid desired, and of giving more or less as it
should be found proper.

" This mode is not new ; it was formerly practised with success by the British government, with respect to Ireland and the
colonies.   We sometimes gave even more than they expected or
thought just to accept ; and in the last war, carried on while we
were united, they gave us back in five years a million sterling.
We should probably have continued such voluntary contributions,
whenever the occasion appeared to require them for the common
good of the empire.   It was not till they chose to force us, and to

deprive us of the merit and pleasure of voluntary contributions, that we refused and resisted. Those contributions, however, were to be disposed of at the pleasure of a government in which we had no representative. I am therefore persuaded that they will not be refused to one in which the representation shall be equal.

" My learned colleague has already mentioned, that the present mode of voting by states, was submitted to originally by congress, under a conviction of its impropriety, inequality, and injustice. This appears in the words of their resolution. It is of Sept. 6th, 1774. The words are—

" *Resolved*, That in determining questions in this congress, each colony or province shall have one vote : the congress not being possessed of, or at present able to procure, materials for ascertaining the importance of each colony."*

On the 2d of July, the question was taken on the motion of Mr. Ellsworth, *that in the senate each state should have one vote*, and five states were in favor of it, five against it, and one divided ; and the motion was lost.† This equal division on a question of such importance, accompanied with so much warmth on both sides, seemed to present an insurmountable obstacle to further proceedings of the convention, without some compromise. To effect this, Charles C. Pinckney of South Carolina, moved for the appointment of a committee to take into consideration the subject of both branches of the legislature. This motion prevailed, though not without opposition. Some of the members were in favor of appointing a committee, though they had little expectation of a favorable result. Mr. Martin of Maryland, declared, that each state must have an equal vote, or the business of the convention was at an end.

Mr. Sherman said, we have got to a point, that we cannot move one way or the other ; a committee is necessary to set us

* This debate on the question of the representation of the states in the senate, is taken from the minutes of Mr. Yates, with the exception of the speech of Dr. Franklin, which is found in his works.

† Connecticut, New York, New Jersey, Delaware, and Maryland, were in the affirmative,—Massachusetts, Pennsylvania, Virginia, North Carolina, and South Carolina, in the negative, and Georgia divided.

right. Mr. Gerry observed, that the world expected something from them—if we do nothing, we must have war and confusion—the old confederation would be at an end. Let us see if concessions cannot be made—accommodation is absolutely necessary, and defects may be amended by a future convention.*

* While the important question of the representation of the states in the senate was the subject of debate, and the states were almost equally divided upon it, Dr. Franklin moved that prayers should be attended in the convention every morning, and in support of his motion, thus addressed the president.

"*Mr. President*—The small progress we have made after four or five weeks close attendance and continual reasonings with each other, our different sentiments on almost every question, several of the last producing as many *noes* as *ayes*, is methinks a melancholy proof of the imperfection of the human understanding. We indeed seem to feel our own want of political wisdom, since we have been running all about in search of it. We have gone back to ancient history for models of government, and examined the different forms of those republics, which, having been originally formed with the seeds of their own dissolution, now no longer exist; and we have viewed modern states all round Europe, but find none of their constitutions suitable to our circumstances. In this situation of this assembly, groping as it were, in the dark, to find political truth, and scarce able to distinguish it when presented to us, how has it happened, sir, that we have not hitherto once thought of humbly applying to the Father of Lights to illuminate our understandings?---In the beginning of the contest with Britain, when we were sensible of danger, we had daily prayers in this room for the divine protection! Our prayers, sir, were heard ;---and they were graciously answered. All of us, who were engaged in the struggle, must have observed frequent instances of a superintending Providence in our favor. To that kind Providence we owe this happy opportunity of consulting in peace on the means of establishing our future national felicity. And have we now forgotten that powerful friend ?---or do we imagine we no longer need its assistance.---I have lived, sir, a long time ; and the longer I live, the more convincing proofs I see of this truth, *that God governs in the affairs of men !* And if a sparrow cannot fall to the ground without his notice, is it probable that an empire can rise without his aid ?---We have been assured, sir, in the sacred writings, that ' except the Lord build the house, they labor in vain that build it.' I firmly believe this ; and I also believe, that without his concurring aid, we shall succeed in this political building no better than the builders of Babel : we shall be divided by our little partial local interests, our projects will be confounded, and we ourselves shall become a reproach and a by-word down to future ages. And what is worse, mankind may hereafter, from this unfortunate instance, despair of establishing government by human wisdom, and leave it to chance, war, and conquest.

" I therefore beg leave to move, that henceforth prayers, imploring the assistance of heaven, and its blessings on our deliberations, be held in this assembly every morning before we proceed to business ; and that one or more of the clergy of this city be requested to officiate in that service."

A committee was chosen by ballot, consisting of one from each state, and the convention adjourned for three days.* Fortunately the committee by way of compromise, agreed upon a report, which was made on the day to which the convention had adjourned. They recommended two propositions, on the express condition that both should be generally adopted. The propositions were—

"I. That in the first branch of the legislature, each of the states now in the union be allowed one member for every forty thousand inhabitants, of the description reported in the seventh resolution of the committee of the whole house—that each state not containing that number shall be allowed one member—that all bills for raising or appropriating money, and for fixing the salaries of the officers of the government of the United States, shall originate in the first branch of the legislature, and shall not be altered or amended by the second branch—and that no money shall be drawn from the public treasury, but in pursuance of appropriations to be originated in the first branch.

" II. That in the second branch of the legislature, each state shall have one vote."

The power of raising and appropriating money, fixing the salaries of the officers, was given to the house of representatives, where the states were represented by the number of their inhabitants, as a balance to the powers of the senate, where they were to be equally represented. On the question of vesting the house with the exclusive power of raising and appropriating money, and fixing the salaries of the officers, the states were divided in the following manner—Connecticut, New Jersey, Delaware, Maryland, and North Carolina, in the affirmative—Pennsylvania, Virginia, and South Carolina, in the negative—Massachusetts, New York, and Georgia, divided—and nine states

* This committee consisted of Mr. Gerry, from Massachusetts ; Mr. Ellsworth, from Connecticut ; Mr. Yates, from New York ; Mr. Patterson, from New Jersey ; Dr. Franklin, from Pennsylvania ; Mr. Bedford, from Delaware ; Mr. Martin, from Maryland ; Mr. Mason, from Virginia ; Mr. Davie, from North Carolina ; Mr. Rutledge, from South Carolina, and Mr. Baldwin, from Georgia.

against two, determined, that this was a decision of the question
in the affirmative. On that part of the report of the committee,
recommending, that each state have an equal vote in the senate
—Connecticut, New York, New Jersey, Delaware, Maryland, and
North Carolina, were in the affirmative—Pennsylvania, Virginia,
and South Carolina, in the negative—Massachusetts and Georgia, divided.

We would here state, that the delegates from the state
of New York, were Mr. Yates, Mr. Lansing, jr., and Mr. Hamilton. Mr. Yates and Mr. Lansing, left the convention about
the 11th of July, but Mr. Hamilton continued to the close and
put his signature to the constitution. The two gentlemen first
named, considered their powers " were explicit, and confined to
the sole and express purpose of *revising* the articles of confederation, and that they had no authority to make so radical a change
in the general government, as a large majority of the convention
contemplated." On this account, they returned home.

Having thus settled the great question of the representation of
the states, in the national legislature, the convention proceeded
to organize this great department more in detail.

The representatives were to be chosen every two years, and
the number designated for the first congress, was sixty-five. They
were afterwards to be apportioned among the states according to
their respective numbers, which was to be determined by adding
to the whole number of free persons, including those bound to
service for a term of years, and excluding Indians not taxed,
three fifths of all other persons. The enumeration was to be made
within three years after the first meeting of congress, and within
every subsequent term of ten years—and *direct taxes* were to be
apportioned among the states in the same manner.

The senate was to be composed of two persons from each
state, chosen by the legislature thereof, for six years. Those first
chosen were to be divided into three classes ; the seats of the
first class to be vacated at the expiration of two years, the second, four years, and the third, six years. The times, places, and
manner of holding elections for senators and representatives was

to be prescribed by the legislature of each state ; but a power of making or altering such regulations was reserved to congress, except as to the *place* of choosing senators.

The power of the house of representatives respecting raising money was finally limited to originating all bills for raising revenue ; but the senate might propose or concur with amendments, as in other bills.

The subject of the powers of the national government, was one of no little difficulty, as well as delicacy. . While on the one hand, it was important they should be adequate to the exigences of the union, so on the other, they should be such, as in all probability, would secure the assent of the American people.

A majority of the convention at last determined that congress should be invested with power, to lay and collect taxes, duties, imposts, and excises—to pay the debts and provide for the common defense and general welfare of the United States ; all duties, imposts, and excises to be uniform throughout the United States—to borrow money on the credit of the United States—to regulate commerce with foreign nations, and among the several states, and with the Indian tribes—to establish a uniform rule of naturalization, and uniform laws on the subject of bankruptcies throughout the United States—to provide for the punishment of counterfeiting the securities and current coin of the United States —to establish post offices and post roads—to promote the progress of science and useful arts, by securing, for limited times, to authors and inventors, the exclusive right to their respective writings and discoveries—to constitute tribunals inferior to the supreme court—to define and punish piracies and felonies committed on the high seas, and offences against the law of nations—to declare war, grant letters of marque and reprisal, and make rules concerning captures on land and water—to raise and support armies ; but no appropriation of money to that use to be for a longer term than two years—to provide and maintain a navy—to make rules for the government and regulation of the land and naval forces—to provide for calling forth the militia to execute the laws of the union, suppress insurrections, and repel invasions

—to provide for organizing, arming, and disciplining the militia, and for governing such part of them as might be employed in the service of the United States—reserving to the states the appointment of the officers, and the authority of training the militia according to the discipline prescribed by congress—to exercise exclusive legislation in all cases whatsoever, over such district, (not exceeding ten miles square,) as might, by cession of particular states, and the acceptance of congress, become the seat of government of the United States, and to exercise like authority over all places purchased, by the consent of the legislatures of the states in which the same shall be, for the erection of forts, magazines, arsenals, dockyards, and all other needful buildings—and to make all laws necessary and proper for carrying into execution these and all other powers vested by the constitution in the government of the United States, or in any department or officer thereof.

While the members of the convention granted these powers to the general government; they, at the same time, by special provisions, limited their powers in certain cases, by declaring, that the importation of slaves should not be prohibited prior to the year 1808; and that no tax should be imposed on such importation, exceeding ten dollars for each person—that the privilege of the writ of habeas corpus should not be suspended but in cases of rebellion or invasion—that no bill of attainder, or *ex post facto* law should be passed—that no capitation, or other direct tax should be laid, unless in proportion to the enumeration directed to be taken for the apportionment of representatives—that no tax or duty should be laid on articles exported from any state— that no preference should be given by any regulation of commerce or revenue to the ports of one state over another; nor should vessels bound to or from one state, be obliged to enter, clear, or pay duties in another—that no money be drawn from the treasury, but in consequence of appropriations made by law. That no title of nobility should be granted by the United States; and so jealous were they of foreign influence in the national administration, that they prohibited persons holding any office of profit or trust under the authority of the United States from receiving, without the consent of congress, any present, emolument, office, or title of any kind whatever, from any king, prince, or foreign state.

While the convention, thus secured the people of the United States against the exercise or abuse of power in the general government ; they deemed it important to restrain the states themselves from doing certain acts, prejudicial to the people or to the union. The states were, therefore, prohibited from entering into any treaty, alliance, or confederation ; granting letters of marque and reprisal ; coining money ; emitting bills of credit ; making any thing but gold and silver a tender in payment of debts—they were not to pass any bill of attainder, *ex post facto* law, or law impairing the obligation of contracts, or grant any title of nobility. Nor was any state permitted, without the consent of congress, to lay any imposts or duties on imports or exports, except what might be absolutely necessary for executing its inspection laws ; and the net produce of all duties and imposts laid by any state, on imports or exports, were to be for the use of the treasury of the United States ; and all such laws were to be subject to the revision and control of congress. No state, without the assent of congress, could lay any duty of tonnage, keep troops or ships of war in time of peace, enter into any agreement or compact with another state, or with a foreign power, or engage in war, unless actually invaded, or in such imminent danger as would not admit of delay.

To prevent the encroachments of the states on the powers of the general government, some of the delegates deemed it absolutely necessary that the national legislature should possess a right to negative all state laws contravening the articles of union, or any treaties subsisting under the authority of the United States ; and this power was embraced in the resolutions submitted to the convention by Mr. Randolph, and agreed to in committee of the whole.

The proposition, however, conferring this power on the national legistature, was finally rejected, seven states against three.*

The organization of a supreme executive presented many difficulties, arising not merely from the nature of the subject, but from the complicated system of the government. The mode of choice, and whether to consist of one or more persons, the time for which the executive should be chosen, whether re-eligible, and the powers to be granted to the person or persons, who should administer the government, were questions of new impression, and which the members of the convention found it extremely difficult to settle in a manner satisfactory even to themselves. After much deliberation, on the 26th of July, a majority of the states, being six against three and one divided, agreed to the following plan—that a national executive be instituted—

To consist of a single person ;

To be chosen by the national legislature ;

For the term of seven years ;

To be ineligible a second time ;

With power to carry into execution the national laws ;

To appoint to offices in cases not otherwise provided for ;

To be removeable on impeachment and conviction of malpractice or neglect of duty ;

To receive a fixed compensation for the devotion of his time to public service ;

To be paid out of the public treasury.†

This plan was referred to the committee appointed to prepare the constitution, and was incorporated in the first draft reported by them.

This important subject remained undecided until the 31st of August, when it was referred to a committee of one from each

---

* The states in favor of it, were Massachusetts, Virginia, and North Carolina---those against it, Connecticut, New Jersey, Pennsylvania, Delaware, Maryland, South Carolina, and Georgia.—*Journals of the Convention, p.* 188.

† On the question of agreeing to this plan, New Hampshire, Connecticut, New Jersey, North Carolina, South Carolina, and Georgia, were in the affirmative---Pennsylvania, Delaware, and Maryland, in the negative---and Virginia was divided.

state ; and on the 4th of September, the committee reported an entire new plan, which, after some amendments, was adopted. It provided that the executive power should be vested in a president of the United States, to hold his office for four years, and with the vice president, chosen for the same term, be elected as follows :—

Each state to appoint, in such manner as the legislature thereof might direct, a number of electors equal to the whole number of senators and representatives to which the state might be entitled in congress, but no senator or representative or person holding any office of trust or profit under the United States, to be appointed an elector.

The electors to meet in their respective states, and vote by ballot for two persons, of whom one at least should not be an inhabitant of the same state with themselves. They were to make a list of all the persons voted for, and of the number of votes for each, which list they were to sign, certify and transmit sealed to the seat of the government of the United States, directed to the president of the senate—the president of the senate, in the presence of the senate and house of representatives, was to open all the certificates and the votes were then to be counted. The person having the greatest number of votes to be president, if such number should be a majority of the whole number of electors appointed; and if more than one have such majority, and have an equal number of votes, then the house of representatives were immediately to choose, by ballot, one of them for president; and if no person had a majority, then from the five highest on the list, the house were, in like manner, to choose the president. But in this choice, the votes were to be by states, the representatives from each state to have one vote—a quorum for this purpose to consist of a number of members from two thirds of the states, and a majority of all the states to be necessary to a choice. In every case, after the choice of the president, the person having the greatest number of the votes of the electers to be vice-president. But if there should be two or more who had an equal vote, the senate were to choose from them, by ballot, the vice-president

Congress were to determine the time of choosing the electors, and the day of giving in their votes, which was to be the same throughout the United States.

No person, except a natural born citizen, or a citizen of the United States at the time of the adoption of the constitution was to be eligible to the office of president, nor was any person to be eligible, who had not attained to the age of thirty five years, and been fourteen years a resident in the United States.

In case of the removal of the president from office, or of his death, resignation, or inability to discharge his duties, the same was to devolve on the vice-president; and congress were to provide by law, for the case of removal, death, resignation, or inability both of the president and vice-president, declaring what officer should then act as president, and such officer was to act, until the disability should be removed, or a president be elected.

The president was to receive a compensation, which was neither to be increased nor diminished, during the period of his election, nor was he to receive in that period any other emolument from the United States; or any of them. He was to take a solemn oath,—" to preserve, protect and defend the constitution of the United States," according to the best of his abilities.

He was to be commander in chief of the army and navy of the United States, and of the militia when called into the service of the union; and he might require the opinion in writing of the principal officers of each of the executive departments, upon any subject relating to the duties of their respective offices; and also could grant reprieves and pardons for offenses against the United States, except in cases of impeachment.

He was likewise invested with power, by and with the advice and consent of the senate, to make treaties, provided two thirds of the senators present concurred; and he was to nominate, and by and with the advice and consent of the senate, appoint ambassadors, and other public ministers and consuls, judges of the supreme court, and all other officers of the United States, whose appointments were not otherwise provided for by the constitution, and which should be established by law. But congress might by law vest the appointment of such inferior officers, as they might think proper, in the president alone, in the courts of law, or in the heads of departments.

The president was to fill up all vacancies happening during the recess of the senate, by commissions, to expire at the end of their next session.

It was likewise made his duty to give to congress from time to time, information of the state of the union, and recommend to their consideration, such measures as he should judge necessary and expedient, and on extraordinary occasions to convene both houses or either of them, and in case of disagreement between them, as to the time of adjournment, to adjourn them—was to receive ambassadors and other public ministers—to take care that the laws be faithfully executed, and to commission all officers of the United States ; and was liable to be removed from office, on impeachment for, and conviction of treason, bribery or other high crimes and misdemeanors.

The president had also a partial negative on all bills or resolutions of both houses of congress.

These were to be presented to him, after they had passed the house and senate, for his approbation—if he approved, he was to sign them ; if not, to return them, with his objections in writing, to the house in which they originated, and if not, on reconsideration, repassed by two thirds of both houses, were not to be laws or valid acts of congress.

Fewer obstacles presented in forming the third co-ordinate branch of the government, a national judiciary. This was to consist of a supreme court, and such inferior courts as congress should from time to time establish ; all the judges to hold their offices during good behavior, and their compensation was not to be diminished during their continuance in office. The judicial power was to extend to all cases in law or equity, arising under the constitution, the laws of the United States, and treaties made, or which should be made under their authority ; to all cases affecting ambassadors, other public ministers and consuls ; to all cases of admiralty and maritime jurisdiction ; to controversies to which the United States should be a party: to controversies between two or more states, between a state and citizens of another state, between citizens of different states, between citizens of the same state claiming lands under grants of different states, and between a state, or the citizens thereof, and foreign states, citizens or subjects.

In all cases affecting ambassadors, other public ministers and consuls, the supreme court had original jurisdiction, and in all other cases, appellate jurisdiction, as to law and fact, with such exceptions, and under such regulations as congress should make. The trial of all crimes, except in cases of impeachment, was to be by jury; and such trial was to be held in the state where the crimes were committed; but when not committed within any state, the trial to be at such place as congress should by law direct.

The convention thought proper to define treason in the constitution, and not leave it to legislative acts. They therefore declared that treason against the United States, should consist only in levying war against them, or in adhering to their enemies, giving them aid and comfort. And no person was to be convicted of this crime unless on the testimony of two witnesses to the same overt act, or on confession in open court.

The constitution also provided, that full faith and credit should be given in each state to the public acts, records and judicial proceedings of every other state—and congress were by general laws, to prescribe the manner in which such acts, records and judicial proceedings should be proved, and their effects. The citizens of each state were entitled to all the privileges and immunities of citizens of the several states; and fugitives from justice were to be delivered up, on demand of the executive authority of the state from which they fled—nor was any person held to service or labor in one state, under the laws of the same, escaping into another, to be discharged from such service, in consequence of any law of the state to which he had escaped, but was to be delivered up, on claim of the party to whom such service might be due. And the United States guarantied to every state a republican form of government, and were to protect each of them against invasion ; and on application of the legislature, or of the executive, (when the legislature could not be convened) against domestic violence.

Congress were authorized to admit new states into the union ; but no new state was to be formed within the jurisdiction of any other state, nor any state to be formed by the junction of two or more states, or parts of states, without the consent of the legislatures of the states concerned.

All debts contracted or engagements entered into, before the adoption of the constitution, were to be as valid against the United States, under the new system, as under the confederation ; and congress were invested with the power of disposing and regulating the territory or other property belonging to the United States.

The constitution itself, and all laws made in pursuance of it, and all treaties made, or to be made under the authority of the United States, were to be the supreme law of the land, and the judges in every state were to be bound thereby, any thing in the constitution or laws of any state to the contrary notwithstanding.

The convention provided that the ratification of nine states should be sufficient for the establishment of the new system among the states so ratifying the same. Having experienced the evils arising from that part of the old system of the general government, which required the assent of every state to any amendment, the members of the convention very wisely ordered in the constitution, that congress, whenever two thirds of both houses deemed it necessary, should propose amendments ; or on the application of the legislatures of two thirds of the several states, should call a convention for proposing amendments, which in either case, should be valid as part of the constitution, when ratified by the legislatures or conventions of three fourths of the several states ; with a proviso, however, that no amendment which should be made prior to the year 1808, should in any manner, effect the rights of the states to bring in slaves ; *and that no state, without its consent, should be deprived of its equal suffrage in the senate.*

In forming so complicated a system of government, many questions were presented, which probably few of the members of the convention had previously contemplated. It is evident, indeed, from the journal of their proceedings, that the great political edifice finally reared and completed by these master builders, was, in many respects, different from that which most of them had originally conceived or planned.

In their deliberations on a subject so new, and with so few guides to direct them, many propositions were made and suggested for examination merely, and afterwards given up by the movers themselves—many, even after being adopted by a majority of the convention, were reconsidered and rejected.

Mr. Hamilton, not perfectly satisfied with the plans submitted by Mr. Randolph or Mr. Patterson, suggested a general plan of his own, which was—that the members of the house of representatives should be elected for three years, and the senators and president or governor during good behavior—the senators to be elected by electors chosen by the people, and for this purpose the states to be divided into election districts—the election of the president to be by electors, chosen by electors, who were to be chosen by the people in the same districts—the president to have a negative on all laws about to be passed, and the execution of all laws passed—to have the power, with the advice of the senate, to make treaties—to have the sole appointment of the heads of departments, and the nomination of all other officers, subject to the approbation of the senate—the senate to have the sole power of declaring war—the supreme judicial authority to be vested in judges to hold their offices during good behavior, to have original jurisdiction in all cases of capture, and appellate jurisdiction in all causes, in which the revenues of the general government, or the citizens of foreign nations were concerned—all impeachments to be tried by a court to consist of the chief or senior judge of the superior court of law in each state, provided such judge hold his office during good behavior, and had a permanent salary—the laws of the states contrary to the constitution or laws of the United States, to be utterly void—the governor of each state to be appointed by the general government, with a negative on the laws about to be passed in the state of which he was governor.

These are the outlines of the plan suggested by Mr. Hamilton, at an early period of the convention, and yet before the close, his opinion with respect to some part of it was changed, particularly as to the continuance of the executive during good behavior.*

* The following letter from Col. Hamilton to Col. Pickering, will serve to show not only his own views on the subject, but the general course of the proceedings in the convention.

" New York, September 16th, 1803.

" *My dear sir*—I will make no apology for my delay in answering your inquiry some time since made, because I could offer none which would satisfy myself. I pray you only to believe that it proceeded from any thing rather than want of respect or regard. I shall now comply with your request.

" The highest toned propositions, which I made in the convention, were for a president, senate, and judges during good behavior---a house of representatives for three years. Though I would have enlarged the legislative power of the general government, yet I never contemplated the abolition of the state governments ; but, on the contrary, they were, in some particulars, constituent parts of my plan.

" This plan was in my conception conformable with the strict theory of a government purely republican ; the essential criteria of which are, that the principal organs of the executive and legislative departments be elected by the people, and hold their offices by a *responsible* and temporary or *defeasible* tenure.

" A vote was taken on the proposition respecting the executive. Five states were in favor of it ; among these Virginia ; and though from the manner of voting, by delegations, individuals were not distinguished, it was morally certain, from the known situation of the Virginia members, (six in number, two of them, *Mason* and *Randolph*, professing popular doctrines,) that Madison must have concurred in the vote of Virginia. Thus, if I sinned against republicanism, Mr. Madison was not less guilty.

" I may truly then say, that I never proposed either a president or senate for life ; and that I neither recommended nor meditated the annihilation of the state governments.

" And I may add, that in the course of the discussions in the convention, neither the propositions thrown out for debate, nor even those voted in the earlier stages of deliberation, were considered as evidences of a definitive opinion in the proposer or voter. It appeared to me to be in some sort understood, that with a view to free investigation, experimental propositions might be made, which were to be received merely as suggestions for consideration.

cles of confederation, the *states* entered into " a firm *league* of friendship with each other, for their common defense, the security of their liberties, and their mutual and general welfare," &c. By the new constitution, as the preamble declares, " the *people*" united and established a government, to ensure domestic tranquility, provide for the general welfare, and secure the blessings of liberty to themselves and their posterity.

As the national legislature was invested with the exclusive power of regulating commerce with foreign nations, and of course could pass *navigation acts*, a difference arose between the navigating and non-navigating states, respecting the exercise of this power. The latter were jealous, that the former might be disposed to secure to themselves improper advantages in the carrying trade. In the first draft of the constitution, therefore, the power of congress was limited in this respect by a special provision, that " *no navigation acts should be passed, without the assent of two thirds of the members present in each house.*"

Some of the slave holding states also wished to secure to themselves the right of importing slaves, free from any tax or duty. A clause was therefore at first inserted, declaring that congress should not prohibit the importation of such persons as the states might think proper to admit, nor lay any tax on the persons so imported.

These two subjects created no little difficulty in the convention, and were at last referred to a committee of one from a state. This committee, by way of compromise, reported that " the migration or importation of such persons as the several states *now existing* shall think proper to admit, shall not be prohibited by the legislature prior to the year 1800 ; but a tax may be imposed on such migration or importation at a rate not exceeding the average of the duties laid on imports."

The same committee also reported against the provision requiring the assent of *two thirds* of the members of each house, to pass *navigation acts*. This report, after an amendment, extending the time of allowing such importation to 1808, and limiting the tax on each person to ten dollars, was adopted by a majority

of the states.* We would here observe, that amendments were
proposed and even adopted until the day when the constitution
was signed. It will be remembered, that in the arrangement
with respect to the ratio of representation in the house, there
was to be one representative for every forty thousand inhabitants.
This remained so, until the last day of the session, when general
Washington rose and said, in effect, that " though he was sensible
of the impropriety of the chairman's intermingling in the debates,
yet he could not help observing, that the small number which
constituted the representative body, appeared to him a defect in
the plan—that it would better suit his ideas, and he believed it
would be more agreeable to the people, if the number should
be increased, and that the ratio should be one for every *thirty
thousand*." The motion for reducing the ratio to this number
was immediately put, and almost unanimously carried. This is
one instance of the influence of that great man in this assembly ;
and there can be no doubt, his influence was also felt in other
instances, though perhaps not in so direct a manner, during the
long deliberations of that body.

  Of the fifty five members who attended this convention, thirty
nine signed the constitution :† of the remaining sixteen, some
in favor of it were obliged from particular business to leave the
convention before it was ready for signing.‡

  The new system was transmitted to congress, accompanied
with the following letter from the president of the convention.

  " We have now the honor to submit to the consideration of
the United States, in congress assembled, that constitution which
has appeared to us the most advisable.

  " The friends of our country have long seen and desired, that
the power of making war, peace and treaties ; that of levying

---

  * The states in favor of allowing the importation of slaves until 1808, were New
Hampshire, Massachusetts, Connecticut, Maryland, North Carolina, South Carolina,
and Georgia—those against it were New Jersey, Pennsylvania, Delaware and Virginia.—*Journals of the Convention, pp.* 285—292.

  † Note 19.

  ‡ This, we are assured, was the case with Caleb Strong of Massachusetts, Oliver
Ellsworth of Connecticut, and Mr. Davie of North Carolina.

money, and regulating commerce, and the correspondent executive and judicial authorities, shall be fully and effectually vested in the general government of the union. But the impropriety of delegating such extensive trust to one body of men, is evident. Thence results the necessity of a different organization. It is obviously impracticable, in the federal government of these states, to secure all the rights of independent sovereignty to each, and yet provide for the interest and safety of all. Individuals entering into society must give up a share of liberty, to preserve the rest. The magnitude of the sacrifice must depend as well on situation and circumstances, as on the object to be obtained. It is at all times difficult to draw with precision the line between those rights which must be surrendered, and those which may be reserved. And on the present occasion this difficulty was increased by a difference among the several states, as to their situation, extent, habits, and particular interests.

In all our deliberations on this subject we kept steadily in our view that which appeared to us the greatest interest of every true American, the consolidation of our union, in which is involved our prosperity, felicity, safety, perhaps our national existence. This important consideration, seriously and deeply impressed on our minds, led each in the convention to be less rigid in points of inferior magnitude, than might have been otherwise expected. And thus the constitution which we now present, is the result of a spirit of amity, and of that mutual deference and concession, which the peculiarity of our political situation rendered indispensable.

That it will meet the full and entire approbation of every state, is not, perhaps, to be expected. But each will doubtless consider, that had her interest alone been consulted, the consequences might have been particularly disagreeable and injurious to others. That it is liable to as few exceptions as could reasonably have been expected, we hope and believe; that it may promote the lasting welfare of that country so dear to us all, and secure her freedom and happiness, is our most ardent wish."

The convention recommended that the constitution should be submitted to state conventions, and that as soon as the same should be ratified by a constitutional majority, congress should take measures for the election of a president, and fix the time for commencing proceedings under it. This requisition was immediately complied with.

It was not to be expected, that so radical a change in the federal government, as that recommended to the consideration of the people, would be adopted without opposition. It could not be supposed, that the same candid and calm deliberation, the same spirit of concession and mutual forbearance would prevail among the great body of the citizens, as among their enlightened representatives in the convention. State pride, state feelings, state interests, as well as state fears and jealousies, would natu- rally have influence in deciding so importont a question. Nor could the minds of a whole community, be easily brought to har- monize, either on the subject of the *organization* of a national government, or with respect to the *powers* proper and necessary to be granted to those who should be entrusted with its adminis- tration. Preconceived opinions, long established prejudices, as well as interested views would govern the minds of many indi- viduals.

The new system was hailed with joy and even with enthusiasm by one part of the community, by another it was viewed with distrust and jealousy. It immediately became the theme of gen- eral conversation and debate, and newspapers and pamphlets were the vehicles of conflicting opinions.

It was a subject, indeed, above all others of a political nature, calculated deeply to excite the feelings of a free people; and the talents of the ablest and wisest men were employed in investigat- ing its merits and its defects. Many of the publications of the day were of a local and transitory nature, others were of a differ- ent character, and would bear a comparison with the productions of statesmen of any age or nation. Among those in favor of the new system, a series of pieces which at first appeared in the newspapers, afterwards called the Federalist, held an eminent rank. They contained a lucid exposition of the views and reasons of the convention in forming the constitution, as well as a clear and systematic development of the principles of the system itself. The public mind was enlightened by these productions, and their beneficial effects were soon visible. These effects were not confined to the period of their first appearance. The Federalist has since been resorted to in doubtful cases of construction, as a valuable commentary on the great charter of the union. It has long since been known, they were written by Mr. Jay, Mr. Madison, and Mr. Hamilton, principally by the two latter gentlemen, who were influential members of the convention.

The new system came before state conventions in 1787 and 1788. It was adopted unanimously by Georgia, New Jersey, and Delaware, and by large majorities in Pennsylvania, Connecticut, Maryland, and South Carolina. The state of Rhode Island declined calling a convention; and it was for a time doubtful whether the other states would assent to it without previous amendments. Such, however, was the situation of the United States, without government, without funds, burdened with debt, and without the power or means of discharging it, despised abroad, and threatened with anarchy at home, small majorities were at last induced to yield their assent, trusting to future amendments.

The convention of Massachusetts met in January, 1788, and in the first place agreed freely to discuss the constitution by paragraphs, until every member had an opportunity of expressing his sentiments upon them—after this to consider and debate the question at large, whether they would adopt and ratify the constitution, before any vote should be taken expressive of the sense of the convention on the whole or any part of it. To the decision of · the people of Massachusetts, the friends of the system looked with extreme solicitude. Their decision, it was supposed, would have great influence in New Hampshire, and in the other states which had not yet acted on the subject. Men of the first talents were in the convention, and great exertions were made by them. Among its advocates were to be found James Bowdoin, Caleb

Strong, Rufus King, Ames, Cabot, Dawes, Dana, Gore, Gorham, Sedgwich, Parsons, Sumner. Such, however, was the peculiar situation of Massachusetts, that its fate in the convention, was for a long time doubtful.

The parties in opposition were thus described at the time by one of its members—" Never was there an assembly in this state in possession of greater abilities and information, than the present convention; yet I am in doubt whether they will approve the constitution. There are unhappily three parties opposed to it. 1. All men who are in favor of paper money and tender laws. These are more or less in every part of the state. 2. All the late insurgents, and their abettors. We have in the convention eighteen or twenty who were actually in Shay's army. 3. A great majority of the members from the province of Maine. Many of them and their constituents are only *squatters* upon other people's land, and they are afraid of being brought to account. They also think, though erroneously, that their favorite plan of being a separate state, will be defeated. Add to these, the honest doubting people, and they make a powerful host."* In this situation of the convention, governor Hancock, who had been chosen president, but had been detained by illness, took his seat, and while the general question was under consideration, proposed certain amendments to be afterwards introduced into the constitution.

Mr. Hancock, it was supposed, was inclined against the system without amendments. His proposition gave a new aspect to the question. The amendments were referred to a committee and reported with some few alterations. It was now supported by some who had before been opposed ; and among these was Samuel Adams who became its warm advocate. The debate took a new turn, and the friends of the constitution again urged with great force, the importance and necessity of accepting it with the proposed amendments. Towards the close of this debate, Mr. Ames thus concluded one of his eloquent

* North American Review for October, 1827.

appeals—" But shall we put every thing to hazard by rejecting this constitution ? We have great advantages by it in respect of navigation ; and it is the general interest of the states that we should have them. But if we reject it, what security have we that we shall obtain them a second time against the local inter- ests and prejudices of the other states? Who is there that really loves liberty, that will not tremble for its safety, if the federal government should be dissolved ? Can liberty be safe without government ?

" The period of our political dissolution is approaching. An- archy and uncertainty attend our future state—but this we know, that liberty, which is the *soul* of our existence, once fled, can re- turn no more.

The union is essential to our being as a nation. The pillars that prop it are crumbling to powder. The union is the vital sap that nourishes the tree. If we reject the constitution, to use the language of the country, we girdle the tree, its leaves will wither, its branches drop off, and the mouldering trunk will be torn down by the tempest. What security has this single state against foreign enemies? Could we defend the mast country, which the British so much desire ? Can we protect our fisheries, or secure by treaties a sale for the produce of our lands in foreign markets? Is there no loss, no danger, by delay ? In spite of our negligence and perverseness, are we to enjoy *at all times* the pri- vilege of forming a constitution, which no other nation has en- joyed at all? We approve our own form of government, and seem to think ourselves in safety under its protection. We talk as if there was no danger of deciding wrong. But when the in- undation comes, shall we stand on dry land ? The state gov- ernment is a beautiful structure. It is situated, however, on the naked beach. The union is the dyke to fence out the flood. That dyke is broken and decayed, and if we do not repair it, when the next spring tide comes, we shall be buried in one com- mon destruction."*

The amendments proposed by the convention, were in sub- stance, that all powers not expressly delegated by the constitu-

* Debates of Massachusetts Convention, p. 201, 202.

tion were reserved to the states—that there should be one representative to every thirty thousand persons, until the whole number of representatives amounted to two hundred—that congress should not exercise the powers vested in them in the 4th section of the first article, unless a state should refuse to make the regulations therein mentioned, or make such as were subversive of the rights of the people to a free and equal representation —that congress lay no direct taxes, but when the monies arising from impost and excise should be insufficient, nor then, until, on a requisition by congress for their proportion, the states should have refused to levy and pay the same ; in which case, congress might assess and levy such state's proportion with interest at 4 per cent. from the time prescribed in such requisition— that congress should create no company with exclusive advantages of commerce—that no person be tried for any crime, by which he might incur an infamous punishment, or loss of life, until indicted by a grand jury, except in the government of the land and naval forces—that the supreme judicial federal court should have no jurisdiction of causes between citizens of different states, unless the matter in dispute be of the value of three thousand dollars at least ; and that the federal judicial powers should not extend to any action between citizens of different states, where the matter in dispute was not of the value of fifteen hundred dollars —that in civil actions between citizens of different states, every issue of fact arising in actions at common law, be tried by a jury if either of the parties required it ; and that congress should at no time consent that any person holding an office of trust or profit under the United States, should accept a title of nobility, or any other title or office, from any king, prince, or foreign state.

The question was taken on the adoption of the constitution, on the 6th of February, 1788, and carried 187 to 168. The amendments were recommended as calculated to " remove the fears and quiet the apprehensions of many of the good people of the commonwealth, and more effectually guard against the administration of the federal government." And the convention enjoined it upon their representatives in congress, at all times, until such amendments should be considered agreeably to the fifth article of the constitution, to exert all their influence, and use all reasonable and legal methods to obtain a ratification of them in the manner provided in the article.

A convention met in New Hampshire soon after the decision in Massachusetts, and after a session of ten days, adjourned for four months. Many of the members were instructed to vote against the proposed system. Some of them, however, on the discussion which took place, changed their opinions, but felt bound by their instructions ; and had the question been then taken, a majority would no doubt, have refused their assent. To give time for further deliberation, and afford an opportunity for the people to reconsider their instructions, a small majority consented to an adjournment.

Having met again in June, the convention of that state adopted the constitution by a majority of eleven only, and nearly in the same form and manner as in Massachusetts. In addition to the amendments proposed by the latter, the former recommended, that no standing army be kept up in time of peace, unless with the consent of three fourths of the members of both houses of congress—that no soldiers in time of peace be quartered in private houses, without the consent of the owners ; and that congress should make no laws touching religion, or infringing the rights of conscience ; nor disarm any citizen, unless such as were, or had been in actual rebellion.

Conventions in Virginia, New York, and North Carolina, did not assemble until the summer of 1788.

Here opposition to the new system was most formidable and persevering.

The convention of Virginia met on the 2d of June, and the talented men of that large state were arranged on opposite sides. Patrick Henry, George Mason, William Grayson, James Munroe, and others, were in the ranks of opposition ; and they were met by Mr. Pendleton, Edmund Randolph, Mr. Madison, John Marshall, Mr. Wythe, George Nicholas, and others. The debates as given to the public, though no doubt imperfect, exhibit a display of eloquence and talents, certainly at that time, unequalled in this country

The debates, though generally courteous, were often animated, sometimes violent. Both parties were determined upon
victory. All the talents and eloquence of Patrick Henry were
exerted against a system which he deprecated.

He commenced by inquiring why the confederation had been
abandoned, and what authority the general convention had to
make a consolidated government.

"And here," said Mr. Henry, "I would make this inquiry of
those worthy characters who composed a part of the late federal
convention. I am sure they were fully impressed with the necessity of forming a *great consolidated government*, instead of a confederation. That this is a consolidated government is demon-
strably clear; and the danger of such a government is, to my
mind very striking. I have the highest veneration for those gentlemen; but, sir, give me leave to demand, what right had they
to say, *we, the people?* My political curiosity, exclusive of my
anxious solicitude for the public welfare, leads me to ask, who authorized them to speak the language of, *we, the people*, instead of,
we, the states? States are the characteristics and the soul of a
confederation. If the states be not the agents of this compact,
it must be one great consolidated government of the *people* of
all the states. I have the highest respect for those gentlemen
who formed the convention, and were not some of them here, I
would express some testimonial of esteem for them. America
had on a former occasion put the utmost confidence in them; a
confidence which was well placed: and I am sure, sir, I could
give up any thing to them; I would cheerfully confide in them
as my representatives. But, sir! on this great occasion, I would
demand the cause of their conduct. Even from that illustrious
man, who saved us by his valor, I would have a reason for his conduct—that liberty which he has given us by his valor, tells me to
ask this reason—and sure I am, were he here, he would give us
this information. The people gave them no power to use their
name. That they exceeded their power is perfectly clear. It is
not mere curiosity that actuates me—I wish to hear the real actual existing danger, which should lead us to take these steps so

dangerous in my conception. Disorders have arisen in other parts of America, but here, sir, no dangers, no insurrection or tumult has happened—every thing has been calm and tranquil. But notwithstanding this, we are wandering on the great ocean of human affairs. I see no land mark to guide us. We are running we know not whither. Difference of opinion has gone to a degree of inflammatory resentment in some parts of the country, which has been occasioned by this perilous innovation. The federal convention ought to have amended the old system—for this purpose they were solely delegated ; the object of their mission extended to no other consideration."

To this direct inquiry, Mr. Randolph, who was a member of the general convention, and who first submitted to that body, propositions for the new system, replied, by saying among other things, that " the members of the general convention were particularly deputed to meliorate the confederation. On a thorough contemplation of the subject, they found it impossible to amend that system : what was to be done ? The dangers of America, which will be shown at another time by particular enumeration, suggested the expedient of forming a *new plan ;* the confederation has done a great deal for us, we will allow, but it was the danger of a powerful enemy, and the spirit of America, sir, and not the energy of that system, that carried us through that perilous war ; for what were its best arms ? The greatest exertions were made, when the danger was most imminent. This system was not signed till March, 1781, Maryland having not acceded to it before ; yet the military achievements and other exertions of America, previous to that period, were as brilliant, as effectual, and successful as they could have been under the most energetic government. This clearly shows, that our perilous situation was the cement of our union. How different the scene, when this peril vanished and peace was restored ! The demands of congress were treated with neglect. One state complained that another had not paid its quota, as well as itself—public credit gone —for I believe were it not for the private credit of individuals, we should have been ruined long before that time. Commerce languishing—produce falling in value, and justice trampled under foot. We became contemptible in the eyes of all foreign nations; they discarded us as little wanton boys who had played for liberty, but who had not sufficient solidity or wisdom to secure it on a permanent basis, and were therefore unworthy of their regard. It was found that congress could not even enforce the observance of their own treaties. That treaty under which we enjoy our present tranquility was disregarded. Making no difference between the justice of paying debts due to people here, and that of paying those due to people on the other side of the Atlantic, I wished to see the treaty complied with, by the payment of the British debts, but have not been able to know why it has been neglected. What was the reply to the demands and requisitions of congress? You are too contemptible, we will despise and disregard you. After meeting in convention," Mr. Randolph added, "the deputies from the states communicated their information to one another; on a review of our *critical situation*, and of the *impossibility* of introducing any degree of improvement into the old system; what ought they to have done? Would it not have been treason to return without proposing some scheme to relieve their distressed country?"

The radical difference between the parties in Virginia, and in other states respecting the new system, was, that it departed from the principles of a confederacy, and constituted a consolidated national government, vested with extensive powers operating not upon the states, but upon individuals; and that the people themselves, on whom it was to operate, were not secured against the improper exercise of those powers, by a bill of rights. The loss of sovereignty and of influence, was felt by the large states; and led them to a more particular examination of the various powers transferred to the different departments of the new government.

Mr. Henry declared the new system produced " a revolution as radical as that which separated us from Great Britain. It is as radical," he added, " if in this transition, our rights and privileges are endangered, and the sovereignty of the states be relinquished: and cannot we plainly see, that this is actually the case!

The rights of conscience, trial by jury, liberty of the press, all your immunities and franchises, all pretensions to human rights and privileges are rendered insecure, if not lost by this change, so loudly talked of by some, and inconsiderately by others. Is this tame relinquishment of rights worthy of freemen? Is it worthy of that manly fortitude that ought to characterize republicans? It is said that eight states have adopted this plan. I declare that if twelve states and a half had adopted it, I would with manly firmness, and in spite of an erring world, reject it."*

Should the system go into operation, Mr. Henry asked, "what will the states have to do? Take care of the *poor*, repair and make *highways*, erect *bridges*, and so on and so on. Abolish the state legislatures at once. For what purposes should they be returned?"

A majority of the convention were in favor of very material amendments, and the question finally was whether it should be adopted *previous* or *subsequent* to such amendments.

After a debate of about twenty days, Mr. Wythe moved that the constitution be ratified, with a preamble, declaring, that the powers granted by it were the gift of the people, and that every power not granted, remained with them—that no right, therefore, of any denomination could be cancelled, abridged, restrained, or modified by congress, or any officer of the United States, except in those instances, in which power was given by the constitution for those purposes. And among other essential rights, liberty of conscience and of the press were mentioned—declaring also that any imperfections which might exist in the constitution, ought rather to be examined in the mode therein prescribed for obtaining amendments, than to bring the union in danger by a delay, with a hope of obtaining previous amendments.

On this motion the debate was renewed with increased zeal and animation. Mr. Henry in opposition to it, observed— "with respect to subsequent amendments, proposed by the wor-

* Debates of the Virginia Convention, p. 43.

thy member, I am distressed when I hear the expression. It is a new one altogether, and such as stands against every idea of fortitude and manliness in the states, or any one else. Evils admitted, in order to be removed *subsequently,* and tyranny submitted to, in order to be excluded by a *subsequent* alteration, are things totally new to me. But I am sure he meant nothing but to amuse the committee. I know his candor. His proposal is an idea dreadful to me. I ask—does experience warrant such a thing from the beginning of the world to this day ? Do you enter into a compact of government first, and afterwards settle the terms of the government ? It is admitted by every one, that this is a compact. Although the confederation be lost, it is a compact, constitution, or something of that nature. I confess I never heard of such an idea before. It is most abhorrent to my mind. You endanger the tranquility of your country—you stab its repose, if you accept this government unaltered."

In the heat of debate he added, "I cannot conclude without saying, that I shall have nothing to do with it, if subsequent amendments be determined on. Oppressions will be carried on as radically by the majority when adjustments and accommodations will be held up. I say I conceive it my duty, if this government is adopted before it is amended, to go home—I shall act as I think my duty requires—every other gentleman will do the same. Previous amendments, in my opinion, are necessary to procure peace and tranquility. I fear, if they be not agreed to, every movement and operation of government will cease, and how long that baneful thing, *civil discord*, will stay from this country, God only knows."

The language of Mr. Henry, however, at the close of this debate, and just before the final question was taken, was dispassionate and truly patriotic. "If I shall be in the minority," he said, "I shall have those painful sensations which arise from a conviction of being overpowered in a good cause. Yet I will be a peaceful citizen ! My head, my hand, and my heart shall be at liberty to retrieve the loss of liberty, and remove the defects of that system in a *constitutional way*. I wish not to go to violence

rill wait with hopes that the spirit which predominated in
evolution, is not yet gone, nor the cause of those who are at-
d to the revolution lost. I shall therefore patiently wait in
ctation of seeing that government changed so as to be com-
le with the safety, liberty, and happiness of the people."*
he object of some of its opponents was, that the states of Vir-
, North Carolina, and New York, should reject the system,
their amendments were agreed to by the other states. This
s supposed would secure the adoption of such amendments
ey required. This, on the other hand, was deemed too haz-
is an experiment ; and it was urged, that it would place the
itself in the greatest danger. To remarks of this kind Mr.
son replied—" The dangers of disunion are painted in strong
s. How is the fact ? It is this—that if Virginia thinks prop-
insist on previous amendments, joined by New York and
h Carolina, she can procure what amendments she pleases.
t is the geographical position of those states ? New York
nands the ocean. Virginia and North Carolina join the
ish dominions. What would be the situation then of the
states ? They would be *topographically* separated, though
cally united with one another. There would be no commu-
ion between the center and the component parts. While
states were thus separated, of what advantage would com-
ial regulations be to them ? Yet will gentlemen pretend to
hat we must adopt first, and then beg amendments ? I see
ason in it. We undervalue our own importance. Consider
ast consequence of Virginia and North Carolina. What
of connection would the rest of the states form ? They would
rrying states without any thing to *carry*. They would have
>mmunication with the other southern states. I therefore
, that if you are not satisfied with the paper as it stands, it is
ear to me as that the sun shines, that by joining those two
s, you may command such amendments as you think neces-
for the happiness of the people. The late convention were
mpowered totally to alter the present confederation. The

* Debates of the Virginia Convention, pp. 423, 465.

idea was to amend. If they have laid before us a thing quite different, we are not bound to accept it—there is nothing dictatorial in refusing it—we wish to remove the spirit of party. In all parts of the world there is a reciprocity in contracts and compacts. If one make a proposition to another, is he bound to receive it?

"Six or seven states have agreed to it. As it is not their interest to stand by themselves, will they not with open arms receive us? Tobacco will always make our peace with them. I hope then that the gentleman will find on reconsideration, that we are not at all in that dangerous situation he represented. In my opinion," he subjoined, "the idea of subsequent amendments is preposterous—they are words without meaning. The *little states* will not agree to an alteration. When they find themselves on an equal footing with the other states in the senate; and all power vested in them—the executive mixed with the legislative, they will never assent. *Why are such extensive powers given to the senate? Because the little states gained their point.* In every light I consider subsequent amendments as unwise and impolitic."

Speaking of the advantages Virginia was to derive from the new system, Mr. Grayson asked, "has Virginia any gain from her riches and commerce? What does she get in return? I can see what she gives up, which is immense. The little states gain in proportion as we lose. Every disproportion is against us. If the effects of such a contrariety of interests be happy, it must be extraordinary and wonderful. From the very nature of the paper, one part whose interests is different from the other, is to govern it. What will be our situation? The northern states are carrying states. We are considered as productive states. They will constantly carry for us. Are manufactures favorable to us? If they reciprocate the act of *Charles II.* and say that no produce of America shall be carried in any foreign bottom, what will be the consequence? This—that all the produce of the southern states will be carried by the northern states on their own terms; which must be very high."

The reply of Mr. Madison to the first part of this speech, no doubt produced a powerful effect in favor of Mr. Wythe's motion. He saw that the fate of the system he had been so instrumental in forming, depended on the question then to be decided. He was too well acquainted with the difficulties in the general convention, to believe that the states could ever unite in the various amendments which would be proposed.

" Nothing has excited more admiration in the world," said Mr. Madison, " than the manner in which free governments have been established in America. For it was the first instance from the creation of the world to the American revolution, that free inhabitants have been seen deliberating on a form of govnrnment, and selecting such of their citizens as possessed their confidence, to determine upon, and give effect to it. But why has this excited so much wonder and applause? Because it is of so much magnitude, and because it is liable to be frustrated by so many accidents. If it has excited so much wonder, that the United States have in the middle of war and confusion, formed free systems of government, how much more astonishment and admiration will be excited, should they be able, peaceably, freely, and satisfactorily, to establish one general government, when there is such a diversity of opinions and interests, when not cemented or stimulated by any common danger? How vast must be the difficulty of concentrating in one government the *interests*, and conciliating the *opinions* of so many different heterogeneous bodies? How have the confederacies of ancient and modern times been formed? As far as ancient history describes the former to us, they were brought about by the wisdom of some eminent sage. How was the imperfect union of the Swiss Cantons formed? By danger. How was the confederacy of the United Netherlands formed? By the same. They were surrounded by dangers. By these and one influential character, they were stimulated to unite. How was the Germanic system formed? By danger, in some degree, but principally by the over-ruling influence of individuals. When we consider this government, we ought to make great allowances. We must calculate the impossibility that every state should be gratified in its wishes, and much less that every individual should receive this gratification. It has never been denied by the friends of the paper on the table, that it has its defects. But they do not think that it contains any real danger. They conceive that they will in all probability be removed when experience will shew it to be necessary. I beg that gentlemen deliberating on this subject, would consider the alternative. Either nine states shall have ratified it or they will not. If nine states will adopt it, can it be reasonably presumed or required, that nine states having freely and fully considered the subject, and come to an affirmative decision, will, upon the demand of a single state, agree that they acted wrong, and could not see its defects—tread back the steps which they have taken, and come forward and reduce it to uncertainty, whether a general system shall be adopted or not? Virginia has always heretofore spoken the language of respect to the other states, and she has always been attended to. Will it be that language, to call on a majority of the states to acknowledge that they have done wrong? Is it the language of confidence to say, that we do not believe that amendments for the preservation of the common liberty and general interest of the states, will be consented to by them? This is neither the language of confidence nor respect. Virginia, when she speaks respectfully, will be as much attended to, as she has hitherto been, when speaking this language. It is a most awful thing that depends on our decision—no less than whether the thirteen states shall unite freely, peaceably, and unanimously, for the security of their common happiness and liberty, or whether every thing is to be put in confusion and disorder! Are we to embark in this dangerous enterprize, uniting various opinions to contrary interests, with the vain hopes of coming to an amicable concurrence?

It is worthy of our consideration, that those who prepared the paper on the table, found *difficulties not to be described, in its formation*—mutual deference and concession were absolutely necessary. Had they been inflexibly tenacious of their individual opinions, they would never have concurred. Under what circumstances was it formed? When no party was formed, or particular proposition made, and men's minds were calm and dispassionate. Yet under these circumstances, it was difficult, *extremely difficult*, to agree to any general system.

"Suppose eight states only should ratify it, and Virginia should propose certain alterations, as the previous condition of her accession. If they should be disposed to accede to her proposition, which is the most favorable conclusion, the difficulty attending it would be immense. Every state, which has decided it, must take up the subject again. They must not only have the mortification of acknowledging that they have done wrong, but the difficulty of having a re-consideration of it among the people, and appointing new conventions to deliberate upon it: They must attend to all the amendments, which may be dictated by as great a diversity of political opinions, as there are local attachments. When brought together in one assembly they must go through, and accede to every one of the amendments. The gentlemen who within this house have thought proper to propose previous amendments, have brought no less than forty amendments—a bill of rights which contains twenty amendments, and twenty other alterations, some of which are improper and inadmissible. Will not every state think herself equally entitled to propose as many amendments? And suppose them to be contradictory. I leave it to this convention, whether it be probable that they can agree, or agree to any thing but the plan on the table ; or whether greater difficulties will not be encountered, than were experienced in the progress of the formation of this constitution."

The motion of Mr. Wythe prevailed by a majority of ten, 88 to 80. In the form of ratification, after stating that every power not granted remained with the people, they added, " with these impressions, with a solemn appeal to the searcher of hearts for the purity of our intentions, and under the conviction that whatsoever imperfections may exist in the constitution, ought rather to be examined in the mode prescribed therein, than to bring the union into danger, by a delay with a hope of obtaining amendments previous to the ratification."

The convention at the same time, agreed upon a bill of rights, consisting of twenty articles, and the same number of amendments to the body of the constitution. The most important of the latter were—that congress should not lay direct taxes, until the states had refused them—that members of the senate and house should be incapable of holding *any civil office* under the authority of the United States—that no commercial treaty should be ratified without the concurrence of *two thirds* of the whole number of the members of the senate, and that no treaty ceding or suspending the territorial rights or claims of the United States, or any of them, or their rights to fishing in the American seas, or navigating the American rivers, should be but in cases of the most extreme necessity, nor should any such treaty be ratified without the concurrence of *three fourths* of the whole number of the members of both houses—that no navigation law, or law regulating commerce should be passed, without the consent of two thirds of the members present in both houses—that no person be capable of being president of the United States for more than eight years in any term of sixteen years—that the judicial power of the United States, should extend to no case, where the cause of action originated before the ratification of the constitution; except in disputes between persons claiming lands under grants of different states, and suits for debts due to the United States— that congress should not alter, modify, or interfere in the times, places, or manner of holding elections for senators or representatives, or either of them, except when the legislature of any state should neglect, refuse or be disabled by invasion or rebellion to prescribe the same—that the clauses which declare that congress should not exercise certain powers, be not interpreted to extend their powers ; but be construed as making exceptions to the specified powers, or inserted merely for greater caution—that the laws ascertaining the compensations of the members be postponed in their operation, until after the election of representatives immediately succeeding the passage of the same—that some tribunal other than the senate, be provided to try impeachment of senators.   The convention enjoined it upon their representatives in the first congress to exert all their influence to obtain a ratification of these amendments, in the manner provided by the constitution; and in all congressional acts to conform, as far as practicable, to the spirit of them.

A majority of the convention of New York, which met on the 17th of June, were strongly opposed to the new system of government. Mr. Jay, Mr. Hamilton, and Chancellor Livingston, were its principal advocates, and governor Clinton, Mr. Yates, Mr. Lansing, Mr. Duane, and Melancthon Smith, were most distinguished in the opposition. The latter gentlemen had great influence in the state ; and the accession of Virginia disappointed their expectations. Ten states had now united, and the constitution must necessarily go into operation—no alternative was, therefore, left for New York, but to unite or secede. The southern district of that state gave strong intimations of a determination to continue a part of the union. Under these circumstances, a small majority concurred with Virginia, in adopting the system, and recommending amendments. This majority was only five, and after a bill of rights and numerous amendments were agreed to, it was moved, "that there should be reserved to the state of New York, a right to *withdraw herself* from the union, after a certain number of years, unless the amendments proposed, should previously be submitted to a general convention." This motion, however, was negatived. The amendments of New York, were more numerous as well as more radical, than those of any other state. In addition to most of the Massachusetts amendments, she proposed, among others of less importance, that no persons, except natural born citizens, or such as were citizens on or before the 4th of July, 1776, or held commissions under the United States during the war, and had since July 4th, 1776, become citizens of some one of the states, should be eligible to the places of president, vice-president, or members of congress—that no standing army be kept up in time of peace, without the assent of two thirds of both houses—that congress should not declare war without the same majority—that the privilege of the writ of habeas corpus should not be suspended for a longer term than six months—that no capitation tax should ever be laid—that no person be eligible as a senator for more than six years in any term of twelve years ; and that the state legislatures might recall their senators—that no member of congress be appointed to *any office* under the authority of the United States—that the power of congress to pass laws of bankruptcy, should only extend to merchants and other traders—that no person be eligible to the office of president a third time—that the president should not command an army in the field without the previous desire of congress—that congress should not constitute any tribunals or inferior courts, with any other than *appellate jurisdiction*, except in causes of admiralty and maritime jurisdiction, and for the trial of piracies and felonies committed on the high seas; and in all other cases, to which the judicial power of the United States extended, and in which the supreme court had not original jurisdiction, the causes should be heard in the state courts, with right of appeal to the supreme or other courts of the United States—that the court for the trial of impeachments should consist of the senate, the judges of the supreme court of the United States, and the senior judge of the highest court in each state—that persons aggrieved by any judgment of the supreme court in any case in which that court had original jurisdiction, should be entitled to a review of the same by commissioners not exceeding seven, to be appointed by the president and senate—that the judicial power should extend to no controversies respecting *land*, unless relating to claims of territory or jurisdiction between states, or between individuals, or between states and individuals under grants of different states—that the militia should not be compelled to serve without the limits of the state for a longer term than *six weeks*, without the consent of the legislature thereof—and that congress should not impose *any excise* on any article, (ardent spirits excepted,) of the growth, production, or manufacture of the United States, or any of them.

To obtain these and other amendments, the convention addressed a circular letter to the governors of all the states, requesting their concurrence in calling another convention. Referring to the new system, they observed, " several articles in it, appear so exceptionable to a majority of us, that nothing but the fullest confidence of obtaining a revision of them by a general convention, and an invincible reluctance to separating from our sister states, have prevailed upon a sufficient number of us, to ratify it, without *stipulating* for *previous amendments.*"

The convention of North Carolina was in session at the same time with that of New York, and on the first of August refused their assent, until a declaration of rights, with amendments to the most *ambiguous* and *exceptionable* parts of the constitution, should be laid before congress or a convention of the states, that might be called for the purpose of amending it, for their consideration.

In this conflict of opinions respecting the new system of government, the views entertained of it by such statesmen as Mr. Adams and Mr. Jefferson, both of whom were in Europe at the time of its formation and adoption, could not fail to have had influence, nor can they now be uninteresting. The views of the latter were disclosed in his letters to his friends, written when the subject was before the state conventions. Some of these have lately been given to the public. He approved the general organization of the government, its division into three branches, and of the powers granted to each. He was particularly pleased with " the *compromise* of the opposite claims of the great and little states ; and of the mode of voting by *persons*, instead of *states.*" He also liked the negative given to the executive " conjointly with a third of either house ;" though he would have preferred to have had the judiciary associated for this purpose, or invested with separate powers.* His great objections were, the want of a *bill* of rights, and the *re-eligibility* of the president. To secure amendments calculated to remove these objections, his first wish was that *nine* states should adopt it, and four refuse their assent, until they were obtained. He afterwards, however, gave a decided preference to the mode adopted by Massachusetts. On the 28th of May, 1788, he wrote from Paris to colonel Edward

* Biography of Mr. Jefferson, vol. 7.   Signers of the Declaration of Independence, pp. 69, 70.

Carrington—" My first wish was, that nine states would adopt it in order to ensure what was good in it, and that the others might by holding off, produce the necessary amendments. But the *plan* of Massachusetts is far preferable, and will, I hope, be followed by those who are yet to decide. There are two amendments only, which I am anxious for. First, a bill of rights, which it is so much the interest of all to have, that I conceive it must be yielded. The first amendment proposed by Massachusetts will in some degree answer this end, but not so well, it will do much in some instances, and too little in others ; it will cripple the federal government in some cases where it ought to be free, and not restrain it where restraint would be right. The second amendment which appears to me essential, is the restoring the principle of necessary rotation, particularly to the senate and presidency ; but most of all to the last. Re-eligibility makes him an officer for life, and the disasters inseparable from an elective monarchy render it preferable, if we cannot tread back that step, that we should go forward and take refuge in an hereditary one."

In another of the 8th of July, he says, " the glorious example of Massachusetts, of accepting *unconditionally*, and pressing for future amendments will, I hope, reconcile all parties. The argument is unanswerable, that it will be easier to obtain amendments from nine states, under the new constitution, than from thirteen after rejecting it."*

While the Americans were about revising their forms of government, Mr. Adams, then in England, wrote his able defense of the constitutions of his country.

His principal object was to refute the erroneous opinions of Turgot and other learned men in Europe, respecting them ; particularly on the subject of the division of the powers of government. Mr. Turgot, in speaking of the new American constitutions, had declared, " that by most of them the customs of England were imitated, without any particular motive. Instead of collecting," he observed, " all authority into one *center*, *that of the nation*, they have established different bodies, a body of rep-

* North American Review for October, 1827, p. 269.

resentatives, a council, and a governor, because there is in England a house of commons, a house of lords and a king." These opinions Mr. Adams combatted with success. The Americans had indeed in their colonial state been accustomed to a division of the powers of government; and the general principle, that the legislative, executive and judicial powers should be kept distinct, had now become a part of their political creed. In framing their constitutions, however, questions arose, how far the executive power might in *particular cases* be controled by a body, constituting a part of the legislature; and on these some of the wisest politicians entertained different opinions.

Whether the senate should have a negative on presidential appointments, was a question on which the members of the general convention were much divided. This power in that body did not accord with Mr. Adams' ideas of a well balanced government.

In this he differed from some of his old friends and compatriots, whom he met in the first congress at New York, under the new constitution, in the summer of 1789. On this point as well as some others, a correspondence at that time took place between him and his friend Roger Sherman of Connecticut, who had been long engaged in political life, was one of the committee that prepared the articles of confederation, and also a member of the general convention.

The following extracts from this correspondence, showing not only the opinions of these experienced statesmen, but also, in some degree, the views of the convention on this important part of the constitution, will not, we trust, be unacceptable in this place.

To some general observations of Mr. Sherman in favor of this power in the senate, Mr. Adams made the following objections.

" The negative of the senate upon appointments," he said, " is liable to the following objections.

" 1. It takes away, or at least it lessens the responsibility of the executive—our constitution obliges me to say, that it lessens the responsibility of the president. The blame of an hasty, injudicious, weak, or wicked appointment, is shared so much between him and the senate, that his part of it will be too small. Who can censure him, without censuring the senate, and the legislatures who appoint them ? all their friends will be interested to vindicate the president, in order to screen them from censure ; besides, if an impeachment is brought before them against an officer, are they not interested to acquit him, lest some part of the odium of his guilt should fall upon them, who advised to his appointment.

" 2. It turns the minds and attention of the people to the senate, a branch of the legislature, in executive matters ; it interests another branch of the legislature in the management of the executive ; it divides the people between the executive and the senate : whereas all the people ought to be united to watch the executive, to oppose its encroachments, and resist its ambition.—Senators and representatives, and their constituents—in short the aristocratical and democratical divisions of society ought to be united, on all occasions to oppose the executive or the monarchial branch when it attempts to overleap its limits. But how can this union be effected, when the aristocratical branch has pledged its reputation to the executive by consenting to an appointment.

" 3. It has a natural tendency, to excite ambition in the senate. An active, ardent spirit, in that house, who is rich, and able, has a great reputation and influence, will be solicited by candidates for office; not to introduce the idea of bribery, because, though it certainly would force itself in, in other countries, and will probably here, when we grow populous and rich, yet it is not yet, I hope, to be dreaded. But ambition must come in, already. A senator of great influence, will be naturally ambitious and desirous of increasing his influence. Will he not be under a temptation to use his influence with the president as well as his brother senators, to appoint persons to office in the several states who will exert themselves in elections to get out his enemies or opposers both in senate and house of representatives, and to get in his friends, perhaps his instruments ? Suppose a senator, to aim at the treasury office, for himself, his brother, father, or son. Suppose him to aim at the president's chair, or vice-president, at the next election—or at the office of war, foreign or domestic affairs, will he not naturally be tempted to make use of his whole patronage, his whole influence, in advising to appointments, both with president and senators, to get such persons nominated, as will exert themselves in elections of president, vice-president, senators, and house of representatives, to increase his interest and promote his views. In this point of view, I am very apprehensive that this defect in our constitution, will have an unhappy tendency to introduce corruption of the grossest kinds, both of ambition and avarice, into all our elections. And this will be the worst of poisons to our constitution ; it will not only destroy the present form of government, but render it almost impossible to substitute in its place any free government, even a better limited monarchy, or any other than a despotism or a simple monarchy.

" 4. To avoid the evil under the last head, it will be in danger of dividing the continent into two or three nations, a case that presents no prospect but of perpetual war.

" 5. This negative on appointments, is in danger of involving the senate in reproach, obloquy, censure, and suspicion, without doing any good. Will the senate use their negative or not—if not ; why should they have it—many will censure them for not using it—many will ridicule them, call them servile, &c., if they do use it. The very first instance of it, will expose the senators to the resentment not only of the disappointed candidate and all his friends, but of the president and all his friends ; and those will be most of the officers of government, through the nation.

" 6. We shall very soon have parties formed—a court and country party—and these parties will have names given them, one party in the house of representatives will support the president and his measures and ministers—the other will oppose them—a similar party will be in the senate—these parties will struggle with all their art, perhaps with intrigue, perhaps with corruption at every election to increase their own friends and diminish their opposers. Suppose such parties formed in senate, and then consider what factions, divisions, we shall have there, upon every nomination.

" 7. The senate have not time. You are of opinion "that the concurrence of the senate in the appointment to office, will strengthen the hands of the executive, and secure the confidence of the people, much better than a select council, and will be less expensive," but in every one of these ideas, I have the misfortune to differ from you. It will weaken the hands of the executive, by lessening the obligation, gratitude, and attachment of the candidate to the president, by dividing his attachment between the executive and legislature which are natural enemies.

" Officers of government, instead of having a single eye and undivided attachment to the executive branch, as they ought to have, consistent with law and the constitution, will be constantly tempted to be factious with their factious patrons in the senate. The president's own officers in a thousand instances will oppose his just and constitutional exertions, and screen themselves under the wings of their patrons and party in the legislature. Nor will it secure the confidence of the people ; the people will have more confidence in the executive, in executive matters, than in the senate. The people will be constantly jealous of factious schemes in the senators to unduly influence the executive, and of corrupt bargains between the senate and executive, to serve each others private views. The people will also be jealous that the influence of the senate will be employed to conceal, connive, and defend guilt in executive officers, instead of being a guard and watch upon them, and a terror to them—a council selected by the president himself at his pleasure, from among the senators, representatives, and nation at large, would be purely responsible—in that case, the senate as a body would not be compromised. The senate would be a terror to privy councillors—its honor would never be pledged to support any measure or instrument of the executive, beyond justice, law, and the constitution. Nor would a privy council be more expensive. The whole senate must now deliberate on every appointment, and, if they ever find time for it, you will find that a great deal of time will be required and consumed in this service. Then the president might have a constant executive council ; now he has none.

" I said under the seventh head that the senate would not have time. You will find that the whole business of this government will be infinitely delayed, by this negative of the senate on treaties and appointments. Indian treaties and consular conventions have been already waiting for months, and the senate have not been able to find a moment of time to attend to them ; and this evil must constantly increase, so that the senate must be constantly sitting, and must be paid as long as they sit.

" But I have tired your patience. Is there any truth or importance in these broken hints and crude surmises or not ? To me they appear well founded and very important."

To these remarks Mr. Sherman replied, that he esteemed " the provision made for appointments to office, to be a matter of very great importance, on which the liberties and safety of the people depended, nearly as much as on legislation. If that was vested in the president alone he might render himself despotic. It was a saying of one of the kings of England, ' *that while the king could appoint the bishops and judges, he might have what religion and laws he pleased.*' To give that observation its full effect, they must hold their offices during his pleasure ; by such appointments without control, a' power might be gradually established, that would be more formidable than a standing army.

" It appears to me that the senate is the most important branch in the government, for the aid and support of the executive, for securing the rights of the individual states, the government of the United States and the liberties of the people. The executive is not to execute its own will, but the will of the legislature declared by the laws, and the senate being a branch of the legislature, will be disposed to accomplish that end ; and advise to such appointments as will be most likely to effect it; from their knowledge of the people in the several states, they can give the best information who are qualified for office. And they will, as you justly observe, in some degree lessen his responsibility, yet will he not have as much remaining as he can well support? and may not their advice enable him to make such judicious appointments as to render responsibility less necessary ? no person can deserve censure when he acts honestly according to his best discretion.

" The senators being chosen by the legislatures of the states, and depending on them for re-election, will naturally be watchful to prevent any infringement of the rights of the states. And the government of the United States being federal, and instituted by a number of sovereign states for the better security of their rights, and advancement of their interests, they may be considered as so many pillars to support it, and by the exercise of the state governments, peace and good order may be preserved in the places most remote from the seat of the federal government as well as at the centre.

" I believe this will be a better balance to secure the government, than three independent negatives would be.

" I think you admit in your defense of the governments of the United States, that even one branch might serve in a diplomatic government like that of the union ; but I think the constitution is much improved by the addition of another branch, and those of the executive and judiciary. This seems to be an improvement on federal government beyond what has been made by any other states. I can see nothing in the constitution that will tend to its dissolution except the article for making amendments.

" That the evils that you suggest may happen in consequence of the power vested in the senate to aid the executive, appear to me to be but barely possible. The senators, from the provision made for their appointment, will commonly be some of the most respectable citizens in the states for wisdom and probity, and superior to faction, intrigue, or low artifice, to obtain appointments for themselves or their friends, and any attempts of that kind would destroy their reputation with a free and enlightened people, and so frustrate the end they would have in view. Their being candidates for re-election, will probably be one of the most powerful motives (next to that of their virtue) to fidelity in office, and by that mean alone would they hope for success. ' He that walketh uprightly, walketh surely,' is the saying of a divinely inspired writer—they will naturally have the confidence of the people, as they will be chosen by their immediate representatives, as well as from their characters, as men of wisdom and integrity. And I see not why all the branches of government should not harmonize in promoting the great end of their institution, the good and happiness of the people.

" The senators and representatives being eligible from the citizens at large, and wealth not being a requisite qualification for either, they will be persons nearly equal as to wealth and other qualifications, so that there seems not to be any principle tending to aristocracy ; which, if I understand the term, is a government by nobles, independent of the people, which cannot take place with us in either respect, without a total subversion of the constitution. I believe the more this provision of the constitution is attended to and experienced, the more the wisdom and utility of it will appear. As senators cannot hold any other office themselves, they will not be influenced in their advice to the president by interested motives. But it is said they may have friends and kindred to provide for ; it is true they may, but when we consider their character and situation, will they not be diffident of nominating a friend or relative who may wish for an office and be well qualified for it, lest it should be suspected to proceed from partiality ? And will not their fellow members have a degree of the same reluctance, lest it should be thought they acted from friendship to a member of their body ? so that their friends and connections would stand a worse chance, in proportion to their real merit, than strangers. But if the president was left to select a council for himself, though he may be supposed to be actuated by the best motives—yet he would be surrounded by flatterers, who would assume the character of friends and patriots, though they had no attachment to the public good, no regard to the laws of their country, but influenced wholly by self interest, would wish to extend the power of the executive in order to increase their own ; they would often advise him to dispense with laws that should thwart their schemes, and in excuse plead that it was done from necessity to promote the public good—they will use their own influence, induce the president to use his to get laws repealed, or the constitution altered to extend his powers and prerogatives, under pretext of advancing the public good, and gradually render the government a despotism. This seems to be according to the course of human affairs, and what may be expected from the nature of things. I think that members of the legislature would be most likely duly to execute the laws both in the executive and judiciary departments."*

The ratification of the constitution by the state of New Hampshire, being the ninth in order, was laid before congress, on the 2d of July, 1788, and with the ratifications of the other states, referred to a committee, to report an act for carrying the new system into operation. An act for this purpose was reported on the 14th of the same month, but in consequence of a division as to the place where the first congress should meet, did not pass until the 13th of September following. By this act, the electors of president were to be appointed on the first Wednesday of January, 1787, and to give in their votes on the first Wednesday of the succeeding February ; the first Wednesday of March, being the 4th day of that month, was fixed as the *time*, and the city of New York, as the *place* for commencing proceedings under the new constitution.

Before noticing these proceedings, we shall give a brief view of the state constitutions.

* MSS Letters.

CHAPTER XIX.

States institute forms of government agreeably to the advice of congress—States of Connecticut and Rhode Island proceed according to their charters—Massachusetts at first conform to their charter as far as practicable—New Hampshire, South Carolina, Virginia, New Jersey, Pennsylvania, Delaware, Maryland, and North Carolina, establish new governments in the course of the year 1776---Those of New Hampshire, South Carolina, and New Jersey, limited to the continuance of the disputes with Great Britain---General principles and outlines of these constitutions---New York establishes a government in 1777---Its general features---Constitution of Massachusetts not finally completed until 1780---Vermont not a part of the union until 1791---Claimed by New York and New Hampshire--Declares independence in 1777---Outlines of her constitution, formed in 1786---Constitution of Georgia as established in 1789---After the formation and adoption of the general government, principles of making constitutions better understood—Pennsylvania, New Hampshire, South Carolina, and Delaware, revise and alter their systems of government.

It will be remembered that on the 10th of May, 1776, congress recommended to the assemblies and conventions of the several colonies where no governments sufficient to the exigences of their affairs had been established, to adopt such systems, as, in the opinion of the representatives of the people would best conduce to the happiness and safety of their constituents in particular, and America in general.

The difficulties in forming state governments or constitutions, were much less than in forming a system, embracing all the states. The people had long been familiar with the civil institutions of their respective states, and could with comparative ease make uch alterations, as would suit their new political situation. The eople of the states of Connecticut and Rhode Island, as we have afore noticed in our colonial summary, had from their first settlement, chosen all their rulers, and'in these states, a change of rms was only requisite.

Massachusetts, after the alteration of her charter by parliament, agreeably to the advice of congress, continued her old system, as r as practicable, until she was able and had leisure to form a new and more permanent one.   From the peculiar situation of New Hampshire, South Carolina, and Virginia, congress in the latter part of the year 1775, recommended to them, if they judged it necessary for their peace and security, to establish governments to continue during the disputes with Great Britain.   In pursuance of these recommendations, the states of New Hampshire, South Carolina, Virginia, New Jersey, Pennsylvania, Delaware, Mary-land, and North Carolina, during the year 1776, established new systems of government.   Those of New Hampshire, South Car-olina, New Jersey and Virginia were adopted before the final declaration of independence, and with the exception of that of Virginia, were expressly limited in their duration to the contin-uance of the dispute between the colonies and Great Britain.

We would here observe, that in all the constitutions thus form-ed, except that of Pennsylvania, the legislative power was vested in two branches, each having a negative.

The constitution of New Hampshire was comprised in a few short paragraphs.   In January, 1776, the representatives who had met in a provincial congress, assumed the name, power and authority of a house of representatives or an assembly of the col-ony of New Hampshire ; and *as a house* proceeded to elect twelve persons from the several counties, who were to constitute a distinct and separate branch of the legislature, by the name of a council, to continue until the third Wednesday of December then next, seven to be a quorum to do business.   The council to appoint their president ; and no act or resolve was to be valid or put in execution, unless passed by both branches—all public officers, with the exception of clerks of courts, to be appointed by the council and assembly—and all money bills to originate in the house.   Should the disputes with Great Britain continue longer than the year 1776, and the general congress should give no instructions to the contrary, it was provided, that the council be chosen by the people in each county, in such manner as the council and house should order—all general and field officers of the militia, in case of vacancy, and all officers of the army to be appointed by the two houses; but in case of emergency, the officers of the army might be appointed otherwise, as the houses should direct—all civil officers, with the exception of some of minor importance, were also to be chosen by the legislature, and all writs of election to be issued in the name of the council and assembly, signed by the president and speaker.

This form of goverment, imperfect as it was, continued through the war of the revolution, and until the year 1792, when a new constitution was substituted, similar to that which had been established in Massachusetts.

In February, 1776, the provincial congress of South Carolina, chose a committee of eleven, " to prepare and report a plan or form of government, as would best promote the happiness of the people, and would most effectually secure peace and good order in the colony, during the continuance of the dispute between Great Britain and the colonies."*

On the 5th of March, this committee reported a plan of civil government, which was under consideration until the 24th, when it was adopted.

While this important subject was under debate, the prohibitory act of parliament of the December preceding arrived, and in a great measure silenced opposition.

This congress, like that of New Hampshire, resolved itself into a " general assembly," to continue until the 21st of October of the same year.

The general assembly, from their own body, elected by ballot, a legislative council, to consist of thirteen members, to continue for the same period—the council and assembly were jointly to elect a president, and commander in chief, and a vice-president; and the legislative authority was vested in the president, the general assembly and legislative council—all money bills to originate in the assembly, and could not be amended or altered by the

* The committee were Charles Cotesworth Pinckney, John Rutledge, Charles Pinckney, Henry Laurens, Christopher Gadsden, Rawlins Lowndes, Arthur Middleton, Henry Middleton, Thomas Bee, Thomas Lynch, Jun. and Thomas Hayward, Jun.—*Drayton's Memoirs of the American Revolution in South Carolina, vol. 2, p. 174.*

council, and all bills having passed both houses, were to receive the assent of the president.

The president, however, had no power to adjourn, prorogue, or dissolve the council and assembly, but might convene them, if necessary, before the time to which they had adjourned.

A privy council was to be formed, to consist of the vice-president, and six others, three chosen by the assembly, and three by the legislative council; but no officer in the service of the united colonies or that of South Carolina, to be eligible as a member. This council was to advise the president when required, but he was not bound to consult them, except in particular cases.

The members of the assembly were to be chosen by the people, after October, 1776, for two years; and the president and vice-president were still to be chosen by the assembly and council.

The executive authority was vested in the president, with the limitations specified in the constitution.

Justices of the peace were to be nominated by the general assembly, and commissioned by the president, during good behavior; all other judicial officers to be elected by the assembly and legislative council, and to receive their commissions from the president, and to hold their offices during good behavior, subject to be removed, on the address of both houses. Sheriffs, commissioners of the treasury, the secretary of the colony, register of mesne conveyances, attorney general, and powder receiver, also to be chosen by joint ballot of the two houses, the sheriffs to continue for two years only, and the others during good behavior.

All field officers in the army and captains in the navy, to be appointed by the legislature, and all other officers either in the army or navy by the president; and the president, with the advice and consent of the privy council, was to fill all vacancies until an election by the legislature. The president was not to make war or peace, or enter into any final treaty, without the assent of the general assembly and legislative council.

This form of government remained until June, 1790, when a new constitution was formed by a convention called for that purpose. The legislative authority of that state, was now vested in a general assembly, consisted of a house of representatives and senate. The members of the house were chosen for two years from certain districts, and the senators from the same districts.

The senate was chosen for four years, and divided into two classes, the seats of the first class to be vacated at the end of two, and of the second at the end of four years.

The executive authority was lodged in a governor, to be chosen once in two years, by joint ballot of both houses. No person was eligible to the office of governor, unless he had attained the age of thirty, had resided in and been a citizen of the state ten years, and possessed of a settled estate in the same, in his own right, of the value of fifteen hundred pounds sterling clear of debt; nor could any person, having served two years as governor, be re-elected, till after the expiration of four years. A lieutenant governor was to be chosen at the same time, and in the same manner, and have the same qualifications as the governor. The governor was commander in chief of the army and navy, and of the militia—had power to grant pardons and reprieves,—was to take care that the laws be faithfully executed, and had power to prohibit the exportation of provisions, for any time not exceeding thirty days—to convene the assembly on extraordinary occasions, and to recommend to their consideration such measures as he should judge necessary.

The judges of the supreme court, commissioners of the treasury, secretary of state, and surveyor general, were to be elected by the joint ballot of both houses—the judges of the superior and inferior courts to hold their offices during good behavior—the commissioners of the treasury, secretary of state, and surveyor general, to continue in office for four years only, and to be ineligible for the same period. The qualifications of an elector, a freehold of fifty acres of land, or a town lot, of which he had been legally seized and possessed six months, or not having a freehold or town lot, a residence of six months, and the payment of a tax of three shillings sterling, the preceding year, towards the support of government. The free exercise and enjoyment of religious profession and worship without discrimination or preference, was to be allowed to all—but no minister of the gospel, or public preacher of any religious profession, was eligible to the office of governor, lieutenant governor, or to a seat in either house of assembly.

The convention of Virginia, on the 15th of May, 1776, appointed a committee to prepare a declaration of rights, and a plan of government calculated " to maintain peace and order in that colony, and secure substantial and equal liberty to the people." A declaration of rights was reported and agreed to on the 12th of June following, and on the 29th of the same month a constitution was unanimously adopted by the convention without any limitation as to time. The preliminary declaration not only contained an enumeration of rights, but also the fundamental principles on which a constitution should be founded. It asserted, among other things, that all men were born equally free and independent, and had certain important and natural rights, of which they could not, by any compact, deprive or divest their posterity ; that among these was the enjoyment of life and liberty, with the means of acquiring and possessing property, and pursuing and obtaining happiness and safety—That all power was vested in and derived from the people, that magistrates were their trustees and servants, and at all times amenable to them.— That government was, or ought to be, instituted for the common benefit, protection and security of the people, nation, or community, and that form the best, which was capable of producing the greatest degree of happiness and safety, and most effectually secured against the danger of mal-administration ; and that a majority of the community had an indubitable, unalienable and indefeasible right to reform, alter or abolish it, in such manner as should be judged most conducive to the public weal.

After declaring that the legislative, executive and judiciary departments should be separate and distinct, the constitution divided the legislative department into two branches, the house of delegates and senate, to be called *the general assembly of Virginia.* The house of delegates to consist of two representatives, to be chosen from each county, annually, one from the city of

Williamsburgh, and one from the borough of Norfolk. The senate to consist of twenty four members, chosen from as many districts; which districts were to be divided into four classes by lot; and at the end of the first year, the members from the first class to be displaced, and the vacancies supplied by others from the same class, and so on in rotation through each class. All laws were to *originate* in the *house of delegates*, to be approved, rejected or amended by the senate; but money bills were not subject to any *alteration*.

A governor and council of state were chosen annually by joint ballot of both houses, but no person was to continue in the office of governor more than three years in succession, nor be eligible, until the expiration of four years after he should be out of office. The governor, with the advice of the council of state, was " to exercise the executive powers of government, according to the laws of the commonwealth, and was not, under any pretence, to exercise any power or prerogative, by virtue of any law, statute or custom of England." The council of state consisted of eight members, and out of their number was annually to choose a president. Two members of the council were to be removed and their vacancies supplied by the joint ballots of both houses, at the end of every three years, and those so removed to be ineligible for the next three years. The powers of the governor and council were very limited, though in general terms constituted the executive department of the government, and vested with executive powers. The legislature appointed the judges of the supreme court of appeals, and general court, judges in chancery, judges in admiralty, secretary, and attorney general, to be commissioned by the governor, and to continue in office during good behavior. The governor and council, in the first instance appointed justices of the peace for the counties, but in case of vacancies, or increase of numbers afterwards, the appointments were to be made on recommendation of the county courts. They also had power to grant reprieves or pardons, to embody the militia, and to direct them when embodied—to supply vacancies occasioned by death, incapacity or resignation, by appointments to be approved or rejected by the legislature. The governor and other officers were made liable to impeachment when out of office, for mal-administration, corruption or other means by which the safety of the state might be endangered.

Sheriffs and coroners were to be appointed by the courts, subject to the approbation of the governor and council.

The qualification of an elector was to continue the same, as then provided by law. This was, as is understood, a freehold of fifty acres of land, or a town lot.

The people of Virginia had always claimed that the charters of Maryland, Pennsylvania, and North and South Carolina, had taken part of the territories originally granted to them. To quiet the inhabitants of the latter states on this subject, the Virginia constitution specially declared, that the territories within the charters, creating those colonies, " were ceded, released, and forever confirmed to the people of those states, with all the rights of property, jurisdiction, and government, which might, at any time before, have been claimed by Virginia, with the exception of the free navigation and use of the rivers Potomac and Pokomoke, with the property of the Virginia shores and strands, bordering on those rivers. The western and northern extent of Virginia was, in all other respects, to stand as fixed by the charter of king James I, in 1609, and by the treaty of peace in 1763 ; unless by acts of the legislature, one or two governments should be established, west of the Allegany mountains."

It is not a little extraordinary, that this form of government has ever since remained the constitution of so large a state as Virginia, without any of those amendments, which experience has proved necessary in most of the other states.

The government of New Jersey, as established by a provincial congress, on the 2d of July, 1776, was vested in a governor, legislative council, and general assembly. The council was to consist of one person, and the assembly of three persons from each county, both to be chosen annually ; but the legislature at any time thereafter, had power to apportion the members of the *assembly* among the counties, provided the number should be never less than thirty-nine.

The council and assembly annually by joint ballot elected a governor ; who was to be president of the council. The governor was vested with the supreme executive power, was *ex officio* chancellor, acted as captain general and commander of the militia and other military force, and was the *ordinary* or *surrogate general*. Any three of the council to be a privy council, whom the governor might consult. The governor and council were also a court of appeals in the last resort.

The judges of the supreme court were to continue in office *seven* years, and the judges of the courts of common pleas in the several counties, justices of the peace, clerks of the supreme court and of the common pleas and quarter sessions, the attorney general and secretary, to hold their offices *five* years, and all of them to be appointed by the legislature, and commissioned by the governor. Sheriffs and coroners to be elected annually by the people in each county, and no person to be sheriff for a longer term than three years in succession, and not again to be eligible until after the lapse of three years. The qualification of an elector, was fifty pounds proclamation money, that of a senator one thousand, and of a member of assembly five hundred pounds of the same money.

No person was to be deprived of the privilege of worshipping God, according to the dictates of his conscience ; or be compelled to attend any place of public worship, contrary to his own faith and judgment, or obliged to pay taxes for building churches or maintenance of ministers contrary to what he believed to be right, or had voluntarily engaged to perform. No religious sect was to have preference to another, and no *protestant* inhabitant was to be denied the enjoyment of any civil rights on account of his religious principles ; but all persons professing a belief in the faith of any protestant sect, demeaning themselves peaceably, were capable of being elected to office and enjoying equal privileges and immunities with others.

The form of government established by Maryland, contained some features different from that of any other state ; particularly with respect to the mode of electing and continuing senators.

The house of delegates consisted of four persons chosen annually from each county, and two from the city of Annapolis, and two from Baltimore; and each must have real or personal property of the value of five hundred pounds current money.

The senators were to be chosen every five years by two electors from every county, and one from Annapolis, and one from Baltimore. These electors were to be chosen in the respective counties every five years; and were to meet and choose by ballot, fifteen senators, *nine* of whom to be resident on the western, and *six* on the eastern shore of the bay of Chesapeake, and each to have real and personal property above the value of one thousand pounds.

After the election and during the five years, the senators were to fill all vacancies in their body, occasioned by refusal, death, resignation, or otherwise.

The senate was not permitted to *amend* or *alter* any money bill; but to prevent the house from taking any improper advantage of this, the constitution expressly provided that the house should not annex to any money bill, any matter or thing, not immediately relating to, and necessary for the imposing and levying taxes or supplies, to be raised for the support of government. The two houses were annually to elect by joint ballot a governor, who must have real and personal property, above the value of five thousand pounds, (one thousand to be freehold estate.) They were, also, annually to elect five persons to be a council to the governor, each to have a freehold in lands and tenements, above the value of one thousand pounds. The governor was to preside in the council, and the members to fill vacancies in their body, during the year.

The governor was not to continue in office longer than three years in succession, nor be eligible until the expiration of four years, after he had been out of office. The governor and council constituted the executive. The chancellor, all judges, the attorney general, clerks of the general court, and of the county courts, registers of the land office, and registers of wills, held their commissions during good behavior, removeable for misbehavior, on conviction in a court of law ; and the chancellor and judges, were removeable by the governor, on the address of two thirds of both houses of the general assembly.

The governor, with the advice and consent of the council, appointed the chancellor, all judges and justices, the attorney general, naval officers, officers of the regular land and sea service, officers of the militia, registers of the land office, surveyors, and all other civil officers of government, with the exception of some of minor importance. The civil officers not holding their offices during good behavior, to be appointed annually. A court of appeals was to be constituted, composed of persons of integrity and sound judgment, to decide in the last resort, in all cases of appeal from the general court, court of chancery, and court of admiralty.

The qualification of an elector was a freehold estate of fifty acres of land in the county ; or property in the state above the value of thirty pounds, and residence. Every governor, senator, delegate to congress or assembly, and every member of the council, was to take an oath, " that he would not receive, directly or indirectly, at any time, any part of the profits of any office, held by any other person, during his office of, &c., or of the profits or any part of the profits, arising from any agency for the supply of clothing or provisions for the army or navy."

This form of government was preceded by a declaration of rights, consisting of forty-two articles. The thirty-third declares, that " all persons professing the christian religion are equally entitled to protection in their religious liberty ; and that no person ought by any law, to be molested in his person or estate, on account of his religious persuasion or profession, or for his religious practice ;" and that no person ought to be compelled " to frequent or maintain, or contribute, unless on contract, to maintain any particular place of worship, or any particular ministry ; yet the legislature may, in their discretion, lay a general tax, for the support of the christian religion ; leaving to each individual the power of appointing the payment over of the money collected from him, to the support of any place of worship or minister, or for the benefit of the poor of his own denomination, or the poor in general of any particular parish ; but that the churches, chapels, glebes, and all other property now belonging to the church of England, ought to remain to the church of England forever." And by the thirty-fourth article, every gift, sale, or devise of lands, and every gift or sale of goods or chattels, to any minister or preacher of the gospel, as such, or to any religious sect for the use or support of such minister, without leave of the legislature, is declared void, except land not exceeding two acres, for a church or other house of worship, and for a burying ground.

This constitution of Maryland, has remained until this time, without any alteration in its general principles, except making a residence of twelve months a qualification of an elector.

The three counties of Newcastle, Kent, and Sussex, upon Delaware, (originally belonging to the proprietors of Pennsylvania,) in September, 1776, by the act of their inhabitants, became a new state, by the name of Delaware. The representatives of the people, at the same time, formed a new system of government, similar in its general principles, to those previously established in other states. The house of assembly consisted of seven representatives from each of the three counties ; and the other branch of the legislature, called the council, of three persons chosen from each county. At the end of one year, after the first election, the seat of the councillor who had the smallest number of votes in each county, was to be vacated, and his place supplied by a new choice, and at the end of the second year, the councillor who stood second in number of votes retired, and at the end of the third year, the seat of the third was vacated, and supplied, and this rotation afterwards continued.

A president was chosen by joint ballot of both houses, for three years, and at the end of that term, was not eligible until the expiration of three years. The president had a privy council of four persons, two chosen by each house, two to be removed, one by the assembly and one by the council, at the end of two years, and the other two at the end of the next year after. The president and privy council had little executive power. The president and the general assembly had the appointment of all the judges and other principal officers, by joint ballot—the judges to hold their offices during good behavior. All persons professing the christian religion were to be entitled to equal privileges, no preference of one religious sect to another to be given, and no clergyman or preacher of the gospel, was to hold any office, or be a member of either branch of the legislature.

The frame of government established by Pennsylvania, in September, 1776, bore a strong resemblance to the proprietary system, the principal features of which were stated in our colonial summary. The supreme legislative power was vested in a single body, consisting of the representatives of the freemen— and the supreme executive power in a president and council. The representatives, who were to constitute the general assembly, were chosen from the cities and counties, in proportion to the number of *taxable* inhabitants ; a return of which was to be made once in seven years. The executive council consisted of twelve persons, one chosen from the city of Philadelphia, and one from each of the three adjoining counties, to continue in office three years—one from each of four other counties particularly named, to continue two years—and one from each of the four remaining counties, for one year ; and as their terms of service expired, their places to be supplied by new elections. A president and vice-president were to be elected annually by joint ballot of the assembly and council, and to be from among the members of the council. That laws, before they were enacted, might " be more maturely considered, and the inconvenience of hasty determinations as much as possible prevented," the constitution provided, " that all bills of a public nature, should be printed for the consideration of the people, before they are read in general assembly the last time for debate and amendment ; and except on occasions of sudden necessity, shall not be passed into laws until the next session of assembly ; and for the more perfect satisfaction of the public, the reasons and motives for making such laws shall be fully and clearly expressed in the preambles."

The judges of the supreme court were to hold their offices for seven years, removable for misbehavior by the general assembly —justices of the peace to be chosen by the freeholders of each city and county, two or more from certain districts to be ascertained by law, and presented to the president in council, who was to select and grant commissions to one or more, for seven years; but they were removable in the same manner as the judges of the supreme court. The freemen in each city and county were to elect two persons annually, to the offices of sheriff and coroner, and one was to be commissioned by the president for each office. The people of Pennsylvania were not inattentive to the important subject of education. One ar-article of the constitution made it the duty of the legislature to establish *schools* in each county for the instruction of youth, " with such salaries to the masters, paid by the public, as may enable them to instruct youth at low prices." The same article also declared, that all useful learning should be duly encouraged and promoted in one or more universities.

The constitution of this state contained one provision entirely new. Every seven years two persons from each county, were to be chosen, to constitute a council of *censors*. It was made the duty of this council, to inquire whether the constitution had been preserved inviolate in every part—whether the legislative and executive branches of the government had performed their duty as guardians of the people, or assumed or exercised greater powers than they were entitled to—whether the public taxes had been justly laid and collected, and whether the laws had been faithfully executed. For these purposes they had power to send for persons and papers; and they were authorized to pass *censures*, to order *impeachments*, to recommend the repealing such laws as appeared to them contrary to the principles of the constitution, and also to call a convention. The powers of the censors were to continue one year. On the subject of religious liberty, the bill of rights declared, that all men had a natural and inalienable right to worship Almighty God according to the dictates of their own consciences and understandings; and

member of the house, one hundred acres for six months. No person who denied the being of a God, or the truth of the protestant religion, or the divine authority of the old or new testament, or who should hold religious principles incompatible with the freedom and safety of the state, was capable of holding any office, or place of trust or profit in the civil departments. The constitution provided there should be no establishment of any one religious church or denomination in preference to another—it also made it the duty of the legislature to establish schools for the convenient instruction of youth, with such salaries to the masters, paid by the public, as that they might instruct at a low price ; and all useful learning was to be duly encouraged and promoted, in one or more universities.

On the 31st of May, 1776, the members of the convention of New York recommended to the electors of that state to authorize them, or such others as they might depute, to take into consideration the necessity and propriety of instituting a new system of government, agreeably to the advice of the general congress; and to direct that the representatives of a majority of the counties, if they should judge it necessary, should establish such government. New representatives were elected and met on the 9th of July, and assumed the name of *the convention of the representatives of the state of New York.*

The subject of forming a new government was postponed to the first of August, and in the mean time, all magistrates were directed to continue the exercise of their functions, and all processes were ordered to issue in the name of the people.

On the first of August a committee was appointed " to take into consideration and report a plan for instituting and framing a form of government, and to prepare and report at the same time, a bill ascertaining and declaring the essential rights and privileges of the good people of that state, as the foundation for such government."[*]

---

[*] Immediately after the battle at Lexington, for the purpose of securing their rights and preserving peace and order, associations were signed by the people of New York in the several counties, in the following form :—

" A general association, agreed to and subscribed by the freeholders and inhabitants

Mr. Jay was placed at the head of this committee. In April, 1777, the convention completed and established a constitution, in many respects more perfect than any previously instituted by any state.

The members of the assembly were distributed among the counties, and were to vary according to the number of electors in each ; the number to be ascertained every seven years. The senate consisted of twenty four persons, to be chosen by the people for *four* years, and were divided into four classes, the seats of each class to be vacated at the end of each of the four years. For the choice of senators the state was divided into four great districts and the number assigned to each, to be afterwards varied in a certain ratio, according to the number of electors. The number of senators was never to exceed one hundred, nor the number of the assembly three hundred. The executive authority was vested in a governor, elected by the people once in three years. A lieutenant governor was also to be chosen for the same period, who was to preside in the senate. A council of *revision* and a council of *appointment* were established. The former, consisting of the governor, chancellor and judges of the supreme court, was to *revise* all bills about to be passed into laws by the legislature. These bills were to be presented to this coun-

of the county of * * Persuaded that the salvation of the rights and liberties of America depends, under God, on the firm union of its inhabitants, in a vigorous prosecution of the measures necessary for its safety ; convinced of the necessity of preventing the anarchy and confusion which attend a dissolution of the powers of government : We the freemen, freeholders and inhabitants of the county of * . * being greatly alarmed at the avowed design of the ministry to raise a revenue in America, and shocked by the bloody scene now acting in Massachusetts Bay—do, in the most solemn manner resolve never to become slaves ; and do associate, under all the ties of religion, honor and love to our country, to adopt and endeavor to carry into execution whatever measures may be recommended by the continental congress, or resolved upon by our provincial convention, for the purpose of preserving our constitution and opposing the execution of the several arbitrary and oppressive acts of the British parliament, until a reconciliation between Great Britain and America, on constitutional principles (which we most earnestly desire) can be obtained---and that we will, in all things follow the advice of our general committee, respecting the purposes aforesaid, the preservation of *peace* and *good order*, and the safety of individuals and private property.----*State papers in the office of the secretary of the state of New York.*

cil for their consideration; and if a majority thought it improper
the bills should become laws, they were to return them to the
legislature with their objections in writing; and unless repassed
by two thirds of both houses, the same were rejected. Four senators, one from each of the senatorial districts, were annually to
be appointed by the assembly, who with the governor, as president,
were to constitute a council for the appointment of officers.

The chancellor, the judges of the supreme court, and the first
judges of the county court, were to hold their offices during good
behavior. The president of the senate, the senators, the chancellor and judges of the supreme court were constituted a court for
the trial of impeachments and for the correction of errors—the
chancellor, and judges in cases of error brought from their decisions, might give their reasons but not their votes.

An elector of members of the assembly, must possess a freehold estate of the value of twenty pounds, or have rented a tena-
ment of the yearly value of forty shillings, and been rated and
actually paid taxes to the state. No persons but those possessed
of a freehold estate of the value of one hundred pounds over
and above all debts charged on the same, could vote for senators
or governor.

The free exercise and enjoyment of religious profession and
worship, without discrimination or preference, was allowed to all
—but no minister of the gospel, or priest of any denomination
whatsoever, was capable of holding any civil or military office or
place.*

The people of Massachusetts did not form a constitution until
1780. A convention for that purpose met in September, 1779,
and was continued by adjournments till March following, when a
frame of government was submitted to the consideration of the
people, and adopted by a large majority.

* This constitution was amended in 1801, by providing that the members of the
assembly should be one hundred, and never exceed one hundred and fifty, and that
the number of senators should be thirty two. The council of appointment has lately
been abolished, and executive appointments vested in the governor and senate, and
the qualifications of electors have been varied, and placed upon an equal footing.

It was more perfect, than any previously established. It commenced with a preamble, declaring, that the end of the institution, maintenance and administration of government was to secure the existence of the body politic, to protect it, and to furnish the individuals who composed it, with the power of enjoying in safety and tranquility their natural rights and the blessings of life ; and that when these objects were not obtained, the people had a right to alter it—that the body politic was formed by a voluntary association of individuals—was a social compact, by which the whole people covenanted with each citizen, and each citizen with the whole people, that all should be governed by certain laws for the common good. With these views and principles, the people of Massachusetts solemnly formed themselves " into a free, sovereign, and independent body politic and state by the name of the Commonwealth of Massachusetts."*

It was preceded by a bill of rights, containing thirty articles, the last of which declared, that the government should be divided into three departments, legislative, executive, and judicial, neither to exercise the powers of the other.

The legislative department, consisting of a senate and house of representatives, was styled the *general court* of Massachusetts ; a name given to the legislature in the first settlement of the colony.

The senate was composed of forty persons chosen annually, from certain districts, into which the state from time to time was to be divided by the general court. In the formation of these districts, a new principle was established. In assigning the number of senators to each, the general court was to be governed by the proportion of the *public taxes* paid by them ; but the number of districts was never to be less than thirteen, nor was any district to have more than six senators. The representatives were elected annually from the towns—every corporate town containing one hundred and fifty rateable polls, to send one representative ; if a town contained three hundred and seventy-five, two ; and if six hundred, three ; and the number to be increased in the ratio of one for two hundred and twenty-five rateable polls. All mo-

---

* This constitution was drawn by a sub-committee, consisting of James Bowdoin,

ney bills were to originate in the house, but the senate might propose or concur with amendments.

The executive authority was lodged in a governor and council
—the governor to be chosen annually by the people—the council
consisted of nine persons, with the lieutenant governor, and were
to be chosen out of those returned for senators, by the joint ballots of both houses ; and if on the first choice, the whole number
who would accept should not be elected, the residue were to be
chosen from among the people at large, not more than two from
any one district.

Judicial officers were to continue during good behavior, but removable on the address of both houses ; commissions of justices,
however, were to expire at the end of seven years.

All judicial officers, the attorney general, the solicitor general,
all sheriffs, coroners, and registers of probate, were to be nominated and appointed by the governor, by and with the advice and
consent of the council; and every nomination was to be made
by the governor at least *seven* days prior to such appointment.
The secretary, treasurer, receiver general, the commissary general, notaries public, and naval officers, were to be chosen annually, by joint ballot of both houses ; and no person was eligible as
treasurer and receiver general, more than five years successively.
The captains and subalterns of the militia were to be chosen by
the companies—the field officers of regiments by the captains and
subalterns, of their respective regiments—and the brigadiers to
be elected by the field officers of their respective brigades—the
major generals by the two houses, each having a negative on the
other.

The governor had a partial negative on the acts of the legislature. Every bill or resolve of the senate and house, was to be
submitted to the governor for his revisal ; and if not approved
by him, he was to return the same, with his objections in writing,
and if not reconsidered and approved by two thirds of both
branches, was not to have the force of a law.

The qualification of an elector was a freehold estate of the annual income of three pounds, or any estate of the value of sixty
pounds.

After confirming the rights and immunities of Harvard college, the constitution made it the express *duty* of the legislature and magistrates, at all future periods, " to cherish the interests of literature and the sciences, and all seminaries of them ; especially the university of Cambridge, *public schools*, and *grammar` schools* in the towns ; to encourage private societies and public institutions, by rewards and immunities for the promotion of agriculture, arts, sciences, commerce, trades, manufactures, and a *natural history* of the country ; to countenance and inculcate the principles of humanity and general benevolence, public and private charity, industry and frugality, honesty and punctuality in their dealings ; sincerity, good humor, and all social affections and generous sentiments among the people."

The second and third articles of the bill of rights embraced the subject of religion and religious liberty. It was declared to be the duty of all men in society publicly, and at stated seasons, to worship the Supreme Being, the Great Creator and Preserver of the universe. But that no one should be hurt, molested, or restrained, in his person, liberty, or estate, for worshipping God, in the manner and seasons, most agreeably to the dictates of his own conscience ; or for his religious professions or sentiments.

The third article declared this great fundamental truth, ' that the happiness of a people, and the good order and preservation of civil government essentially depended upon piety, religion, and morality.' The same article, also, asserted, that as these could not be diffused throughout a community, but by the institution of the public worship of God, the people had a right to invest their legislature with power to authorize and require the several towns, parishes, &c., " to make suitable provision for the institution of the public worship of God, and for the support and maintenance of public protestant teachers of piety, religion, and morality, in all cases, where such provision shall not be made voluntarily."

The people, however, were to have the exclusive right of selecting their public teachers, and of contracting with them for their support ; and all monies paid by any person, for the support of public worship, and of public teachers, was to be applied if he required it, to the support of the teacher of his own religious sect or denomination, if there was any, on whose instructions he attended, otherwise to be paid to the teachers of the parish, where the money was raised. And every denomination of christians was to be " equally under the protection of the law ; and no subordination of any sect or denomination to another to be established by law."

Vermont did not become a member of the union until 1791. This state was originally settled under grants from New Hampshire, and principally by the hardy yeomanry of New England, who became acquainted with the country, in the war of 1756. It was a long time known by the name of " the New Hampshire Grants ;" and its inhabitants were called "the Green Mountain boys." It was claimed by New York, under the old grant to the duke of York ; and in 1764, on an *ex parte* application to the king and council, the country, as far east as Connecticut river, was placed under the jurisdiction of that province. This was done not only without the knowledge, but contrary to the wishes of the inhabitants ; and they uniformly refused to submit to the jurisdiction of that state. The government of New York attempted to enforce obedience but in vain. Civil process was resisted by force, and the people at the revolution, declared themselves independent, and in 1777, established a temporary government. They afterwards requested to be admitted a member of the confederacy, but congress were unwilling to offend the states of New York and New Hampshire, who opposed it. July 4th, 1786, a frame of government was established, containing provisions taken principally from those of Pennsylvania and Connecticut.

The supreme legislative power was vested in a single body, consisting of representatives from the several counties, to be called the general assembly; and the supreme executive power in a governor and council. A governor, lieutenant governor, and twelve councillors, were to be chosen annually, by the people. All bills before they became laws, were to be laid before the governor and council for their revision and concurrence, or proposals of amendments. If the amendments proposed by the council were not agreed to b the assembly, the governor and council had a right to suspend the passage of the bill until the next session of the legislature. The general assembly, in conjunction with the council, were annually to appoint judges and other principal officers, to be commissioned by the governor—every man of the age of twenty-one, having resided in the state one year, and of quiet and peaceable behavior, was an elector. No person could be compelled to attend any religious worship, or support any place of worship, or maintain any minister. Schools were to be maintained in the towns, and one or more grammar schools incorporated and properly supported in each county.

A council of censors was to be chosen every seven years, with the same powers as in Pennsylvania.

By the constitution of Georgia, established in May, 1789, the representatives were elected annually, and the senators every third year. The governor, in whom the executive power was lodged, was elected every two years in the following manner;—the house was to vote by ballot for three persons, and a list of the persons voted for sent to the senate, and out of the three persons having the highest number of votes, the senate was to elect a governor.

The state officers were to be oppointed as follows,—the house of representatives to vote for three persons; and a list of the three persons having the highest number of votes, was to be transmitted to the senate, from which the senate was to choose one. The governor, however, was to appoint military officers, and his secretary; and the legislature might vest the appointment of inferior officers in the governor, the courts of justic, or in such other manner as they might by law direct. The governor was to revise all bills passed by both houses, and without his assent, such bills could not become laws, unless re-passed by two thirds of both branches.

Electors must have resided in the county six months, and paid a tax for the year preceding the election. The judges of the supreme court and the attorney general, were to hold their offices three years; and all persons to have the free exercise of their religion, without being obliged to contribute to any religious profession but their own.

By the investigations and discussions which took place in the general and state conventions, relative to the new system of general government, the leading principles in the formation of American constitutions became better understood by the people of the United States. Many of the states, soon after the new government went into successful operation, revised the systems they had hastily established at an early period of the revolution.

Pennsylvania and South Carolina formed new constitutions in 1790, New Hampshire and Delaware in 1792. The alterations in that of South Carolina we have before noticed. Pennsylvania now divided her legislature into two branches, and gave her governor a qualified negative to legislative acts. The governor of that state was to be chosen by the people for three years, but was not capable of holding the office longer than nine years out of twelve, and was vested with the power of appointing most of the state officers. The council of censors was abolished. The constitution of Delaware was made in a great measure conformable to that of Pennsylvania, with the exception of the partial negative of the chief magistrate to legislative acts. Vermont revised her system in 1793, but retained most of the principles contained in that of 1786. The constitutions of the new states of Kentucky and Tennessee, admitted into the union during the administration of president Washington, conformed in their general principles to that of the United States. With respect to slavery, the constitution of Kentucky prohibited the legislature from passing laws for the emancipation of slaves without the consent of their owners, or without paying them a full equivalent in money for those emancipated. Nor could they prevent emigrants from bringing with them slaves, so long as slavery existed in the state. The legislature, however, were directed to pass laws permitting the owners of slaves to emancipate them, securing the rights of creditors, and preventing them from being a charge to any county; and the legislature had power also to prevent them from being brought into the state as *merchandize*, as well as from being brought there from a foreign country.

CHAPTER XX.

First congress under the new constitution meet at New York, on the 4th of March, 1789---George Washington chosen president, and John Adams vice-president---President's inaugural speech, and answers of both houses---Congress lay tonnage and other duties---Give a preference to American shipping---Establish different departments---Determine the question about the removal of the heads of these departments---Power of removal vested in the president alone---Debate on this subject---The senate about equally divided upon it---Amendments to the constitution proposed---A national judiciary established---Its powers and jurisdiction---Vessels of North Carolina and Rhode Island placed on the same footing with those of the United States, until the 15th of January, 1790---Congress direct the secretary of the treasury to report, at their next session, a plan for the support of public credit---Request the president to recommend the observance of a day of public thanksgiving and prayer---Adjourn to the first Monday of January, 1790---North Carolina adopts the constitution in November---Speech of the president at the opening of the second session of congress---He recommends the promotion of such manufactures, as would render the United States independent on others for essential articles, the establishment of a good militia system, and adequate provision for the support of public credit---Financial plan of the secretary of the treasury, submitted to the house in January---Outlines of this plan---Secretary recommends funding the debt of the United States, and the assumption of the state debts---This creates great divisions and long debates in congress---Motion to discriminate between the original holders and the assignees of the domestic debt negatived---Assumption of the state debts violently opposed---Debates on this question---Finally carried---Terms of funding the debts---Commissioners appointed to settle the accounts between the states, and principles of settlement adopted---Census of the inhabitants to be taken on the first Monday of August, 1790---Third session commences the first Monday of December, 1790---Vermont and Kentucky admitted into the union---National bank established---Strongly opposed as unconstitutional---Cabinet divided on the question---President decides in favor of its constitutionality---Duties laid on spirits distilled within the United States---Opposed in congress, and in some of the states---Speech of the president at the opening of the first session of the second congress in October, 1791---Ratio of representation settled---Difference between the houses and the president as to the constitutional rule of apportionment---Gen. St. Clair and his army defeated by the Indians---Opposition to the internal duties increases---The two great parties in the United States more distinctly marked---Cabinet divided---An inquiry into the official conduct of the secretary of the treasury, instituted in the house of representatives---Charges exhibited against him---Negatived by a large majority---Supreme court decides, that a state is liable to a suit in favor of individuals---An amendment altering the constitution in this respect proposed and adopted---The first term of president Washington's administration expires on the 4th of March, 1793.

The national legislature under the new system of government, convened at New York, on the 4th day of March, 1789, and consisted of senators and representatives from eleven states.

A quorum of both houses did not attend until the 6th of April, when, on counting the electoral votes it appeared, that George Washington was unanimously chosen president, and that John Adams was elected vice-president.

Whatever difference of opinion existed among the people of the United States, with respect to the government itself, there was none as to the person, who as their first chief magistrate, was to be selected to administer it. All eyes, from the beginning, were turned to general Washington, as the first president ; and he received, what perhaps no individual in so high a station in any age ever before received, the unanimous and voluntary suffrages of a whole nation.

Informed of his election by a special messenger, the president immediately left his beloved retreat, and set out for the seat of government. He was received on his way, by the sincere congratulations of numerous public bodies, as well as individuals.*

He was met at Elizabethtown, by a committee from both houses of congress, and escorted into the city of New York, amidst the acclamations of thousands.

On the 30th of April, the oath of office was administered to him by the chancellor of the state of New York, in the gallery in

* His reception at Trenton was peculiarly interesting. The inhabitants of that village had not forgotten the memorable scenes of December, 1776.

On the bridge over the creek where the progress of the enemy was arrested twelve years before, the ladies of Trenton erected a triumphal arch, ornamented with flowers, on the front of which was inscribed, " the defender of the mothers will be the protector of the daughters." He was here met by the ladies, attended by their little daughters, who as he passed, literally strewed his way with flowers, as they sung the following ode---

    " Welcome mighty chief, once more
    Welcome to this grateful shore ;
    Now no mercenary foe
    Aims again the fatal blow,
    Aims at thee the fatal blow.

    " Virgins fair and matrons grave
    Those thy conquering arms did save,
    Build for thee triumphal bowers ;
    Strew ye fair his way with flowers,
    Strew your Hero's way with flowers."

front of the senate chamber, in the presence of the members of the senate and house of representatives, and a vast concourse of citizens ; and he was proclaimed president of the United States. Every countenance beamed with inexpressible joy, at the sight of the venerated chief, to whom, under God, they were so much indebted not only for their independence, but that form of government, in the administration of which he had consented to take a share, and which he had in their presence solemnly sworn to support. Soon after taking the oath, he retired to the senate chamber, and made the following address to both houses.

" *Fellow citizens of the senate,*
     and house of representatives,

" Among the vicissitudes incident to life, no event could have filled me with greater anxieties, than that of which the notification was transmitted by your order, and received on the 14th day of the present month. On the one hand, I was summoned by my country, whose voice I can never hear but with veneration and love, from a retreat which I had chosen with the fondest predilection, and, in my flattering hopes, with an immutable decision, as the asylum of my declining years, a retreat which was rendered every day more necessary as well as more dear to me, by the addition of habit to inclination, and of frequent interruptions in my health to the gradual waste committed on it by time. On the other hand, the magnitude and difficulty of the trust to which the voice of my country called me, being sufficient to awaken in the wisest and most experienced of her citizens, a distrustful scrutiny into his qualifications, could not but overwhelm with despondence, one, who, inheriting inferior endowments from nature, and unpractised in the duties of civil administration, ought to be peculiarly conscious of his own deficiencies. In this conflict of emotions, all I dare aver, is, that it has been my faithful study to collect my duty from a just appreciation of every circumstance by which it might be affected. All I dare hope, is, that, if in executing this task, I have been too much swayed by a grateful remembrance of former instances, or by an affectionate sensibility to this transcendant proof of the confidence of my fellow citizens,

and have thence too little consulted my incapacity as well as disinclination, for the weighty and untried cares before me, my error
will be palliated by the motives which misled me, and its consequences be judged by my country, with some share of the partiality in which they originated.

"Such being the impressions under which I have, in obedience
to the public summons, repaired to the present station, it would
be peculiarly improper to omit, in this first official act, my fervent
supplications to that Almighty Being, who rules over the universe,
who presides in the councils of nations, and whose providential
aids can supply every human defect, that his benediction may
consecrate to the liberties and happiness of the people of the
United States, a government instituted by themselves for these
essential purposes, and may enable every instrument employed in
its administration, to execute with success the functions allotted
to his charge.   In tendering this homage to the great Author of
every public and private good, I assure myself that it expresses
your sentiments not less than my own; nor those of my fellow
citizens at large, less than either.   No people can be bound to
acknowledge and adore the invisible hand, which conducts the
affairs of men, more than the people of the United States.   Every step, by which they have advanced to the character of an independent nation, seems to have been distinguished by some token
of providential agency.   And in the important revolution just accomplished in the system of their united government, the tranquil
deliberations, and voluntary consent of so many distinct communities, from which the event has resulted, cannot be compared
with the means by which most governments have been established, without some return of pious gratitude, along with a humble
anticipation of the future blessings which the past seem to pre-
sage.   These reflections arising out of the present crisis, have
forced themselves too strongly on my mind to be suppressed.   You
will join with me, I trust, in thinking that there are none under
the influence of which the proceedings of a new and free government can more auspiciously commence.

"By the article establishing the executive department, it is
made the duty of the president, 'to recommend to your consid-

eration such measures as he shall judge necessary and expedient.' The circumstances under which I now meet you, will acquit me from entering into that subject, further than to refer to the great constitutional charter under which you are assembled, and which, in defining your powers, designates the objects to which your attention is to be given. It will be more consistent with those circumstances, and far more congenial with the feelings which actuate me, to substitute, in place of a recommendation of particular measures, the tribute that is due to the talents, the rectitude, and the patriotism which adorn the characters selected to devise and adopt them. In these honorable qualifications, I behold the surest pledges, that as on one side no local prejudices or attachments, no separate views, nor party animosities, will misdirect the comprehensive and equal eye which ought to watch over this great assemblage of communities and interests; so on another, that the foundations of our national policy will be laid in the pure and immutable principles of private morality ; and the pre-eminence of free government be exemplified by all the attributes which can win the affections of its citizens, and command the respect of the world.

" I dwell on this prospect with every satisfaction which an ardent love for my country can inspire. Since there is no truth more thoroughly established, than that there exists in the economy and course of nature, an indissoluble union between virtue and happiness—between duty and advantage—between the genuine maxims of an honest and magnanimous policy, and the solid rewards of public prosperity and felicity. Since we ought to be no less persuaded that the propitious smiles of heaven can never be expected on a nation that disregards the eternal rules of order and right which heaven itself has ordained. And since the preservation of the sacred fire of liberty, and the destiny of the republican model of government, are justly considered as *deeply*, perhaps as *finally*, staked on the experiment intrusted to the hands of the American people.

" Besides the ordinary objects submitted to your care, it will remain with your judgment to decide, how far an exercise of the occasional power delegated by the fifth article of the constitution, is rendered expedient at the present juncture by the nature of objections which have been urged against the system, or by the degree of inquietude which has given birth to them. Instead of undertaking particular recommendations on this subject, in which I could be guided by no lights derived from official opportunities, I shall again give way to my entire confidence in your discernment and pursuit of the public good. For I assure myself, that whilst you carefully avoid every alteration which might endanger the benefits of an united and effective government, or which ought to await the future lessons of experience ; a reverence for the characteristic rights of freemen, and a regard for the public harmony, will sufficiently influence your deliberations on the question, how far the former can be more impregnably fortified, or the latter be safely and advantageously promoted.

" To the preceding observations I have one to add, which will be most properly addressed to the house of representatives. It concerns myself, and will therefore be as brief as possible. When I was first honored with a call into the service of my country, then on the eve of an arduous struggle for its liberties, the light in which I contemplated my duty, required that I should renounce every pecuniary compensation. From this resolution I have in no instance departed. And being still under the impressions which produced it, I must decline as inapplicable to myself, any share in the personal emoluments, which may be indispensably included in a permanent provision for the executive department ; and must accordingly pray, that the pecuniary estimates for the station in which I am placed, may, during my continuance in it, be limited to such actual expenditures as the public good may be thought to require.

" Having thus imparted to you my sentiments, as they have been awakened by the occasion which brings us together, I shall take my present leave ; but not without resorting once more to the benign Parent of the human race, in humble supplication, that since he has been pleased to favor the American people with opportunities for deliberating in perfect tranquility, and dispositions for deciding with unparalleled unanimity on a form of government, for the security of their union, and the advancement of their happiness ; so his divine blessing may be equally *conspicuous* in the enlarged views, the temperate consultations, and the wise measures on which the success of this government must depend. GEORGE WASHINGTON."

Immediately after the address, he, with the members of both houses, attended divine service at St. Paul's chapel. Thus commenced the government under the new constitution.

Both houses of the national legislature were unanimous in their answers to the inaugural speech of the president.

After congratulating him on the complete organization of the federal government, and felicitating themselves and their country, on his elevation to the office of president, the senate say, " the unanimous suffrage of the elective body in your favor, is peculiarly expressive of the gratitude, confidence, and affection of the citizens of America, and it is the highest testimonial at once of your merit and of your esteem. We are sensible, sir, that nothing but the voice of your fellow citizens, could have called you from a retreat, chosen with the fondest predilection, endeared by habit, and consecrated to the repose of declining years : we rejoice, and with us all America, that, in obedience to the call of our common country, you have returned once more to public life. In you all parties confide, in you all interests unite, and we have no doubt, that your past services great as they have been, will be equalled by your future exertions ; and that your prudence and sagacity as a statesman will tend to avert the dangers to which we were exposed, to give stability to the present government, and dignity and splendor to that country, which your skill and valor as a soldier, so eminently contributed to raise to independence."

The representatives in their answer, expressed not merely their own feelings of veneration and affection, but those of the whole American people.

"You have long held," they said, "the first place in their esteem—you have often received tokens of their affection—you now possess the only proof that remained of their gratitude for your past services, of their reverence for your wisdom, and of their confidence in your virtues.   You enjoy the highest, because the truest, honor of being the first magistrate, by the unanimous choice of the freest people on the face of the earth.

"We well knew the anxieties with which you must have obeyed a summons from a repose reserved for your declining years, into public scenes, of which you had taken your leave forever. It is already applauded by the universal joy which welcomes you to your station.   And we cannot doubt that it will be rewarded with all the satisfaction with which an ardent love for your fellow citizens must revive successful efforts to promote their happiness.

"This anticipation is not justified merely by the past experience of your signal services.   It is particularly suggested by the pious impressions under which you commence your administration, and the enlightened maxims by which you mean to conduct it.   We feel with you the strongest obligations to adore the invisible hand which has led the American people through so many difficulties, to cherish a conscious responsibility for the destiny of republican liberty ; and to seek the only sure means of preserving and recommending the precious deposit in a system of legislation founded on the principles of an honest policy, and directed by the spirit of diffusive patriotism.

"The question arising out of the fifth article of the constitution, will receive all the attention demanded by its importance ; and will we trust, be decided under the influence of all the considerations to which you allude.

"In forming the pecuniary provisions for the executive department, we shall not lose sight of a wish resulting from motives which give it a peculiar claim on our regard.   Your resolution, in a moment critical to the liberties of your country, to renounce all personal emolument, was among the many presages of your patriotic services, which have been amply fulfilled; and your scrupulous adherence now to the law then imposed on yourself, cannot fail to demonstrate the purity, whilst it increases the lustre of a character, which has so many titles to admiration.

" Such are the sentiments which we have thought fit to address you. They flow from our own hearts ; and we verily believe that among the millions we represent, there is not a virtuous citizen whose heart will disown them.

" All that remains is, that we join in your fervent supplication for the blessings of heaven on our country ; and that we add our own for the choicest of these blessings on the most beloved of her citizens."

The national legislature during its first session, was principally occupied in providing revenues for the long exhausted treasury, in establishing a judiciary, in organizing the executive departments in detail, and in framing amendments to the constitution, agreeably to the suggestion of the president. The members immediately entered upon the exercise of those powers, so long refused under the old system of general government. They imposed a tonnage duty, as well as duties on various imported articles. In the exercise of these powers, they did not lose sight of the navigating interest of their country, which had so long been at the mercy of other nations.

Higher tonnage duties were imposed on foreign than on American bottoms ; and goods imported in vessels belonging to citizens of the United States, paid ten per cent. less duty, than the same goods brought in those owned by foreigners. These discriminating duties, were intended to counteract the commercial regulations of foreign nations, and encourage American shipping. It was proposed in the house of representatives, and after long debate carried by a small majority, to make a difference in the duties, in favor of nations having commercial treaties with the United States. This discrimination, however, was negatived in the senate.

To aid in the management of the affairs of the government, three executive departments were established, styled departments of war, of foreign affairs, and of the treasury, with a secretary at the head of each.

The heads of these departments, in addition to the duties specially assigned them, were intended to constitute a council, to be consulted by the president whenever he thought proper; and indeed by the constitution, the president was authorized to require the opinions in writing of the principal officers in the executive departments, on subjects relating to the duties of their offices. These duties were designated in the acts establishing the departments themselves. In framing these acts, it became an important subject of inquiry, in what manner, or by whom, these important officers, could be removed from office. This was a question as new as it was important, and was applicable to all other officers of executive appointment. It depended on the construction of the constitution itself, and occasioned long and learned debates, as well as great divisions in both branches of the national legislature. As the doors of the senate were not open, the debates of that body, on this and other questions, were not known. Some of the members in the house of representatives, were of opinion that they could not be removed, without impeachment. The principal question, however, on which congress were divided, was, whether they were removable by the president alone, or by the president in concurrence with the senate. A majority, however, in both houses, decided, that this power was in the president alone. In the house the majority in favor of this construction was twelve.

When the question first came before the senate, on the bill establishing the department of foreign affairs, some of the members were absent, and that body was equally divided, and the casting vote was given by the vice-president. On a subsequent bill, there was a majority of two in favor of the same construction. That it might not be considered a grant of power by congress, the law was so worded, as to imply a constitutional power, already existing in the president; the expressions being, " that whenever the secretary shall be removed by the president of the United States," &c. In opposition to this clause, it was urged in the first place, that it was improper for the legislature, in this manner, to give a construction to the constitution. That it should be left with the judiciary, another co-ordinate department of the government ; or it should remain to be decided by the president and senate, whenever the occasion occurred, in which a decision should be necessary. In the second place it was said that this great and important power, by a fair construction of the constitution, was in the president and senate. It was an established principle, its opponents said, that the power of removal necessarily rested with those to whom was entrusted the power of appointment, except when there was an express restriction, as in the case of the judges, who held their offices during good behavior. That the senate had, in effect, an equal voice with the president, in the appointment of officers, when their appointment was not by law vested in the president alone, or in some other department of the government; as no appointment could be made without the assent of that body. It was further said, that the constitution being silent on the question, it was contrary to sound policy, as well as inconsistent with the principles of a free government, to give, by construction, such power to any one individual. That it was liable to great abuses, and would render officers entirely dependent on the will, perhaps the whim and caprice of one man. Whatever confidence might be placed in the chief magistrate, then at the head of the government, equal confidence could not be expected in his successors. That a concurrence of the senate was as necessary and proper, in the removal of a person from office, as in his appointment.

The advocates for this clause in the bill, agreed in its importance, and considered the genius and character of the government itself, in no small degree, to depend upon it. In ordinary cases, they said, constitutional questions might be left with the judiciary department without a legislative expression of opinion ; but that this one was of no ordinary character or magnitude ; one, which it would be difficult to bring properly before the courts. It was one, on which it was highly proper that the legislature, particularly the house of representatives, should express an opinion. This opinion, if assented to by the president and senate, would put the question at rest. That if left to be settled at a future time by the president and senate, a difference might arise between them, which would create infinite difficulties and delays, in the administration of the government. They also contended, that by a fair construction of the constitution, this power was in the president alone. It was a political axiom, they said, not to be disputed, that the legislative, executive and judicial powers of government, should be kept distinct, and blended as little as possible. That by the constitution, the executive power was vested in the president ; and the association of the senate, in one executive function, was an exception to the general principle, and that exceptions to general rules were taken strictly. So by the constitution, all legislative power was vested in congress ; and the qualified negative given to the president was only a special restriction to this general power.

The power of appointment, they also said, was substantially in the president alone. He was authorized to nominate, and by and with the advice and consent of the senate, *to appoint.* The president was the agent, and the senate had only a negative on his agency.

Other parts of the constitution were referred to in support of this construction. The president, they said, was directed to take care, that the laws be faithfully executed ; and it must have been the intention of the framers of the new system, to give him power, to an extent necessary for the accomplishment of that object. If an officer, once appointed, was not to depend on the president alone for his official existence, it would be difficult to see how he could be answerable for a faithful execution of the laws.

It was urged with great force also, that if the power of removal was divided between the president and senate, responsibility would be destroyed, and the benefits expected from its exercise, in a great measure, lost. Secrecy and despatch were often necessary to secure and preserve the public interest. Facts relative to the mal-conduct of an officer, might come to the knowledge of the president, rendering an immediate removal indispensable ; and the delay in convening the senate, might be fatal to the best interests of the community. In answer to the objection, that this power would be liable to great abuse, in the hands of an individual, it was said, that all power wherever placed, was liable to this objection ; but that the mode of choosing the chief magistrate would ensure the election of an individual of integrity as well as talents ; and that the tenure of office would be as secure, and the liberties of the people as safe, in the hands of a president thus chosen, as with the president and senate.

With respect to removals, from whim, caprice or any unworthy motives, it was alleged, that sufficient checks were provided against such a wanton abuse of this power. That the principal if not the only inducement for the removal of a meritorious officer, would be, to place some favorite in his room. The president, indeed, might remove, but he could not supply the vacancy without the assent of the senate. The nomination of a successor, would elicit inquiry in that body, and produce a rejection of the favorite nominated to fill the vacancy.

It was also stated by some members, particularly by Mr. Lawrence and Mr. Madison, that for such wanton abuse of power, the president himself would be liable to impeachment and removal from office.

"If the president," said Mr. Lawrence, "abuse his trust, will he escape the popular censure, when the period which terminates his elevation arrives ? And would he not be liable to impeachment for displacing a worthy and able man, who enjoyed the confidence of the people ?"

"The danger, then," Mr. Madison observed, "consists in this, the president can displace from office, a man whose merits require that he should be continued in it. What will be the motives which the president can feel for such abuse of his power, and the restraints to operate to prevent it ? In the first place, he will be impeachable by this house, before the senate, for such an act of mal-administration ; for I contend, that the wanton removal of meritorious officers, would subject him to impeachment and removal from his own high trust."*

* Congressional Register, vol. 1, p. 503.

This decision of a great constitutional question, has been acquiesced in, and its consequences has been of greater importance than almost any other, since the establishment of the new government. From the manner in which this power has been exercised, it has given a tone and character to the executive branch of
the government, not contemplated, it is believed, by the framers of
the constitution, or by those who composed the first congress under it. It has greatly increased the influence and patronage of
the president, and in no small degree made him the center,
around which the other branches of the government revolve.

The experience of a few years has evinced that the supposed checks to executive influence, have, in many instances,
been too feeble and inefficient, nor can it be expected, they will
be more efficacious in future. While so many members of the
national legislature are themselves candidates for office, the balance of power will incline to the side of the executive.

The constitution is not only silent on the subject, but it does
not appear from the proceedings of the general convention, that
the question was agitated in that body. The members of that
convention, who were members of the house of representatives,
differed in opinion on this point. Mr. Madison and Mr. Baldwin
supported the construction finally adopted by congress, and
Mr. Sherman and Mr. Gerry opposed it. The opinion of Mr.
Hamilton, as given in the Federalist, was the same as that of
the two latter gentlemen. The author of number seventy seven,
(Mr. Hamilton) says, " it has been mentioned, as one of the advantages to be expected from the co-operation of the senate, in
the business of appointments, that it would contribute to the stability of the administration.

" The consent of that body would be necessary to *displace*, as
well as to *appoint*. A change of the chief magistrate, therefore,
would not occasion so vehement or general a revolution in the
officers of the government, as might be expected, if he were the
sole disposer of offices. When a man, in any situation, had
given satisfactory evidence of his fitness for it, a new president

would be restrained from attempting a change, in favor of a person more agreeable to him, by the apprehension, that the discountenance of the senate might frustrate the attempt, and bring discredit upon himself."

The question, indeed, presented difficulties of no ordinary magnitude, and not easy of solution.

And it is, perhaps, not less difficult to provide a remedy for the evils which have and may arise, in the administration of the government, from the extent and influence of executive power. The legislative body should be particularly guarded against its improper effects. The hope or expectation of office, from presidential favor, should never be suffered to enter the minds of the members of the legislative department. The constitution, indeed, attempted to provide against this influence, in that branch of the government, by declaring, "that no senator or representative should, during the time for which he was elected, be appointed to any *civil* office, under the authority of the United States, which should have been created, or the emoluments whereof had been increased, during such time."

This subject created no little difficulty as well as division among the framers of the constitution.

The general convention, in the first instance, provided, that the members of each house should be incapable of holding *any office*, under the authority of the United States, during the time for which they should be elected ; and that the members of the senate should be incapable of holding any office, for *one year* afterwards. This was finally restricted in the manner above stated.

The benefits of this restriction, however, were principally limited to the early period of the government, when most of the offices now in existence were created, and the emoluments settled; and this provision now affords but a feeble check against the evil intended to be remedied.

The subject of amending the constitution, was brought before congress during this session, by petitions from the states of Virginia and New York, requesting that another convention might be called to take into consideration and report such amendments as they might think proper and best calculated " to promote our common interests, and to secure to ourselves and our latest posterity, the great and unalienable rights of mankind." The states of Virginia and New York were both opposed to the constitution without the amendments proposed in their respective conventions. This opposition was strongly manifested in the legislature of Virginia, in the first choice of senators. Mr. Madison, who had been so instrumental, not only in forming the new system, but in procuring its ratification, though a candidate, lost his election. His opponents, Richard Henry Lee and William Grayson, were chosen. The same legislature requested another general convention.

Congress, however, had no authority to call a convention. Mr. Madison submitted to the house several amendments, which, together with those presented by the several states, were referred to a committee consisting of one member from a state, with general instructions. Amendments were reported by this committee, and after long debates and various alterations, twelve articles were agreed to by both houses, to be submitted to the states. These were in substance, that congress should make no law respecting an establishment of religion, or prohibit the free exercise thereof, or abridging the freedom of speech or of the press; or the right of the people peaceably to assemble, and to petition for a redress of grievances.

That the right of the people to keep and bear arms should not be infringed.

That no soldier, in time of peace be quartered in any house, without the consent of the owner; nor in time of war, but in a manner prescribed by law.

The right of the people to be secure in their persons, houses, papers, and effects, against unreasonable searches and seizures, not to be violated; and no warrants to issue, but upon probable cause, supported by oath or affirmation, and particularly describing the place to be searched, and the persons or things to be seized.

No person to be held to answer for a capital or other infamous crime, unless on presentment of a grand jury, except in cases arising in the land or naval forces, or in the militia, when in actual service ; no person to be subject to be put twice in jeopardy of life or limb for the same offence ; or compelled in any criminal case, to be a witness against himself ; nor be deprived of life, liberty, or property without due process of law ; nor private property be taken for public use, without just compensation.

In all criminal prosecutions, the accused to enjoy the right to a speedy and public trial by an impartial jury in the state where the crime was committed ; to be informed of the nature of the accusation ; be confronted with the witnesses against him ; to have compulsory process for his witnesses, and to have council for his defense.

The right of trial by jury to be preserved, in all suits at common law, where the value in controversy exceeded twenty dollars ; and no fact tried by a jury to be otherwise re-examined in any court of the United States, than according to the rules of common law.

Excessive bail not to be required ; nor excessive fines imposed, nor unusual punishments inflicted.

The enumeration of certain rights in the constitution, not to be construed to deny or disparage others retained by the people.

The powers not delegated to the United States by the constitution, nor prohibited by it to the states, were reserved to the states, or to the people.

As to numbers in the house of representatives, one article provided, that after the first enumeration, there should be one representative for every thirty thousand, until the whole number should be one hundred, after which there should be not less than one hundred, nor more than one representative for every forty thousand, until the whole number was two hundred, after this the whole not to be less than two hundred, nor more than one for every fifty thousand.

No law varying the compensation for the services of the members of congress, was to take effect, until after an election of representatives should have intervened. These amendments, it will be perceived, were principally confined to a declaration of rights, and did not include those various alterations in the body of the constitution proposed by some of the states, particularly by Virginia and New York.

In the senate, the various amendments adopted by the Virginia convention were moved and rejected. This gave great dissatisfaction to the senators as well as the people of that state.

In transmitting those proposed by congress, to the speaker of the house of representatives, the Virginia senators observed, " it is impossible for us not to see the necessary tendency to consolidated empire, in the natural operation of the constitution, if not further amended than is now proposed ; it is equally impossible for us, not to be apprehensive for civil liberty, when we know of no instance in the records of history, that shows a people ruled in freedom, when subject to one undivided government, and inhabiting territory so extensive as that of the United States, and when, as seems to us, the nature of man and of things prevent it. The impracticability in such case, of carrying representation sufficiently near to the people for procuring their confidence and consequent obedience, compels a resort to fear resulting from great force, and excessive power in government. Confederated republics, where the federal hand is not possessed of absorbing power, may admit the existence of freedom, whilst it preserves union, strength, and safety. Such amendments, therefore, as may secure against the annihilation of the state governments, we devoutly wish to see adopted. If a persevering application to congress from the states that have desired such amendments, should fail of its objects, we are disposed to think, reasoning from causes to effects, that unless a dangerous apathy should invade the public mind, it will not be many years before the constitutional number of legislatures will be found to demand a convention for the purpose."*

Ten of the articles proposed by congress were ratified by the constitutional majority of the states. Those relating to the number of the house of representatives, and to compensation for

* Life of Richard H. Lee, vol. 2, p. 100.

the services of the members of the national legislature were rejected.

A national judiciary was, also, established during this session, consisting of a supreme court, circuit, and district courts. The bill for carrying this part of the constitution into effect, originated in the senate, and was drawn up by a committee, of which Mr. Ellsworth was chairman. The district courts were to consist of one judge in each state. The states were divided into circuits, in each of which, one of the judges of the supreme court, and the district judge of the state, in which the court was held, constituted the circuit courts. In certain cases, this court had original jurisdiction, and also took cognizance of appeals from the district courts. The supreme court was composed of a chief justice and five associate judges, and was to hold two sessions annually, at the seat of government. This court had exclusive jurisdiction in certain cases, and appellate jurisdiction from the circuit courts, and also, from the state courts, in cases, where the validity of treaties and the laws of the United States were drawn in question. This organization of the federal judiciary has remained nearly the same, to the present time, except for a short period, when a different system relative to the circuit courts was established, but which was soon abolished, and the old system restored.

Much debate was had this session, on the subject of designating a place for the permanent seat of the national government; and congress were about equally divided, between a situation on the banks of the Susquehannah and Potomac; but rose without a decision.

The fixing the salaries of the president and vice-president, members of congress, and the great officers of the government created some difficulty. The compensation to the president was settled at twenty-five thousand dollars a year, and to vice-president five thousand. The representatives had six dollars per day, and six dollars for every twenty miles travel, and the senate seven dollars per day and the same for travel. To each of the heads of departments was allowed a salary of three thousand five hundred dollars, to the chief justice of the supreme court four thousand dollars, and the associate judges three thousand five hundred.

The states of North Carolina and Rhode Island having refused to adopt the constitution, were not a part of the union, and of course, not subject to its laws. In their intercourse with the United States, therefore, they were considered in some respects as foreign states. By the law for the collection of duties, all goods imported from these states, except those of their own growth or manufacture, were subject to foreign duties. Towards the close of the session, however, on the application of individuals belonging to these states, their vessels were placed on the same footing with those of the United States, until the 15th of January, 1790.

The various offices created during this session, were filled by the executive, and men of the first talents and respectability, in different parts of the union, were called to take a share in the administration of the new government ; and in these appointments, president Washington did not forget those, who had participated with him, in the toils and dangers of achieving the independence of their country.

Mr. Jefferson was placed at the head of the department of foreign affairs, Mr. Hamilton at the head of the treasury, and Mr. Knox was made secretary of the war department. John Jay was appointed chief justice, John Rutledge, James Wilson, William Cushing, Robert H. Harrison, and John Blair, associate judges of the supreme court, and Edmund Randolph, attorney general. Nicholas Eveleigh was appointed comptroller; Oliver Wolcott, auditor ; and Joseph Nourse, register. Congress did not lose sight of the principal object in view, in forming the new government, the support of public credit. Just before they rose, a resolution passed the house of representatives, directing the secretary of the treasury to prepare a plan for this purpose, and report the same to the next session.

Nor were they unmindful, that the people of the United States owed the blessings they now enjoyed to that Supreme Being, who guides and directs the affairs of men and nations ; and that it was their duty publicly to acknowledge from whence those blessings flowed. The president, therefore, by a resolution of both houses, was requested to recommend to the people of the United States, a day of public thanksgiving and prayer, to be observed, "by acknowledging with grateful hearts, the many and signal favors of Almighty God, especially by affording them, an opportunity peaceably to establish a constitution of government, for their safety and happiness." Having fixed the first Monday of January, 1790, for their next meeting, congress adjourned the 29th of September. Before the time of their next meeting, the state of North Carolina ratified the constitution.

The proceedings of the first congress were generally approved, and the benefits of the new system began to be felt and realized.

At the opening of the next session, the president congratulated congress, on the favorable prospect of public affairs ; and among other things, recommended to their attention, the important subject of providing for the common defense, by the establishment of a good militia system, and the promotion of such manufactures as would render America independent on others for essentials, particularly military supplies. He, also, recommended the adoption of all proper means, for the advancement of agriculture, commerce, and manufactures, and the promotion of science and literature, and above all, that provision be made for the support of public credit.

The last subject referred to by the president, received early attention. The report of the secretary of the treasury respecting public credit, was submitted to the house, on the 15th of January. The public debt of the United States, was estimated by the secretary, at more than fifty-four millions of dollars. Of this sum the foreign debt, principally due to France and the Hollanders, constituted eleven millions and three quarters, including more than a million and a half of interest ; and the domestic liquidated debt, including about thirteen millions of arrears of interest, more than forty millions ; and the unliquidated debt, two millions. The secretary recommended the assumption of the debts of the several states, to be paid equally with those of the union, as " a measure of sound policy and substantial justice." These were estimated at twenty-five millions of dollars. Doubts were expressed by the secretary, whether, in addition to all other expenses, it was in the power of the United States, to make a secure and effectual provision for the payment of the interest of so large a sum, on the terms of the original contracts. He, therefore, submitted to the house, several plans for the modification, security, and payment of the domestic debt.

One proposition was, to lower the rate of interest on the whole debt, another, to postpone the payment of the interest, on a portion of the principal to a distant day. No new modification, however, was to be made, without the assent of the creditors. This important subject was under the consideration of congress, until the 4th of August, 1790, when a law, making provision for the debt of the United States, was passed.

By this act, a new loan of the whole of the domestic debt, was proposed on the following terms—two thirds of the principal, to draw an interest of six per cent., after the first of January, 1791, and the other third, to draw the same interest, after the year 1800; the arrears of interest to draw three per cent., after January, 1791. The debt drawing six per cent., to be redeemable by payments, not exceeding in one year, eight per cent., on account both of principal and interest; and the three per cents. were made redeemable, at the pleasure of the government.

By the same act, congress assumed twenty one millions and a half of the state debts; and this sum was apportioned among the states, having regard to the amount of the debts of each.* The sum thus assumed, was also to be loaned to the United States, by individuals holding certain evidences of state debts, but on terms

---

* The following is the apportionment among the states :—

New Hampshire,	$300,000	Delaware,	$200,000
Massachusetts,	4,000,000	Maryland,	800,000
Rhode Island,	200,000	Virginia,	3,000,000
Connecticut,	1,600,000	North Carolina,	2,400,000
New York,	1,200,000	South Carolina,	4,000,000
New Jersey,	800,000	Georgia,	300,000
Pennsylvania,	2,200,000		

somewhat different from those of the domestic debt. Four ninths was to bear an interest of six per cent. commencing on the first of January, 1792, two ninths to draw the same interest after the year 1800, and the other three ninths an interest of three per cent. from January, 1792.

The national legislature were much divided as to the mode and manner of providing for the security and payment of so large a debt, deemed of little value, under the old federal government; and particularly on the question of assuming the payment of the state debts. The public creditors, as well as the community at large, had waited with no small degree of solicitude, for the first financial report from the head of the treasury department, and this solicitude was not diminished by the proceedings of congress on the subject. Unfortunately, the public debt again became an object of extensive speculation.

That some provision would be made for the payment of this debt, under the new government, was the general expectation; and the propriety of making a discrimination between the original holders and the purchasers, had been suggested in private circles, as well as in the public newspapers. The idea of making such a discrimination, was opposed by the secratary, as unjust, impolitic and ruinous to public credit.

In an early stage of the proceedings on his report, this question was submitted to the house of representatives. Mr. Madison proposed that the purchasers should receive the highest average price at which the debt had been sold, and the original holders the residue, both to have interest at six per cent. The government was to have no advantage from this arrangement.

In favor of the proposition, it was, among other things, urged, that the case was in many respects so extraordinary, the usual maxims were not strictly applicable. The debt originally contracted, it was said, was to be paid in gold and silver; but instead of this, paper had been substituted, and which the creditors were compelled to take. That they had no alternative. This paper they had parted with, either from necessity or a well grounded distrust of the public. In either case, they

had been injured, and suffered loss from the default of the debt-
or; and in justice, the debtor ought not to take advantage of
this default. The original debt had never been discharged,
because the paper had been forced upon the creditors. A
composition, therefore, between the purchasers and the original
holders, by allowing the former an average price at which the
debt had been sold, and paying the latter the residue, would do
equal justice to both. In opposition to the measure, it was said
in the first place, that the discrimination proposed was a violation of the original contract, on the part of the public. That by
the terms of the certificates given to the original creditors, the
debt was made payable to assignees or to bearer; and of course
the contract was made with the purchaser as well as with the
original holder. That it was impossible for government to examine into the private transactions between the original creditor
and his assignee. The debt had been purchased at the market
price, and the creditor had parted with his security for what he
deemed an equivalent; and however unfortunate might be the
situation of some, who from necessity had been obliged to part
with their securities, redress could not be afforded them in the
manner contemplated. In most instances, the purchaser had
placed greater confidence in the government, than the original
holder, and had run the risk of eventual payment, and which,
but for a change in the federal government, would perhaps never
have been made.

The impolicy of the measure was also strongly urged, as tending
greatly to impair, if not totally destroy, public credit hereafter.
The interest of individuals, as well as the community, required
that a public debt should be transferable; and its value in market
would depend on a variety of circumstances. If government
should thus interfere, in case of transfers, all confidence in public
engagements would be destroyed. It was likewise said, that
great injustice would be done in carrying the plan into effect in
the manner proposed. That many of the original certificates
were issued to persons who in fact had no interest in them, being
for the benefit of others, to whom, for various considerations,

they were to transfer the same. That the intermediate purchasers had, in many instances, suffered as much or more than the original holders, and that no provision was proposed for them. The proposition was negatived by a large majority. The irredeemability of the debt, except to the amount of eight per cent. on account both principal and interest, occasioned also much opposition and debate.

The assumption of the state debts, however, was a subject which gave rise to more serious debate, and created divisions both in and out of congress, the effects of which were long felt in the administration of the general government.

The debts of the several states were very unequal. Those of Massachusetts and South Carolina amounted to more than ten millions and a half, while the debts of all the other states, were only estimated at between fourteen and fifteen millions. The first proposition on this subject in the house of representatives, was to assume the whole of these debts. This was at first adopted, in committee of the whole, by a small majority. Afterwards, when the members from North Carolina took their seats, the subject was recommitted, and negatived by a majority of two—thirty one to twenty nine. Propositions were afterwards made, to assume specific sums from each, but were negatived. These various propositions occasioned long and violent debates among the members from different states, and lead to an inquiry into the origin of the state debts and to a comparative view of the different exertions and expenses of the states themselves, in their struggle for independence. The assumption of specific sums from each, was finally carried in the senate, by a majority of two, and was concurred in by the house by a majority of six.

Those in favor of the assumption contended that it was a measure of *justice* as well as *policy*. That it was just in respect to the creditors themselves, as well as to the states. These debts, it was said, were incurred for services rendered, supplies furnished, or loans made, not for the particular benefit of the individual states, but for the benefit of the union, for the common cause in which all were embarked. Justice, therefore, required that the persons to whom they were due, should be placed on the same footing with those who had a direct claim on the United States; and that both be paid out of a common fund. That although some states might be able to provide ample funds for the payment of their debts; yet others, destitute of like resources, burthened with a larger debt, occasioned, perhaps, by greater exertions in the common cause, might be unable to make adequate provision. One class of creditors, therefore, who happened to live in a large state, abounding in wealth and resources, and, perhaps, with a comparatively small debt, might be paid in full; while another, equally meritorious, living in a small state, having a large debt, and destitute of resources, might receive little or nothing. It would be just, in respect to the states, as in this way each would bear its proportion of the expenses incurred for one common object. It was to be considered also, it was said, that no inconsiderable proportion of the state debts, were incurred at a time when the United States had little or no credit. It was also strongly contended, that as the constitution had transferred to congress the principal funds on which the states had relied for the payment of their debts, it was just that the debts should follow the funds.

The policy of the measure, its advocates said, was not less apparent than its justice.

A provision for these debts by the states themselves, would necessarily create an interference between the general and state governments in their revenue systems, highly injurious, if not ruinous to both. The United States having the *exclusive* power to lay imposts, most of the states must have recourse to excises and direct taxes. These, it was said, must be very unequal in different states, in consequence of the inequality, of their debts. Great burdens, therefore, would be thrown on those states whose exertions had been greatest in the common cause; and jealousies and dissatisfaction must be the necessary consequence. In those states where recourse was had to direct taxes, a greater burden would be thrown on the landed interest, and this would produce emigration to other states less opppressed with taxes of this description. Where resort was had to excises, which would be laid on foreign as well as domestic articles, greater inducements would be held out to smuggling, materially affecting the revenue of the United States. In addition to this, commercial advantages might be greater in some states than in others, and a transfer of capital from one state to another be thereby encouraged. The collection of the same amount of taxes, it was said, might be made with less expense, under the direction of one government, than under several; and by having the general management of the revenues of the country in their hands, the national legislature would be enabled more fully to promote domestic industry and improvement throughout every part of the union.

In the course of the debates on this interesting question, it was stated by the advocates of the assumption, that a difference in the amount of state debts did not arise solely from a difference in exertions during the war,—but that the debts of some states were lessened by the avails of confiscated property and from territorial asquisitions. And it was asked, whether those, by whose offenses a confiscation of property had been incurred, had not offended against United America, and not merely against that state, where the offense was committed, and which alone received the benefit of the confiscation? And whether the acquisition of territory, was not owing to the exertions of the national force, under national direction ?

The opponents of the measure were not less decided in opinion that it was both *unjust* and *impolitic*, whether it went to a general or a partial assumption.

They denied that the state debts could be considered, in any way, the debts of the union, or that the United States were under obligations to discharge any part of them, except the balance, which, on a final settlement, should be found due to particular states. If they were the debts of the United States, in the hands of individuals, it was asked, whether they were not equally so when in the state treasuries? Whether the United States were not equally bound to provide for them in both situations? Before the adoption of the constitution, it was said, they had never been so considered. They contended, also, that not being the

.debts of the union, congress were not warranted by the constitution, in assuming the payment of them.

As to the policy of the measure, its opponents said, among other things, if a public debt was a public evil, the assumption would increase and perpetuate the evil. That the United States, and the individual states together, could discharge a debt of eighty millions much sooner than the United States alone. That after the general government had resorted to all the means of revenue in its power, the individual states would have other financial resources still remaining. It was, also, particularly urged, that each state could raise money, in a way most convenient for itself, and to which they had been accustomed. Some of the states, they said, were hostile to excises, others to direct taxes ; and that no general system of internal taxation could be established, adapted to the circumstances of each state, or which would give general satisfaction.

Some of the states had, by their exertions, paid a greater proportion of their debts, than others, and it would be unjust, they alleged, to compel them to contribute to the payment of the debts of the delinquent states. In answer to the suggestion, that unless the measure should be carried, great dissatisfaction would exist in some of the states—it was said, that much greater dissatisfaction would follow from its adoption. A majority of the people of the United States, it was believed, was opposed to it ; and the discordant interests, as well as jealousies among the states, now too much felt, would be thereby greatly increased.

The opposers of the assumption, also stated, that the adoption of the measure, would render state creditors more dependent on the general government ; that it would greatly lessen the influence and importance of the states, and tend to consolidate the union. The debts of Massachusetts, South Carolina, and Connecticut, as reported by the secretary, amounted to about one half of those of all the others. These states, therefore, felt a deep interest in the question. The legislature of South Carolina, in January, 1790, instructed their representatives in congress, to solicit the national legislature to assume their debt, " it having been incurred," as they said, " in consequence of the war between the United States and Great Britain."

In the course of the debate, Mr. Sedgwick declared, that the insurrection, which had then just taken place in Massachusetts, was occasioned by the burden of taxes necessarily imposed on the people of that state, to pay a debt, incurred merely for national purposes. Mr. Ames, in his usual strain of eloquence, asked, " but were the state debts contracted for the war? It appears, by the books in the public offices, that they were. Will any one say, that the whole expense of defending our common liberty, ought not to be a common charge?' Part of this charge was contracted by Massachusetts, before congress assumed the exercise of its powers. The first ammunition that repulsed the enemy at Lexington, and made such havoc at Bunker Hill, was purchased by the state, and appears in the form of the state debt." The states of Virginia, North Carolina, and Georgia, were most strenuous in their opposition.

This interesting question was finally decided in the senate, 14 to 12. In this body, the states of Massachusetts, Connecticut, New York, New Jersey, and South Carolina, were unanimously in the affirmative—Rhode Island, Virginia, North Carolina, and Georgia, with equal unanimity in the negative—and Pennsylvania, Delaware, and Maryland, divided.

Previous to its final decision, a bill had passed, fixing the temporary seat of government at Philadelphia, until 1800, and after that time, permanently on the river Potomac.

This subject had long been agitated in the old congress, and until this session, had not been settled. It has been supposed, and probably with truth, that this decision had some influence on the settlement of the question, concerning the assumption of the state debts. No question had created so great a division in congress, as well as among the people of the United States, under the new system of government. The house of delegates in Virginia, in November, 1790, declared, that so much of the act passed by congress, making provision for the debt of the United States, as assumed the payment of the state debts, was repug-

nant to the constitution of the United States, as it went to
the exercise of a power not expressly granted to the general government. They, also, declared, that so much of the
act, as limited the power of the United States, in redeeming
the public debt, was dangerous to the rights and subversive
of the interest of the people, and demanded the marked disapprobation of the general assembly. They, at the same time
resolved, that so far as the act pledged the faith of the United
States, and appropriated funds for the payment of certain
debts, due by the several states, would, in its operation, be highly
injurious to those states, which had redeemed a considerable portion of their debt, incurred during the late war, and particularly
produce great injury to the state of Virginia. This, it is believed, was the first act of a state legislature, importing censure on
the proceedings of the general government. The amount of the
debt of each state assumed, and subscribed to the loan, was to be
a charge against such state, in account with the United States.
To complete a settlement of the accounts between the states
and the United States, a board, consisting of three commissioners, was established during this session ; the determination of a
majority of them to be final and conclusive. In this settlement
the commissioners were empowered to decide, according to the
principles of general equity. The rules prescribed for their proceeding were, to debit each state with all advances, which had
been or might be made to it, by the United States, with the interest thereon, to the last day of the year 1789 ; and to credit
each state, for its disbursements and advances, with interest to
the same period ; and having struck the balance due to each
state, were to find the aggregate of all the balances, and this aggregate was to be apportioned between the states, by the same
rule, as prescribed in the constitution, for the apportionment of
representation and direct taxes, and according to the first enumeration which should be made. The balances found due to
the states, were to be funded on the same terms as the other part
of the domestic debt, but not to be transferable.*

* The commissioners completed a settlement in 1793, and for the result, See
Note 20

A cession of western lands by North Carolina, was received during this session, and approved by congress ; and the territory south of the river Ohio, was formed into a territorial government, with the same powers and privileges, as had been granted to the territory north of that river. Congress, also, proceeded to exercise some of the other powers vested in them by the constitution. Among other things, they directed an enumeration of the inhabitants to be made, on the first Monday of August, 1790 ; and established an uniform rule of naturalization. Aliens, being free white persons, who should have resided two years, in the United States, might be admitted citizens thereof, under certain regulations and restrictions. A fund for sinking the national debt was established. For this purpose, the surplus produce of the duties on imports, after satisfying all other demands, was appropriated to be applied to the purchase of the debt, under the direction of the president of the senate, the chief justice, the secretary of state and treasury, and attorney general, for the time being ; purchases to be made by any three of them, with the approbation of the president. Acts also were passed, authorizing the president to borrow money in Europe, at a rate of interest less than six per cent., to be applied also to the purchase of the debt.

In May, 1790, the state of Rhode Island adopted the constitution, and thus completed the union of all the states, under the new government.

This interesting session, did not close until August 12th, 1790. One of the first acts of the next session, which commenced on the first Monday of December following, was the admission of two new states into the union. Vermont, having amicably settled its disputes with New York, was admitted on the 4th of March, 1791 ; and Kentucky, with the consent of Virginia, on the first day of June, 1792 ; each to have two representatives, until an apportionment of representation should be made agreeably to the constitution.

The most important measures of this session, were the establishment of a national bank, and the imposition of a tax, on spirits distilled within the United States, from foreign and domestic materials.

To aid in the management of the national finances, the secretary of the treasury had previously recommended the establishment of a bank ; and in February, 1791, an act passed for that purpose. The preamble disclosed the principal reasons for its adoption, declaring, " that it would be conducive to the successful conducting of the national finances, give facility to the obtaining of loans for the use of the government, in sudden emergencies," and would also, " be productive of considerable advantage to trade and industry in general."

The capital stock of the bank was ten millions of dollars ; two millions to be subscribed for the benefit of the United States, and the residue by individuals. One fourth of the sums subscribed by individuals, was to be paid in gold and silver, and three fourths in the public debt. By the act of incorporation, it was to be a bank of discount as well as deposit, and its bills which were payable in gold and silver on demand, were made receivable in all payments to the United States. The bank was located at Philadelphia, with power in the directors, to establish offices of discount and deposit only, wherever they should think fit, within the United States.

The duration of the charter was limited to the 4th of March, 1811 ; and the faith of the United States was pledged, that during that period, no other bank should be established under their authority. One of the fundamental articles of the incorporation, was, that no loan should be made to the United States, for more than one hundred thousand dollars, or to any particular state for more than fifty thousand, or to any foreign prince or state, unless previously authorized by a law of the United States. The books were opened for subscriptions, in July, 1791, and a much larger sum subscribed, than was allowed by the charter ; and the bank went into successful operation. This measure was not adopted without warm and violent debates.

It was said in opposition, in the first place, that congress had no power under the constitution, to create this or any other corporation ; in the second place, that so large a monied institution, wouid, in its effects, be highly injurious to the community.

Its advocates, on the other hand, contended generally, that the establishment of an institution of this kind, though not within the express words of the constitution, was among the incidental powers contemplated by that part of the instrument, which enabled congress to make all laws *necessary* and *proper*, for carrying into execution, the powers expressly granted.

An institution of this kind, they said, was necessary and proper, for the attainment of the important ends contemplated in the constitution ; and that similar establishments, in all well regulated communities, had been found necessary, in the management of their finances, and for the attainment of the great ends of civil government. In answer, its opponents said, that the constitution was not only silent on the subject, but that no such power was intended to be granted by the framers of that instrument. That in the general convention, a proposition to give congress power to create corporations, was made and negatived. It was a power, they said, too important to be assumed, by implication ; nor could they agree to so broad a construction as was given by the advocates of the measure, to the words " *necessary* and *proper*," as used in the constitution. No means, they considered, to be *necessary* for the purpose of carrying into execution the *specified powers*, except those without which, the powers granted, would be *nugatory*, or the ends contemplated *absolutely unattainable.*

The president, before approving the bill, requested the opinions of the members of his cabinet, in writing, as to its constitutionality. The secretary of state and attorney general, were of opinion, that the bill was unconstitutional, while the secretaries of the treasury and war, were of a different opinion, and concurred with the majority in congress.

After the most mature deliberation, the president put his signature to the bill ; and experience has proved the expediency if not the absolute necessity of an institution of this kind, to enable the government to manage its great concerns ; and has likewise evinced the profound, and almost unerring judgment of that great man, who, as chief magistrate, gave it his sanction. Though this question, for many years afterwards, agitated the public mind, and divided the national councils ; yet the late establishment of a national bank, with a capital of thirty-five millions, with the approbation and consent of those, heretofore opposed to it on constitutional grounds, must rescue the names of the authors of the first bank, from the reproach then cast upon them, for a violation of the constitution ; and has, it is presumed, put the question at rest.

The act laying a duty on spirits distilled within the United States, and which was the commencement of a system of internal taxation, was a subject of much debate, and called forth the local feelings and prejudices of the members from different parts of the union.   It was not only strongly opposed in the national legislature, but opposition was afterwards carried so far as to produce in the state of Pennsylvania, an open insurrection, requiring the imposition of a military force on the part of the government.

At the opening of the first session of the second congress, in October, 1791, the president in his speech, notices with pleasure, the prosperous situation of the country under the new system of government.

" Your own observation in your respective districts," he observed, " will have satisfied you of the progressive state of agriculture, manufactures, commerce, and navigation : in tracing their causes, you will have remarked, with particular pleasure, the happy effects of that revival of confidence, public as well as private, to which the constitution and laws of the United States, so obviously contributed.   And you will have observed, with no less interest, new and decisive proofs of the increasing reputation and credit of the nation."

Referring to the depredations of the Indians on the frontiers, and the necessity he-was under of commencing offensive operations against them, he said, " it is sincerely to be desired, that all need of coercion in future, may cease, and that an intimate intercourse may succeed, calculated to advance the happiness of the Indians, and to attach them to the United States."

With this view, he proposed the adoption of regulations securing them against imposition, in the alienation of their lands, and extending to this unenlightened race the benefits of commerce and civilization, and inflicting punishment on those, who should violate their rights. This humane policy, was afterwards pursued by the government. This session was principally spent in carrying into effect the new system of government, extending its benefits to every part of the union, and securing to all, the fruits of their own industry. For these purposes, laws were passed concerning the fisheries, and the government and regulation of fishermen employed therein—declaring what officer should act as president of the United States, in case of a vacancy—establishing a mint, and regulating the coins of the United States—apportioning the representatives among the several states, according to the first enumeration—providing more effectually for the national defense, by establishing an uniform militia system, and for calling forth the militia in the exigences mentioned in the constitution. On the subject of apportioning the representatives, a difference arose between the senate and house, with respect to the *ratio* to be adopted, and the *mode* of applying it. A bill passed both houses, fixing the ratio at one member for every thirty thousand ; and the whole federal number in the United States, was divided by this sum, and the numbers produced by this division, was apportioned among the states by this ratio, giving to each state its number, and the residue was apportioned among the states which had large fractions. The president very justly considered this *mode* of apportionment, as contrary to the constitution, and returned the bill to congress with his objections. The first was that the constitution had prescribed, that representatives should be apportioned among the several states, according to their respective numbers ; and that there was no one proportion or division, which applied to the respective states, would yield the number and allotment of representatives proposed by the bill. The second, that by the constitution, the number of representatives should not exceed one for every thirty thousand ; which restriction, by the fair and obvious construction, was to be applied to the separate and respective states ; and that the bill had alloted to eight states, more than one for every thirty thousand. This was the first instance, in which the president had exercised his qualified veto, to any act of congress. The bill not being repassed by two thirds of both houses, was rejected. A bill was afterwards passed, apportioning the representatives, agreeably to a ratio of one for every thirty thousand in each state, which received the sanction of the president ; and this mode of apportionment has since been pursued.

Early in the session, the president communicated to congress, the unfortunate defeat of general St. Clair and his army, by the Indians. In consequence of this, the frontiers were left more exposed to Indian depredations ; and the number of the regular troops was augmented, and additional duties laid on various imported articles, to defray the expense.

The administration of the general government was disturbed this year, not only by the continuance of Indian hostilities, but by an increased opposition, in some parts of the union, to the laws laying a duty on domestic spirits. This opposition had been carried so far, as to require a proclamation from the president, warning all persons against unlawful combinations and proceedings, tending to obstruct the operation of the laws. These subjects, among others, were noticed by the president, in his communication to congress, at the commencement of their session on the 6th of November, 1792.

It was apparent that the two great parties, originally formed at the time of the adoption of the constitution, and which from various causes, had since increased, began now to be more distinctly marked. Those originally opposed to the new government, as was to be expected, watched with a jealous eye, every exercise of power under it.

Individuals who had foretold the evil consequences of adopting the system, without previous amendments, and who had been disappointed, in the alterations proposed by congress, would naturally lay hold of every act of the government, tending to shew the truth of their predictions : and pride of opinion would be in-

terested, not only in proclaiming, but magnifying real or supposed evils.

Nor was the opposition limited to the unconstitutionality of the
acts of the general government,—it extended to many of the
great and important measures of its administration.

The funding system generally, the assumption of the state
debts, the bank, and duties on domestic spirits, were objects of
the, most severe attack ; and the secretary of the treasury, who
was considered as the author of them, had become very unpopular in some parts of the union.

The difference between the heads of the departments of state
and treasury, on some important questions, which had been agitated in the cabinet, was well known and felt in congress, and
elsewhere. The public conduct and political characters of the gentlemen at the head of these departments, in the course of the year
1792, had been the subject of severe newspaper animadversions.
Mr. Hamilton was viewed not only as the author of the funding
system, the bank, and other measures deemed either unconstitutional, or highly injurious to the public interest, but was charged
with hostility to republican principles and state rights. Mr.
Jefferson, on the other hand, was considered hostile to the constitution, and was accused of being opposed to the administration of
which he was a member, and of taking measures to reduce the
powers of the general government, within too narrow limits.

During this session, an inquiry was instituted in the house of
representatives, into the official conduct of the secretary of the
treasury. This was commenced by Mr. Giles, by calling for information from the president and secretary, relative to loans, negociated in pursuance of the acts of the 4th and 12th of August,
1790, and the management and application of these loans ; as
well as the application and management of the revenue generally.
The resolutions introduced for the purpose of obtaining this information, were adopted by the house. The object of the mover
was disclosed in his remarks in support of them. These remarks he concluded by saying—" Candor, however, induces me
to acknowledge, that impressions, resulting from my inquiries

into this subject, have been made upon my mind, by no means favorable to the arrangements made by the gentleman at the head of the treasury department."

The report of the secretary, in answer to this call for information, evinced that his pride was not a little wounded by the remarks of Mr. Giles. " The resolutions," he said, " to which I am to answer, were not moved without a pretty copious display of the reasons on which they were founded. These reasons are of a nature to excite attention, to. beget alarm, to inspire doubts.

" Deductions of a very extraordinary complexion, may, without forcing the sense, be drawn from them. I feel it incumbent upon me, to meet the suggestions which have been thrown out, with decision and explicitness. And while I hope I shall let fall nothing inconsistent with the cordial and unqualified respect which I feel for the house of representatives, while I acquiesce in the sufficiency of the motives that induced, on their part, the giving a prompt and free course to the investigation proposed, I cannot but resolve to treat the subject with a freedom which is due to truth, and the consciousness of a pure zeal for the public interest."

Having endeavored to shew the fallacy of the statements made by the mover of the resolutions, in conclusion he observed,—" Thus have I not only furnished a just and affirmative view of the real situation of the public accounts, but have likewise shewn, I trust, in a conspicuous manner, fallacies enough in the statements, from which the inference of an unaccounted for balance is drawn, to evince that it is one tissue of error."

Soon after this report was made, Mr. Giles submitted to the house several resolutions, containing charges against the secretary. The substance of them was, that he had failed to give congress information, in due time, of monies drawn from Europe —that he had violated the law of the 4th of August, 1790, by an unauthorized application of money borrowed under it,—that he had drawn part of the money into the United States, without any instructions from the president—that he had exceeded his authority in making loans, under the acts—that without instructions from the president, he had drawn more of the money borrowed in Holland, than he was authorized by those acts, and that he had been guilty of an indecorum to the house, in undertaking to judge its motives in calling for information. The charges contained in these resolutions being considered either frivolous or unsupported, the resolutions themselves were negatived by large majorities.

The states were not a little alarmed at a decision of the supreme court of the United States, at their session in February, 1793. The court at this sesion, four judges against one, decided, that a state was liable to a suit, in favor of an individual. This important and interesting question came before the court, in a suit instituted by a citizen of South Carolina, against the state of Georgia. The process was served, by leaving a copy with the governor, and also with the attorney general of that state—it was made returnable to August term, 1792 ; and was continued to February following. The state of Georgia did not appear, and the question was argued solely by the attorney general of the United States, in favor of the plaintiff.

The decision was grounded on that part of the constitution, establishing the federal judiciary, which declares, that the judicial power should extend among other cases, " to controversies between a state and citizens of another state." The court were of opinion, that this was not limited to controversies, where the state was plaintiff.

In consequence of this decision, in the summer of 1793, a suit was also commenced by an individual against the state of Massachusetts, and suits against other states, were no doubt, in contemplation. Congress, at their next session, proposed an amendment to the constitution, declaring, that the judicial power of the general government, should not be construed to extend to any suit, in law or equity, against any state, by the citizens of another state, or by citizens or subjects of any foreign state. This was afterwards ratified by the states, and became a part of the constitution.

The 4th of March, 1793, closed the sessions of the second congress, as well as the first term of the administration of president Washington

CHAPTER XXI.

GENERAL WASHINGTON had consented, though with great reluctance, not to decline a second election. He again received the unanimous vote of the electors. Mr. Adams was also again elected vice-president, but not with equal unanimity. Of one hundred thirty two votes, Mr. Adams had seventy seven, Mr. Clinton, of New York, fifty, Mr. Jefferson four, and Aaron Burr one. The states of New York, Virginia, North Carolina, and Georgia, were unanimous in favor of Mr. Clinton, and Kentucky voted for Mr. Jefferson.

On the 5th of March, the president took the oath of office, and entered upon the second term of his administration. It was fortunate for the United States that he yielded to the wishes of his country, not to decline a second election. The great events which had taken place in Europe, the effects of which were soon to be felt in America, required, in a chief magistrate, all the wisdom and firmness, for which he was so eminently distinguished, as well as all that popularity and weight of character, which he had so justly acquired. A most extraordinary revolution in France, was coeval with a change of government in the United States. A new constitution, with the assent of the king, was established by the French people. The legislative power was vested in a single body, styled a national assembly, and to their acts a partial negative only was reserved to the crown.

This assembly was dissolved in 1792, and a national convention substituted. Soon after this, royalty itself was abolished, and the French nation declared a republic. The king and queen were arrested, and before this convention accused of various crimes against the state; and on the 21st of January, 1793, the king was brought to the guillotine, and the queen, not long after, shared a similar fate. The convention soon after the death of the king, declared war against Great Britain and Holland. The news of these important transactions reached America not long after president Washington had entered upon the second term of his administration; and presented a new state of things to the consideration of the government and people of the United States.

Enjoying the blessings of liberty and self-government themselves, and remembering with gratitude the aid afforded by France in the attainment of them, the citizens of America had seen with satisfaction and even enthusiasm, a revolution, by which the people of that country participated in the same blessings. And although in the progress of this revolution, in consequence of the frequent changes, as well as great defects in their systems of government, from the ferocity and cruelty of the rival factions, from the imprisonment and beheading of the king and queen, some were led to doubt whether a republican or representative government, could be permanently maintained in that country; yet a great proportion of the American people seemed to have no doubt on the subject.

They viewed France in the same situation America formerly was, contending for her rights against the tyranny of Great Britain and the rest of Europe, and many individuals were ready to join with her in the contest, or to engage in privateering against the commerce of the belligerent powers, regardless of the consequences to themselves or their country.

The president, however, from his high station, was called upon to view these great events as they might affect his own country, whose destinies, under God, were entrusted to his care ; and he felt himself bound to consult the dictates of his judgment, rather than the impulse of his feelings. He foresaw that the storm which was gathering in Europe, must soon reach the United States, and he felt it his duty, as far as possible, here to prevent its desolating effects. In the mighty conflict which was to ensue, a conflict in which all the great European powers either were or must necessarily be engaged, he was satisfied the best interests of his country dictated a state of neutrality ; and he was convinced that this course might be pursued without a violation either of national faith, or national honor.

Neutrality, however, he knew, to be just, must be impartial ; and he was sensible, that from the state of public feeling in America, it would be extremely difficult to preserve a state of strict neutrality, or to avoid collisions with some of the contending powers, particularly France or Great Britain. Aware of the importance and delicacy of the crisis, he assembled his cabinet in April, for their advice. To them he submitted certain questions, particularly with respect to the existing relations with France.* These were of course communicated confidentially, but they afterwards clandestinely found their way to the public.

The answers of the members of the cabinet to these questions were requested in writing. On some of them, the opinions of the members were unanimous ; on others, a difference prevailed. All were in favor of issuing a proclamation of neutrality, of receiving a minister from the existing French government, and against convening congress. Some of the cabinet, however, were for receiving the minister with some degree of qualification, from a doubt, whether the government of France could be considered

* Note 21.

as finally settled by the deliberate sense of the nation. The president, however, concluded to receive him in an unqualified manner. As to the clause of guarantee, in the treaty of 1778, a difference of opinion also existed in the cabinet. The secretaries of the treasury and of war, considered the clause as only applicable to a *defensive war*, and therefore, not binding in a contest commenced by France herself; while the secretary of state and the attorney general, thought it unnecessary, at that time, to decide the question. The views of the members of the cabinet were indeed different, on the great question of the French revolution, and this served to increase the divisions already existing.

A proclamation was issued by the president, on the 22d of April, declaring it to be the duty and interest of the United States, to pursue a conduct friendly and impartial towards the belligerent powers of Europe, and that it was their disposition to observe such conduct; warning the citizens to avoid all acts tending to contravene such a disposition; and declaring that those who might render themselves liable to punishment, by committing, aiding, or abetting hostilities against any of the belligerents, or by carrying contraband of war, would not receive the protection of the United States. The wisdom and policy of this measure, soon became manifest.

After France became a republic, Mr. Genet was sent minister to the United States, in the room of Mr. Ternant, who had been appointed by the king.

The new minister arrived at Charleston, South Carolina, on the 8th of April, where he remained some weeks; and from thence went by land to Philadelphia.

He was presented in form to the president, on the 18th of May, and received as the representative of the French republic. In his first interview, he assured the president, that " on account of the remote situation of the United States, and other circumstances, France did not expect that they should become *a party* in the war, but wished to see them preserve their prosperity and happiness in peace."

This was in accordance with the declaration made by the national convention, contained in a public letter addressed to the people of the United States, of which Mr. Genet was to be the bearer. In this letter, after speaking of the abolition of royalty, and the establishment of a republic, they say to the people of America, " the immense distance which parts us, prevents your taking in this glorious regeneration of Europe, that concern which your principles and past conduct reserved to you."

This letter was published at Paris, December 23d, 1792, and before the arrival of the new minister, was republished in the United States. Notwithstanding these declarations, Genet had in his pocket, *secret* instructions, by which he was charged to take such steps, as should induce the American government finally, to make *common cause* with France. These instructions being afterwards made public, by Genet himself, in vindication of his conduct, disclosed the real views of the French government, in sending a new minister to America. Extracts from them, cannot be uninteresting to the reader.

They were drawn by the executive council, who appointed the new minister, and after speaking of the means of renewing and consolidating the *commercial ties* between the two countries, proceed to disclose the further views of the council—" the executive council are disposed to set on foot, a negociation upon these foundations, and they do not know, but that such a treaty admits a *latitude* still more extensive, in becoming a national agreement, in which the two *great* people shall suspend their commercial and political interests, and establish a mutual understanding to befriend the empire of liberty, wherever it can be embraced, to guaranty the sovereignty of the people, and punish those powers, who still keep up an exclusive colonial and commercial system, by declaring that their vessels shall not be received, in the ports of the contracting parties. Such a compact, which the people of France will support with all the energy which distinguishes them, and of which they have given so many proofs, will contribute to the general emancipation of the new world. However vast this project may be, it will not be difficult to execute, if the Americans determine on it ; and it is to convince them of its practicability, that citizen Genet must direct all his attention."

After stating that France had a particular interest, in acting efficiently against England and Spain, and that the Americans were equally interested in disconcerting the destructive projects of George III, the executive council added, " as it is possible, however, that the false representations, which have been made to congress of the situation of our internal affairs, of the state of our maritime power, of our finances, and especially of the storms with which we are threatened, may make her ministers in the negociations which citizen Genet is entrusted to open, adopt a timid and wavering conduct, the executive council charges him, *in expectation, that the American government will finally determine to make a common cause with us,* to take such steps as will appear to him, the exigences may require, to serve the cause of liberty and the freedom of the people."

The real and ultimate views of the French government in sending a new minister to the United States, are here disclosed.

The "steps" he was charged to take in case of the "timid and wavering conduct" of the American government, referred no doubt, to enlisting the American people on the side of France, and through their influence, to induce, if not compel the government finally to make *common cause* with her ; and the conduct of the French minister was in conformity with this ultimate object. And, but for the wisdom and prudence of the chief magistrate, and the indiscretion of the minister himself, the United States would probably at that period, have been involved in the destructive wars of Europe.

The French nation, being at war with the great maritime powers, perceived the importance and even the necessity of a relaxation of its colonial system. Immediately after the declaration of war against Great Britain and Holland, the national convention, therefore, passed a decree opening their ports in the East and West Indies, and granted special privileges to the vessels of the United States.

The communication of Mr. Genet, enclosing this decree, clearly evinced that a *political* as well as *commercial* compact between the two countries, was contemplated by the French government, and was at the same time, to be a subject of negociation.

" The French republic," says Mr. Genet, in his letter to the secretary of state, of the 23d of May, 1793, " seeing in the Americans but brothers, has opened to them by the decrees now enclosed, all her ports in the two worlds ; has granted them all the favors which her own citizens enjoy, in her vast possessions ; has invited them to participate the benefits of her navigation, in granting to their vessels, the same rights as to her own ; and has charged me, to propose to your government, to establish in a true *family compact*, that is, in a national compact, the liberal and fraternal basis on which she wishes to see raised the *commercial* and *political* system of two people, all whose interests are confounded." He added, " that he was invested with the powers necessary to undertake this important negociation, of which the sad annals of humanity offer no example before the brilliant era at length opening upon it."

The first instructions of Genet, extracts from which we have just given, bore date the 4th day of January, 1793. On the 17th of the same month, he was furnished with additional instructions, more explicit as to the *objects* and *conditions* of the *new compact* he was directed to propose to the United States. The old treaty of alliance was to be more fully *defined* and *enlarged ;* and a *new guaranty* of the French West India Islands was to be a *sine qua non* of the American commerce with these islands.

These instructions serve to explain the French ministers letter above mentioned, concerning the new " *family compact.*"

" The executive council," say the last instructions, " wish that a new treaty, founded upon a basis more *liberal* and more *fraternal*, than that of 1778, may be concluded as *soon as possible.*— As, however, they cannot conceal, that in the actual state of Europe, a negociation of this kind may be subject to many impediments, whether brought about by secret manœuvres of the English minister and his partizans in Philadelphia, by the timidity certain members of the federal government, who, notwithstanding their known patriotism, have always shown the strongest aversion to every measure which might be unpleasing to England, they think it right for the present, that citizen Genet should draw every advantage which the provisions of the subsisting treaty secure to the republic, until a new *compact* has more clearly and fully *defined* and *enlarged* them. In this view, which existing circumstances render particularly important, citizen Genet is expressly enjoined to make himself thoroughly master of the sense of the treaty of 1778, and to be watchful in the execution of the articles, which are favorable to the commerce and navigation of the French republic, and he shall endeavor to satisfy the Americans, that the engagements which may appear burdensome to them are the just price of that independence, which the French contributed to acquire for them."

With respect to the *terms* of this new *family compact*, the executive council in their last instructions say, " the *reciprocal guaranty* of the *possessions* of the two nations stipulated in the 11th article of the treaty of 1778, can be established upon generous principles, which have been already pointed out, and shall equally be an *essential* clause in the new treaty which will be proposed. The executive council in consequence, recommend especially to citizen Genet, to *sound early* the disposition of the American government, and to make it a *condition sine qua non, of their free commerce with the West Indies*, so essential to the United States. It nearly concerns the peace and prosperity of the French nation, that a people whose resources increase beyond all calculation, and whom nature hath placed so near our rich colonies, should become interested *by their own engagements*, in the preservation of these islands. The citizen Genet will find the less difficulty in making this proposition relished in the United States, as the great trade which will be the reward of it, will indemnify them ultimately for the sacrifices they may make at the outset, and the Americans cannot be ignorant of the great disproportion between their resources and those of the French republic ; and that for a long period, the *guaranty asked of them*, will be little else than *nomin-*

al for them, while that on our part will be *real*, and we shall immediately put ourselves in a state to fulfil it, in sending to the American ports a *sufficient force to put them beyond insult, and to facilitate their communication with the Islands and with France.*"

The French minister was also furnished with blank letters of marque, to be delivered " to such French or American owners as should apply for the same." There were also delivered to him by the minister at war, " officer's commissions in blank for several grades in the army."

At that period of the government the president had never made a treaty without previously consulting the senate. The French minister was, therefore, informed, that as " the senate was in recess, and could not meet again till the fall, the participation, in matters of treaty, given by the constitution to that branch of the government, would, of course, delay any definite answer to his friendly propositions."

The American executive was, at the same time, well aware that a *political* and not a *commercial* connection with the United States, was the *real* or principal object of the newly established republic. During the preceding year, the American government had repeatedly made overtures for new commercial arrangements with France, particularly with respect to her colonies. But these had been neglected. In the unsettled state of the new government, the president very wisely delayed meeting the propositions of Genet.

His views on the subject, greatly misrepresented at the time, were communicated to Mr. Munroe, while minister in France, in a letter from the secretary of state, of June 1st, 1795. Referring to these propositions, the secretary says,—" It is impossible to look into this subject, without remarking, that other principles may be conceived, upon which the executive might have refused to act immediately ; but which do not *appear* to have influenced his designs. His attention must have been arrested by the diction of Mr. Genet's overtures. The president and the French republic had hitherto agitated a change in *commercial* regulations only ; when Mr. Genet announces a desire to modify the *political* connection also. The precise meaning of the word *political,* was not very obvious ; though the most natural interpretation was, that the *political* relation, established by the treaty of alliance, was proposed to be revised.

"The project, therefore," the secretary added, "of a treaty on the basis of Mr. Genet's propositions, ought to have been well explored before the first advance. To assent to them, if it would not have been a departure from neutrality, would at least have magnified the suspicion of our faith, without a confidence in which, that neutrality must always be insecure : To reject them was to incur discontent, possibly a breach with an ally. The councils of nations ought to be superior to the passions which drive *individuals. Permanent* good being the polar star of the former, they will often have to encounter the impetuosity of the latter, *who substitute feelings for sound policy.*"*

Mr. Genet was instructed " to solicit the American government for the payment of the sums remaining due to France, though all the times stipulated for the reimbursement had not yet expired." As an inducement for anticipating these payments, it was proposed by the French government, that the whole of the money thus paid, should be expended in purchasing the various productions of the United States. One of the first official acts of the new minister, therefore, was, an application to the executive for this object. He proposed, that the whole of the debt due to France, be paid in specie or bank bills of equal currency with specie, or in government bonds, bearing interest and payable at certain specified periods ; on condition that the sums advanced should be invested in the productions of America, for the supply of the French dominions. In answer to this proposition, the French minister was informed that the payment of the instalments, as they fell due, could then only be effected by new loans ; and that it was not in the power of the United States to anticipate the payment of the whole sum at once. That the issue of government bonds to so large an amount, would tend greatly to injure

* Munroe's View, pp. 240, 241, 242.

public credit ; and that, therefore, the advantages offered, were insufficient to induce an acceptance of the proposition.

The reply of the minister, as well as his other communications made about the same time, evinced the spirit with which he was governed.

" Without entering into the financial reasons," he said in a letter of the 14th of June, " which operate this refusal, without endeavoring to prove to you, that it tends to accomplish the infernal system of the king of England, and of the other kings, his accomplices to destroy, by famine, the French republicans and liberty, I attend, on the present occasion, only to the calls of my country," &c.

He requested the president to direct an adjustment of the amount due to France, to enable him to make assignments of the same to American merchants or farmers, in payment for provisions they might furnish, agreeably to his instructions.

Questions of serious importance soon arose, not only with regard to belligerent and neutral rights and duties under the general law of nations ; but also under the treaties existing between the two countries, on which the American executive and the French minister unfortunately differed. In a conference with the secretary of state, soon after his reception, Mr. Genet spoke of his proceedings at Charleston, and expressed a hope, " that the president had not so absolutely decided against the measure, but . that he would hear what was to be said in support of it." He added, that he would write him a note, justifying his conduct under the treaty between the two nations ; but if the president should finally determine otherwise, he must submit, as his instructions enjoined him to do what was agreeable to the Americans.

In pursuance of this intimation, he soon after addressed a note to the secretary of state, in answer to one of the 15th of May, to Mr. Ternant, his predecessor. This was the commencement of a correspondence between the new French minister and the American executive ; a correspondence which, whether viewed in relation to the claims and complaints on the part of the French government, or to the style and manner in which they were presented, stands unequalled in the history of diplomacy.

That language, such as this correspondence contained, should have been used by a foreign minister to the president of the United States, could hardly have obtained belief among those unacquainted with the spirit of that period, had not the correspondence itself been submitted to their examination.

The French minister claimed the right of arming vessels in our ports, and of enlisting American citizens to cruize against nations with whom the United States were at peace ; and insisted that the American government could neither prohibit such armaments, or punish those who should thus engage in the war, on the side of France. In his first note on this subject, after acknowledging that by his order, vessels had been armed and commissioned in the port of Charleston, and that these vessels, manned in part by American citizens, had taken and brought prizes into American ports, he says, " I ought, by a sincere exposition of my conduct, to put you in a capacity to judge, whether I have encroached on the sovereignty of the American nation, its laws, and its principles of government. The vessels armed at Charleston belong to French houses; they are commanded and manned by French citizens, or by Americans, who, at the moment they entered the service of France, in order to defend their brothers and their friends, knew only the treaties and the laws of the United States, no article of which imposes on them the painful injustice *of abandoning us*, in the midst of the dangers which surround us. It is then evident, sir, that these armaments cannot be matter of offense in the citizens of the United States ; and that those who are on board of our vessels, have *renounced the immediate protection* of their country, on taking part *with us*."

These novel doctrines were resisted by the American executive; and the secretary of state, in reply informed the French minister, that arming and equipping vessels in the ports of the United States, to cruise against nations with whom they were at peace, was incompatible with their territorial sovereignty.

That it was the *right* of every nation "to prohibit acts of sovereignty from being exercised by any other within its limits, and the *duty* of a neutral nation to prohibit such as would injure one of the warring powers; that the granting military commissions within the United States, by any other authority than their own, was an *infringement* on their sovereignty, and particularly so, when granted to their *own citizens*, to lead them to commit acts contrary to the duties they owed their own country; that the departure of vessels, thus illegally equipped, from the ports of the United States, would be but an acknowledgment of respect, analogous to the breach of it, while it is necessary, on their part, as an evidence of their faithful neutrality."

The French minister, instead of submitting to the opinion of the president, declared to the secretary of state, that this opinion was contrary to the *principles of natural right*, to the *usage* of nations, to the *connection* which united the two countries, and even to the president's *proclamation*.

"Every obstruction by the government of the United States," he said, "to the arming of French vessels, must be an attempt on the rights of man, upon which repose the independence and laws of the United States; a violation of the ties, which unite the people of France and of America; and even a manifest contradiction of the system of neutrality of the president; for, in fact, if our merchant vessels, or others, are not allowed to arm themselves, when the French alone are resisting the league of all the tyrants against the liberty of the people, they will be exposed to inevitable ruin in going out of the United States, which is certainly *not the intention of the people of America*.

"Their fraternal voice has resounded from every quarter around me, and their accents are not equivocal—they are as pure as the hearts of those by whom they are expressed, and the more they have touched my sensibility, the more they must interest, in the happiness of America, the nation I represent; the more I wish, sir, that the federal government should observe, as far as in their power, the public engagements contracted by both nations; and that by this generous and prudent conduct, they will give, at least to the world, the example of a true neutrality, which does not consist in a *cowardly abandonment of their friends* in the moment when danger menaces them, but adhering strictly, *if they can do no better*, to the obligations they have contracted with them."

The right of arming in American ports, was claimed also by Mr. Genet, under the 17th and 22d articles of the treaty of amity and commerce between the two countries. The president, on the other hand, viewed the 17th article as merely giving to the contracting parties, the right of entering the ports of the other with their prizes, and departing with them freely, but not of arming and manning vessels in their respective ports. A construction was also given by the executive to the 22d article, different from that contended for by the French minister. While the latter claimed that this article expressly gave France the right of arming in the ports of the United States, the president said that it only prohibited foreign privateers from arming in the ports of either party ; but did not grant such permission to the contracting parties themselves—that on this point it was silent, and left open and free, to be decided according to circumstances. That a negative stipulation as to privateers of the enemies of France, was not an affirmative one in favor of France herself. This, it was also said, could not have been the intention of the parties when the treaty was made ; as such a stipulation on the part of France, would have been inconsistent with her treaties with other powers, then in force. In case of war between the United States and Spain, France by her treaty with the latter, could not permit the vessels of the United States to be armed in her ports.

This, the American government said, must have been the construction put upon this article by France herself, in her treaty with Great Britain, in 1786 ; by which persons " not being subjects of either crown," were prohibited from arming in the ports of the other. If this had amounted to an affirmative stipulation, that the subjects of the crown of Great Britain, being at war with the United States, might arm in her ports against them, it would have been a direct violation of that article.   Bound by treaty to refuse to one belligerent the right of arming in our ports, and at liberty to refuse it to the other, the executive said, it would be a breach of neutrality, not to refuse it to the latter.   This reasoning, however conclusive, not being in accordance with the views of the French minister, was by no means satisfactory to him.

Nor was he better satisfied with the reasoning of the American executive, as to the *right* and *duty* of the United States, to restrain their citizens from hostile acts against nations, with whom they were at peace.   " The United States," says the secretary, " being in a state of peace with most of the belligerent powers by treaty, and with all of them by the laws of nature ; murders and robberies committed within our territory, or on the high seas, on those with whom we are so at peace, are punishable equally as if committed on our own inhabitants.   If I might venture to reason a little formally, without being charged with running into ' subtleties and aphorisms,' I would say, that if one citizen has a right to go to war of his own authority, every citizen has the same.   If every citizen has that right, then the nation (which is composed of all its citizens,) has a right to go to war by the authority of its individual citizens.   But this is not true, either on the general principles of society or by our constitution, which gives that power to congress alone, and not to the citizens individually.   The first position is not true ; and no citizen has a right to go to war of his own authority ; and for what he does without right, he ought to be punished.   Indeed, nothing can be more obviously absurd, than to say that *all the citizens may be at war, and yet the nation at peace.*"   To these reasonings, or rather axioms, which it must now appear strange, could be controverted by any one, the French minister applied the epithet of " diplomatic subtleties."

And when the secretary enforced the principles of neutrality advanced by him, by quotations from Vattel, and the most approved writers on national law, Genet calls them " the aphorisms of Vattel, &c."   " All the reasonings," he said to the secretary in his answer, " contained in your letter, are ingenious, but I do not hesitate to tell you, that they rest on *a basis* which I cannot admit."

" You oppose to my complaints, to my just reclamations, upon the footing of right, the *private* or *public* opinion of the president of the United States ; and this *egis*, not appearing to you sufficient, you bring forward *aphorisms of Vattel*, to justify or excuse infractions committed on positive treaties." And he has the affrontery to add, " do not punish the brave individuals of your nation, who arrange themselves under our banner, knowing perfectly well, that no law of the United States gives to the government, the sad power of arresting their zeal, by acts of rigor. The Americans are free ; they are not attached to the globe, like the slaves of Russia ; they may change their situation when they please, and by accepting at this moment, the succor of their arms in the habit of trampling on tyrants, we do not commit the plagiat of which you speak. The true robbery, the true crime, would be to enchain the courage of these good citizens, of these sincere friends of the best of causes."*

Not only were French vessels armed in American ports, and manned by American citizens, to cruise against nations in amity with the United States ; but these vessels returned into port with their prizes, some of which were taken on the high seas, and others within the jurisdictional limits of the United States.

In some instances, also, the public armed ships of France, took vessels on our shores, and in our waters, and brought them in as prizes.

When our neutrality was thus violated, either by a public or private armed ship, the president deemed it his duty, as far as practicable, to cause the vessels to be restored ; and for this purpose only, the courts of the United States, made inquiry and took cognizance of prizes thus made.

The French minister complained loudly of this conduct of the American government ; declaring, that French consuls alone, could decide whether these vessels were lawful prize or not. In

---

* American State Papers, vol. 1, p. 98.

vain did the president in reply, say, that by the consular convention, no such power was given to French consuls—in vain did
he refer to the established law of nations, " that it was an essential attribute of the jurisdiction of every country, to preserve peace,
to punish acts in breach of it, and to restore property taken by
force, within its limits"—in vain did he refer for a recognition of
the same principles, to the 6th article of the treaty between
the two countries, by which each party stipulates by all the means
in their power, to protect and defend each others vessels and effects, in their respective ports or roads, or on the seas near their
countries, and to recover and restore the same to the right owners.

These well known principles, recognized by a solemn compact
between France and America, were entirely disregarded by the
French minister and consular agents ; and the president was at
last compelled to give notice to the consuls, that if they continued to exercise " within the United States, a general admiralty
jurisdiction, and in particular, to assume to try the validity of
prizes, and to give sentence thereon as judges of admiralty," or
should undertake " to give commissions within the United States,
and to enlist or encourage the enlistment of men, natives, or inhabitants of the states, to commit hostilities on nations, with
whom the United States were at peace, their exequaturs should
be revoked, and their persons be submitted to such prosecutions
and punishments as the laws should prescribe for the case." Notwithstanding this, French consuls not only continued to exercise
admiralty jurisdiction, and to determine the validity of prizes,
but did actually resist the process of the federal courts, supposed
to interfere with the exercise of such jurisdiction.   A regular writ
of replevin was issued at Boston, by virtue of which, the schoon-
er Greyhound, brought into Boston harbor as a French prize, was
taken possession of by the marshal of the district of Massachusetts. By orders from the French consul Duplaine, this vessel was
forcibly taken from the custody of the marshal, by the French
frigate Concord, then in the harbor, and was for some time detained by force, under the protection of the frigate. Informed
of this outrage on the laws of the country, the president imme-

diately revoked and annulled the exequatur of the consul, and prohibited his further exercise. of consular powers. The French minister himself, also, forbade an officer of justice to serve a process, on a vessel taken within a mile of the American shores, and brought into New York as a prize ; and gave orders to a French squadron, then in the harbor, to protect this vessel against any person, who should attempt to take her into custody.*

Convinced that it was a breach of neutrality, to permit either of the belligerents to arm in our ports, the president requested the governors of the several states, to take measures to prevent the same ; and also directed instructions to be sent to the collectors of the customs, to give notice of all acts, contravening the laws of neutrality in their respective ports, to the governors of the states, and to the attornies of the United States.

These instructions were accompanied with certain rules, relative to the arming of vessels, and to the enlistment of men.

Mr. Genet complained, likewise, that French property was taken from American vessels, on the high seas, by belligerents, contrary to the law of nations, "that free ships should make free goods ;" and that this was permitted by the American government, to the great injury of France. In communicating these complaints, the language of the minister was, in the highest degree, insulting to the American executive and nation.

· " On all the seas," he said, in his note to the secretary of state of July 25th, " an audacious piracy pursues, even in your vessels, French property, and also that of the Americans destined for our ports. Your political rights are counted for nothing ; in vain do the principles of neutrality establish, that *friendly vessels make friendly goods* ; in vain, sir, does the president of the United States endeavor, by his proclamation, to reclaim the observation of this maxim ; in vain does the desire of preserving peace, tend to sacrifice the interests of France, to that of the moment; in vain does the thirst of riches preponderate over honor, in the political balance of America ; all this management, all this condesension, end in nothing ; our enemies laugh at it ; and the French, too

* American State Papers, vol. 1, 167, 168, and 169.

confident, are punished, for having believed, that the *nation had a flag, that they had some respect for their laws, some conviction of their strength, and entertained some sentiment of dignity.* It is not possible for me, sir, to paint to you all my sensibility on this scandal, which tends to the diminution of your commerce, to the oppression of ours, and to the debasement and vilification of republicans." He added, in the conclusion of this extraordinary communication, " But if our fellow citizens have been deceived, if you are not in condition to maintain the *sovereignty of your people, speak ;* we have guarantied it when slaves, we shall be able to render it formidable, having become freemen."

He demanded, at the same time, to be informed, what measures the American government had taken to obtain restitution of the property plundered from his fellow citizens, under the protection of its flag. In answer to this insolent letter, the secretary remarked—" I believe it cannot be doubted, but that, by the general law of nations, the goods of a friend found in the vessel of an enemy are free, and that the goods of an enemy, found in the vessel of a friend, are lawful prize. Upon this principle, I presume, the British armed vessels have taken the property of French citizens found in our vessels, in the case above mentioned, and I confess I should be at a loss, on what principle to reclaim it." The secretary added, that sundry nations had changed this principle by special treaties. That this modification of national law, had been adopted in treaties the United States had made with France, the United Netherlands, and Prussia ; but that with England, Portugal and Austria, they had no treaties, and, therefore, " had nothing to oppose to their acting according to the law of nations, that enemy's goods were lawful prize, though found in the bottom of a friend."*

Remonstrances against these proceedings of the French minister, were made in vain—he seemed determined to set the

---

* To preserve peace within our waters, as far as possible, as the American ports were the resort of the armed vessels of all the belligerents, the president established a rule, that no hostile public armed vessel should sail from the same port within twenty four hours of each other. This rule was highly displeasing to the French minister.

law and the government of the country at defiance. At Philadelphia, under the eye of the government, he caused a vessel, taken from the British, called the Little Democrat, to be armed; and directly contrary to the remonstrances of the president and the governor of Pennsylvania, he ordered her departure. In a conference with the governor of Pennsylvania, or his secretary, on this subject, his language towards the president was extremely intemperate; and he threatened *to appeal*, from his ` decision to that of the American people.

Wearied, at last, with the conduct of the French minister, his insulting language, his outrage upon the laws, his assumption of the sovereignty of the country, and his threats of appealing from the government to the people; the president came to the resolution of soliciting his recall. On the 16th of August, Mr. Morriss, the American minister in France, was requested to communicate these wishes of the president to the French government.

In a letter to Mr. Morriss, the president presented a detailed account of the conduct of the minister, and directed him immediately to lay the same before the French government. After stating that Mr. Genet had acted as co-sovereign of the country, had armed vessels, levied men, given commissions of war, independent of the government and in opposition to its orders and efforts, and had endeavored to excite discord and distrust between the American people and their government, and between the two nations; the president concluded by saying, " that his government would see that the case was pressing. That it was impossible for two sovereign and independent authorities to be going on, within one territory, at the same time, without collision. They will perceive, that if Mr. Genet perseveres in his proceedings, the consequences would be too hazardous to us, the example so humiliating and pernicious, that he might be forced even to suspend his functions, before a successor could arrive to continue them. If our citizens," he said, " had not already been shedding each other's blood, it was not owing to the moderation of Mr. Genet, but to the forbearance of the government. That it was well known, that if the authority of the laws had been resorted to, to stop the Little Democrat, its officers and agents were to have been resisted by the crew of the vessel, consisting partly of American citizens."* A copy of this letter was immediately communicated to Mr. Genet, and called from him a reply dated September 16th, but which did not reach the president until December following. The history of diplomacy, it is believed, may be searched in vain, for a more insulting and insolent communication, from a foreign agent to the government to which he was accredited. After accusing the president of assuming the exercise of powers not belonging to him, of bending treaties to circumstances and of changing their sense, of preparing accusations against the *American people*, rather than against him ; after declaring that the conduct attributed to him was that of *gratitude* against *ingratitude*, of *truth* against *error*, he demanded, " as an act of justice, which the American people, which the French people, which all free people are interested to reclaim, that there be made a particular inquiry, in the next session of congress, of the *motives*, on which the head of the executive power of the United States has taken on himself to demand the recall of a public minister, whom the *sovereign people of the* United States had received *fraternally*, and *recognized*, before the diplomatic forms had been fulfilled, with respect to him, at Philadelphia. It is in the name of the French people," he added, " that I am sent to their brethren—to free and sovereign men ; it is, then, for the representatives of the American people, and not for a *single man*, to exhibit against me an act of accusation, if I have merited it. A despot may singly permit himself to demand from another despot, the recall of his representative, and to order his expulsion in case of refusal." He also charged him with issuing " premature proclamations," with "a partial impartiality," which soured his friends, without satisfying his enemies ; and in conclusion, he enumerated many executive acts, at which he had been extremely wounded, some of which were, indeed, of an extraordinary and ridiculous nature. He complained, that the president was in a

* American State Papers, vol. 1, p. 155.

hurry, before knowing what he had to transmit to him, to proclaim sentiments, over which decency and friendship should at least have drawn a veil—that he decorated his parlor with medallions of Capet and his family—that American citizens, who had ranged themselves under the banners of France, by his instructions, had been prosecuted and arrested, and that, in spite of "respectful insinuations, he had *deferred* to convoke congress immediately, in order to take the true sentiments of the people, to fix the *political system* of the United States, and to decide, whether they would *break*, *suspend* or *tighten* their *cords* with France."

The French minister, however, still continued to exercise the highest acts of sovereignty, within the United States. Not content with arming vessels in our ports, and manning them with American citizens, to cruise against nations at peace with their country, he, in the latter part of the year, projected an hostile expedition from South Carolina and Georgia, against the Floridas. To carry this project into effect, he secretly issued commissions to several citizens of South Carolina, with instructions to raise, organize, train and conduct troops within the United States, with the avowed object to proceed, with hostile intentions, against the Spanish dominions. Several persons in South Carolina received these commissions, and proceeded to enlist men in that state under them. To induce enlistments, not only the pay, rations, and clothing were stated, but a share of the conquests, was allotted to the officers and men who should engage. The whole was to be conducted with the utmost secrecy; small parties were to assemble on the shores near Charleston or elsewhere, and a French fleet was to take and convey them to the place of their destination. A rumor of these proceedings having reached the legislature of South Carolina while in session, an inquiry was instituted before a committee of the house of representatives. This committee found the facts above stated, and reported the same to the legislature, with the names of several citizens who had actually received commissions from the French minister. This report was accepted by the legislature, and the

governor requested to issue a proclamation, prohibiting all as-
semblages of troops, unauthorized by government, and to exert
the whole force of the state, if necessary, to enforce obedience to
his commands.

They also recommended, that prosecutions be commenced
against the persons named in the report. The governor, on the
9th of December, issued a proclamation, and prosecutions were
instituted against those principally concerned.

The proceedings of the legislature of South Carolina, were
immediately forwarded to the president. As soon as the French
minister heard of them, he addressed a note to the secretary of
state, in which he declared, that he had not " authorized, in
any manner, the recruiting, the formation, or the collecting of
an armed force, or of any corps, *in the territory of the United
States ;* but, at the same time," he added, " I am too frank to
disguise from you, that, *authorized by the French nation*, to deliver commissions to those of your fellow citizens who should
feel themselves animated with a desire of serving the best of
causes, I have granted them to several brave republicans of South
Carolina, whose intention appeared to me to be to *expatriate
themselves*, and to go among the independent tribes, ancient
friends and allies of France, in order to retaliate, if they could,
in concert with us, on the Spanish and English, the injury which
the government of these two nations had the baseness to commit
on your fellow citizens, under the name of those savages, in like
manner as is lately done under that of the Algerines."

As those who should engage in this enterprize were to assemble, *in small parties*, along the coast, and be taken on board of
vessels, the French minister, it seems, did not consider this as recruiting, forming, or collecting an armed force, in the territory
of the United States.

The reasons avowed for his conduct are, indeed, very extraordinary, as well as inconsistent. The persons to whom he gave
commissions,.were to *expatriate* themselves, and yet they were
only to go among certain Indian tribes ; and for what purpose ?
Not to aid or avenge the cause of France, but to *retaliate* upon

the *Spaniards* and *English*, the injuries committed by their government upon *American citizens*, under the name of those savages; and this was to be done in concert with France. The real object was, by the aid of American citizens, to wrest by force, the Floridas from the Spaniards, against whom the American government had, indeed, just cause of complaint, for their intrigues with the Indians on the southern borders.

The French minister projected also an hostile expedition against New Orleans and Louisiana from the state of Kentucky. This was put in a train of execution in a more bold and daring manner, than the enterprise against the Floridas from South Carolina and Georgia. Genet soon became acquainted with the views and feelings of the people of the west, concerning the navigation of the Mississippi, as well as their suspicions, that the general government had neglected to urge this subject with Spain in a manner its importance demanded.

Taking advantage of these feelings, as well as the opposition of the people to the general government, as early as August, 1793, he formed a plan of an expedition from the west, against the Spanish possessions at the mouth of the Mississippi.

The president, apprized of this, on the 29th of August gave information to the governor of Kentucky that measures were then taking in Philadelphia, to excite the inhabitants of that state, to join in the enterprize. And the governor was desired to attend particularly to any such attempts among the citizens of that state, and to put them on their guard against the consequences of committing acts of hostility against nations at peace with the United States, and to take all legal measures necessary to prevent them. Democratic societies were about the same time formed in Kentucky, and the subject of the navigation of the Mississippi claimed their attention.

In October, 1793, the society at Lexington declared, "That the right of the people on the waters of the Mississippi to the navigation, was undoubted ; and that it ought to be *peremptorily* demanded of Spain, by the government of the United States."

Other publications appeared about the same time, calculated to inflame the people at the west, on a subject in which they felt so deep an interest.

In this state of public sentiment, the French minister, about the first of November, sent four persons to Kentucky, by the names of La Chaise, Charles Depeau, Mathurin and Gignoux, with orders to engage men in an expedition against New Orleans and the Spanish possessions; and for this purpose they carried with them blank commissions. The governor of Kentucky was again informed of these movements by the secretary of state, in a letter of the 6th of November, and was furnished not only with the names of the persons then on their way, but a particular description of them—and he was requested to prevent any such enterprise from that state, and if necessary, to employ the militia for that purpose. These emissaries arrived in Kentucky about the last of November, and found not only many of the people of that state ready to engage in the expedition, but the governor himself disposed, if not to countenance, at least to connive at it. Aware, no doubt, of this disposition, two of these Frenchmen, La Chaise and Depeau, on the 25th of November, addressed notes to the governor himself.

Depeau informed him that he had been despatched by the French ambassador, in company with other Frenchmen to join the expedition of the Mississippi—but as strange reports had reached him, that his excellency had orders to arrest all who might incline to assist them, he wished to be satisfied on the subject.*

---

* The following is the extraordinary letter of Depeau, as found in H. Marshall's history of Kentucky.

" *Citizen governor*---It may appear quite strange to write to you on a subject in which, although it is of some consequence.

" With confidence from the French ambassador, I have been despatched in company with more Frenchmen to join the expedition of the Mississippi.

" As I am to procure the provision, I am happy to communicate to you, whatever you shall think worthy of my notice, or in which your advice may be of use to me, as I hope I have no way disobliged you ; if I have, I will most willingly ask your pardon. For nobody can be more than I am willing for your prosperity and happiness.

The answer of the governor to Depeau's letter, three days after, was as extraordinary as the letter itself.

He informed the agent of the French minister, of the "*charge*" he had received from the secretary of state, in the month of August preceding, in nearly the very words of the secretary himself, and he only added, "*to which charge I must pay that attention which my present situation obliges me.*"

This answer, no doubt, satisfied the French emissaries, and others who saw it, they had nothing to fear from the governor of Kentucky. The project which now began to be developed, was, to raise two thousand men, under French authority ; and for this purpose, French commissions were distributed and received among the citizens of that state. George Rogers Clark, who had been a revolutionary officer, agreed to command the expedition, and issued *proposals* for raising troops. In these he styled himself, "*major general in the armies of France, and commander in chief of the revolutionary legions on the Mississippi.*"

The proposals were, "for raising volunteers for the reduction of the Spanish posts on the Mississippi, for opening the trade of that river, and giving freedom to its inhabitants, &c."

The pay and the share of plunder was also settled. All who served in the expedition were entitled to one thousand acres of land—those who would engage for one year, to have two thousand—and those who served two years, or during the war with France, were to have three thousand acres of any unappropriated lands that might be *conquered*—the officers in proportion, and pay as other French troops. All *plunder* to be divided according to the cus-

"As some strange reports has reached my ears, that your excellence has positive orders to arrest all citizens inclining to our assistance, and as my remembrance know by your conduct, in justice you will satisfy me in this *uncommon request.*

"Please let me know, as I shall not make my supply till your excellence please to honor me with a small answer.

"I am your well wisher in remaining for the French cause, a true citizen democrat.   CHARLE DEPEAU.

"*Postcript.*---Please to participate some of these handbills, to that noble society of democrats ; I also enclose a paper from Pittsburgh."---*H. Marshall's History of Kentucky, vol. 2, p. 100.*

tom of war. Those who preferred money to land, were to receive one dollar per day.*

Governor Shelby, in his answer to the letter of the secretary of state of the 29th of August, dated the 5th of October, referring to the supposed enterprise from Kentucky, says, " I think it my duty to take this early opportunity to assure you, that I shall be particularly attentive to prevent any attempts of that nature from this country. I am well persuaded, at present, none such is in contemplation in this state. The citizens of Kentucky possess too just a sense of the obligations they owe the general government, to embark in any enterprise that would be so injurious to the United States." After these assurances of co-operation, what must have been the surprise of the president, on receiving the following letter from the same governor, dated the 13th of January, 1794. "After the date of my last letter to you," he says to the secretary of state, " I received information that a commission had been sent to general Clarke, with powers to name and commission other officers, and to raise a body of men ; no steps having been taken by him, (as far as come to my knowledge,) to carry this plan into execution, I did not conceive it was either proper or necessary for me to do any thing in the business.

" Two Frenchmen, La Chaise and Depeau, have lately come into this state ; I am told they declare publicly, they are in daily expectation of receiving a supply of money, and that as soon as they do receive it, they shall raise a body of men and proceed with them down the river. Whether they have any sufficient reason to expect to get a supply, or any *serious intention of applying it in that manner, if they do receive it, I can form no opinion.*" After requesting the president to give him *full and explicit directions* as to the steps he wished taken, to prevent the contemplated expedition, he added, " I have great doubts, even if they do attempt to carry their plan into execution, (provided they manage their business with prudence,) whether there is any legal authority to restrain or punish them, at least before they have *actually*

* H. Marshall's History of Kentucky, vol. 2, pp. 100, 102, and 103.

accomplished it. For if it is lawful for any one citizen of this state to leave it, it is equally so for any number of them to do it. It is also lawful for them to carry with them any quantity of provisions, arms, and ammunition ; and if the act is lawful in itself, there is nothing but the particular intention with which it is done that can possibly make it unlawful ; but I know of no law which inflicts a punishment on intention only, or any criterion by which to decide what would be sufficient evidence of that intention, if it was a proper subject of legal censure.

" I shall upon all occasions, be averse to the exercise of any power which I do not consider myself as being clearly and explicitly invested with, much less would I assume a power to exercise it against men who I consider as friends and brethren, in favor of a man who I view as an *enemy* and a tyrant. I shall also feel but little inclination to take an active part in punishing or restraining any of my fellow citizens for a supposed intention only, to gratify or remove the fears of the minister of a prince, who openly withholds from us, an invaluable right, and who secretly instigates against us a most savage and cruel enemy.

" But whatever may be my private opinion as a man, as a friend to liberty, an American citizen, and an inhabitant of the western waters, I shall at all times hold it as my duty to perform whatever may be *constitutionally* required of me as governor of Kentucky, by the president of the United States."*

This letter precluded all expectation of aid against the meditated hostile expedition, from the state authorities of Kentucky. The president, therefore, on the 24th of March, 1794, issued his own proclamation, apprizing the people at the west of the unlawful project, and warning them of the consequences of engaging in it. He, about the same time, directed general Wayne to establish a strong military post at fort Massac, on the Ohio, and gave him orders to prevent by force, if necessary, all hostile movements down that river. Soon after these orders were known, an address, "to the inhabitants of western America," supposed to

* American State Papers, vol. 2, pp. 37, 39, 40.

have originated from one of the democratic societies, appeared in the gazettes, in which the people at the west, were told that " the time is come when we ought to relinquish our claim to those blessings, proffered to us by nature, or endeavor to obtain them *at every hazard.* The principles of our confederation have been *totally perverted* by our Atlantic brethren. It is a fact incontestable, that they have endeavored to deprive us of all that can be important to us as a people.

" To you then, inhabitants of the west ! is reserved the display of those virtues, once the pride and boast of America, uncontaminated with Atlantic luxury—beyond the reach of European influence, the pampered vultures of commercial countries have not found access to your retreat.   A noble and just occasion presents itself to assert your rights ; and with your own, perhaps establish those of thousands of your fellow mortals.

" Reflect that you may be the glorious instruments in the hands of Providence, of relieving from the galling chains of slavery, your brethren of Louisiana."

The author of this address, alluding to the proclamation of the president, and his orders to general Wayne, says, " before I close this address, I cannot but observe with what indignation must the citizens of Kentucky view the conduct of the *general government,* towards them in particular.   In answer to their decent and spirited exertions, they receive, instead of assurances of relief from oppression, denunciations from the executive ; and are held up to public view, as the disturbers of the peace of America. And a *miserable fragment* of the mighty legions of the United States, is destined to awe the hosts of freemen who seek but their right."[*]

Previous to this address, the president had informed the governor of Kentucky, that negociations with Spain were pending, and that every exertion was making to bring them to a close, and to secure the free navigation of the Mississippi.   This extraordinary enterprise was not finally relinquished, until it was disavow-

* H. Marshall's History of Kentucky, vol. 2, pp. 118, 119.

ed by the successor of Genet, and the French commissions were recalled.

This reiterated violation of the national sovereignty, by a foreign minister, was no longer to be endured. The proceedings of the legislature of South Carolina, were laid before congress by the president, on the 15th of January, 1794; and he soon after, determined to hold no further intercourse with Mr. Genet, and had prepared a message to congress on the subject. The news of his recall prevented the necessity of presenting it.

The president had not only to suffer the mortification of seeing himself thus insulted, the authority of the laws outraged, and the government of his country usurped by a foreign minister; but also to endure the painful reflection, that this conduct was encouraged and supported by many of his fellow citizens.

The manner in which the new minister of the French republic was received at Charleston, and on his way to the seat of government, manifested the deep interest felt by the American people in the cause of France. On his first arrival at Philadelphia, and even before he was presented to the president, or acknowledged as a public minister, he received a congratulatory address from a number of the inhabitants of that city, previously prepared by a committee appointed for that purpose, and to which he returned an answer.

From these manifestations in favor of the French cause, Mr. Genet believed the American people were ready to make common cause with the republic.

Situated as the United States were at that period, with a government new, untried, and powerfully opposed, without a single ship of war, burdened with debt, embarrassed with serious disputes with two of the most powerful European nations, and harrassed with an Indian war, it would seem impossible for any one even to doubt the wisdom and policy of the measures adopted by the president and his cabinet. Yet soon after the proclamation appeared, not only its justice and policy was disputed, but the power of the president to issue it denied.

The prejudices of the people against Great Britain, arising from recent as well as ancient causes of controversy, and their partialities in favor of France, were made subservient to the views of the leaders of the opposition, and brought to bear against the administration of the general government. And though few would openly declare that the United States ought to make common cause with the new republic, yet many openly took part with the French minister against their own government, and advocated measures, which, if adopted, would necessarily bring them in collision with the enemies of France. While the president was using all the means in his power to preserve his country from the calamities of war, he was accused of particular friendship for Great Britain, and of hostility to France, of favoring the one at the expense of the other; nay, was charged with an intention of joining the coalition against France.

The following extracts from two of the leading and most influential opposition newspapers of the day, will serve, among others of a similar character, to shew the spirit which prevailed against the father of his country.

As early as July, 1793, the National Gazette, printed at the seat of government, and edited by one of the clerks in the department of state, had the following paragraph—" The minister of France, I hope, will act with firmness and with spirit. The people are his friends, or the friends of France, and he will have nothing to apprehend; for as yet, the people are sovereign of the United States. Too much complacency is an injury done his cause, for as every advantage is already taken of France, (not by the people) further condescension may lead to further abuse. If one of the leading features of our government is pusillanimity, when the British lion shows his teeth, let France and her minister act as becomes the dignity and justice of their cause, and the honor and faith of nations."

" It is no longer possible to doubt," said the General Advertiser, also published at Philadelphia, " that the intention of the executive of the United States is, to look upon the treaty of amity and commerce which exists between France and America, as a nullity ; and that they are prepared to join the league of kings against France."

Societies, in imitation of the Jacobin clubs in Paris, were formed in different parts of the United States, (no doubt by the direction and advice of Mr. Genet,) styled democratic societies, ostensibly for the purpose of securing liberty, but really, with a view more effectually to oppose the measures of the administration, and to promote the views of the French minister. The acts and proceedings of these societies breathed a spirit of hostility against the president, and were calculated to destroy all regular government.

No circumstances were left unattended to on the part of the French republic, or its minister, to engage the people in their favor. Their interest, their pride, their prejudices, their sense of gratitude for past services, and their natural sympathies towards a nation struggling for liberty, were all addressed.

• The French frigate, which brought Genet to this country, was an object of curiosity, as she entered the American ports, and the inscriptions on her masts, proclaimed the principles by which the republic professed to be governed, and were calculated to catch the attention and interest the feelings of the numerous spectators, who daily crowded her decks.*

The conduct, however, of the French minister towards the chief magistrate, the unparalleled atrocities committed by the rival factions in France, and the beheading of the king and queen, who had been considered the greatest benefactors of America in the war of the revolution, at length greatly weakened the cause of the French republic, in the minds of the dispassionate and considerate portion of the American people. In August a rumor was in circulation in New York, that Mr. Genet, dissatisfied with the decision of the president, on some important question, had threatened to *appeal* to the people. This being denied, Mr. Jay and Mr. King, who had then just returned from Philadelphia, were

---

* On the fore mast was inscribed,—*Enemies of equality, change or tremble.*
On the main mast,—*Free people, you see in us, brothers and friends.*
On the mizen mast,—*We are armed to support the rights of man.*

called upon for information. They gave a certificate under their hands, which was immediately published, that the same was true.

These proceedings drew from Mr. Genet a letter, addressed to the president himself, in which, calling these rumors " *dark calumnies*," which he wished to dissipate, he requested from him the following explicit declaration, " that I have never intimated to you an intention of appealing to the people-; that it is not true, that a difference of opinion in political sentiments, has ever betrayed me to forget what was due to your character, or to the exalted reputation you have acquired, by humbling a tyrant, against whom you have fought, in the cause of liberty." " To you alone," he added, in the same letter, "through the secretary of state, have I declared, that the federal government, far from manifesting any regard for our generous conduct towards this country—for the new advantages which are offering to her commerce —or for the reiterated demonstrations of our real and disinterested friendship, were sacrificing our interests to those of our enemies,* by their interpretation of the treaties which exist between us. To you I have represented, without reserve, that this conduct did not appear to correspond with the views of the people of America, with their desire to observe, with fidelity, their public engagements, or with their affectionate regard for the cause of liberty, upon which their very existence depend." In answer to this communication, the secretary of state was directed to inform Mr. Genet, that no direct correspondence took place between the president and foreign ministers. He was directed also to add, " The president does not conceive it to be within the line of propriety or duty for him to bear evidence against a declaration, which, whether made to him, or others, is perhaps immaterial, he therefore, declines interfering in the case."

The certificate given by Mr. Jay and Mr. King, drew upon them the indignation of the French minister and his adherents. Pretending still to deny the charge, Genet requested of the president, that prosecutiont be instituted against the authors of it. This subject, for form's sake, probably, was referred to the attorney general. Mr. Jay and Mr. King, conceiving their characters for veracity to be indirectly called in question, held a correspondence and conference with the president; and they were furnished with a copy of a report made to him, by the secretary of state, in the affair of the vessel called the *Little Democrat*; in which it was particularly stated, that such a threat had been made by the French minister. The publication of Mr. Genet's letter to the president, and the answer of the secretary, disclosed *distinctly* to the American people, that a serious misunderstanding existed between the American executive and the French minister; and they were perfectly satisfied, that if this threat had not been made to the president himself, it was made to others. The great mass of American citizens were indignant at this attempt, on the part of a foreign minister, to separate them from the government and rulers of their choice, particularly from their chief magistrate, in whom they placed the highest confidence.

Meetings of the citizens were held in different parts of the union, and resolutions passed, expressing an entire approbation of the proclamation and of the measures taken by the executive to preserve their country in peace.

The president himself always remained satisfied with the propriety and policy of this great and important measure of his administration.

In his farewell address to the American people on retiring from office, he expressed his most unqualified approbation of it. " In relation to the still subsisting war in Europe," he said, " my proclamation of the 22d of April, 1793, is the index to my plan. Sanctioned by your approving voice, and by that of your representatives in both houses of congress, the spirit of that measure has continually governed me ; uninfluenced by any attempts to deter me from it."

CHAPTER XXII.

Political relations with Great Britain under the new government—The president informally sounds the British government relative to the inexecution of the treaty, and a commercial intercourse—Discriminating duties in the United States claim the attention of the British ministry—Referred to the committee of trade and plantations in September, 1789—Report of the committee on this subject, and also with regard to the terms of a commercial treaty with the United States—West India trade not to be open to the Americans, nor the principle admitted that free ships should make free goods—English minister arrives in the United States—Enters into discussion with the secretary of state, on the subject of the treaty—This discussion broken off, by the new state of things in Europe—British orders of June 8th, 1793, relative to certain articles of provisions destined to France—American government remonstrates against these orders—Treaties between Great Britain and Russia, and other powers on this subject—Similar orders issued by Russia and other nations in Europe—Reasons given in justification of them—Answers of some of the European neutrals—Algerine cruisers let loose upon American commerce in the Atlantic, in consequence of a truce between Algiers and Portugal—This truce made by a British agent—Many American vessels captured, and their crews made slaves—Speech of the president at the opening of congress in December, 1793—Report of the secretary of state concerning foreign restrictions on American commerce—Mr. Jefferson resigns—Mr. Madison's commercial resolutions—New British orders respecting the West India trade—American vessels bound to the West Indies taken and condemned—Congress divided as to the mode of resisting these aggressions on neutral rights, and obtaining satisfaction and indemnity---Various plans proposed in the house of representatives---British establish a new military post at the rapids of the Miami of the lake---Mr. Jay nominated minister extraordinary to London---Reasons of the president for this mission---Mr. Jay's instructions---Non-intercourse bill passed by the house, but rejected in the senate—Congress take measures of defense—Lay additional internal taxes—Pass acts to prevent the violation of the neutrality and sovereignty of the country—Fauchet arrives as successor to Genet—Has orders to send Genet to France—Requests liberty of the president to take him by force or stratagem—President refuses his request—Views of the French government not changed—Mr. Morriss recalled from France, and Mr. Munroe appointed his successor—His instructions.

FOR the purpose of presenting a connected view of the prominent measures of the new government, as well as of the political relations of the United States with France, to the close of the year 1793 ; we have omitted to notice the state of their relations with Great Britain, during this period.

It now becomes necessary to revert to this interesting part of Washington's administration. The American minister, Mr. Adams, as before stated, returned from England without accomplishing the objects of his mission. The British court having declined sending a minister to this country under the old government, the president would not renew the negociations by a formal mission, under the new system. He thought proper, however, in an informal manner, to sound the British government, on the subject of the non-fulfilment of the treaty of peace, and with respect to a commercial intercourse between the two countries.

Governeur Morriss, who was about to visit London, in October, 1789, was instructed by a private letter from the president himself, to converse with his Brittannic majesty's ministers, on the following points—" Whether there be any, and what objections to now performing those articles in the treaty, which remain to be performed on his part ; and whether they incline to a treaty of commerce with the United States, on any, and on what terms."

With respect to a commmercial treaty, the president in his instructions, says, " in treating this subject, let it be strongly impressed on your mind, that the privilege of carrying our productions in our vessels to their islands, and bringing in return the productions of these islands to our ports and markets, is regarded here as of the highest importance ; and you will be careful not to countenance any idea of our dispensing with it in a treaty." In pursuance of these instructions, Mr. Morriss had several conferences with the British ministers, the result of which was, that they did not intend to surrender the western posts, until the United States had made compensation for infractions of the treaty on their part.

On the subject of a treaty of commerce, the answers of the British ministers were evasive, and their remarks general. It was evident, they were not yet prepared to commence that business in earnest. They, however, expressed to Mr. Morriss, their intention of sending a minister to the United States. The acts of the American government, giving a preference to their own vessels, in tonnage and other duties, over those of foreign nations, had not passed unnoticed by the British cabinet, ever extremely jealous of any act of a foreign government, tending in the smallest degree to affect their commercial or navigating interest. As early as the 30th of September, 1789, these acts were referred to the lords of the committee of privy council, on the subject of trade and foreign plantations, to consider and report their opinion on the same. While this subject was before the committee, the British cabinet having concluded to send a minister to America, they were commanded, also, to take into consideration and report, " what were the proposals of a commercial nature, it would be proper to be made by their government to the United States."

On the 25th of January, 1791, this committee made a report on all the subjects referred to them, and which formed the basis of instructions to the minister about to be sent to the United States. A few copies were at first printed, but afterwards, probably because it contained the substance of instructions to their minister, were suppressed.

It was drawn with no ordinary ability, and no doubt, fully disclosed the views then entertained by the British government, respecting a commercial intercourse with the United States.

The event of a negociation was recommended by the committee, before resorting to retaliatory measures, against the American discriminating duties.

The merchants of London, Liverpool, Bristol, and Glasgow, were consulted by the committee, and a great majority of them were of opinion, that attempts should be made by negociation, to effect some equitable commercial arrangement, previous to a resort to measures of a retaliatory nature.

The navigating interest of Great Britain, did not escape the particular attention of this committee. On this subject, they say—" after full consideration of all that has been offered on the subject of *navigation*, the committee think, that there is but one proposition, which it will be advisable to make on this head, to the government of the United States, in any negociation for a commercial treaty between the two countries, viz., that British ships trading to the ports of the United States, shall be treated with respect to duties of tonnage and impost, in like manner as ships of the United States shall be treated in the ports of Great Britain." With respect to the West India trade, they observed, "if congress should propose, (as they certainly will,) that this principle of equality should be extended to the ports of our colonies and islands, and that the ships of the United States should be *there* treated as British ships, it should be answered, that this demand *cannot be admitted*, even as a subject of negociation."

The committee were of opinion, that all the articles of maritime law, then lately inserted in their treaties with other foreign powers, might be also inserted, if required, in a commercial treaty with the United States, "except that any article allowing the ships of the United States to *protect the property of the enemies of Great Britain in time of war*, should on no account be admitted: it would be more dangerous," they said, "to concede *this privilege* to the ships of the United States, than to those of any other foreign country; from their situation, the ships of these states would be able to cover the whole trade of France and Spain with their islands and colonies in America and the West Indies, whenever Great Britain should be engaged in a war with either of these powers; and the navy of Great Britain would in such case, be deprived of the means of distressing the enemy, by destroying his commerce, and thereby diminish his resources."

The committee advise the king to open a negociation, for the purpose of making a commercial treaty with the United States, "but it will be right," they repeat, "in an early stage of this negociation, to declare explicitly, that Great Britain can never *submit to treat*, on what appears to be the favorite object of the people of those states, that is, the admisson of the ships of the United States into the ports of your majesty's colonies and islands."*

Agreeably to the intimation given to Mr. Morriss, Mr. Hammond arrived in the United States, in 1791, as minister from

* Acheson's Collections of Papers.

Great Britain ; and the next year, Thomas Pinckney of South Carolina, was sent in the same character, to the court of London. Soon after the arrival of Mr. Hammond, a correspondence commenced between him and the American secretary of state, on the subjects in controversy between the two countries, particularly concerning the inexecution of the treaty of peace.

The British minister having no authority to *conclude* a commercial treaty, the consideration of that subject was postponed.

In answer to the question put by the American secretary, as to the intentions of the British government, in relation to the non-fulfilment of that article of the treaty of peace, concerning the surrender of the western posts, the British minister said, that the execution of this article was suspended, in consequence of a breach of the 4th, 5th, and 6th articles, on the part of the United States ; and that in all their discussions and subsequent arrangements, these subjects could not be separated.

It was agreed, that each should state the particular acts done by the other, supposed to be in contravention of the treaty. Mr. Jefferson commenced on the part of the American government, in December, 1791, by repeating, that the garrisons had not been withdrawn from the western posts, according to the stipulations in the 7th article, that British officers had exercised jurisdiction over the country and inhabitants, belonging to the United States, in the vicinity of these posts, that American citizens had been excluded from the navigation of the great lakes ; and that, contrary to the same article, a great number of negroes, the property of the citizens of the United States, had been carried away at the time of the evacuation of the city of New York.

The supposed infractions on the part of the United States, complained of by the British minister, were—

1st, Impediments to the collection of debts, contracted before the date of the treaty, by the acts and proceedings of the several states.

2d, The non-restitution of the estates of the royalists, confiscated during the war.

3d, The prosecution of the royalists, and the confiscation of their property subsequent to the peace.

A statement of these infractions, was made by the British minister, in March, 1792, with a reference to the various acts of the states on these subjects. In May following, an answer to this was given by the American secretary, showing that, with respect to property confiscated by the individual states, the fifth article merely stipulated, that congress should *recommend* to the legislatures of the several states, to provide for its restitution. That congress had done all in their power, and all they were bound by treaty to do, by recommending a compliance on the part of the states ; but that it was left with the states themselves to comply or not, as they might think proper, and that this was so understood by the British negociators, and by the British ministry, at the time the treaty was completed.

The secretary stated, that no confiscations had taken place subsequent to the peace.

He also claimed, that the first infractions were on the part of the British government, by withholding the western posts, and by the transportation of negroes ; and that the delays and impediments which had taken place, in the collection of British debts, were justifiable on that account. With respect to the allowance of interest on the debts, during the time the two countries were engaged in war, this, he said, was a point much litigated in the courts, and in some states was allowed, and in others disallowed.

This answer of the American secretary was transmitted to the British court by Mr. Hammond ; and the new state of things, which soon after arose in Europe, prevented a reply or a renewal of these negociations in America. Great Britain having become a party in the war against France, new and important subjects of controversy arose which claimed the attention of the American government. The extraordinary revolution and proceedings in France, to which we have before alluded, united all the great powers of Europe against that nation. And the allies, in order to compel the French to submit to their terms, early in 1793, adopted a new and extraordinary mode of warfare against them, being nothing less than to deprive them of the means of support, by preventing all foreign supplies of corn, flour, meal and other provisions.

In pursuance of this plan, the British court, on the 8th of June, 1793, declared it to be lawful for all his majesty's ships of war and privateers, " to stop and detain all vessels loaded wholly or in part with *corn, flour,* or *meal,* bound to any port of France, or any port occupied by the armies of France, and to send them to such ports as should be most convenient, in order that such *corn, meal,* or *flour* might be purchased on behalf of his majesty's government, and the ships to be released after such purchase, and after a due allowance for freight ; or that the masters of such ships, on giving due security, to be approved by the court of admiralty, be permitted to dispose of their cargoes of *corn, meal,* or *flour,* in the ports of any country in amity with his majesty."

These instructions, though bearing date early in June, were not finally issued to the admiralty until about the last of that month ; and they did not reach the United States until the first of September, and twelve days after, were formally communicated, by Mr. Hammond, to the American government.

This extraordinary plan of subduing a whole nation by famine, was concerted between Great Britain and Russia, as early as the 25th of March, 1793.

The following articles constitute part of a convention between his Britannic majesty and the empress of Russia, entered into on that day; and are too extraordinary to be here omitted.

" Art. III. Their said majesties engage to shut all their ports against French ships ; not to permit the exportation, in any case, from the said ports for France, of any military or naval stores, or *corn, grain, salt meat* or other *provisions ;* and to take all other measures, in their power, for injuring the commerce of France, and for bringing her, *by such means,* to just conditions of peace.

" Art. IV. Their majesties engage to unite all their efforts to prevent *other powers,* not implicated in this war, from giving, on this occasion of common concern to every civilized state, any *protection* whatever, directly or indirectly, in consequence of their neutrality, to the commerce or property of the French, on the sea, or in their ports."

The same articles were inserted in treaties which Great Britain made with Spain, Prussia, and the emperor of Germany, in the summer of the same year.

In consequence of his engagements in these treaties, his Britannic majesty issued the instructions before recited. An informal account of them had no sooner reached the United States, than the president, perceiving how materially they would affect American commerce, directed a remonstrance to be presented to the British government, against such a palpable violation of neutral rights. The American minister at London was directed to declare to the British court, that "reason and usage had established, that when two nations went to war, those who choose to live in peace, retain their natural rights to pursue their agriculture, manufactures and other ordinary vocations, to carry the produce of their industry, for exchange, to all nations, belligerents or neutrals, as usual, to go and come freely, without injury or molestation : and in short, that war among others should be for them as if it did not exist."

There was but one restriction to these natural rights, the American secretary said, which was, that neutrals should not furnish either party with *implements* merely of war, for the annoyance of the other, nor *any thing* whatever to a place blockaded by its enemy ; and he also declared, that *corn, flour* and *meal*, were not contraband of war. Mr. Pinckney was also particularly directed to require of the British government, an explanation of these orders.

Mr. Hammond attempted a justification of them, by remarking, " that by the law of nations, as laid down by the most modern writers, it was expressly stated, that all provisions were to be considered as contraband, and liable to confiscation, in case where the depriving of an enemy of those supplies, was one of the means intended to be employed for reducing him to reasonable terms of peace." Lord Grenville, also, in a conference with Mr. Pinckney, justified them on the same ground; and said, they did not go so far as the strict law of nations would warrant, not extending to all *kinds* of *provisions*, or to *confiscation.*

These principles, however, were resisted by the American government, as totally unwarranted by the law of nations; and Mr. Pinckney, in answer to lord Grenville, on the subject of reducing France by famine, stated, that provisions were then cheaper in the ports of that country, than in those of England.

Notwithstanding these remonstrances on the part of the United States, the orders were rigidly enforced, and English ports were soon filled with American vessels, originally bound to France.

The manner in which this new mode of warfare was enforced in Europe by the allied powers, as well as a brief view of the principles upon which it was there attempted to be supported, cannot be foreign from our design.

The orders of the empress of Russia extended farther than those of Great Britain; and to enforce them she fitted out a fleet of twenty five sail of the line, with a number of frigates, to cruise in the east and north seas, " for the purpose (in conjunction with the English maritime force) of preventing the sending of any *provisions* or *ammunition* to France."*

The Russian charge'des affaires, in his note of July 30th, 1793, informed the court of Sweden, that the commanders of the Russian fleet were instructed, " to stop all neutral vessels having a cargo for the ports of France, to force them either to return to the ports from whence they came, or to unload their cargoes in any neutral port they should think fit to point out." The empress having before been the great champion and supporter of neutral rights, found it necessary to make some apology for her de-

---

* She requested the king of Sweden, "not to permit his ships of war to take any Swedish merchantmen, laden with such commodities, under their convoy." She also gave orders to search *all merchant vessels*, to see if their cargoes consisted of such goods; " all which is done," she added, " for this reason, namely, that no *neutrality* can take place with respect to a government consisting only of rebels."

parture from the principles she formerly professed. "After all the proofs," her minister added, "which her majesty has given of the generous and disinterested care she has taken to secure the rights of neutral states in time of war, by establishing a particular code of navigation laws, which received the approbation of most of the maritime powers, by solemn treaties—she has no reason to fear lest her present conduct might excite any suspicion of her intending to infringe that generous and beneficial system, since that system can, by no means, be applicable to the present circumstances.

"In order to prove this assertion, it will be sufficient to allege, that the usurpers of the government of France, after having overthrown every order in that country, after having dipped their murderous hands in the blood of their king, have, by a solemn decree, declared themselves the protectors and supporters of all those who should attempt like crimes against their sovereigns and governors in other states. This they not only promised, but they have actually attacked most of their neighboring powers, with armed forces, and by this have placed themselves in a state of war against all the powers of Europe; no *neutrality*, consequently, could exist from that time, in any power, with regard to them, except where prudence, and the benefit of the common cause, prescribed *a feigned* peaceable disposition. But this motive is no longer in existence, since the combination of the formidable powers of Europe, to make it their *common cause* against the enemies of the safety and happiness of nations."*

The language of the British court to his Danish majesty, was similar to that held by the empress of Russia.

"It can by no means be mistaken," said the British ambassador, (Hailes,) at the court of Copenhagen, "how much the circumstances of the present war are different from those wars, in which Europe can depend on the established laws and rights of nations; nor can it more be denied, that this palpable difference ought to have a *material and powerful influence* on the enjoyment of the privileges allowed to neutral nations, by the same general laws and rights of nations, or by particular treaties."

The British ambassador, also, after stating that there was no government in France, acknowledged either by neutrals or belligerents, and that neither, could have any assurance of the observation of the laws and rights of nations, not only justified the determination of the coalesced powers, to reduce France, by prohibiting supplies of provisions; but also intimated, that the Danish court could not even admit French privateers into their ports, as, for want of a legal government, they could have no *legal commissions*, and must be considered as *pirates*.

The answer of Bernstorf, the Danish minister, was worthy of that great and illustrious statesman.

" The law of nations," says the Danish minister, " is unalterable. Its principles do not depend on circumstances. An enemy engaged in war can exercise vengeance upon those who do not expect it; but in this case, and without violating the rigid law, a fatal reciprocity may take place; but a neutral power, which lives in peace, cannot admit of, nor acknowledge such a compensation, it can only screen itself, by its impartiality, and by its treaties. It is not pardonable for her to renounce her rights in favor of any belligerent power. *The basis of her rights is the universal and public law, before which all authority must vanish* : it is neither a party nor a judge ; nor do the treaties give room to privileges and favors."

The views of Bernstorf, on the new mode of warfare of the coalesced powers, were peculiarly just, and in accordance with those of president Washington.

" The want of grain," he added, " as a consequence of the failure of domestic productions, is not a thing unusual, which might only take place in the present moment ; or which might be occasioned by the ground which constitute the difference so often alleged between the present and former wars. France is almost constantly able to make imports from abroad. Africa, Italy, and America, furnish her with much more corn than the Baltic.

" In the year 1709, France was more exposed to famine than it now is ; and yet England could not then avail herself of the same grounds. On the contrary, when soon after Frederick IV, king of Denmark, on account of his war with Sweden, which required almost constantly importations from abroad like France, could believe that he might adopt the principle, that exportation can be lawfully prevented, if one has hopes to conquer an enemy by so doing ; and he intended to apply, with regard to the whole country, this principle, which is only considered as valid with regard to blockaded ports ; all the powers remonstrated, especially Great Britain, and unanimously declared this principle to be *new and inadmissible ;* so that the king, convinced to the contrary, desisted from it. A war," added Bernstorf, " can certainly differ from others, with regard to its occasion, tendency, necessity, justice, or injustice. This can be a most important concern to the belligerent powers. It can and must have influence upon the peace, upon the indemnifications, and other necessary circumstances. But all this is absolutely of no concern to the neutral powers. They will, upon the whole, give the utmost deference to those on whose side justice seems to be ; but they have *no right to give way to this sentiment.* When a neutrality is not *quite perfect*, it ceases to be neutrality."

The Danish minister appealed to the conduct of Great Britain herself, on the subject of French privateers. " They cannot be considered as pirates," he said, " by the neutral powers, as long as England does not consider and treat them as such. In England, the prisoners are deemed to be prisoners of war ; they are exchanged, and negociations have been entered into for this purpose. The usual laws of war are there observed in all respects, and by this rule alone we ought to go."*

This reasoning, however, was as unavailing in Europe, as in America. The orders of the coalesced powers, were rigidly enforced, and neutral rights and interests sacrificed. Those of the British government particularly affected and embarrassed the American commerce ; and justly excited the resentment of the people of the United States. This state of public feeling in

* British Senator, vol. 8, p. 40.---State Papers.

America, was increased by a belief, that the Indian war, which desolated their western frontiers, was also encouraged, if not instigated by the British in Canada. Another event likewise occured, this year, peculiarly distressing to American commerce and seamen, and added not a little to this excitement. For many years, war had existed between Portugal and Algiers. In consequence of this, Algerine cruizers had been confined to the Mediterranean by a Portuguese fleet; and the commerce of the United States, as well as that of Portugal herself, had been protected in the Atlantic, from the depredations of this regency. In September, 1793, an unexpected truce for a year, was concluded between Portugal and Algiers. The dey's cruizers, therefore, immediately, and without previous notice, passed into the Atlantic; and American vessels, while on their way to Portugal and other parts of Europe, and without the smallest suspicion of danger, became a prey to these lawless freebooters, and many American seamen were doomed to slavery.

This unexpected and extraordinary measure was brought about by a British agent at Algiers; and the Portuguese minister declared to the American consul at Lisbon, that the same had been effected without his knowledge. The Portuguese government, he said, about six months before, had requested the aid of Great Britain and Spain, in bringing about a peace with that regency; but as no person had been appointed on the part of Portugal, to effect this object, he supposed the business remained only in embryo. Some provisions in the treaty itself, indicated pretty strongly, the truth of this statement of the minister. The British government had guarantied the performance of it on the part of Portugal; and by a most extraordinary clause, the Portuguese government was restrained from affording *protection* to any nation against Algerine cruizers.*

The British minister, Grenville, disavowed any intention to injure the United States; declaring, that being desired by their friend and ally, to procure a peace with Algiers, the British gov-

* American State Papers, vol. 10, p. 279.

ernment had instructed their agent to effect this object, and thereby enable the Portuguese fleet to co-operate with them against France ; and that finding a permanent peace unattainable, he had concluded a truce for a short period.

The British ministry, however, must have foreseen, that this measure in its immediate consequences, would be fatal to American commerce in the Atlantic ; and that hundreds of American seamen must necessarily be consigned to slavery. Nor is it possible to believe, that it should not have occured to them, that an Algerine fleet, would also effectually co-operate in their favorite plan against France. Whatever were the real views of Portugal, she was too dependent on Great Britain, to refuse a ratification of the treaty. On the application of the American consul, the Portuguese government furnished a convoy for the vessels of the United States trading tothat country, until the treaty should be ratified.

The Americans were very justly incensed, that their property should be thus exposed to Algerine rapacity, and their fellow citizens doomed to slavery without the least warning.

In this state of public affairs, both at home and abroad, the president met congress on the 3d of December, 1793. Never, since the period of the American revolution, had the affairs of the United States been in a more critical and delicate situation, or presented greater difficulties to those entrusted with the administration of government. The president, in his speech to both houses, informed them of the course he had pursued, in the " new and delicate" situation, in which the United States had been placed, in consequence of the war, which, in the course of the year, had embraced most of the nations in Europe, particularly those with which they had the most extensive relations and connections. That he had thought it his duty to admonish his fellow citizens of the consequences of a contraband trade, and particularly of hostile acts to either party ; and that to preserve the country in peace, he had adopted some general rules, which, while they conformed to existing treaties, asserted the privileges of the United States. That it must now rest with congress to

correct, improve, or enforce these rules ; suggesting at the same
time, that some further legislative aid would be found expedient,
especially in cases, where individuals, within the United States,
should array themselves in hostility against any of the powers
at war, enter upon military expeditions or enterprises, or usurp
or exercise judicial authority therein ; and where the penalties
for a violation of the laws of nations were indistinctly marked, or were inadequate. He at the same time recommended, that while the United States adopted measures for the
fulfilment of their duties towards others, they should not neglect those which were necessary for placing the country in a
competent state of defense ; and that they should exact from
others the fulfilment of duties towards themselves.

" The United States," he observed, " ought not to indulge the
persuasion, that contrary to the order of human events, they will
forever keep at a distance, those painful appeals to arms, with
which the history of other nations abounds.   There is a rank due
to the United States among nations, which will be withheld, if
not absolutely lost, by the reputation of weakness.

" If we desire to avoid insult, we must be able to repel it ; if
we desire to secure peace, one of the most powerful instruments
of our prosperity, it must be known, that we are at all times ready
for war."

After stating the continuance of Indian hostilities, and recommending among other things, that provision be made for the regular redemption of the public debt, and for the purchase of arms
and military stores, he concludes—

" The several subjects to which I have now referred, open a
wide range to your deliberations ; and involve some of the
choicest interests of our common country.   Permit me to bring
to your remembrance the magnitude of your task.

" Without an unprejudiced coolness, the welfare of the government may be hazarded ; without harmony, as far as consists
with freedom of sentiment, its dignity may be lost.   But, as the
legislative proceedings of the United States will never, I trust, be
reproached for the want of temper or candor, so shall not the pub-

lic happiness languish, from the want of my strenuous and warmest co-operation."

The particular situation of the United States with Great Britain
and France, in consequence of the new state of things in Europe,
was the subject of a distinct and separate communication.

In this communication, made the 5th of December, the president referred to the extraordinary orders and decrees of those
two belligerents, which had affected the commerce of the United States ; and with respect to the conduct of the French minister sent to this country by the representative and executive
bodies of France, he observed—" It is with extreme concern
I have to inform you, that the proceedings of the person, whom
they have unfortunately appointed their minister plenipotentiary here, have breathed nothing of the friendly spirit of the
nation, which sent him ; their tendency, on the contrary, has
been to involve us in *war* abroad, and in *discord* and *anarchy* at
home. So far as his acts, or those of his agents, have threatened our immediate commitment in the war, or flagrant insult to
the authority of the laws, their effect has been counteracted by
the ordinary cognizance of the laws, and by an exertion of the
powers confided to me. Where their danger was not imminent,
they have been borne with, from sentiments of regard to his nation ; from a sense of their friendship towards us ; from a conviction, that they would not suffer us to remain long exposed to the
action of a person, who has so little respect for our mutual dispositions ; and I will add, from a reliance on the firmness of my
fellow citizens in their principles of peace and order."

. The members of the house of representatives in their answer to
the president's speech, were unanimous.* " The United States,"
they said, " having taken no part in the war which has embraced
in Europe the powers with whom they have the most extensive relations, the maintenance of peace was justly to be regarded as one
of the most important duties of the magistrate, charged with the
faithful execution of the laws. We, accordingly, witness with ap-

* This was drawn by a committee consisting of Mr. Madison, Mr. Sedgwick, Mr.
Hartley, Mr. Watts, and Samuel Smith.

probation and pleasure, the vigilance with which you have guarded an interruption of that blessing, by your proclamation, admonishing our fellow citizens of the consequences of illicit and hostile acts towards the belligerent parties; and promoting, by a declaration of the existing legal state of things, an easier admission of our right to the immunities belonging to our situation."

The senate declared the proclamation to be a " measure well timed and wise, manifesting a watchful solicitude for the welfare of the nation, and calculated to promote it."

The same unanimity, unfortunately, did not prevail in the subsequent proceedings of the national legislature during this session. The secretary of state, by a resolution of the house, in February, 1791, had been instructed to make a report as to the nature and extent of the privileges granted to American commerce, as well as the restrictions imposed upon it by foreign nations; and also as to the measures, in his opinion, proper for the improvement of the commerce and navigation of the United States. Early in this session, the secretary submitted to the house a report on this subject, and which was referred to the consideration of the committee of the whole.

This report had reference to a state of things, prior to the new system of the coalesced powers, and presented a view of the extent and value of the trade of the United States, with each of those countries, with whom they had any considerable commercial connection, and a detailed account of the privileges granted by each to American commerce, and the restrictions imposed upon it. The secretary presented two methods of removing, modifying and counteracting these restrictions.

1st. By amicable arrangements, as being the most eligible, if practicable.

2d. By countervailing acts, on the part of the American government, where friendly arrangements could not be made.

This report was one of the last official acts of Mr. Jefferson. At the close of this year, according to previous intimations given to the president, he retired from office; and Edmund Randolph was soon after appointed his successor.

This report of Mr. Jefferson, formed the basis of the celebrated commercial resolutions, as they were called, submitted to the house by Mr. Madison early in January, 1794. The substance of the first of these resolutions was, that the interest of the United States would be promoted by further restrictions and higher duties, in certain cases, on the *manufactures* and *navigation* of foreign nations. The additional duties were to be laid on certain articles manufactured by those European nations, *which had no commercial treaties with the United States.* The articles selected were those manufactured principally from leather, wool, cotton, silk, hemp, flax, iron, steel, pewter, copper, and brass. These resolutions required reciprocity in navigation, except with respect to the West India trade. On foreign vessels, employed in this trade, higher tonnage duties were to be imposed, as well as additional duties on their cargoes. The last of the resolutions declared, that provision ought to be made, for ascertaining the losses sustained by American citizens, from the operation of particular regulations of any country, contravening the law of nations; and that these losses be reimbursed, in the first instance, out of the additional duties on the manufactures and vessels of the nation establishing such regulations. The debates on these resolutions were long and animated. On the 3d of February, the first was adopted, by a majority of five only.

When the second came under consideration, Mr. Fitzimons, a member from Pennsylvania, moved an amendment, the effect of which was, to extend its operation to all nations. This motion gave way to one made by Mr. Nicholas of Virginia, exempting all nations from its operation, except Great Britain. While this was under consideration, the whole subject was postponed until the first Monday of March, by a majority of five; the advocates of the measure voting for the postponement, and its opponents against it.

In discussing these resolutions a wide range was taken; their *political* as well as *commercial* effects upon foreign nations, were brought into view. In the course of the debate it was soon apparent, that their political bearing was considered as the most

important, particularly on that nation to which its operation was
finally limited, by the motion of Mr. Nicholas.   Before this subject again came before the House, news of additional British
instructions of the 6th of November, relative to the French West
India trade, arrived in the United States, and demanded something more than mere commercial regulations.   By these the
commanders of British ships of war, and privateers, were directed " to stop and detain all ships laden with goods, the produce
of any colony belonging to France, or carrying provisions, or
other supplies, for the use of such colony, and to bring the same,
with their cargoes, *to legal adjudication*, in the British courts of admiralty."   These instructions, though dated the 6th of November, were not made public, or even known to the American minister in England, until the last of December following.   If the
orders of June preceding were a violation of neutral rights,
these were much more so.   American vessels, bound to the
French West Indies were, under the new orders, without previous
notice, seized and carried into British ports, in the West Indies;
many of them condemned on the most frivolous pretences, and
others detained and harrassed a long time before the courts of admiralty.   Such was the threatening aspect of political affairs, that
early in the session, a committee of the House was instructed to
prepare and report an estimate of the expense requisite to place
the principal sea-ports of the country in a state of defense.   The
orders of the 6th of November rendered the importance and
necessity of a measure of this kind more apparent.

    That some measures of resistance to these aggressions should
be adopted, all agreed ; but a difference of opinion existed in congress, what those measures should be.   The opponents of the administration, urged the adoption of commercial restrictions, while
its supporters, with the President himself were in favor of a different course.   Various plans were submitted to the House, by
members in accordance with their different views of the subject.
On the 12th of March Mr. Sedgwick proposed sundry resolutions,
the purport of which was, that fifteen regiments of auxiliary troops
be enlisted for two years, on condition, that if war should break out

within that time, between the United States and any foreign European nation, they should be bound to serve three years, after the commencement of the war, should the same so long continue ; the troops however, to receive no pay, until the war happened, except half a dollar per day, for each days exercise in military disclipline.

By the last of the resolutions, the President was authorised to lay an embargo, for forty days, in case he deemed the safety and welfare of the country required it. After an ineffectual attempt to take up this resolution, the house, on the 14th of March, resumed the discussion of Mr. Madison's commercial plan ; but without coming to a decision. The debates upon it were renewed with increased heat on both sides. The opponents of the measure urged the impropriety of its adoption, in the alarming state of affairs with Great Britain ; if viewed as a peace measure, they said, it was impolitic, if a war measure, inefficient. The great injuries the United States had received, and were receiving from British spoliations, demanded a much more energetic course of conduct—that the time had arrived when they must seriously prepare for war—that without a speedy redress for these injuries, war was inevitable. While the advocates of the plan, urged its efficiency, they declared, that its doption would not preclude any other, which might be proposed. To prevent American commerce from being further exposed to depredation, congress on the 26th of March laid an embargo on all ships and vessels in the ports of the United States, bound to any foreign port or place for the term of thirty days. The resolutions of Mr. Sedgwick for raising troops being negatived, he immediately proposed, in general terms, " that measures ought immediately to be taken, to render the force of the United States more efficient." This proposition being adopted, a committee, to whom it was referred, reported that an addition be made to the regular military force, including a corps of artillerists and engineers—that the President be authorised to call on the executives of the several states, to organize, and hold in readiness to march at a moments warning, eighty thousand militia.

Soon after this report was submitted, Mr. Madison expressed his determination to call up his commercial regulations, unless gentlemen had something else to propose, which, in the juncture of affairs, might be deemed more urgent. Mr. Smith, of South Carolina, then rose and observed, that the subject of indemnity to the owners of vessels and cargoes, which had been captured by some of the belligerent powers, was, in his opinion, very urgent, and entitled to the immediate attention of congress. He was strongly impressed, he said, with the principle, that those who were thus despoiled of their property, while pursuing a lawful trade, without being protected, had a right to look to their government for compensation, and that the government must look to the aggressor. He, therefore, read in his place, a resolution he intended to propose, declaring that " provision ought to be made for the indemnification of all citizens of the United States, whose vessels or cargoes had been seized and confiscated by any of the belligerent powers, contrary to the law of nations."

Mr. Dayton said, he could not agree to such a proposition, without designating the fund from which the indemnity was to be made, he, therefore, submitted to the house, the two following resolutions.

" 1st. That provision ought to be made by law, for the sequestration of all the debts due from the citizens of the United States to the subjects of the king of Great Britain.

" 2d. That provision ought, in like manner, to be made, for securing the payment of all such debts into the treasury of the United States, there to be held as a pledge for the indemnification of such of the citizens of the said states, as shall have suffered from the ships of war, privateers, or from any person or description of persons, acting under the commission or authority of the British king, in contravention of the law of nations, and in violation of the rights of neutrality."

These resolutions were immediately taken into consideration, and debated with great warmth and even acrimony. They were opposed upon principle, as well as policy, and were finally postponed.

Pending the resolutions of Mr. Dayton, intelligence arrived, that the British ministers, in answer to inquiries of the London merchants, had informed them, that *condemnation* of property, under the orders of the 6th of November, had not been contemplated. Indeed, on the 8th of January, 1794, these orders were revoked, and others substituted, directing the commanders of British ships, to bring in for adjudication such vessels only, as were laden with goods, the produce of the French islands, and coming *directly* from the same, to any port *in Europe ;* or such vessels, as were laden with the produce of the islands, the property of *French subjects*, wherever bound. This left the *direct* trade between the United States and the French islands, free to American vessels laden with property belonging to American citizens. By the new orders, vessels attempting to enter a blockadaded port in the French islands,.or laden in whole or in part, with *naval or military stores*, bound to the same, were also made liable to seizure, and to be proceeded with according to the law of nations.

The new instructions were transmitted to the American executive, on the 9th of January, by Mr. Pinckney; and with other communications from him, were submitted to congress, on the 4th of April. If the principles of the orders of the 6th of November, were unjustifiable, much less could the concealment of them, for so long a time after they were issued and in force, admit of justification or even apology. Mr. Pinckney had no knowledge of them, until about the 26th of December, nor had he an opportunity of obtaining from the minister, any explanation respecting them, until about the time of their revocation. In a conference with Mr. Grenville, he was informed, that they were intended to prevent abuses, which might take place from the sailing of the St. Domingo fleet to the United States, and to aid in a contemplated attack upon the French Islands, by Sir John Jarvis and Sir Charles Grey ; and that neutral vessels brought in under them, were not to be condemned, unless otherwise legally liable to condemnation. This explanation was far from being satisfactory to the American government; and the new orders, though less objectionable, because less extensive, still embraced principles not warranted by the law of nations.

The movements of the British in Canada, during the winter of 1794, produced also no little excitement in congress, as well as throughout the United States, and gave unequivocal indications of an expected rupture between the two countries. On the 10th of February, lord Dorchester, in a speech to several Indian tribes assembled at Quebec, declared, he should not be surprised, if Great Britain and the United States were at war in the course of the year; and told them, in that event, *a line must be drawn by the warriors.* Soon after this, governor Simcoe established a military post at the rapids of the Miami of the lake, many miles within the American limits, evidently with an intent to encourage, and if necessary, to support the Indians, then at war with the United States. On these subjects, a correspondence took place between the American secretary and Mr. Hammond. The latter attempted to justify the advance of governor Simcoe, as necessary to protect British subjects residing in districts dependent on the fort at Detroit ; or to prevent that fort from being straitened by the approach of the American army. In either case he intimated, that *the status quo* would apply, until a final arrangement of the points in dispute between the two countries, could be made.

In this serious and threatening aspect of affairs, the advocates for commercial restrictions considered the resolutions of Mr. Madison too limited. On the 7th of April, therefore, a proposition was submitted to the house, by Mr. Clark, declaring that until the British government should make restitution for all losses and damages sustained by the citizens of the United States from British armed vessels, contrary to the law of nations, and also, until the western posts be given up by the British, all *commercial intercourse* between the United States and Great Britain, so far as respects the products of Great Britain and Ireland, should be prohibited. This proposition produced a protracted as well as ardent debate, involving the great and interesting question, as to the most efficient and honorable course to be pursued, in the critical state of affairs with Great Britain.

Pending this important discussion, the president, in accordance with that course of policy he had uniformly pursued, of preserving his country in peace, so long as the same could be done, consistently with honor, and a just regard to its rights, determined to make the last and only effort for this purpose, which afforded any prospect of success.

On the 16th of April, he nominated Mr. Jay, as minister extraordinary to the British court. "The communications" he said in his message to the senate, making this nomination, "which I have made to you, during the present session, from the despatches of our minister at London, contain a serious aspect of our affairs with Great Britain. But as peace ought to be pursued with unremitted zeal, before the last resource, which has so often been the scourge of nations, and cannot fail to check the advanced prosperity of the United States, is contemplated, I have thought proper to nominate, &c.

"My confidence," he subjoined, "in our minister plenipotentiary in London, continues undiminished ; but a mission like this, while it corresponds with the solemnity of the occasion, will announce to the world a solicitude for a friendly adjustment of our complaints, and a reluctance to hostility. Going immediately from the United States, such an envoy will carry with him a full knowledge of the existing temper and sensibility of our country ; and will thus be taught to vindicate our rights with firmness, and to cultivate peace with sincerity." The views of the president on this trying occasion, were more particularly stated, in a note to the secretary of state, the day preceding this nomination. "My objects are," said the president, " to prevent a war, if justice can be obtained by fair and strong representations, (to be made by a special envoy,) of the injuries, which this country has sustained from Great Britain, in various ways : to put it in a complete state of military defense—and to provide eventually such measures, as seem to be now pending in congress for execution, if negociation in a reasonable time, proves unsuccessful."* These views of the president were in accordance with those of the members of congress, who usually supported his administration, and should free their names from the imputation, then cast upon them, of being willing to submit to the unjust aggressions of Great Britain. As early as the 10th of March, Mr. Ellsworth, a member of the senate, at the request of Mr. Strong, Mr. Cabot, and Mr. King, who were also among the most influential members of that body, had a conference with the president, on the critical state of affairs with Great Britain ; and the result of this conference was, that unless redress for injuries received could be obtained, by a special mission to the court of London, war was unavoidable ; and to meet the latter event, however calamitous it might be, the country must be prepared.

Mr. Jefferson and Mr. Hamilton, as well as Mr. Jay, were mentioned to the president by different persons, as proper envoys, on this extraordinary mission. The long experience of Mr. Jay, in diplomatic affairs, probably gave him the preference, in the mind of the president. His nomination was approved in the senate, eighteen to eight.

Mr. Jay accepted the appointment with great reluctance, and not without a full knowledge of the infinite difficulties in the way of accomplishing the objects of his mission in a manner which should be satisfactory. No treaty with any foreign power had yet been made under the new government. Treaties had only been formed with the Indian tribes; and in these instances, as well as in the instance of an attempt to obtain the release of American prisoners by a treaty with the regency of Algiers, the president had in person attended the senate, and requested their advice as to the terms he was about to propose. In this mode of proceeding, serious difficulties had arisen ; and on reconsideration, it had been deemed most consistent with the constitution, not to consult the senate in a formal manner, until a treaty had actual-

* Randolph's Vindication.

ly been made. The senate, therefore, in this instance, were not previously consulted by the president, as to the terms of a treaty with Great Britain. This has ever since been considered the true construction of the constitution, and the course then adopted invariably pursued.

The mission to England was opposed to the sense of a majority of the house of representatives, and in the senate it met with the opposition of Mr. Munroe, Mr. Burr, and others. The two great and primary objects of this mission were, the vexations and spoliations committed on American commerce, under British orders; and the adjustment of all differences concerning the treaty of peace. Should these points " be so accommodated, as to promise the continuance of tranquility between the United States and Great Britain," " the subject of a commercial treaty," according to Mr. Jay's instructions, " might then be listened to, or even broken to the British ministry."

Aware that the British government might wish to detach the United States from France, and even make some overtures of that kind, Mr. Jay was specially instructed to say, " that the government of the United States would not derogate from their treaties and engagements with France."

The advocates of commercial restrictions, did not relax their exertions, in consequence of the new mission to England. They viewed it as an improper interference with their favorite system, which they resolved still to carry into effect. The proposition made by Mr. Clark, after much debate, was so modified in the house, as to read, " whereas the injuries which have been suffered and may be suffered, by the United States, from violations committed by Great Britain on their neutral rights and commercial interests, as well as from her failure to execute the seventh article of the treaty of peace, render it inexpedient for the interest of the United States, that the commercial intercourse between the two countries, should continue to be carried on, in the extent at present allowed—

" *Resolved*, That from and after the first day of November, 1794, all commercial intercourse between the citizens of the United States, and the subjects of the king of Great Britain, or the citizens or subjects of any other nation, so far as the same respects articles of the growth or manufacture of Great Britain or Ireland, shall be prohibited."

This resolution was adopted by the house on the 21st of April, by a majority of twenty; and a bill passed in pursuance of it; but it was negatived in the senate, by the casting vote of the vice-president. To meet that state of things, which seemed unavoidable, in the failure of the negociation, congress, after the appointment of Mr. Jay, proceeded to place the country in a posture of defense. The principal ports and harbors were directed to be fortified. A detachment of eighty thousand militia was required from the several states, to be ready, at a moment's warning; the exportation of arms was prohibited for a year, and the importation of brass cannon, muskets, swords, cutlasses, musket ball, lead, and gun powder, was encouraged, by permitting them to come in duty-free; and a corps of artillerists and engineers was established. The president was also authorized to purchase a number of gallies, and to lay an embargo, whenever, in his opinion, the public safety should require it, during the recess of congress. To meet the necessary expenses, the internal taxes were increased by laying duties on carriages, snuff, refined sugar, on sales at auction, and on licenses for selling wines and spirituous liquors by retail. These duties were violently opposed; and that on carriages was declared, by its opponents, unconstitutional; and in Virginia the collection of this tax was disputed, until a decision of the supreme court of the United States in favor of it. The national legislature also, agreeably to the recommendations of the president, at the opening of the session, took measures to prevent the laws and sovereignty of the country from being again outraged by foreigners, as well as to secure the neutrality of the United States from being compromitted by acts of their own citizens. The enlistment of men, either as soldiers or seamen, within the territory or jurisdiction of the United States, in the service of any foreign prince or state, was prohibited under a penalty of one thousand dollars, and imprisonment not exceeding three years,—the arming of vessels, in American ports, to be employed in the service of any foreign state, to commit hostilities upon the subjects or citizens of any nation, with whom the United States were at peace ; and the issuing of a commission, within the United States, for any vessel to be so employed, were also prohibited under severe penalties ; nor was the armament of any foreign vessel to be increased in American ports. Persons who should begin or set on foot, any military expedition or enterprize, to be carried on from the United States, against the dominions of any foreign power at peace with them, were, likewise, subjected to severe punishments ; and the president was authorized to employ the land and naval force of the union, to compel the observance of these laws.

During this session Mr. Giles again moved for an investigation into the official conduct of the secretary of the treasury. A committee for this purpose was appointed, (Mr. Hamilton himself desiring an inquiry,) and Mr. Giles was placed at the head of the committee. The result of this investigation, by the political enemies of the secretary, was highly honorable to the talents and integrity of that great financier.

This interesting session of the national legislature closed on the 9th of June, 1794. The independent conduct of the executive, had, for a time, at least, stayed the calamities of war.

It is proper here to state, that Mr. Genet being recalled, his place was supplied by a successor, Mr. Fauchet, who arrived in the United States in February, 1794.

The Brissotine party in France, which sent Genet to America, had been supplanted by that of Robertspiere ; and many of the Brissotines were sent to the guillotine ; and there can be no doubt, that Genet himself was doomed to the same fate.*

His successor had special orders to send him back to France, and for this purpose to use force, if necessary.

---

* It is not a little singular, that the Jacobin clubs in France, in the formation of which Genet himself had, probably, no inconsiderable share, had denounced him, because he had embroiled his country with general Washington.—*Diplomacy of the United States.*

Fauchet, therefore, immediately after his arrival, finding that Mr. Genet did not intend to return, requested liberty to arrest and send him back, agreeably to his instructions. This was refused by the president. Still desirous of effecting his object, he enquired whether the executive would oppose his decoying him on board of a French vessel, under the pretence of honoring him with an entertainment, and then sailing with him for France. The president not only refused to wink at this clandestine mode of proceeding, but declared he would resist it, if necessary, by force. By this upright and impartial conduct, the president, no doubt saved Mr. Genet from the guillotine.

The conduct of the new French minister was, at first more concialitory than that of his predecessor. It was soon apparant however, that a change of men, had not produced a real change in the measures or views of the French government, by whomsoever administered, in regard to the United States. The real object of France was, to induce the Americans to make common cause with her against her enemies, particularly Great Britain. Complaints were still urged against the conduct of the American executive, as hostile to France and friendly to England. The mission to the court of London, was viewed with particular jealousy and distrust, by the French republic. Aware that this would be the case, the president, about the last of May, 1794, appointed Mr. Munroe, successor to Mr. Morriss, who, at the request of the French government, had been recalled.

The appointment of this gentleman it was supposed might tend to remove these jealousies. His instructions contained an explicit declaration of the president, in favour of the revolution in France. " The president" says the secretary in his letter of instructions, " has been an early and decided friend of the French revolution ; and whatever reasons there may have been under an ignorance of facts and policy, to suspend an opinion upon some of its important transactions, yet is he immutable in his wishes for its accomplishment ; incapable of assenting to the right of any foreign prince, to meddle with its interior arrangement ; and persuaded that success will attend their efforts, and particularly, that union among themselves is an impregnable barrier against external assaults."

With respect to the conduct of the American government towards France, and the mission of Mr. Jay, the instructions say, " from Messrs. Genet and Fauchet we have uniformly learned, that France did not desire us to depart from neutrality ; and it would have been unwise to have asked us to do otherwise. For our ports are open to her prizes, while they are shut to those of Great Britain, and supplies of grain could not be forwarded to France with so much certainty, were we at war, as they can even now, notwithstanding the British restrictions ; and as they may be, if the demand to be made upon Great Britain should succeed. We have therefore pursued neutrality with faithfulness ; we have paid more of our debt to France than was absolutely due, as the secretary of the treasury asserts ; and we should have paid more, if the state of our affairs did not require us to be prepared with funds for the possible event of war. We mean to retain the same line of conduct in future, and to remove all jealousy, with respect to Mr. Jay's mission to London, you may say, that he is positively forbidden to weaken the engagements between this country and France. It is not improbable, that you will be obliged to encounter, on this head, suspicions of various kinds. But you may declare the motives of that mission to be, to obtain immediate compensation for our plundered property, and restitution of the posts. You may intimate by way of argument, but without ascribing it to the government, that if war should be necessary, the affections of the people of the United States towards it, would be better secured by a manifestation, that every step had been taken to avoid it ; and that the British nation would be divided, when they found, that we had been forced into it. This may be briefly touched upon, as the path of prudence with respect to ourselves ; and also, with respect to France, since we are unable to give her aid, of men or money. To this matter you cannot be too attentive, and you will be amply justified in repelling with firmness any imputation of the most distant intention to sacrifice our connection with

France to any connection with England."* After stating, that the
subjects of treaties of commerce, of alliance, and of the execution of the guaranty of the French Islands, were to be referred
to the American government, at home, it is added at the close,
" In short it is expected, with a sure reliance on your discretion,
that you will not commit the United States, by any specific declarations, except where you are particularly instructed, and except in giving testimony of our attachment to their cause."

* Munroe's View.

CHAPTER XXIII.

WHILE the president was exerting himself to prevent a foreign war, he was threatened with a civil war at home. For about three years, the inhabitants of the counties in Pennsylvania, lying west of the Allegany mountains, had opposed the execution of the laws imposing duties on domestic spirits. This opposition, notwithstanding all the exertions of congress and the executive to render the operation of those laws as little burdensome as possible, was now carried to such a length, as seriously to put at hazard the peace, if not the existence of the union. The revenue officers, in attempting to do their duty, were threatened not only with the loss of their property, but their lives ; and in many instances, were personally abused and compelled to renounce their offices. In the summer of 1794, the marshal of the district, in attempting to execute process on the delinquents, was attacked by an armed force, and fired upon, but fortunately without injury. He was soon after taken prisoner by an armed mob, his life threatened, and compelled, under the fear of immediate death, to engage, not to serve any process on the west side of the Allegany mountains. In July, the house of general Neville, the inspector, near Pittsburgh, was attacked, but defended with so much spirit, that the assailants were obliged to retire. Apprehending a second and more powerful attack, the inspector applied to the judges, civil magistrates, and military officers for protection. But he was informed that the combination against the execution of the laws, was so general in that quarter, that no protection could be given. The attack was soon after renewed, by about five hundred men. The inspector considering it impossible to resist with effect so large a force, and that his life must be the sacrifice, by the advice of his friends, retired to a place of concealment. About eleven men from the garrison at Pittsburgh, remained with a hope of saving the property.

The assailants demanded that the inspector should come out and renounce his office, but were informed, that he had retired on their approach, to some place unknown. The papers belonging to his office were then required, and after a short but indecisive parly on the subject, the house was attacked, and a firing commenced between its occupants and the insurgents ; in consequence of which, one of the assailants was killed, and a number on both sides wounded. The house was at last set on fire and consumed. The marshal and inspector made their escape down the Ohio, and by a circuitous route, reached the seat of government. The excise laws, as they were called, were unpopular in some of the other states, and strong indications were given of a more extensive and open opposition.

The insurgents were no doubt, encouraged by individuals, particularly by the democratic societies, in different parts of the union.

This created no little alarm in the mind of the president, and he entertained serious doubts, whether the militia, if called upon to suppress the insurrection, would obey the orders of the executive. Such, however, was the conduct of the insurgents, that no alternative was left, but either to surrender the government itself into the hands of the lawless and disobedient, or compel submission by military force.

The experiment was new but necessary, and the fate of the republic depended upon the issue. The law had wisely provided, that before resort could be had to the last alternative, an associate justice or district judge of the United States must declare and give notice, that the laws were opposed, and the execution thereof obstructed by combinations too powerful to be suppressed by the ordinary course of judicial proceedings, or the powers vested in the marshals; and that the president should also by proclamation, command the insurgents to disperse and retire peaceably to their respective homes, within a limited time.

Such a declaration or notice was given by James Wilson, an associate justice; and on the 7th of August, a proclamation was issued, in which, after stating the various acts and combinations of the insurgents, the president declared—" and whereas it is, in my judgment, necessary under the circumstances of the case, to take measures for calling forth the militia, in order to suppress the combinations aforesaid, and to cause the laws to be duly executed ; and I have accordingly determined so to do, feeling the deepest regret for the occasion, but with the most solemn conviction, that the essential interests of the union demand it—that the very existence of the government, and the fundamental principles of social order, are materially involved in the issue ; and that the patriotism and firmness of all good citizens are seriously called upon, as occasion may require, to aid in the effectual suppression of so fatal a spirit." The insurgents were required to disperse and retire to their respective homes, by the first of the following September. At the time of issuing the proclamation, requisitions were made on the governors of New Jersey, Pennsylvania, Maryland, and Virginia, for their quotas of about twelve thousand men, to be organized to march at a minutes warning. The number of troops was afterwards augmented to fifteen thousand.

Unwilling however, to resort to military coercion, until every òther expedient had failed, the president, with a truly paternal care, made one more peaceable effort to bring the disaffected to a sense of their duty. He appointed James Ross, Jasper Yates, and William Bradford, gentlemen distinguished for their talents and integrity, commissioners to repair to the scene of the insurrection, for the purpose of conferring with the insurgents, to represent to them how painful to the president was the idea of exercising military power, and that it was his earnest wish to render it unnecessary, by those endeavors which humanity, a love of peace and tranquility, and the happiness of his fellow citizens, dictated. The commissioners were empowered to promise an amnesty, and perpetual oblivion of the past, on condition of future submission to the laws. Two commissioners were appointed by the state of Pennsylvania, to join with those on the part of the United States.

Previous to this, by the orders of Bradford, one of the principal leaders of the opposition, the mail was stopped by force, and sundry letters from gentlemen at Pittsburgh, giving an account of the proceedings of the insurgents, were taken out and opened.

The authors of these letters became extremely obnoxious to Bradford and his associates; and soon after, a circular letter, signed by him and six others, was addressed to the militia officers, stating, their suspicions that the Pittsburgh post would carry the sentiments of some of the people, relative to the situation of affairs in that country, and that letters by that post were in their possession, by which " certain secrets were discovered hostile to their interest ;" and that a crisis had arrived, in which every citizen must express his sentiments, " not by his *words*, but his *actions*." The officers were, therefore, called upon to render their personal services, with as many volunteers as they could raise, to rendezvous at the celebrated Braddock's field, with *arms* and *accoutrements* in good order. The real object of this meeting, as previously arranged by the signers of the circular letter, though disclosed to a few only, was to attack the garrison at Pittsburgh, and seize the arms and ammunition there, for their own defense. In justification of this bold measure, they referred to the former conduct of the colonists, at the commencement of the revolution, in seizing British posts and arms, until their grievances were redressed, as applicable to their situation. This project, however, when disclosed to some who were less rash and impetuous, was considered too daring to be carried into execution; and before the time of the meeting, was relinquished. Several thousands, however, met at the place of rendezvous, many with arms, and were harangued and reviewed by Bradford, who assumed the command. Little was actually done at this meeting, except ordering general Gibson and colonel Nevil, the authors of the letters robbed from the mail, to be expelled from Pittsburgh.

A meeting of delegates from four of the western counties, and from the county of Ohio, in Virginia, was held at Parkinson's ferry, on the 14th of August. This meeting, consisting of about two hundred delegates, was composed of some of the more moderate, as well as the most daring and turbulent. Edward Cooke was elected chairman, and Albert Gallatin secretary. The meeting, which was held in the field, was opened by Bradford, in an inflammatory harangue, and comments on the letters taken from the mail. Mr. Marshall, one of those who called the meeting at Braddock's field, then introduced sundry resolutions, one of which was, "that a standing committee be appointed, to consist of members from each county, to be denominated a committee of *public safety ; whose duty it shall be to call forth the resources of the western country to repel any hostile attempts that might be made against the citizens, or the body of the people.*" The latter part of this resolution, which was an open and avowed act of rebellion, was opposed by Mr. Gallatin, and after some delay, the mover proposed to withdraw it, provided a committee of sixty should be appointed, with power to call another meeting.

The resolutions offerred by Mr. Marshall, were referred to a committee, and after being amended and modified, were passed.*

* The proceedings of the executive respecting the insurgents, and Findley's History of the insurrection.

The first declared, that taking citizens from their respective abodes or vicinage, to be tried for real or supposed offenses, was a violation of their rights, a forced and dangerous construction of the constitution, and ought not, under any pretence whatever, to be exercised by the judicial authority.

The second appointed a standing committee of one from each township, to draft a remonstrance to congress, praying for a repeal of the excise laws, and the substitution of a tax less odious ; and to give assurances, that such a tax should be faithfully paid—To make a statement of the late transactions in relation to these laws, with the causes which led to them, and to make a representation to the president on the subject ; with power also to call another meeting.

The third recommended to their fellow citizens to exert themselves in support of the municipal laws of the respective states, and especially in preventing any violation or outrage against the property or person of any individual.

And the fourth appointed a committee of three from each county, to meet the commissioners of the government, and to report the result of their conference to the standing committee. This meeting was attended by many spectators. The feelings of individuals were expressed in a variety of ways, on this occasion. A liberty pole was erected in view of the meeting, with a motto, " *liberty and no excise, and no asylum for cowards or traitors.*"

The meeting being dissolved, the standing committee, consisting of sixty, agreed to meet at Redstone Old Fort, on the second of September. The commissioners of the general government, as well as of the state of Pennsylvania, agreeably to previous arrangement, met the conferees at Pittsburgh ; and the former proposed a general amnesty, on condition of submission to the laws.

This proposition met with the entire approbation of all the conferees, with the exception of Bradford, and they engaged to recommend a compliance on the part of the people. The result of the conference was made known to the standing committee at

Redstone on the 28th of August, (a meeting of that body having been called four days earlier than that agreed to) and produced very warm and violent debates   The restless and turbulent spirits were not yet willing to yield.   Bradford, in particular, was mad enough, not only to recommend a perseverance in their opposition to the laws, but to urge the establishment of an independent governmet ; declaring, that the general government had been only trifling with Spain about the Mississippi, and with Great Britain respecting the Indians.   Being independent, he said, they could settle these disputes, in a short period.

Although the committee urged the acceptance of the proposition of the commissioners in full, yet a small majority only could be procured to declare, as their opinion, it was for the *interest* of the people to accede to it.   This question was taken by ballot, by which the votes were concealed, and each had an opportunity of sheltering himself from the resentment of those, from whom violence was apprehended ; and it was supposed, that had it been taken publicly, it would have been negatived.

As no reliance could be placed on the proceedings of the general committee, it was deemed proper to refer the subject to the people themselves.   A second committee was appointed to confer with the commissioners, and it was agreed between them, that the sense of the people should be taken publicly in townships, and that each individual should subscribe the following written or printed declaration—" I do solemnly promise henceforth to submit to the laws of the United States ; that I will not indirectly oppose the execution of the acts for raising a revenue on distilled spirits and stills, and that I will support, as far as the law requires, the civil authority, in affording the protection due to all officers and other citizens."   This question was to be proposed to all citizens of the age of eighteen years and upwards, by two or more members of the meeting at Parkinson's ferry, or a justice of the peace of the township where the people should be assembled, and a report of the numbers voting in the affirmative and negative, was to be made by them to the commissioners, by the 16th of September ; together with their opinion, whether there was such a general submission of the people, in their respective counties, that an office of inspection might be immediately and safely established there.

From various causes, a compliance with the terms proposed, was so limited and partial in the *survey*, embracing the several counties, in which the opposition had prevailed, the commissioners in their report to the president, deemed it their duty to declare their opinion, that such was the state of things in that *survey*, " that there is no probability, that the act for raising a revenue on distilled spirits and on stills, can at present be enforced by the usual course of civil authority, and that some more competent force is necessary to cause the laws to be duly executed, and to insure to the officers and well disposed citizens that protection which it is the duty of government to afford."

On the receipt of this report, the president was under the painful necessity of putting the military force in motion ; and his second proclamation, declaring this event, was issued on the 25th of September ; announcing to the world, that this step was taken " in obedience to that high and irresistible duty consigned to him by the constitution, to take care that the laws be faithfully executed ;" deploring that the American name should be sullied by the outrages of citizens on their own government, and commiserating such as remained obstinate from delusion ; at the same time declaring his resolution, in perfect reliance on that gracious Providence, which had so signally displayed its goodness towards his country, to reduce the refractory to a due subordination to the law.

It does not fall within the limits of our design, to present a view of the military operations which followed. We shall only observe, that the call of the father of his country, was cheerfully as well as promptly obeyed by the militia, that he attended the army in person, and that by his wise and energetic measures, and by the prudent conduct of the militia themselves, this formidable insurrection was suppressed without bloodshed, and the government and laws preserved.*

* Bradford made his escape into the Spanish dominions, two others of the principal insurgents, Philip Vigol and John Mitchell, were tried for treason and found guilty, but afterwards pardoned by the president.

We would here state, that during the summer of this year, general Wayne obtained a complete victory over the hostile Indians, near the Miami of the lake, and almost under the guns of the British fort, then lately erected in that country. This decisive victory put an end to a war, which had so long desolated the frontiers, although a treaty with the hostile tribes, was not concluded until the following year.

The national legislature had adjourned to meet on the first Monday in November, 1794, but a quorum of the senate was not formed until the 18th of that month. The president's speech to both houses, contained a particular review of the insurrection in Pennsylvania, and of the measures taken to suppress it. The promptitude with which his call for support from his fellow citizens had been obeyed, demonstrated, he said, that they understood the true principles of government and liberty, and " that notwithstanding all the devices which have been used to sway them from their interest and duty, they are now as ready to maintain the authority of the laws against licentious invasions, as they were to defend their rights against usurpation." While he thus offered the meed of praise to the militia, he also said—" to every description of citizens let praise be given ; but let them persevere in their affectionate vigilance over that precious depository of American happiness, the constitution of the United States. Let them cherish it too, for the sake of those, who from every clime are daily seeking a dwelling in our land. And when in the calm moments of reflection, they shall have retraced the origin and progress of the insurrection, let them determine whether it has not been fomented by *combinations of men*, who, careless of consequences, and disregarding the unerring truth, that those who rouse, cannot always appease a civil convulsion, have disseminated, from an ignorance or perversion of facts, suspicions, jealousies, and accusations of the whole government."

In calling out the militia in this emergency, the defects of the militia system itself became more apparent, and the president most earnestly recommended a revision.

He likewise called the atttention of congress, to the important subject of providing for the redemption of the public debt.

" The time," he remarked, " which has elapsed since the commencement of our fiscal measures, has developed our pecuniary
resources, so as to open a way for a definitive plan for the redemption of the public debt. It is believed, that the result is
such as to encourage congress to consummate this work without
delay. Nothing can more promote the permanent welfare of
the nation, and nothing would be more grateful to our constituents." While he reserved certain circumstances concerning intercourse with foreign nations, for a future communication, he
thought proper to announce to congress, that his policy, in foreign
transactions, had been, " to cultivate peace with all the world ; to
check every deviation from the line of impartiality ; to explain
what may have been misapprehended, and correct what may
have been injurious to any nation ; and having thus acquired the
right, to lose no time in acquiring the *ability*, to insist upon
justice being done to ourselves." Nor did he omit, in the interesting and critical situation in which his country was placed, in
conclusion, to request all to unite, " in imploring the Supreme
Ruler of nations, to spread his holy protection over these United
States ; to turn the machinations of the wicked to the confirming
our constitution ; to enable us, at all times, to root out internal
sedition, and put invasion to flight ; to perpetuate to our country
that prosperity which his goodness has already conferred, and to
verify the anticipations of this government being a safeguard to
human rights."

The answer of the senate, reported by Mr. King, Mr. Ellsworth,
and Mr. Izard, expressed an entire approbation of the policy
of the president, with respect to foreign nations, as well as his
conduct in relation to the insurgents.

" Our anxiety," they said, " arising from the licentiousness and
open resistence to the laws, in the western counties of Pennsylvania, had been increased by the proceedings of certain self-created societies, relative to the laws and administration of the government ; proceedings, in our apprehension, founded in political
error, calculated, if not intended, to disorganize our government,
and which, by inspiring delusive hopes of support, have been

instrumental in misleading our fellow citizens in the scene of insurrection."

The declaration in the speech relative to the influence of combinations of men, in fomenting the insurrection, created no little feeling, both in and out of congress.

The answer of the house, as reported by Mr. Madison, Mr. Sedgwick, and Mr. Scott, was silent, not only with respect to those combinations, but also as to the success of general Wayne, and the policy of the executive, in relation to foreign nations. The mission of Mr. Jay, to which a majority had been opposed, as an improper interference with their favorite system of commercial restrictions, was not yet forgotten, and the same majority refused to express their approbation of the policy of the executive, in regard to foreign nations. Nor could a vote of direct censure of self-created societies be procured, without confining it to those in the four *western counties of Pennsylvania, and parts adjacent.*

The subject of making provision for the redemption of the public debt, occasioned much debate, as well as great division in the house.

It was a favorite measure with the secretary of the treasury, as well as with the president. The former, on the 15th of January, 1795, submitted to congress a plan for this purpose, drawn with his usual ability.

The secretary proposed, an increase of the sinking fund, by adding to it, duties on imports and tonnage, on spirits distilled within the United States, and on stills, the avails of the sales of the public lands, the dividends on bank stock belonging to the United States, and the interest of the money, which should be redeemed, together with all monies which should be received from debts due to the United States antecedent to the constitution, and all surplusses of the amount of revenues, which should remain at the end of every calendar year beyond the amount of appropriations charged upon them, and which during the session of congress commencing next thereafter, should not be especially appropriated. This fund was to be applied to the payment of the six per cent and deferred stock, according to the right reserved to the United States, that is, to the payment of eight per cent. on account of the principal and interest, and to continue until the whole should be paid and redeemed ; and after such redemption, the same fund to continue appropriated until the residue of the debt of the United States, foreign and domestic, funded and infunded should be redeemed and discharged. The faith of the United States was to be firmly pledged to the creditors for the inviolable application of this fund to the payment of the debts, until the same should be fully conpleted ; and for this purpose, the fund was to be vested in the commissioners of the sinking fund as "*property in trust.*"

The importance of this measure, for the purpose of preventing the evils arising, from a great accumulation of debt, was pressed upon the legislature by the secretary, in a manner calculated to produce conviction.

"There is no sentiment" he remarked " which can better deserve the serious attention of the legislature of a country, than the one expresed in the speech of the president ; which indicates the danger to every government, from the progressive accumulation of debt. A tendency to it is perhaps *the natural disease* of all governments ; and it is not easy to conceive any thing more likely than this, to lead to great and convulsive revolutions of empires. On the one hand, the exigencies of a nation creating new causes of expenditure, as well from its own, as from the ambition, rapacity, injustice, intemperance and folly of other nations, proceed in increasing and rapid succession. On the other, there is a general propensity in those who administer the affairs of government, founded in the constitution of man, to shift off the burden from the present to a future day ; a propensity, which may be expected to be strong in proportion as the form of the state is popular."

The difficulties arising from this propensity in a republican government, as well as the inconsistency of those, who, to obtain popularity, will loudly declaim against the accumulation of debt, and in favor of its reduction as *abstract questions ;* and yet from the same motives, will as loudly declaim against the very means, which can alone prevent the one, and effect the other, are stated by the Secretary, with great perspicuity and truth.

"To extinguish a debt" he observed, "which exists, and to avoid contracting more, are ideas almost, always favored by public feeling and opinion, but to pay taxes for the one or the other purpose, which are the only means to avoid the evil, is always more or less unpopular. These contradictions are in human nature. And the lot of a country would be enviable indeed, in which there were not always men, ready to turn them to the account of their own popularity, or to some other sinister account. Hence it is no uncommon spectacle to see the same man clamoring for occasions of expense, when they happen to be in unison with the present humour of the community, well or ill directed, declaiming against a public debt, and for the reduction of it ; yet vehement against every plan of taxation, which is proposed to discharge old debts, or to avoid new, by defraying the expenses of exigencies as they emerge."

An act finally passed, on this important subject, during this session, substantially in accordance with the plan suggested by the secretary, though congress were divided on the question of pledging the internal duties. The funds appropriated for the reimbursement and redemption of the debt, were by law *vested* in the commissioners of the sinking fund, *in trust* for that object, and the faith of the United States was pledged, that the funds should inviolably so remain appropriated and vested, until the whole debt should be paid.

These funds were to be applied to the payment of eight per cent. per annum, on account of the principal and interest of the six per cent and deferred stock, and the surpluss to the payment of the other debts foreign and domestic. In pursuance of this compact with the public creditors, the six per cent. stock was fully paid in the year 1818, and the deferred stock in 1824.

The total amount of the unredeemed debt of the United States (including the assumed debt,) in 1795, was $76,096,468 17.

During this session of congress, Mr. Hamilton the secretary of the treasury, gave in his resignation, and Mr. Oliver Wolcott who had been comptroller from the commencement of the government, was appointed his successor. On the first of January of this year, general Knox, who had been long secretary at war, also resigned his place, and colonel Pickering was appointed in his room.

It will be remembered that the disputes with Spain, concerning limits and the navigation of the Mississippi, were by the old congress, just at the close of their existence, referred to the new government. Since the peace of 1783, the Spaniards had kept possession of the country north of latitude 31°, to the mouth of the river Yazoo, and had built a fort at the Walnut Hills. They had also, in May, 1790, made a treaty with the Chickesaw and Cherokee nations of Indians, and taken them under their protection. By this treaty these tribes acknowledged, that the territory south of the Yazoo belonged to the Spaniards, and promised to support them in the possession of it. The Spaniards, on the other hand, engaged to protect these Indians, in the possession of their lands. Individuals also, supposed to be under the influence of the Spanish government, fomented difficulties among the Creeks, in consequence of a treaty they had made with the United States, in August of the same year, and instigated them to acts of hostility.

An expected rupture between Great Britain and Spain, in the year 1790, in consequence of disputes relative to Nootka Sound, seemed to present a favorable moment for the renewal of the negociations with the latter. The president, therefore, gave special instructions to the American representative at the Spanish court on the subject, and sent them by colonel Humphreys, then appointed a minister resident at the court of Portugal. The amicable adjustment of the disputes between Great Britain and Spain, prevented any thing being done under these instructions.

Intimations, however, having been given to the American executive the next year, that the Spanish court was disposed to renew the negociations at Madrid, Messrs. Carmichael and Short were appointed commissioners plenipotentiary, on the part of the United States. Their instructions extended to the subject of commerce, as well as limits and the navigation of the Mississippi. They were directed to *insist* on the right of the United States to the free navigation of that river, and to extend their southern limits to latitude 31°. The claim to extend so far south, was founded on ancient charters, and the settlement of the line between Georgia and West Florida, by the royal proclamation of October, 1763.

Their right to navigate the Mississippi, was claimed,

1. Under the treaty of Paris in 1763.
2. Under the treaty of peace in 1782—3.
3. By the law of nature and nations.

Mr. Gardoqui was again appointed negociator on the part of Spain. When pressed, in the course of the negociation, on the subject of limits and navigation, he again assured the American commissioners, that the right of the United States to navigate the Mississippi, would never be yielded by his catholic majesty. As to limits, he declared the right of Spain to the country possessed by her, north of the thirty first degree of north latitude, rested on her conquest of it, as territory originally belonging to Great Britain; or if it was not a part of West Florida, he intimated that Spain, until she had acknowledged the independence of the United States, had a right to make conquests within their limits.*

This important negociation remained in this situation until Spain joined the coalition against France, and entered into a treaty with Great Britain. By this treaty she also engaged to take every measure in her power to distress the trade of France; and for this purpose to prevent neutral powers from affording any protection to French commerce and property.

In consequence of this, American commerce became the prey of Spanish, as well as British cruizers; and new subjects of complaint engaged the attention of the American commissioners at the court of Madrid.

In the progress of the war, however, Spain became dissatisfied with the conduct of Great Britain, and the invasion of her terri-

* State Papers, vol. 1, p. 160.

tory by France, gave serious alarm to the Spanish court.   In the summer of 1794 the commissioners of his catholic majesty, informally made certain propositions to the American executive; in consequence of which, the president determined to send an envoy extraordinary, to conclude the negociations at Madrid.   Mr. Thomas Pinckney, then minister at London, was selected for this purpose.   Mr. Pinckney arrived at Madrid about the last of June, 1795, and the negociation was renewed between him and the duke de la Alcudia.   In consequence of the success of the French arms, Spain at this time was obliged to make peace with France; and this circumstance was favorable to the American mission.   In their first conference, the duke intimated to Mr. Pinckney, that their accommodation with France was connected with the American negociation, and he desired both might proceed together; he afterwards expressed a wish to establish *a triple alliance* between France, Spain and America. This idea was thrown out, no doubt, at the suggestion of the French government, who had promised to assist the Americans in their disputes with Spain; and probably with a view of inducing them, by important concessions on the part of the latter, to join in the war, or at least to reject the British treaty.

The Spanish minister also requested, that in any treaty to be made, the United States should guaranty the possessions of Spain in America.   With this request, the American minister was not authorized to comply.

After many conferences as to details, a treaty was at last concluded between the two governments, on the 27th of October, 1795.   It was confined principally to the two great subjects in dispute, and was styled a treaty of friendship, limits and navigation.   By this, the line between the United States and East and West Florida, was the same as that settled by the treaty of peace with Great Britain, and the troops and garrisons of either party were to be withdrawn, within six months after the ratification of the treaty.   The line was to be ascertained by a commissioner and surveyor, to be appointed by each of the contracting parties, and who, for that purpose were to meet at Natchez, within six months from the time of ratification.

The western boundary of the United States, which separated them from the colony of Louisiana, was fixed in the middle of the channel of the river Mississippi, to the thirty-first degree of north latitude ; and it was also agreed, that the navigation of that river from its source to the ocean, should be free only to the subjects and citizens of the two countries. To enable the citizens of the United States, to enjoy the benefits of this navigation below the thirty-first degree of latitude, liberty was granted them for the term of three years, to deposit their merchandize and effects, in the port of New Orleans, and to export the same without paying any other duty than a fair price for storage ; and at the end of three years, the king was, at his option, either to continue this permission, or to assign an equivalent establishment on some other part of the banks of the Mississippi. It was stipulated among other things, that both parties should use all the means in their power, to maintain peace and harmony among the Indian nations on their borders ; and both parties bound themselves to restrain even by force, the Indians within their limits, from acts of hostilities against the other—and it was also agreed, that neither party would thereafter make any treaties with those who did not live within their respective limits. Provision was also made, that free ships should make free goods, and that no citizen or subject of either party, should take a commission or letters of marque for arming any vessel, to act as a privateer, from their respective enemies, under the penalty of being considered and punished as *a pirate.*

Thus, after a tedious and unpleasant negociation of about fifteen years, the boundaries between the countries belonging to the United States and Spain, in America, were settled ; and the right of navigating every part of the Mississippi, a right so important to a vast extent of country at the west, was secured to the United States.

The president was able, also, during this year, to bring to a close the long negociations with the Dey of Algiers ; by which

peace was established with that regency, and the release of
American captives obtained. This was effected through the
agency of colonel Humphreys, Mr. Barlow, and Mr. Donalson.
About one hundred and twenty American citizens were released from slavery ; some of whom had been subjected to this
ignominious state, more than ten years. As early as the summer
of 1785, two American vessels were taken by the Algerines, and
their crews, twenty-one in number, doomed to slavery. Many
causes combined to prevent the release of these men, or those who
had survived, until this time, some of which produced great distress and misery to the captives themselves. The American ministers in Europe, were authorized to make treaties with the Bar-
bary powers ; but their authority did not extend to the ransom
of prisoners. They sent an agent, however, for the purpose of
ransoming the crews of these vessels ; but the sum he was authorized to give for their release, was far below the demands of
the rapacious Dey. He was resolved to make the most of his
new prisoners ; and refused their release without the enormous
sum of nearly sixty thousand dollars. The American government
were unwilling to give a sum so much higher than had been given
by other powers, and thereby establish a precedent, which would
serve in future, but to increase the rapacity of this lawless free-
booter, and induce him to prey upon American vessels, rather
than those of any other power. The Dey believed that the United States would submit to any terms, rather than leave their citizens in slavery. It was thought best, therefore, to attempt their
release secretly, and by the agency of some individuals, who
should appear to act for themselves alone, and not for the United
States. For this purpose, Mr. Jefferson, the American minister
at Paris, with the approbation of congress, applied to a religious
order in France, called Mathurins, instituted in ancient times, for
the redemption of christian captives from the infidel powers. The
principal of this order, readily undertook the business, and without any reward for his services.

The American prisoners had heretofore been supplied by the
Spanish consul at Algiers ; and his bills, for expenses thus incur-

red, had been paid. The principal of the Mathurins, informed Mr. Jefferson, that these supplies, as he had understood from his agent, had been so liberal, as to convince the Dey, they came from a public source. He therefore recommended a discontinuance of this mode of supply, and that he be permitted to furnish them. That the daily allowance furnished by him, would be much less than they had heretofore received ; and that being thus supported, as it would appear, by his charity, the demands of the Dey for their ransom might be lessened. To this arrangement the government assented, and agreed for a time, to appear to abandon them to their fate ; and the captives themselves, and their friends, from this conduct of their government, were led to believe this to be really the case.

This belief affected the prisoners much more than slavery itself; and drew from them the most severe and bitter reproaches against their government and country. Unfortunately the exertions of the Mathurins were unsuccessful. Other individuals in Europe also attempted to ransom them, but without success. The Dey still believed their support came from the United States ; and refused to reduce his demands within reasonable limits. During the interregnum which took place between the expiration of the old, and the final establishment of the new government, these poor captives seemed almost to have been forgotten. In the mean time, six of them had died. The subject of redeeming the survivors, was brought before the national legislature, under the new government, by the president, and the sum of forty thousand dollars was appropriated for their release. Admiral sir Paul Jones, and Mr. Barclay, were successively intrusted with this interesting negociation ; but both of them, unfortunately, died before they reached Algiers ; and thus the wretched situation of these men was prolonged. The business was then placed in the hands of colonel Humphreys, minister at Lisbon. While at Gibraltar, on his way to Algiers, in October, 1793, he met with the intelligence, that a truce, which we have before mentioned, between Portugal and Algiers, for one year, had taken place, and that an Algerine fleet had passed the straits into the Atlantic

Within one month from this time, ten American vessels fell into the hands of these piratical freebooters, and more than one hundred American citizens were added to their fellow sufferers in slavery. Colonel Humphreys immediately sent a memorial to the Dey, requesting a passport for Algiers, for the purpose of negociating a peace, and the ransom of American prisoners. This was intrusted to the Swedish consul at that place, Mr. Skjoldebrand, who, with his brother, were friendly to America, and had generously assisted the 'American captives. On the presentation of this memorial, the Dey declared he would not make peace with the Americans, or any other nation, at any price. He not only refused the passport, but declared " that he would not allow any American ambassador, under any flag whatever." This conduct of the Dey precluded all hope of relief for the American captives, except from the effectual interposition of their own government. To obtain this, they sent, through the hands of colonel Humphreys, their petition to congress. The letter to him, enclosing this petition, signed by thirteen masters of vessels, for themselves and " brother sufferers," evinced a spirit worthy of those who had been born and educated in a land of freedom.

In addition to the horrors of slavery, they were threatened with the plague, then in the vicinity of Algiers. Crowded as they were, during the night, in slave prisons, with hundreds of captives of other nations, they deemed it next to impossible they should escape the contagion, should it enter the city. They requested, therefore, that a separate house might be obtained for their residence. They added, however, " at the same time, honored sir, and friend, be you assured, that we the American captives in this city of *bondage*, will bear our sufferings with fortitude and resignation, as becoming a race of men, endowed with superior souls, in adversity."

Unable to go to Algiers with safety, colonel Humphreys went back to Lisbon, and afterwards returned to the United States. Congress appropriated about a million of dollars, to be applied under the direction of the president, to procure their release.

The money was borrowed of the bank of the United States, and was to be furnished in London, principally by the sale of public stock.   Colonel Humphreys was empowered to conclude a treaty of peace with the Dey of Algiers, and for this purpose he left the United States in April, 1795.   He was accompanied by Joseph Donaldson, consul for Tunis and Tripoli; who was to be employed to negociate the treaty, while colonel Humphreys himself went to France, to obtain the aid of the French government.

In the mean time, Mr. Donaldson proceeded to Algiers, and on the 5th of September concluded a treaty with the Dey.   He engaged that the money for the ransom should be paid in three or four months, presuming it would be ready in London before that time.   Joel Barlow was employed by colonel Humphreys to go from France, to assist in the negociation, but the treaty was concluded before his arrival at Algiers.

The failure in the payment of the money by the time stipulated, greatly incensed the Dey, and he threatened to abandon the treaty; and it was with great difficulty that Mr. Barlow and Mr. Donaldson procured a delay until the 8th of April, and the Dey then declared, that unless the money was paid within thirty days, he never would be at peace with America.   In this situation the American captives were thrown into a state of despair; and the agents were only able to save the treaty and procure their release by a promise to present him a frigate of thirty six guns.

By this they obtained a delay of three months, and in the mean time the money negociations were arranged, and the poor captives finally released.   This was not done, however, but at the expense and sacrifice of about one million of dollars.*

* American State Papers, vol. 10, p. 452.

CHAPTER XXIV.

MR. JAY arrived in Great Britain, on the 15th of June, 1794, and on the 19th of November following, concluded and signed with lord Grenville, " a treaty of amity, commerce, and navigation between his Britannic majesty and the United States." It was received by the president on the 7th of March, 1795, and on the 8th of June, was submitted to the senate, and on the 24th of the same month, that body advised its ratification, with the exception of the 12th article, relating to the West India trade. This interesting subject occasioned violent debates in the senate, and the treaty itself was finally sanctioned in that body, (excluding the article relating to the West India trade,) by a bare constitutional majority, twenty against ten.

The preamble stated that the two governments " being desirous, by a treaty of amity, commerce, and navigation, to terminate their differences in such a manner, as, without reference to the merits of their respective complaints and pretensions, may be the best calculated to produce mutual satisfaction and good understanding," &c.

The western posts were to be surrendered to the United States, on or before the first of June, 1796 ; but no compensation was made for negroes carried away by the British commander, after the peace of 1783.   The United States were to compensate British creditors for losses occasioned by legal impediments to the collection of debts, contracted before the revolutionary war ; to be settled and adjusted by commissioners ; and Great Britain was to make compensation to American merchants, for illegal captures of their property, to be adjusted also in the same mode. In both cases, the commissioners to consist of five persons, two to be appointed by each government, and the fifth by the unanimous voice of the four ; but if they should not agree, then the commissioners named by the two governments, to propose one, and of the two names thus proposed, one to be drawn by lot. Provision was also made for ascertaining more accurately the boundaries between the United States, and the British North American possessions.

British subjects holding lands in the territories of the United States, and American citizens holding lands in the British dominions, were to continue to hold them, according to the nature and tenure of their respective estates and titles therein, with power to sell, grant, or devise the same ; and by the 10th article, it was expressly provided, that neither the debts due from individuals of the one nation, to individuals of the other, nor shares or monies in the public funds, or in the public or private banks, should, in any event of war or national differences, be sequestered or confisca ted, "it being unjust and impolitic," as asserted in this article, "that debts and engagements contracted and made by individuals, having confidence in each other and in their respective governments, should ever be destroyed or impaired by national authority, on account of national differences and discontents."

Both parties had liberty to trade with the Indians, in their respective territories in America, (with the exception of the country within the limits of the Hudson bay company,) and the river Mississippi to be also open to both nations.

The ten first articles, principally embracing these important
subjects, were made permanent.

The other eighteen articles related to the future intercourse between the two countries, and in their duration, were limited to twelve years, or two years after the termination of the war in which the British nation were then engaged. By the 12th article, a direct trade was permitted between the United States and the British West India Islands, in American vessels not above the burden of seventy tons, and in goods or merchandize of the growth, manufacture, or produce of the states, and in the productions of the islands; but the United States were restrained from carrying molasses, sugar, coffee, cocoa, or cotton, either from the islands, or from the United States to any part of the world.

As a considerable quantity of cotton, at that time, was produced in the southern states, and had then began to be exported, and the quantity would probably increase, the 12th article was excluded. The American negociator, it was said, was then ignorant that cotton of the growth of the United States, had or would become an article of export.

A reciprocal and perfect liberty of commerce and navigation between the United and the British dominions in Europe, was established, neither to be subject to higher duties than other nations, the British government reserving the right of countervailing the American foreign duties. And American vessels were freely admitted into the ports of the British territories in the East Indies, but not to carry on the coasting trade.

Timber for ship building, tar, rosin, copper in sheets, sails, hemp, and cordage, and generally whatever might serve directly to the equipment of vessels, (unwrought iron and pine planks only excepted,) were included in the list of contraband. With respect to provisions and other articles, not generally contraband, on "account of the difficulty of agreeing on the precise cases, in which they should be regarded as such," and for the purpose of providing against the inconveniences and misunderstandings which might thence arise, it was declared, that whenever such articles should become contraband, according to the existing law of nations, the same should not be confiscated, but the owners be completely indemnified by the captors, or the government.

Prizes made by ships of war and privateers of either party, might enter and depart from the ports of each other, without examination; and no shelter or refuge was allowed to such vessels as had made a prize upon the subjects or citizens of the parties. Nothing, however, in the treaty was to operate contrary to former and existing treaties with other nations.

Mr. Jay was unable to obtain a stipulation, that free ships should make free goods. Indeed after the declaration of the lords of the committee of trade and plantations on this subject, contained in their report which we have before mentioned, it was hardly to be expected that Great Britain in time of war, would consent to any relaxation of the rigid rule of law, on this subject. Notwithstanding the opinion of the same committee, that their colonial ports were not to be opened to the Americans, and that this was not to be a subject even of negociation, yet a direct trade was permitted between the United States and the British West India Islands, in vessels of a certain description. But the article granting this privilege, for the reasons before mentioned, was excluded.

These are the principal features of a treaty, which gave such high offense to the rulers of France, and created such divisions in the United States, as to put in jeopardy the government itself.

Unfortunately, it left the important question with respect to provisions being contraband, as it found it, resting on the existing law of nations; but Mr. Jay, to whom had been assigned a most difficult as well as most delicate task; in a private letter to the president on the subject of the treaty, said, " to do more was impossible."* He also added, " I ought not to conceal from you, that the confidence reposed in your personal character was visible and useful throughout the negociations."

The treaty was approved by Thomas Pinckney, the resident minister at the court of London. In his letter to the secretary of state he observed, " although some points might have been arranged more beneficially for us, if the treaty had been dictated

* Marshall, vol. 5. p. 616.

entirely by the United States, yet when it is considered as a composition of differences, where mutual complaints had rendered
mutual concessions necessary to establish a good understanding,
I think it may fairly be said, that as little has been conceded by
Mr. Jay, and as much obtained for the United States, as under
all circumstances considered could be expected."

Although secrecy was enjoined, yet one member of the senate
soon after that body had advised its ratification, caused the treaty to be published in one of the public newspapers in Philadelphia, and it immediately became a subject of discussion.

Many of the opponents of the administration and those, who had
been hostile to the mission of Mr. Jay, were prepared to pronounce its condemnation; and such was the state of public feeling against Great Britain, that a temperate, impartial and
unimpassioned examination of its merits was not to be expected.
The people at large, unaccustomed to view a subject of this nature and magnitude, in all its bearings, to compare its advantages
and disadvantages, could easily be induced to pronounce a ver-
dict against a treaty, that did not contain every concession from
their adversary.

Meetings of the citizens were held in different parts of the
union, on the subject. At some of these meeting the passions,
rather than the understandings of the people, were addressed, and
resolutions were passed, condemning the treaty in the most unqualified manner. The people were made to believe, that the
advantages were entirely on the side of Great Britain, and that
the interest of France had been sacrificed. Numerous resolutions
and addresses against the treaty were presented to the president,
requesting him to withhold his assent. Early in July the citizens
of Boston, at a town meeting, passed resolutions against it, and
sent them to him by express. His answer to the citizens of this
town, disclosed the course he intended to pursue on this occasion,
so interesting to his country; a course, alike firm and dignified.
After stating that in every act of his administration, he had sought
the happiness of his fellow citizens; and that, to obtain this ob-

ject, overlooking all local, partial or personal considerations, he had contemplated the United States as one great whole, and confiding that sudden impressions, when erroneous, would yield to candid reflection, he had consulted only the substantial and permanent interests of his country, he added,—" Without a predilection for my own judgement, I have weighed with attention, every argument which has, at any time, been brought into view. But the constitution is the guide, which I never can abandon. It has assigned to the president the power of making treaties, with the advice and consent of the senate. It was doubtless supposed that these two branches of government would combine without passion, and with the best means of information, those facts and principles upon which the success of our foreign relations will always depend ; that they ought not to substitute for their own conviction the opinions of others ; or to seek truth through any channel, but that of a temperate and well informed investigation. Under this persuasion, I have resolved on the manner of executing the duty before me. To the high responsibility attached to it, I freely submit ; and you, gentlemen, are at liberty to make these sentiments known, as the ground of my procedure. While I feel the most lively gratitude for the many instances of approbation from my country, I can no otherwise deserve it, than by obeying the dictates of my conscience."

While this subject was under the consideration of the president, news arrived of the renewal of the British orders, for stopping provisions destined for France. This created doubts in the mind of the president, whether he should ratify the treaty, until satisfactory explanations were given on this part of it. He directed a memorial or remonstrance to be prepared against the renewal of these orders. In the mean time, his private business called him to Mount Vernon. He here constantly met with the proceedings of the people in different parts of the union against the treaty ; and the extent and nature of the opposition, as well as his own feelings and reflections on the subject, are disclosed in his private letters to the secretary of state.

In one of the 29th of July, he says—" I view the opposition which the treaty is receiving from the meetings in different parts of the union, in a very serious light. Not because there is more weight in any of the objections that are made to it, than were presented at first; for there are none in some of them, gross misrepresentations in others. Nor as it respects myself personally; for this shall have no influence on my conduct; plainly perceiving, and I am accordingly preparing my mind for the obloquy, which disappointment and malice are collecting, to heap upon my character. But I am alarmed on account of the effect it may have on the advantage the French government may be disposed to make of the spirit which is at work; to cherish a belief in them, that the treaty is calculated to favor Great Britain, at their expense. Whether they believe or disbelieve these tales, the effect it will have upon the nation will be nearly the same; for while they are at war with that power, or so long as the animosity between the two nations exists, it will, no matter at whose expense, be their policy, and it is feared it will be their conduct, to prevent us from being on good terms with Great Britain, or from her deriving any advantage from our commerce, which they can prevent, however much we may be benefitted ourselves. To what length this policy and interest may carry them, is problematical; but when they see the people of this country divided, and such a violent opposition given to the measures of their own government, particularly in their favor, it may be extremely embarrassing, to say no more of it.

" To sum the whole up in a few words. I have never seen a crisis, which in my judgment, has been so pregnant of interesting events; nor one from which more is to be apprehended; whether viewed on one side or the other.''

In another, written three days after this, he observes, " To be wise and temperate, as well as firm, the crisis most eminently calls for; for there is too much reason to believe, from the pains which have been taken before, at and since the advice of the senate respecting the treaty, that the prejudices against it are more extensive than is generally imagined. This, from men who are of no party, but well disposed to the government, I have lately learned is the case. How should it be otherwise? when no stone has been left unturned, that would impress the people's minds with the most arrant misrepresentations of facts—that their rights have not only been *neglected*, but absolutely *sold*—that there are no reciprocal advantages in the treaty; that the benefits are all on the side of Great Britain; and what seems to have more weight than all the rest, and has been most pressed, is, that this treaty is made with a design to oppress the French, in open violation of a treaty with that nation, and contrary too, to every principle of gratitude and sound policy. In time, when passion shall have yielded to sober reason, the current may possibly turn; but in the mean while, this government, in relation to France and England, may be compared to a ship between the rocks of Sylla and Charybdis. If the treaty is ratified, the partizans of France (or rather of war and confusion) will excite them to hostile measures; or, at least, to unfriendly sentiments. If it is not, there is no foreseeing all the consequences that may follow, as it respects Great Britain. It is not to be inferred from this that I am, or shall be disposed to quit the ground I have taken; unless circumstances, more imperious than have yet come to my knowledge, shall compel it; for there is but one straight course in these things and that is, to seek truth, and pursue it steadily."

The president returned to Philadelphia, on the 11th of August, and the treaty was ratified on the 14th, on the terms proposed by the senate. In the negociations with Great Britain, perfect good faith was observed towards France. The French minister here, was informed, that Mr. Jay had instructions not to weaken the engagements with his nation; and Mr. Munroe was directed to make a similar communication to the French government at Paris. Soon after the senate advised its ratification, a copy of it was submitted to Mr. Adet by direction of the president, with a request that he would state his objections. On the 30th of June, he, in a note to the secretary of state, referred to such parts as appeared to him, to destroy the effect of the treaty with France. The stipulations referred to, were those which made naval stores contraband of war, excluded from that list in the

French treaty; which subjected to seizure enemy's property in neutral bottoms, and admitted prizes in American ports. To the first and second, the American secretary immediately answered, that naval stores were contraband by the law of nations, that by the same law, enemy's property in neutral bottoms was good prize, and that on these points, Great Britain could not be prevailed upon to relax ; and with respect to the admission of prizes into American ports, this privilege did not extend to those made from the French, during the present or any future war, because contrary to the existing treaty with France.

It is proper here to state, that in the summer of this year, a treaty was made with the western Indians. In consequence of this, and the treaties made with Great Britain, Spain, and Algiers, the United States were not only relieved from Indian hostilities, but in a degree, from their embarrassments with foreign nations, and left more at liberty to attend to their domestic concerns. Alluding to these important events, as well as to the internal prosperity of the country, the president, at the opening of the session of congress, in December, 1795, expressed a persuasion, that he had never met the national legislature, when the public affairs of the United States, afforded more just cause of mutual congratulation, or called for more " profound gratitude to the author of all good, for the numerous and extraordinary blessings they enjoyed." He officially announced, that after full and mature reflection, he had added his sanction to the treaty with Great Britain ; and that when ratified on the part of the British government, it would be placed before congress. After recommending to their attention the military establishment, the system of intercourse with the Indians, and additional provisions for the redemption of the public debt, the president concluded by observing that, " temperate discussion of the important subjects which would arise in the course of the session ; and mutual forbearance, where there was a difference of opinion, were too obvious and necessary for the peace, happiness, and welfare of the country, to need any recommendation from him." While the majority in the senate in favor of the administration had increased, the result of the last elections had again placed a majority in the house of representatives in opposition. This was manifest from the answers returned by the respective houses to the president's speech.

That of the senate, adopted fourteen to eight, expressed an entire approbation of the conduct of the executive.

The answer reported by a committee of the house, contained expressions of *undiminished* confidence in the president. But a motion was made to strike out this part; and in the debate on this motion, some of the members did not hesitate to say, that their confidence in the chief magistrate had diminished; and it was evident, that a majority were in favor of the motion. The answer was, therefore, recommitted, and so varied as to meet the unanimous assent of the house.

Mr. Munroe, we would here state, arrived in France about the first of August, 1794, and was received by the convention with great cordiality and affection.

He afterwards presented to the French government the American colors, which were placed with those of France, in the hall of the national convention. Mr. Munroe was the bearer of answers from the senate and house of representatives, to a letter previously addressed to them by the committee of public safety, expressing their friendship and good will, as well as the deep interest they took in the happiness and prosperity of the French republic.

In October, 1794, the committee of public safety again addressed a letter to "the representatives of the United States in congress assembled." "The connections," they said, "which nature, reciprocal wants, and a happy concurrence of circumstances, have formed between two nations, cannot but be indissoluble. You have strengthened those sacred ties, by the declarations which the minister plenipotentiary of the United States has made in your name, to the national convention, and to the French people. They have been received with rapture by a nation, who know how to appreciate every testimony which the United States have given to them of their affection. The colors of both nations, united in the centre of the national convention, will be an everlasting evidance of the part which the United States have taken in the success of the French republic." Mr. Adet was the bearer of this letter, as a minister plenipotentiary, and was " specially instructed to *tighten* the *bands* of fraternity and mutual benevolence," between the two countries. He did not arrive in the United States, until June, 1795, and was directed to present to the government, the flag of the republic. This was not done, however, until the first of January, 1796, when it was, in a formal manner, presented to the president, together with the letter of the committee of public safety addressed to congress. In presenting the flag, Mr. Adet, in his address, delivered on the occasion, after stating that France only saw in the Americans " friends and brothers," proceeded to say, " long accustomed to regard the American people as her most faithful allies, she has sought to draw closer the ties already formed in the fields of America, under the auspices of victory, over the ruins of tyranny.

" The national convention, the organ of the will of the French nation, have more than once expressed their sentiments to the American people ; but above all, these burst forth on that august day, when the minister of the United States presented to the national representation the colors of his country. Desiring never to lose recollections as dear to Frenchmen, as they must be to Americans, the convention ordered that these colors should be placed in the hall of their sittings. They had experienced sensations, too agreeable not to cause them to be partaken of by their allies, and decreed that to them the national colors should be presented."

To this address the president immediately returned an answer ; in which, after expressing his own and the sympathetic feelings of the Americans in general, in favor of the French republic, and congratulating him on the brilliant exploits of his nation, and on the security of their liberty in a regularly organized government, he thus concludes, " I receive, sir, with lively sensibility, the symbol of the triumphs and of the enfranchisement of your nation, the colors of France, which you have now presented to the United States.

The transaction will be announced to congress; and the colors will be deposited with those archives of the United States, which are at once the evidences and the memorials of their freedom and independence. May these be perpetual! and may the friendship of the two republics be commensurate with their existence."

On the 4th of January, the president, by a special message, communicated to both houses, the letter of the committee of public safety, and informed them that he had received the colors of France, and had directed them to be deposited among the archieves of the United States.

The president was requested, by an unanimous resolution, to make known to the representatives of the French people, that the *house* received, with the most sincere and lively sensation, the communication of the committee of public safety; and to assure them that the house rejoiced in the opportunity of congratulating the French nation upon their brilliant and glorious achievements; and hoped that these achievements would be attended with the establishment of the liberty and happiness of that great and magnanimous people.

The *senate* also received with pleasure, the evidence of the continued friendship of the French republic, and expressed a wish that the colors of France, presented as a symbol of the triumphs of that great people, and given as a pledge of faithful friendship, might contribute to cherish and perpetuate the sincere affection by which the two republics were so happily united.

The French minister was disappointed that the colors of the republic had not the honor of a conspicuous place in the hall of the house of representatives; and in a note informed the president he could not remain silent on a circumstance which must make all France discontented. That as the American flag was placed in the hall of the legislative body of France, the French flag should receive the same honor. He was informed that the president was the constitutional organ of communication with foreign nations, and for this purpose was the sole representative of the American people; that he had deposited the French flag with the evidences and memorials of the freedom and independence of his own country. That the people of the United States did not exhibit in their deliberative assemblies, " any public spectacles or tokens of their victories, the symbols of their triumphs or the monuments of their freedom."

On the first of March the president informed congress, by message, that the treaty with Great Britain had been duly ratified, that he had directed it to be promulgated, and had transmitted a copy thereof for their information. This important subject, in various ways, occupied the attention of the house for a great part of the remainder of the session. Soon after its ratification by the president was known, petitions against it were circulated throughout the United States, for signatures. These petitions, all couched in the same language, were addressed to the house of representatives. The petitioners, after stating that certain stipulations in the treaty tended to involve their country in the political intrigues of European nations, to infract the treaty of alliance with France, and to produce the sad spectacle of war, between that magnanimous republic and the republic of the United States, 'proceeded to declare, that many of its stipulations were manifest encroachments on the constitutional powers of congress. After enumerating also the instances of such encroachments, which principally referred to the legislative powers vested in the national legislature,* the petitioners in conclusion said, " Wherefore solemnly protesting against the exercise of pow-

* The instances mentioned are—

1. In the regulation of commerce with foreign nations.

2. In the regulation of trade and intercourse with the Indian tribes.

3. In regulating the territory of the United States and of individual states.

4. In establishing duties and imposts.

5. In establishing a rule of naturalization.

6. In constituting a tribunal of appeal, paramount to the supreme judicial court of the United States.

7. In changing the terms of, and establishing a rule to hold real estate.

8. In defining piracies committed on the high seas, and declaring the punishment thereof.

9. In depriving free citizens of the privilege of the writ of habeas corpus, in the case of piracy, as defined and punished by the said treaty ; and

10. In attempting, in various other instances, to restrain and limit the legislative authority of congress.

er by the president and senate, in any of the foregoing cases, without the concurrence of congress, as manifestly tending to absorb all the powers of government in that department alone ; to establish, as the sole rule of legislation over all the great foreign and domestic concerns of the United States, the mere will and absolute discretion of the president and senate, in conjunction with a foreign power; and finally to overturn and effect a total change in the present happy constitution of the United States— We most earnestly pray, that the representatives of the people, in congress assembled, will, in their wisdom, adopt such measures, touching the said treaty, as shall most effectually secure from encroachment, the constitutional delegated powers of congress, and the rights of the people, and preserve to our country an *uninterrupted continuance of the blessings of peace.*"

Many of these petitions were presented in the winter of 1796, from different parts of the union, and laid the foundation of the proceedings of the house in relation to the treaty. Before the merits of the treaty itself became a subject of debate, an important preliminary question arose upon a resolution calling on the president for the instructions of Mr. Jay, and the correspondence and documents relating to it.

This resolution was offered by Mr. Livingston of New York, on the 2d of March, and was debated until the 24th of that month, when it passed, sixty two to thirty seven.

The principal question on this resolution was, as to the constitutional power of the house, in relation to treaties. The public feeling on the treaty, was brought into the house; and never, since the adoption of the constitution, had so much talent been displayed, or so much warmth manifested, as in the debates on this preliminary question, and on the merits of the treaty itself.

The speakers on both sides were numerous, and a very wide range was taken in debate. Every article and every word in the constitution, having the least bearing on the question, was critically examined.

These debates at large have been given to the public, and a sketch of the principal arguments can only here be presented.

In opposition to the call, it was said, that the constitution, in plain and explicit terms, had declared, that the president should have power, by and with the advice and consent of the senate, to make treaties; and that all treaties made, or which should be made, under the authority of the United States, should be the supreme law of the land. That the power of making treaties was an important act of sovereignty in every government, and in most countries was very properly intrusted with the executive branch. That the American constitution had vested this power with the chief magistrate, in concurrence with two thirds of the senate. That a treaty fairly made, and embracing those things which are the proper objects of compact between nations, when thus assented to, and duly ratified, became a solemn compact binding on the United States, was the supreme law of the land, and ought to be carried into execution. That legislative aid or assent, was not necessary to give it *validity* or *binding force*, though sometimes required, agreeably to the form of our government, to carry it into complete effect. Where laws or appropriations of money were requisite for this purpose, it was, in all ordinary cases, the duty of the legislative branch of the government, to pass such laws and to make such appropriations; and that a failure so to do, would be a breach of national faith; as much so as to refuse to make appropriations for the payment of a debt legally contracted.

Extraordinary cases, it was said, might occur, in which the legislature might be justified in refusing its aid to carry a treaty into effect. The conduct of a nation, with which the compact was made, might be such, after the completion of the treaty; or the stipulations in it might be so ruinous to the state, as to render it proper, and even make it a duty, for the legislative branch, to withhold its aid. These cases, however, it was said, were not to be governed by ordinary rules, but when they occurred, would make a law for themselves.

The house of representatives, were not making a constitution, but expounding one already made; and while they should watch with a jealous eye, every encroachment on their rights by another branch of the government, they should be cautious, not to usurp power constitutionally vested in others. That the treaties referred to in the constitution, included all those usually made,— treaties of peace, alliance and commerce, and that no precise limits to this power, were fixed, and from the nature of the case, could not be. The people of the United States, who adopted the constitution, considered their interest and rights sufficiently secured, by placing this necessary and important power in the hands of the president, and one branch of the legislature; and that this necessarily excluded the other legislative branch. It was well known, it was also urged, that most of the treaties usually made, must necessarily include regulations concerning many objects, intrusted likewise, by the constitution, to legislative regulations; and if the treaty power could not operate on these, the power itself, would be reduced to very narrow limits; and no treaty with a foreign nation, could be made, embracing these objects; as congress, to whom all legislative power was given, had no authority to make treaties. It was necessary, also, it was said, to consider, that the legislative power, and treaty power, operated differently and for different purposes. The former was limited to its own jurisdiction, and could not extend to a foreign jurisdiction and government. A legislature could, indeed grant privileges to foreigners, within its jurisdictional limits, but could not secure reciprocal privileges in a foreign country; this could only be done, with the assent of a foreign government; and this assent was not usually given except by treaty.

Treaties being the supreme law of the land, must also, it was said, be paramount to the laws of the United States, as well as the constitution and laws of the individual states. That congress, under the confederation, was invested with the power of " entering into treaties, and alliances," on condition, " that no treaty of commerce should be made, whereby the legislative power of the respective states should be restrained from imposing such imposts and duties on foreigners, as their own people were subjected to, or from prohibiting the exportation of any species of goods, or commodities whatsoever." With these exceptions, the power was general, and treaties made in pursuance of it, had been considered paramount to state laws, without the assent of the states themselves. When some of the state laws, were supposed to contravene the treaty of peace with Great Britain, congress, in their address to the states on the subject, declared that " when a treaty was constitutionally made, ratified and published, it immediately became binding on the whole nation, and superadded to the laws of the land, without the intervention of state legislatures. That treaties derived their obligations from being compacts between the sovereigns of this and of another nation ; whereas laws or statutes derived their force, from being the acts of a legislature competent to the passing them." They, therefore, unanimously " resolved, that the legislatures of the several states cannot of right pass any act or acts, for interpreting, explaining, or construing a national treaty, or any part or clause of it ; nor for restraining, limiting, or, in any manner, impeding, retarding or countervailing the operation or execution of the same ; for that, on being constitutionally made, ratified and published, they become, in virtue of the confederation, part of the laws of the land, and are not only independent of the will and power of such legislatures, but, also binding and obligatory on them." To remove all ground of complaint, however, on the part of Great Britain, congress recommended to the States, to pass general acts, repealing all laws, repugnant to that treaty. That, afterwards, in a discusion, with the British, minister on this subject, Mr. Jefferson, then secretary of state, speaking of the repealing acts of the states, said, " indeed, all this was supererogation. It resulted from the instrument of confederation among the states, that treaties made by congress, according to the confederation, were superior to the laws of the states."

The opponents of the resolution, also contended, that the the constitution, was so understood not only in the general convention, but in the state conventions, which ratified that instrument; and in some of the latter, this was made a strong ground of objection, particularly those of Virginia, and North Carolina. One of the amendments proposed by the Virginia convention, was, " that no commercial treaty should be ratified, without the concurrence of two thirds of the whole number of senators ; and no treaty, ceding, restraining, or suspending the territorial rights or claims of the United States, or any of their rights or claims to fishing in the American seas, or navigating the American rivers, shall be, but in case of the most urgent and extreme necessity, nor shall any such treaty be ratified without the concurrence of three fourths of the whole number of the members of both houses respectively." The convention of North Carolina proposed an amendment, " that no treaties which shall be directly opposed to the existing laws of the United States in congress assembled, shall be valid until such laws shall be repealed, or made conformable to such treaty ; nor shall any treaty be valid, which is contradictory to the constitution of the United States."

The same construction, it was said, had uniformly been given to this part of the constitution, by the house of representatives ; that various treaties had been made with the Indian tribes, embracing a surrender of lands, settlement of boundaries, grants of money, &c.—and when made and ratified by the president and senate, had been considered as laws of the land, without the sanction of the house ; and money, when necessary, had been appropriated as a matter of course ; that the constitution made no distinction between treaties with foreign nations and with Indian tribes, the same clause applying to both. And that the house, in June, 1790, declared by a resolution, " that all treaties made, or which should be made and *promulgated*, under the authority of the United States, should from time to time, be published and annexed to *the code of laws*, by the secretary of state." That the secretaries had accordingly, always annexed treaties to the laws, as soon as ratified by the president and senate, and promulgated by the former.

The resolution was not only supported by the mover, and others, but had the aid of all the ingenuity and talents of Mr. Madison and Mr. Gallatin. The latter, alluding to the great constitutional question made by the opponents of the resolution, said, he had hoped in that stage of the business, this would have been avoided ; but as gentlemen in opposition, " had come forward on that ground, he had no objection to follow them in it, and rest the decision of the constitutional powers of congress, on the fate of the present question. He would, therefore," he said, " state his opinion, that the house had a right to ask for the papers proposed to be called for, because their co-operation and sanction was necessary, to carry the treaty into effect, to render it *a binding instrument*, and to make it, properly speaking, *a law of the land ;* because they had a full discretion, either to refuse that co-operation, because they must be guided, in the exercise of that discretion, by the merits and expediency of the treaty itself, and therefore, had a right to ask for every information, which could assist them in deciding that question.

" The general power of making treaties," he observed, " undefined as it is, by the clause which grants it, may either be *expressly limited* by some other positive clauses of the constitution ; or it may be checked by some powers vested in other branches of the government, which, although not diminishing, may control the treaty-making power. That the specific legislative powers delegated to congress, were limitations of the undefined power of making treaties vested in the president and senate ; and that the general power of granting money, also, vested in congress, would at all events, be used, if necessary, as a check upon, and as controling the exercise of the powers claimed by the president and senate."

After stating that a treaty could not repeal a law of the United States, Mr. Gallatin asked, " to what would a contrary doctrine lead ? If the power of making treaties is to reside in the president and senate unlimitedly, in other words, if in the exercise of this power, the president and senate are to be restrained by no other branch of the government, the president and senate may absorb all legislative power; the executive has nothing to do, but to substitute a foreign nation to the house of representatives, and they may legislate to any extent." Mr. Gallatin further remarked, that " he should not say that the treaty is unconstitutional; but he would say, that it was not the supreme law of the land, until it received the sanction of the legislature. That the constitution and laws made in pursuance thereof, and treaties made under the authority of the United States, are declared to be the supreme law of the land. The words are, ' under the authority of the United States,' not signed and ratified by the president; so that a treaty clashing in any of its provisions, with the express powers of congress, until it has so far obtained the sanction of congress, is not a treaty, under the authority of the United States."

He also added, that treaties were the supreme law of the land, only when they came in competition with the constitutions and laws of the individual states, but were not supreme or paramount to the laws of the United States, because it is declared, in the same clause of the constitution, " and the judges in every state, shall be bound thereby, any thing in the constitution and laws of any state, to the contrary notwithstanding."

" It would have been childish," he said, " if the constitution had confined itself to expressing the first part of the clause, because no doubt could arise, whether the constitution, laws, and treaties were the supreme law of the land; but as the general government sprung out of a confederation of states, it was necessary to give that government sufficient authority to provide for the general welfare, that the laws of the union, should supersede the laws of the particular states. But the clause does not compare a treaty with the law of the United States, or either of them with the constitution; it only compares all the acts of the federal government with the acts of the individual states, and declares that either of the first, whether under the name of constitution, law, or treaty, shall be paramount to, and supercede the constitution and laws of the individual states."

The views of Mr. Madison on this important question, were generally in accordance with those expressed by Mr. Gallatin.

He regretted, " that on a question of such magnitude, there should be any apparent inconsistency or inexplicitness in the constitution, that could leave room for different constructions.

" As the case, however, had happened, all that could be done," he said, " was to examine the different constructions with accuracy and fairness, according to the rules established therefor, and to adhere to that which should be found most rational, consistent, and satisfactory." Mr. Madison confined his remarks principally, to two different constructions, one, and that supported as he said, by the opponents of the resolution, that the treaty-power was "both unlimited in its objects, and completely paramount in its authority ;" the other, that the congressional power was co-operative with the treaty power, on the legislative subjects submitted to congress by the constitution.

As to the first, he said, " it was important and appeared to him to be a decisive view of the subject, that if the treaty power alone could perform any one act, for which the authority of congress is required by the constitution, it may perform any act, for which the authority of that part of the government is required. Congress have power to regulate trade, to declare war, to raise armies, to levy, borrow, and appropriate money, &c. If by treaty, therefore, as paramount to the legislative power, the president and senate can regulate trade ; they can also declare war, they can raise armies to carry on war, and they can procure money to support armies." Mr. Madison was unable, he said, " to draw a line between any of the enumerated powers of congress ; and did not see, but the president and senate might, by a treaty of alliance with a nation at war, make the United States a party in that war. They might stipulate subsidies, and even borrow money to pay them : they might furnish troops to be carried to Europe, Asia, or Africa—they might even attempt to keep up a standing army in time of peace, for the purpose of co-operating on given contingencies with an ally, for mutual safety, or other common objects."

" The force of this reasoning," he added, " is not obviated by saying, that the president and senate could only pledge the public faith, and that the agency of congress would be necessary to carry it into operation : For, what difference does this make, if the obligation imposed be, as is alledged, a constitutional one ; if congress have no will but to obey, and if to disobey be treason and rebellion against the constituted authorities. Under a constitutional obligation, with such sanctions to it, congress, in case the president and senate should enter into an alliance for war, would be nothing more than the mere heralds for proclaiming it."

He considered that construction the most consistent, most in accordance with the spirit of the constitution, and freest from difficulties, " which left with the president and senate the power of making treaties, but required, at the same time, the *legislative sanction* and co-operation, in those cases where the constitution had given express and specified powers to the legislature. It was to be presumed," he said, " that in all such cases, the legislature would exercise its authority with discretion, allowing due weight to the reasons which led to the treaty. Still, however, this house, in its legislative capacity, must exercise its reason; it must deliberate ; for deliberation is implied in legislation. If it *must* carry all treaties into effect, it would no longer exercise a legislative power ; it would be the mere instrument of the will of another department, and would have no will of its own. When the constitution contains a specific and peremptory injunction on congress to do a particular act, congress must, of course, do the act, because the constitution, which is paramount over all the departments, has expressly taken away the legislative discretion of congress. The case is essentially different when the act of one department of government, interferes with a power expressly vested in another, and no where expressly taken away : Here the latter power must be exercised according to its nature ; and if it be a legislative power, it must be exercised with that deliberation and discretion, which is essential to legislative power."

The general doctrine of the advocates of the resolution was, that the power to make treaties was limited to *such objects* as were not comprehended and included in the specified powers given to congress ; or that a treaty, embracing such objects, was not valid; that is, was not the supreme law of the land, unless sanctioned by the house.*

The advocates of the resolution also said, that this was the first time this question had come before the house for their determination; and that whatever opinions might heretofore have been expressed by individuals or by public bodies, could have little weight.

The constitution having fixed no precise limits to the treaty-powers, the constructive limitations contended for by the advocates of the resolution, were deemed totally inadmissible by its opponents. If this extensive power was liable to abuse in the hands of the president and senate, they remarked, the same might be said of all the general powers given to congress. In answer to the limited construction given to the words, " under the authority of the United States," confining their operation to the constitutions and laws of the individual states, it was said, that they referred to treaties already made under the confederation, as well as those to be made under the new government. With respect to the co-operative powers of congress, or of the house, in giving validity to treaties, it was asked, in what way this power was to be exercised? Congress could only act in their legislative capacity, and their sanction must be given by a law. This law might be passed by a bare majority of both houses, and if not approved by the president, might still be repassed by two thirds, and become a law, without the assent of the president.

According to this doctrine, it was also said, a treaty might be sanctioned without the consent of *two thirds* of the senate, as a law might be passed by a bare majority of the senate and house, and be approved by the president.

This call for executive papers, with its avowed object, placed the president in a delicate situation. Satisfied, after mature reflection, with regard to his constitutional duty, he did not hesitate as to the course to be pursued. In answer, therefore, on the 30th of March, he sent to the house the following message, assigning his reasons for not complying with their request.

* See printed Debates on the British Treaty.

" *Gentlemen of the house of representatives :—*

"With the utmost attention I have considered your resolution of the 24th instant, requesting me to lay before your house a copy of the instructions to the minister who negociated the treaty with the king of Great Britain, together with the correspondence and other documents relative to that treaty, excepting such of the said papers as any existing negociation may render improper to be disclosed.

"In deliberating upon this subject, it was impossible to lose sight of the principle which some have avowed in its discussion, or to avoid extending my views to the consequences which must follow from the admission of that principle.

"I trust that no part of my conduct has ever indicated a disposition to withhold any information, which the constitution has enjoined upon the president as a duty to give, or which could be required of him, by either house of congress, as a right; and with truth I affirm that it has been, as it will continue to be, while I have the honor to preside in the government, my constant endeavor to harmonize with the other branches thereof, so far as the trust delegated to me by the people of the United States, and my sense of the obligation it imposes 'to preserve, protect, and defend the constitution,' will permit.

"The nature of foreign negociations require caution; and their success must often depend on secrecy; and even when brought to a conclusion, a full disclosure of all the measures, demands, or eventual concessions, which may have been proposed or contemplated, would be extremely impolitic; for this might have a pernicious influence on future negociations, or produce immediate inconveniences, perhaps danger and mischief, in relation to other powers. The necessity of such caution and security was one cogent reason for vesting the power of making treaties with the president, with the advice and consent of the senate; the principle on which that body was formed confining it to a small number of members.

"To admit, then, a right in the house of representatives, to demand, and to have, as a matter of course, all the papers respecting a negociation with a foreign power, would be to establish a dangerous precedent.

" It does not occur, that the inspection of the papers asked for, can be relative to any purpose under the cognizance of the house of representatives except an impeachment, which the resolution has not expressed. I repeat, that I have no disposition to withhold any information which the duty of my station will permit, or the public good shall require, to be disclosed ; and, in fact, all the papers affecting the negociation with Great Britain, were laid before the senate, when the treaty itself was communicated, for their consideration and advice.

" The course which the debate has taken on the resolution of the house, leads to some observations on the mode of making treaties under the constitution of the United States. Having been a member of the general convention, and knowing the principles on which the constitution was formed, I have ever entertained but one opinion on this subject ; and from the first establishment of the government to this moment, my conduct has exemplified that opinion, that the power of making treaties is *exclusively* vested in the president, by and with the advice and consent of the senate, provided two thirds of the senate present concur; and that every treaty so made and promulgated, thenceforward becomes the law of the land. It is thus that the treaty making power has been understood by foreign nations ; and in all treaties made with them, *we* have declared, and *they* have believed, that when ratified by the president, with the advice and consent of the senate, they become obligatory.

" In this construction of the constitution, every house of representatives has heretofore acquiesced ; and until the present time, not a doubt or suspicion has appeared, to my knowledge, that this construction of the constitution was not the true one. Nay, they have more than acquiesced ; for till now, without controverting the obligation of such treaties, they have made all the requisite provisions for carrying them into effect.

" There is, also, reason to believe that this construction agrees with the opinions entertained by the state conventions, when they were deliberating on the constitution ; especially by those who objected to it, because there was not required in *commercial treaties*, the consent of two thirds of the whole number of the members of the senate, instead of two thirds of the senators present ; and because in treaties respecting territorial and certain other rights and claims, the concurrence of three fourths of the whole number of the members of both houses respectively, was not made necessary. It is a fact declared by the general convention, and universally understood, that the constitution of the United States was the result of a spirit of amity and mutual concession. And it is well known that under this influence, the smaller states were admitted to an equal representation in the senate, with the larger states ; and that this branch of the government was invested with great powers ; for on the equal participation of these powers the sovereignty and political safety of the smaller states were deemed essentially to depend. If other proofs than these, and the plain letter of the constitution itself, be necessary to ascertain the point under consideration, they may be found in the journals of the general convention, which I have deposited in the office of the department of state.

" In these journals, it will appear that a proposition was made, ' that no treaty should be binding on the United States, which was not ratified by a law,' and that the proposition was explicitly rejected.

" As, therefore, it is perfectly clear to my understanding, that the assent of the house of representatives is not necessary to the validity of a treaty ; as the treaty with Great Britain exhibits in itself, all the objects requiring legislative provision, and on these the papers called for can throw no light ; and as it is essential to the due administration of the government, that the boundaries fixed by the constitution between the different departments, should be preserved—a just regard to the constitution and to the duty of my office, under all the circumstances of this case, forbid a compliance with your request."*

* American State Papers, vol. 2, pp. 102—105.

The opinion of the president, on this important constitutional question, however satisfactory it may now be to those who examine it without any particular bias, was by no means, in accordance with that of the house. A resolution was submitted, declaring the constitutional power of that body, in relation to treaties; and on the 7th of April, was adopted, fifty-seven to thirty-five, and entered on the journals. After referring to the section of the constitution concerning treaties, it declared, "that the house of representatives do not claim any agency in making treaties; but that when a treaty stipulates regulations on any of the subjects submitted by the constitution to the power of congress, it must depend for its *execution*, as to such stipulations, on a law or laws to be passed by congress; and it is the constitutional right and duty of the house of representatives, in all such cases, to deliberate on the *expediency* or *inexpediency* of carrying such treaty into effect, and to determine and act thereon, as in their judgment may be most conducive to the public good."

A second resolution was added, asserting that it was not necessary to the propriety of any application from the house to the executive for information desired by them, and which might relate to any constitutional functions of the house, that the purposes for which such information might be wanted, or to which it might be applied, should be stated in the application.

The opinion expressed in this resolution, relative to the power of the house regarding treaties, was somewhat equivocal, and seemed to be confined to the *expediency* merely, of making the requisite provision for carrying them into effect, whenever legislative aid was necessary for that purpose.*

* The question regarding the constitutional powers of congress or of the house, in relation to treaties, came before congress in 1814, when the commercial treaty or convention with Great Britain of July, 1815, was laid before that body by the president. The house, at first differed with the senate, as to the form of a law, for carrying into effect, that part of the convention, which stipulated an equality of duties, in certain cases. The house at first, passed a bill, equalizing the duties, without referring to the convention.

The senate negatived this, and passed a declaratory bill, and to which, after a con-

The president, during this session, had submitted to the house, copies of the treaties with Spain, with the Dey and Regency of Algiers, and with the Indians north-west of the Ohio. On the 13th of April, a resolution was submitted by Mr. Sedgwick, declaring, that provision ought to be made by law, for carrying into effect these treaties, as well as that with Great Britain, embracing them all in the same resolution.

After much altercation on the subject of thus joining all these treaties together, a division was made, and the question taken on each. The resolution was amended by a majority of eighteen, so as to read, 'that it is *expedient* to pass the laws necessary for carrying into effect,' &c.

The subject of the British treaty was taken up on the 15th of April, and debated in committee of the whole, until the 29th of the same month, when the question was decided in the affirmative, by the casting vote of the chairman, Mr. Muhlenburgh, who declared he was not satisfied with the resolution as it then stood, but should vote for it, that it might go to the house and be there modified, so as to meet his approbation.

The next day, an amendment was proposed by Mr. Dearborn, by way of preamble—" Whereas, in the opinion of this house, the treaty is highly objectionable, and may prove injurious to the United States ; yet considering all circumstances relating thereto, and particularly, that the last eighteen articles are to continue in force only during the present war, and two years thereafter ; and confiding, also, in the efficiency of measures which may be taken, for bringing about a discontinuance of the violations committed on our neutral rights, in regard to vessels and seamen, therefore," &c. After striking out the words, " highly objectionable, and may prove injurious to the United States,". the preamble was negatived, fifty to forty-nine, and the

ference, the house agreed 100 to 85. This bill, merely " enacted and declared, that so much of any act as imposes a higher duty of tonnage, or of impost on vessels and articles imported in vessels of the United States, contrary to the provisions of the convention, should be *deemed* and *taken* to be of no force and effect."

resolution as reported to the house, passed fifty-one to forty-eight, and bills ordered to be prepared accordingly.

Those in favor of the treaty, seemed not disposed to enter into a discussion of its merits, alleging that every member, had made up his mind on the subject, that despatch was necessary, in case the treaty was carried into effect. The posts were to be delivered up on the first of June, and this required previous arrangements on the part of the American government. Mr. Murray said, " that the subject was completely understood, both by the house and country, and the time so extremely pressing, that the execution of the treaty was more valuable, than any explanation which members could give. The country requires of us at this crisis, acts not speeches."

Mr. Giles, in reply, hoped " a question which had already produced so much agitation, would be taken up and decided upon, in a manner suitable to its importance. He thought it would not be treating the public mind with a sufficient degree of respect, to take a hasty vote upon the subject. He did not think that gentlemen in favor of the treaty, would have wished to have got rid of it, in this way. He avowed, he could not discover those merits in the treaty, which other gentlemen cried up ; but he pledged himself, that if they would convince him, that the treaty was a good one, he would vote for it. He was desirous of knowing, in what latent corner its good features lay, as he had not been able to find them. He thought he should be able to show features in it, which were not calculated for the good, but for the mischief of the country. He hoped, therefore, the committee would rise and suffer a proper discussion." Mr. Tracy said, " he hoped the committee would rise. The gentleman from Virginia wished to deliver his sentiments on the occasion, and he wished to hear him. He was, also, willing to give him time ; for if he had the task upon him, to prove the British treaty as bad, as it had been represented to be, he ought not to be hurried." Mr. Murray, in reply, " would vote for the committee to rise, as he despaired of taking a vote or hearing a word said to day, on the merits of the resolution offered. Gentlemen will, of course, come prepared, and he trusted, that however terrible the treaty may have struck them in the dark, a little discussion might diminish their horrors. He could not, however, suppress his surprise, that none of those, and in particular the gentleman from Virginia, (Mr. Giles,) who had entertained opinions so hostile to this treaty so long, should be at a loss to enter on its discussion, with an eagerness proportioned to their zeal and conviction of its mighty faults. But the gentleman, it seems, has left his paints and brushes at home, and cannot now attempt, though the canvass is before him, to give us those *features* of the treaty, which had been so caricatured out of doors."

" He would agree that the committee should rise, hoping that the delay was owing to an aversion to do mischief, and relying on the effects of a night's reflection ; the pillow is the friend of conscience."*

With a temper and with feelings thus indicated, did the house enter upon the discussion of this interesting and important subject. The debate was opened, the next day, by Mr. Madison, against the treaty, and in the course of the discusssion he was followed on the same side by Mr. Swanwick, Mr. Nicholas, Mr. Giles, Mr. Heath, Mr. Page, Mr. Findley, Mr. Rutherford, Mr. Moore, Mr. Holland, Mr. S. Smith, Mr. Gallatin, and Mr. Preston—while the resolution was supported by Mr. Ames, Mr. Coit, Mr. Dwight, Mr. Foster, Mr. Gilbert, Mr. Goodhue, Mr. Griswold, Mr. Harper, Mr. Henderson, Mr. Hillhouse, Mr. Kittera, Mr. Murray, Mr. N. Smith, Mr. T. Smith, Mr. Swift, Mr. Tracy, Mr. Williams, Mr. S. Lyman, Mr. Cooper, Mr. Bourne, Mr. Kitchell, and Mr. Dayton.

In this debate not only the constitutional powers of the house, in relation to treaties, were again discussed, but every article, and every clause in the treaty examined, and its merits and demerits developed. The arguments on both sides were pushed to an extreme, and partook not a little of personal as well as political feelings.

* See printed Debates on the British Treaty.

The objections of those opposed to carrying the treaty into effect were generally, that it wanted reciprocity,—that it gave up all claim of compensation for negroes carried away contrary to the treaty of peace, and for the detention of the western posts—that it contravened the French treaty, and sacrificed the interest of an ally to that of Great Britain—that it gave up, in several important instances, the law of nations, particularly in relation to free ships making free goods, cases of blockade, and contraband of war—that it improperly interfered with the legislative powers of congress, especially by prohibiting the sequestration of debts—and that the commercial part gave few if any advantages to the United States.

On the other hand it was urged, that the treaty had been constitutionally made and promulgated, that a regard to public faith, and the best interests of the country, under all circumstances, required it should be carried into effect, although not, in all respects perfectly satisfactory—that it settled disputes between the two governments of a long standing, of a very interesting nature, and which it was particularly important for the United States to bring to a close—that provision also was made for a settlement of those of more recent date, not less affecting the sensibility as well as honor of the country; and in which the commercial part of the community had a deep interest—that in no case had the law of nations been given up—that the question as to provisions being contraband, although not settled, was left as before the treaty—that the conventional rights of France were saved by an express clause, and as to the sequestration of private debts, it was said, this was contrary to every principle of morality and good faith, and ought never to take place—that the commercial part would, probably, be mutually beneficial, was a matter of experiment, and was to continue only two years after the close of the war in Europe. That in fine, on the part of the United States, the only choice left was treaty or war.

A want of reciprocity in the West India trade was particularly urged against the treaty.

A treaty of commerce with Great Britain, excluding a reciprocity for American vessels in the West Indies, was a phenomenon, they said, which filled them with more surprise than they knew how to express.*

No question in congress had ever elicited more talents or created greater solicitude than this. The loss of national character from a breach of plighted faith, was strongly urged by those who believed the house bound to carry the treaty into effect. Should the treaty be rejected, war, it was also said, could not be avoided consistently with the character and honor of the American nation. The western posts would be retained, the Indians again placed under the control of the British, millions unjustly taken from the merchants would be lost, and perhaps as many millions more added by future spoliations ; redress for past, and security against future injuries, must, it was said, be obtained, either by *treaty* or by *war*. It was impossible that the American people could sit down quietly, without an effort to right themselves.

On these topics all the talents and all the eloquence of the advocates of the treaty, were exerted and displayed.

" To expatiate on the value of public faith," said Mr. Ames, " may pass with some men for declamation—to such men I have nothing to say. To others I will urge—can any circumstance mark upon a people more turpitude and debasement? can any thing tend more to make men think themselves mean, or degrade to a lower point their estimation of virtue, and their standard of action? It would not merely demoralize mankind, it tends to break all the ligaments of society, to dissolve that mysterious charm which attracts individuals to the nation, and to inspire in its stead a repulsive sense of shame and disgust. What is patriotism? Is it a narrow affection for the spot where man was born? are the clods where we tread, entitled to this ardent preference, because they are greener? No, sir, this is not the character of the virtue, and it soars higher for its object. It is

* The subject of the West India trade still remains unsettled. In 1815, during the presidency of Mr. Madison, a commercial treaty was made with Great Britain, and which received his approbation, in which this trade was not secured to the United States.

an extended self-love, mingling with all the enjoyments of life, and twisting itself with the minutest filaments of the heart.   It is thus we obey the laws of society, because, they are the laws of virtue.   In their authority we see, not the array of force and terror, but the venerable image of our country's honor.   Every good citizen makes that honor his own, and cherishes it not only as precious, but as sacred.   He is willing to risque his life in its defense, and is conscious that he gains protection while he gives it.   For what rights of a citizen will be deemed inviolable, when a state removes the principles that constitute their security ?   Or if his life should not be invaded, what would its enjoyment be, in a country odious in the eyes of strangers, and dishonorable in his own ?   Could he look with affection and veneration to such a country as his parent?   The sense of having one would die within him, he would blush for his patriotism, if he retained any, and justly for it would be a vice.   He would be a banished man in his native land.

" I see no exception to the respect that is paid among nations to the laws of good faith.   If there are cases in this enlightened period where it is violated, there are none where it is denied.   It is the philosophy of politics, the religion of government.   It is observed by barbarians—a whiff of tobacco smoke, or a string of beads, gives not merely binding force, but sanctity to treaties. Even in Algiers, a truce may be bought for money, but when ratified, even Algiers is too wise, or too just to disown and annul its obligation.   Thus we see neither the ignorance of savages, nor the principles of an association for piracy and rapine, permit a nation to despise its engagements.

" Will the tendency to Indian hostilities," he added, " be contested by any one ?   Experience gives the answer.   The frontiers were scourged with war, till the negociation with Great Britain was far advanced, and then the state of hostility ceased.   Perhaps the public agents of both nations are innocent of fomenting the Indian war, and perhaps they are not.   We ought not, however, to expect that neighboring nations, highly agitated against each other, will neglect the friendship of the savages ; the traders will gain an influence and will abuse it; and who is ignorant that their passions are easily raised, and hardly restrained from violence? This situation will oblige them to choose between this country and Great Britain, in case the treaty should be rejected. They will not be our friends and at the same time the friends of our enemies.

"But am I reduced to the necessity of proving this point? Certainly the very men, who charged the Indian war on the detention of the posts, will call for no other proof than the recital of their own speeches. It is remembered with what emphasis, with what acrimony, they expatiated on the burden of taxes, and the drain of blood and treasure into the western country, in consequence of Britain's holding the posts. Until the posts are restored, they exclaimed, the treasury and frontiers must bleed.

"If any, against all these proofs, should maintain that the peace with the Indians will be stable without the posts, to them, I will urge another reply. From arguments calculated to produce conviction, I will appeal directly to the hearts of those who hear me, and ask whether it is not already planted there. I resort especially to the conviction of the western gentlemen, whether, supposing no posts and no treaty, the settlers will remain in security? Can they take it upon themselves to say, that an Indian peace, under these circumstances, will prove firm? No Sir, it will not be peace, but a sword. It will be no better than a lure to draw victims within the reach of the tomahawk. On this theme, my feelings are unutterable; if I could find words for them, if my powers bore any proportion to my zeal, I would swell my voice to such a note of remonstrance, it should reach every log-house beyond the mountains. I would say to the inhabitants, wake from your false security. Your cruel dangers, your more cruel apprehensions, are soon to be renewed. The wounds, yet unhealed, are to be torn open again. In the day time, your path through the woods will be ambushed. The darkness of the night will glitter with the blaze of your dwellings. You are a father—the blood of your sons will fatten your cornfields. You are a mother—the war whoop shall wake the sleep of the cradle. On this subject you need not suspect any deception on your feelings. It is a spectacle of horror which cannot be overdrawn. If you have nature in your hearts it will speak a language compared with which, all I have said or can say, will be poor and frigid. Will it be whispered that the treaty has made me a new champion for the protection of the frontiers ? It is known that my voice as well as vote have been uniformly given in conformity with the ideas I have expressed. Protection is the right of the frontiers ; it is our duty to give it.

"It is vain" he said " to offer as an excuse, that public men, are not to be reproached for the evils that may happen to ensue from their measures. This is very true, when they are unforeseen or inevitable. Those I have depicted, are not unforeseen, they are so far from inevitable, we are going to bring them into being by our vote. We choose the consequences, and become as justly answerable for them, as for the measures we know will produce them. By rejecting the posts, we light the savage fires, we bind the victims. This day we undertake to render account to the widows and orphans whom our decision will make, to the wretches that will be roasted at the stake, to our country, and I do not deem it too serious to say, to conscience and to God. We are answerable, and if duty be any thing more than a word of imposture, if conscience be not a bugbear, we are preparing to make ourselves as wretched as our country. There is no mistake in this case, there can be none. Experience has already been the prophet of events, and the cries of our future victims have already reached us. The voice of humanity issues from the shade of their wilderness. It exclaims, that while one hand is held up to reject the treaty, the other grasps a tomahawk. It summons our imagination to the scenes that will open. It is no great effort of the imagination to conceive, that events so near, are already begun. I fancy that I listen to the yells of savage vengeance, and the shrieks of torture. Already they seem to sigh in the western wind—already they mingle with every echo from the mountains."

After adverting to other probable and almost certain consequences of a rejection of the treaty—dissentions between the different branches of the government—war abroad and anarchy at home, the orator reverses the picture—" let me cheer the mind," he concludes " weary, no doubt and ready to despond, on this prospect, by presenting another which it is yet in our power to realize. Is it possible for a real American to look at the prosperity of this country, without some desire for its continuance, without some respect for the measures, which many will say produced, and all will confess, have preserved it? Will he not feel some dread that a change of system will reverse the scene? The well grounded fears of our citizens in 1794, were removed by the treaty, but are not forgotten. Then they deemed war nearly inevitable, and would not this adjustment have been considered, at that day as a happy escape from the calamity?

" The great interest and general desire of our people was to enjoy the advantage of neutrality. This instrument, however misrepresented, affords America that inestimable security. The causes of our disputes are either cut up by the roots, or referred to a new negociation, after the end of the European war. This was gaining every thing, because it confirmed our neutrality, by which our citizens are gaining every thing. This alone would justify the engagements of the government. For when the fiery vapours of the war lowered in the skirts of our horizon, all our wishes were concentrated in this one, that we might escape the desolation of this storm. This treaty, like a rainbow on the edge of the cloud, marked to our eyes the space where it was raging, and afforded at the same time, the sure prognostic of fair weather. If we reject it, the vivid colours will grow pale, it will be a baleful meteor, portending tempest and war."

The speech of Mr. Ames, though, delivered at nearly the close of this debate, was listened to by the house, and by a crowded audience, with a most silent and untired attention. Its eloquence was admired by all, though its effects were dreaded by some. When he took his seat, the question was loudly called for; but Mr. Venable expressed a hope, that the question might not

be taken that day. " Mischievous effects," he said " stared them
in the face, look which way they would ; for if they refused to
carry the treaty into effect, evils might be dreaded ; and if they
carried it into effect, serious evils would certainly arise. The
question was, to choose the least of the two evils. He himself
was not determined, at present which was the least, and wished
for another days consideration."

The question was postponed until the next day, and decided in
the manner before stated.

The delay occasioned by these debates was favorable to the
treaty.   It gave time for reflection among those opposed,
and also, afforded an opportunity for others, who had hitherto
been silent, willing to leave the decision with the constituted authorities, to express their sentiments.   The great mass of the people began seriously to reflect, on the consequences of its rejection ; nor could they be induced to believe that the president, who
had once saved his country from the tyranny of Great Britain, had
now sacrificed its best interests to the same power. During the
discussion therefore, numerous petitions were presented to the
house from different parts of the union, praying that the treaty
might be carried into effect. This changed the votes, if not
the opinions of some of the members.

Mr. Christie of Maryland, declared, he still considered it " as
the worst of all hard bargains, yet, as he was satisfied that a large
majority of his constituents wished it to be carried into effect, he
should give his vote for that purpose, and leave the responsibility
upon them."

This interesting session did not close, until the first of June.
The final vote on the question of carrying the British treaty into
effect, probably saved the United States, from being involved in
the war, which then and so long afterwards desolated Europe.

CHAPTER XXV.

THE two great belligerents, and particularly France, had viewed the contest in America, with respect to the British treaty, with peculiar solicitude. In its final ratification, the French government saw an end to all their hopes of "a family or national compact" with the Americans—and Great Britain could view its rejection, as only a prelude to war with the United States.

The jealousy of the rulers of France respecting the negociations of Mr. Jay, had been manifested in a variety of ways, from the commencement of his mission.

Mr. Munroe, as we have before stated, was instructed to solicit the aid of France, in securing the navigation of the Mississippi.

On the 25th of January, 1795, he submitted to the committee of public safety, the wishes of his government on this subject; and stated the importance of the navigation of that river to the United States. The answer of Merlin de Douay, one of the committee, shows, that the conduct of France would be governed by that of the United States, in regard to the treaty with England. In his note of the 22d of February, 1795, in answer to obser-

vations on this subject, he said, "the ideas which they present are not new to me, nor to the committee of public safety;
and I have reason to think they will be taken into profound consideration, in suitable time and place.   I ought not to dissemble,
however," he added, " that this may depend upon the *conduct*
which the American government will observe in regard to *the
treaty* which its minister Jay has concluded with England.   You
know, sir, in effect, that there ought to be a *reciprocity* of *services*
and of *obligations* between *nations*, as between *individuals*.   I
speak, however, here as an individual."*   The French government were soon after somewhat more explicit on this subject.
About the 9th of March, Mr. Munroe was informed by one of the
members of the diplomatic section of the committee of public
safety, " that in confidence, Mr. Jay's treaty contained nothing
which would give uneasiness here, they had expressly instructed
their agent then negociating with Spain, to use his utmost efforts
to secure the points in controversy between the United States and
that power."†   On the 12th of September, 1795, the secretary
of state informed Mr. Munroe, that the president had ratified the
treaty, and also furnished him with his reasons for so doing, with
a view, that they might be presented to the French government.
France was at that time particularly engaged in forming a new
constitution, which went into operation, on the 27th of October,
1795.   The legislature was divided into two branches, and the
executive power lodged with five persons called a directory.   Soon
after this, de la Croix was appointed minister of foreign affairs.
In February, 1796, this minister informed Mr. Munroe, that the
directory had determined how to act in regard to the American
treaty with Great Britain.   They had, he said, considered the alliance between France and the United States at an end, from the
moment that treaty was ratified ; and intimated that a special envoy would be sent to announce this to the American government.
Soon after, he presented to the American minister, a summary
exposition of the complaints of the French government against

* Munroe's Views, p. 139.   † Do. p. 133.

the United States. The British treaty was the most prominent subject of complaint; by which, he said, the United States had *knowingly* and *evidently* sacrificed their connection with the republic, particularly in abandoning the principles established by the armed neutrality, that free ships should make free goods, and in making articles necessary for the equipment and construction of vessels, and even provisions, contraband of war. Mr. Munroe gave the same answer, that the American government had always given to complaints of this kind, that the treaty had not in these particulars violated or changed the law of nations. That the principles of the armed neutrality had never been recognized by Great Britain—that every article in the list of contraband, was warranted by the law of nations; and as to provisions, they were not made contraband in any case, where they were not so before, by the existing law. Though the French government had announced to the American minister, that the British treaty had put an end to the alliance; their ultimate measures in consequence of it, were delayed, until it should be known, whether congress, particularly the house of representatives would by their acts carry it into effect. The directory were no doubt well informed of the proceedings in America, and were led to believe that the house, at least, would refuse its assent to such acts. The final vote of the house on this question disappointed their expectations, and measures of retaliation were immediately taken. On the 25th of June, 1796, the French minister inquired of Mr. Munroe, whether the intelligence contained in the American gazettes, was true, that the house had consented to carry the treaty into effect. " After the chamber of representatives," he added, " has given its consent to this treaty, we ought no doubt, *to consider it in full force :* and as the *state of things* which results from it, merits our profound attention, I wish to learn from you what light we are to consider the event, which the public papers announce, before I call the *attention* of the directory *to those consequences which ought specially to interest this republic.*" Although the American minister was unable to give any official information on the subject; yet, no doubt, informed by their own minister in the United States, that the intelligence was true, the directory at once took those measures of retaliation they had contemplated ; and on the 2d of July, issued their celebrated decree, that " all neutral or allied powers shall, without delay, be notified, that the flag of the French republic will treat *neutral* vessels, either as to *confiscation*, as to *searches*, or *capture*, in the same manner as they shall suffer the English to treat them."

In the preamble to this decree, the executive directory declared, that " if it becomes the faith of the French nation to respect treaties or conventions which secure to the flags of some neutral or friendly powers, commercial advantages, the result of which is to be common to the contracting powers ; these same advantages, if they should turn to the benefit of our enemies, either through the *weakness of our allies,* or of neutrals, or through *fear,* through *interested views,* or through whatever motives, would in fact warrant the inexecution of the articles in which they were stipulated."   Rumors, indeed, had before this reached the United States, that measures hostile to American commerce, were contemplated by the French government.   To ascertain the truth of these rumors, Col. Pickering, secretary of state, as early as the first of July, 1796, addressed a note to Mr. Adet, inquiring whether the government of France, had decreed any new regulations or orders relative to the commerce of the United States, and if so, what they were.*

Mr. Adet, in his answer of the 14th of the same month, declared he was ignorant of the nature of the orders which might have been given by the government of France, to the officers of the ships of war of the republic, or what conduct it had prescribed to them to hold with regard to neutral vessels trading with their enemies.

Secret orders to capture American vessels, had probably been sent to the West Indies previous to this ; as in June preceding, a valuable ship called the Mount Vernon, was captured off the

* American State Papers, vol. 2, pp. 475, 476.

capes of Delaware, by a privateer from St. Domingo, commissioned by the French republic.

The nations in Europe, under the influence of France, were required about the same time, to pursue a similar conduct towards the Americans. The Batavian Republic, on the 27th of September, 1796, in a note to John Quincy Adams, then American minister in Holland, insisted that the United States should cause their flag to be respected, and intimated that they should also make *common cause* with the French republic. " We cannot let the present opportunity pass," said the minister of foreign affairs, " without requesting you to state to your government, how useful it would be to the interests of the inhabitants of the two republics, that the United States should *at last* seriously take to heart the numberless insults daily committed on their flag by the English—to represent to them that when circumstances oblige our commerce to confide its interests to the neutral flag of American vessels, it has a just right to insist that *that flag* be protected with *energy*, and that it be not insulted at the expense of a friendly and allied nation. Deign to recall," he added, " to the remembrance of the nation of which you are a minister, that the numerous services which our republic has rendered to it, our reciprocal relations, as well as mutual utility, imperiously require, that it should cease to view with indifference the manner in which the English act, who carry off with impunity from on board American vessels, the property of Batavians—lead them to perceive that reasons of convenience, treaties concluded and ratified between our two nations, between two nations who have equally suffered from the arrogance and despotism on the seas of proud albion—in a word, between two nations, who, making *common cause* with the French republic, and governing themselves by the imprescriptible rights of nature and of man, may render to the two hemispheres a peace for which humanity languishes."

In communicating this extraordinary note, Mr. Adams informed the American government, that a general disposition prevailed, even among the *patriotic party* in Holland, in favor of the neutrality of the United States. That their interest favored this, as they were continually receiving remittances of interest on their monies loaned to the Americans, which they apprehended might be suspended by a state of war. But at the same time, he added, this party could have " no avowed will, different from that which may give satisfaction to the government of France. They feel a dependence so absolute and irremoveable upon their good will, that they sacrifice every other inclination, and silence every other interest, when the *pleasure* of the French government is signified to them, in such a manner as makes an *election necessary*."

If any thing were wanting to prove the determination of the French government to defeat the treaty the United States had made with Great Britain, the following paragraph from the same letter must be amply sufficient.

" I received not long ago, " says Mr. Adams, " an intimation that one of the committee of foreign affairs had confidentially communicated to a friend, a circumstance which was intended to be *kept profoundly secret*. It was, that the French government had determined to *defeat*, if possible, the treaty lately concluded between the United States and Great Britain, and had signified to the committee of foreign affairs here, their expectations that they would *concur* with all their influence towards the same object. The tenor of their letter strongly serves to show the accuracy of the information."*

France and Spain, on the 19th of August, 1796, concluded a treaty of alliance, *offensive* and *defensive*. This treaty contained a mutual guaranty of all the states, territories, islands and places which they respectively possessed, or should possess. By the fifteenth article, both powers engaged " to make a common cause to repress and annihilate the *maxims* adopted by any country whatever, which might be subversive of their *present principles*, and which might endanger the *safety of the neutral flag*, and the respect which is due to it; as well as to raise and re-establish the colonial system of Spain on the footing on which it has subsisted, or ought to subsist, according to treaties."

* American State Papers, vol. 3, p. 123.

Soon after this, Spain also complained to the American government, that the British treaty had sacrificed her interests, as well as those of France; particularly in abandoning the principle that free ships should make free goods, and by enlarging the list of contraband; and she made this a ground for delaying the delivery of the posts on the Mississippi and running the line, according to the treaty of October, 1795. In this she was, no doubt, influenced by France. Indeed, at the time of forming the offensive and defensive alliance above mentioned, France contemplated obtaining from Spain, Louisiana and the Floridas;* and the delay in fulfilling the terms of that treaty were probably occa_sioned also by this circumstance, as well as from an expectation that the people at the west might still be induced to separate themselves from their Atlantic brethren. Such a separation, had . been previously contemplated by the Spanish governors of Louisiana, and suggested to some individuals at the west, particulaly judge Sebastian and general Wilkinson, who favored the project, and who, in fact, were for a long time Spanish pensioners. The free navigation of the Mississippi was held out as an inducement to this step.

It is believed, that but few of the western people ever seriously listened to a proposition of this kind. Before the delivery of the Spanish posts, however, a final attempt was made to effect such a separation, and to induce the inhabitants, in conjunction with Spain, to form an independent empire west of the mountains; and there can be little doubt, that France encouraged, if indeed, she did not suggest the project. The baron de Carondelet, governor of Louisiana, in the spring of 1797, gave instructions to his agent Thomas Powers, to confer with the western people on this subject, and to make to them certain propositions for forming such an independent empire. These instructions were brought to light in consequence of an inquiry before congress, in 1808, concerning the connection of general Wilkinson with the Spanish government.

* Munroe's View.

The following extract from these instructions, it is presumed, will not be deemed an uninteresting part of American political history at this period. The *ostensible* object of the mission of Powers was, to convey a letter to general Wilkinson, requesting him to delay the march of American troops for the purpose of taking possession of the forts on the Mississippi, until it should be ascertained whether, before delivery, they were to be dismantled; but the *real* object, to sound the people on the subject of a separation from the Atlantic states.

"On your journey," said the governor to Powers, "you will give to understand *adroitly*, to those persons to whom you have an opportunity of speaking, that the delivery of the *posts* which the Spaniards occupy on the Mississippi, to the troops of the United States, is directly opposed to the interest of those of the west, who, as they must one day separate from the Atlantic states, would find themselves without any communication with lower Louisiana, from whence they ought to expect to receive powerful succours in artillery, arms, ammunition and money, either *publicly* or *secretly*, as soon as ever the western states should determine on a separation, which must insure their prosperity and their independence; that for this reason, congress is resolved on risking every thing to take those posts from Spain; and that it would be *forging fetters* for themselves, to furnish it with militia and means, which it can only find in the western states. These same reasons, diffused abroad by means of the public papers, might make the strongest impression on the people, and induce them to throw off the *yoke* of the Atlantic states; but at the very least, if we are able to dissuade them from taking part in this expedition, I doubt *whether the states could give law to us*, with such troops as they have now on foot.

"*If a hundred thousand dollars* distributed in Kentucky would cause it to rise in insurrection, I am very certain, that the minister, in the present circumstances, would sacrifice them with pleasure; and you may, without exposing yourself too much, promise them to those, who enjoy the confidence of the people.

with another equal sum to arm them, in case of necessity, and twenty pieces of field artillery.

" You will arrive without danger as bearer of a despatch for the general, where the army may be, whose force, discipline and disposition you will examine with care ; and you will endeavor to discover, with your natural penetration, the general's disposition, I doubt that a person of his disposition would prefer, through vanity, the advantage of commanding the army of the Atlantic states, to that of being the *founder*, the *liberator*, in fine the *Washington* of the western states—his part is as brilliant as it is easy—all eyes are drawn towards him—he possesses the confidence of his fellow citizens, and of the Kentucky volunteers— at the slightest movement, the people will name him the general of the new republic—his reputation will raise an army for him ; and Spain, as well as *France*, will furnish him the means of paying it. On taking fort Massac, we will send him instantly arms and artillery ; and Spain limiting herself to the possession of the forts of Natchez and Walnut Hills, as far as fort Confederation, will cede to the western states all the eastern bank to the Ohio, which will form a very extensive and powerful republic, connected by its situation and by its interest, with Spain, and in concert with it, will force the savages to become a party to it, and to confound themselves in time with its citizens.

" The public is discontented with the *new taxes—Spain and France* are *enraged* at the connection of the United States with England—the army is weak and devoted to Wilkinson—the threats of congress authorize me to succour on the spot and openly the western states—money will not then be wanting to me, for I shall send without delay, a ship to Vera Cruz in search of it, as well as of ammunition ; nothing more will consequently be required, but an instant of firmness and resolution, to make the people of the west perfectly happy. If they suffer this instant to escape them, and we are forced to deliver up the posts, Kentucky and Tennessee, surrounded by the said posts, and without communication with Lower Louisiana, will ever remain under the oppression of the atlantic states." In his journey through the western country, Powers intimated that from the change of circumstances and political situation of Europe, there was reason to suppose that the treaty with Spain would not be carried into effect by his catholic majesty.

This mission, however, entirely failed—no one listened to the propositions of the Spanish governor, except judge Sebastian. Wilkinson being now at the head of the American army, and the object so long desired by him and the people of the west, secured by treaty, refused to countenance the plan. The mission of Powers was known to the president, and the governor of the north western territory had orders to arrest and send him to Philadelphia. Of this, Wilkinson gave him notice, and to aid his escape, seut him back, under a military escort by the way of Vincennes and New Madrid.* Notwithstanding the failure of this extraordinary mission, the Spanish government on various pretexts delayed the delivery of the posts until 1788.

The president was dissatisfied with the conduct of the American minister in France, particularly in delaying to present to the French government an explanation of his views in concluding a treaty with Great Britain. He, therefore, in June, 1796, determined to send a new minister to France ; and at first contemplated doing this, without recalling Mr. Munroe. But finding this could not be done in the recess of the senate, he appointed Charles Cotesworth Pinckney, of South Carolina, to succeed Mr. Munroe, whom he recalled.

Mr. Pinckney arrived at Paris about the first of December, and soon after, in company with Mr. Munroe, waited upon the minister of foreign affairs, and presented his credentials. These were laid before the directory, and on the 11th Mr. Munroe was informed by de la Croix, that the directory would " no longer recognize a minister plenipotentiary from the United States, until after a reparation of the grievances demanded of the American government, and which the French republic has a right to expect." The French minister, however, declared, " that this determina-

* Clark's proofs against Wilkinson, and H. Marshall's history of Kentucky, vol. 2. pp. 219, 220, 223.

tion, which is become necessary, does not oppose the continuance of the affection between the French republic and the *American people*, which is grounded on former good offices, and reciprocal interest; an affection which you have taken pleasure in cultivating, by all the means in your power." Informed of this determination of the directory, Mr. Pinckney addressed a note to the French minister, requesting information whether it was their intention that he should quit the territories of the republic. He was immediately informed by a secretary in the foreign department, that the minister could hold no direct communication with him, as this would be acknowledging him as a minister. With respect to his remaining in France, he was told, there was a general law prohibiting all *foreigners* from remaining at Paris, without *special permission*; and as the directory did not intend to grant this *permission*, the general law would apply to him. Mr. Pinckney stated to the secretary, that the directory was in possession of his credentials as a minister of the United States; and, therefore, could not consider him in the light of an ordinary stranger, subject to the laws of the police. Possessed of high honorable feelings, and duly appreciating the character in which he appeared, Mr. Pinckney refused to quit France without a written order from the government. In this unpleasant situation he remained for some time, not without serious apprehensions, he might be arrested and sent away by order of the police officers.

About the last of December, Mr. Munroe took leave of the directory, with much ceremony. Mutual addresses were delivered on the occasion. After expressing his wishes " for a continuance of a close union and perfect harmony between the two nations," Mr. Munroe concluded his address by saying—" I beg leave to make to you, citizen directors, my particular acknowledgments for the confidence and attention with which you have honored my mission during its continuance, and at the same time to assure you, that as I shall always take a deep and sincere interest in whatever concerns the prosperity and welfare of the French republic, so I shall never cease, in my retirement, to pay

in return for the attention you have shewn me, the only acceptable recompence to generous minds, the tribute of a grateful remembrance."

The address of the president of the directory, was calculated
to flatter the people of the United States, whilst it severely cen-
sured their government.

" By presenting this day to the executive directory, your letters
of recall," the president said, " you offer a very strange spectacle to Europe. France, rich in her freedom, surrounded by the
train of her victories, and strong in the esteem of her allies, will
not stoop to calculate the consequences of the condescension of
the *American government* to the wishes of its ancient tyrants.
The French republic expects, however, that the successors of
Columbus, Raleigh and Penn, always proud of their liberty, will
never forget that they owe it to France. They will weigh in
their wisdom the magnanimous friendship of the French people,
with the caresses of perfidious men, who meditate to bring them
under their former yoke. Assure the *good people* of America,
Mr. Minister, that, like them, we adore liberty ; that they will
always possess our esteem, and find in the French people that
republican generosity which knows how to grant peace, as well
as to cause its sovereignty to be respected.

" As for you, Mr. Minister plenipotentiary, you have contended for principles ; you have known the true interests of your
country—depart with our regret ; we restore, in you, a representative to America ; and we preserve the remembrance of the
citizen, whose personal qualities did honor to that title."*

Mr. Pinckney was permitted to reside at Paris until about the
first of February, 1797, when the directory, elated by their victories in Italy, gave him written orders to quit the territories of the
republic. He immediately retired to Amsterdam, where he remained until joined by Mr. Marshall and Mr. Gerry, who, under
the administration of Mr. Adams, were associated with him as
envoys extraordinary to the French republic.

* Munroe's View, pp. 398, 399.

In the spring of 1796, Rufus King was appointed minister to the court of London, in the room of Thomas Pinckney, who, at his own request, was permitted to return home. Mr. King had been an active member of the senate of the United States, from the commencement of the new government. He was well acquainted with the views of president Washington, and from his talents and extensive political information, was peculiarly qualified for the important station assigned him. During a residence of several years as American minister in England, he maintained the rights of his country with great firmness, and sustained a high character among the diplomatic corps at the British court.

The particular friends of president Washington, had long known that he would utterly decline another election. His determination, however, on this subject, was not publicly announced until September, 1796. Unanimity in the choice of his successor was not to be expected. The two great parties in the United States, were now at once arrayed against each other, on the great question of the presidential election. They were divided between Mr. Adams and Mr. Jefferson. Nor did foreign nations view this contest with indifference. Their interests were supposed, in some measure, involved in the issue.

The views of one candidate were considered favorable to Great Britain, those of the other to France. And the difference between these parties, with respect to the conduct of the executive towards these two nations, served to increase the bitterness of this contest.

The French minister took this opportunity to present more in detail, the various complaints of France, against the conduct of the American government. These complaints were embodied in a letter to the secretary of state, bearing date the 15th of November, 1796; and the letter itself, by direction of the minister, was immediately published in the newspapers. It was no doubt, intended to excite the feelings of the people in favor of France, to convince them of the injustice and ingratitude of their own government towards that nation, and to produce an influence on the pending presidential election. Mr. Adet now *formally* notified the American government, that the executive directory regarded the British treaty as a violation of that made with France in 1778, and equivalent to a treaty of alliance with Great Britain; and that justly offended at this conduct of the American executive, they had given him orders from that time, to suspend his ministerial functions, with the federal government. He, at the same time declared, that notwithstanding the wrongs of the *government*, " the directory did not wish to break with *a people* whom they love to salute with the appellation of friend."

He therefore announced, that the government and people of the United States, were not to regard the suspension of his functions as a rupture between the two countries; " but a *mark* of discontent, which was to last until the *government* of the United States returned to sentiments and to measures more conformable to the interests of the alliance and the sworn friendship between the two nations."

After alluding to the enthusiasm with which the American minister was received in the bosom of the national convention, and the joy inspired by the American flag, " when it waved unfurled in the French senate ;" and after enumerating the various complaints of France against the conduct of the American government, and referring to her services in the war of the revolution, he thus concludes—" Alas ! time has not yet demolished the fortifications with which the English roughened this country—nor those the Americans raised for their defense ; their half rounded summits still appear in every quarter, amidst plains, on the tops of mountains.   The traveller need not search for the ditch which served to encompass them ; it is still open under his feet.   Scattered ruins of houses laid waste, which the fire had partly respected, in order to leave monuments of British fury, are still to be found.—Men still exist, who can say, here a ferocious Englishman slaughtered my father ; there my wife tore her bleeding daughter from the hands of an unbridled Englishman.   Alas ! the soldiers who fell under the sword of the Britons are not yet reduced to dust : the laborer, in turning up his field, still draws from the bosom of the earth their whitened bones ; while the ploughman, with tears of tenderness and gratitude, still recollects that his fields, now covered with rich harvests, have been moistened with French blood; while every thing around the inhabitants of this country, animates them to speak of the tyranny of Great Britain and of the generosity of Frenchmen; when England has declared a war of death to that nation, to avenge herself for having cemented with its blood the independence of the United States.—It was at this moment their *government* made a treaty of amity with their ancient tyrant, the implacable enemy of their ancient ally. O! Americans covered with noble scars! O! you who have so often flown to death and to victory with French soldiers! You who know those generous sentiments which distinguish the true warrior! Whose hearts have always vibrated with those of your companions in arms! Consult them to-day to know what they experience; recollect at the same time, that if magnanimous souls with liveliness resent an affront, they also know how to forget one. *Let your government return to itself,* and you will still find in Frenchmen, faithful friends and generous allies."

This manifest attempt on the part of a foreign minister, to separate the people from their government, and to influence the election of a president, failed of its object. The more reflecting and dispassionate part of the Americans, viewed it as an improper interference of a foreign power, in one of their dearest and most important rights; and some, who had been opposed to the administration, used their influence against the candidate supposed to be favored by France.

On the 7th of December, 1796, president Washington met, and for the last time addressed the national legislature. He adverted in his speech to the treaties which had adjusted most of the disputes betweed the United States and foreign nations; and informed congress, they were in a train of execution. The defenseless state in which the war in Europe found the American commerce, and the lawless depredations made upon it, by the belligerents, had more fully convinced the president, that a naval force was necessary for its protection. The extent of this commerce had no doubt excited the jealousy of the navigating interest of Great Britain; and the belligerents considered the United States most vulnerable on the ocean. Both France and Great Britain, therefore, for any supposed injuries received from the Americans, immediately retaliated by a lawless attack on their unprotected trade.

This important subject was strongly pressed upon the attention of congress, by the president, at this time.

" To an active external commerce," he observed, " the protection of a naval force is indispensable. This is manifest with respect to wars in which a state is a party. But besides this, it is evident in our own experience, that the most sincere neutrality is not a sufficient guard against the depredations of nations at war. To secure respect to a neutral flag, requires a naval force, organized and ready to vindicate it from insult or aggression. This may even prevent the necessity of going to war, by discouraging belligerent powers from committing such violations of the rights of the neutral party, as may, first or last, leave no option. From the best information I have been able to obtain, it would seem as if our trade to the Mediterranean, without a protecting force, will always be insecure, and our citizens exposed to the calamities from which numbers of them have just been relieved."

With these views he suggested the propriety of gradually creating a navy, by providing and laying up materials for building and equipping ships of war, and to proceed in the work as our resources should increase.

He invited the attention of the national legislature also to the encouragement of manufactures and agriculture, as well as to the establishment of a military academy and a national university.

He alluded to the late conduct of the French government by saying, that while in our external relations some serious inconveniences and embarrassments had been overcome, and others lessened, he had with much pain and regret to mention, " that circumstances of a very unwelcome nature had lately occurred. Our trade has suffered and is suffering extensive injuries in the West Indies, from the cruizers and agents of the French republic; and communications have been received from its minister here, which indicate the danger of a further disturbance of our commerce by its authority, and which are far from agreeable."

This subject, however, was reserved for a more particular communication.

The president in conclusion said—"The situation in which I now stand, for the last time, in the midst of the representatives of the people of the United States, naturally recalls the period when the administration of the present form of government commenced ; and I cannot omit the occasion to congratulate you and my country, on the success of the experiment, nor to repeat my fervent supplication to the Supreme Ruler of the universe and Sovereign Arbiter of nations, that his providential care may still be extended to the United States ; that the virtue and happiness of the people may be preserved ; and that the government which they have instituted for the protection of their liberties may be perpetual."

The answers of both houses, notwithstanding the conflict of parties, were adopted with great unanimity, and evinced an undiminished veneration for the character of the president. Both expressed their grateful sense of the eminent services he had rendered his country, their extreme regret at his retiring from office, and their ardent wishes for his future personal happiness.

Perfect unanimity, however, did not prevail in the house of representatives. Mr. Giles moved to strike out several clauses in the answer, among which was the following—"And while we entertain a grateful conviction that your wise, firm and patriotic administration has been signally conducive to the success of the present form of government, we cannot forbear to express the deep sensations of regret with which we contemplate your intended retirement from office."

Mr. Giles said, "If he stood alone in the opinion, he would declare, that he was not convinced that the administration of the government for these six years had been wise and firm."—"He did not regret," he added, "the president's retiring from office. He hoped he would retire and enjoy the happiness that awaited his retirement. He believed it would more conduce to that happiness, that he should retire, than if he should remain in office." In this opinion of Mr. Giles, only eleven concurred, and with him

Under the decree of the directory of the second of July, 1796, before noticed, the American commerce at once became a prey to French public and private armed vessels. Additional decrees were also issued by French agents in the West Indies; and American vessels were taken and condemned, even because bound to a British port, and on various other new and frivolous pretences. The want of, or informality in a bill of lading—the want of a certified list of the passengers and crew—the supercargo being by birth a foreigner, although a naturalized citizen of the United States—the destruction of a paper of any kind whatever, and the want of a sea-letter, were sufficient reasons for condemnation.

On the 19th of January, 1797, the president, agreeably to the intimation in his speech at the opening of the session, communicated to the national legislature, the state of the relations of the country with the French republic. This embraced an elaborate review of the conduct of France and her ministers towards the United states, and of their various complaints against the American government, from an early period of the European war; and which was embodied in a letter from the secretary of state to Mr. Pinckney, the American minister in France. It contained not only an able review, but an ample refutation of the various charges made by France, as well as a complete justification of the conduct of president Washington towards that nation, during a period most interesting to his country, and most trying to himself.

This exposition was made to enable the American minister at Paris more fully to make explanations to the French government, as well as to present to the American people the views of the president in his conduct towards France; views, which had been so grossly misrepresented. It created no change, however, in the conduct of France, and produced little effect on the parties in America. The great contest between these parties, relative to the successor of president Washington, at that time absorbed every other consideration. On counting the electoral votes, in February, it appeared that John Adams, by a small majority, was elected president, and that Thomas Jefferson was chosen vice-president.

On the 4th of March, 1797, the administration of president Washington closed—a period to which he had looked forward with inexpressible pleasure.

On retiring from office he received addresses from the legislatures of many of the states, as well as from numerous other public bodies in different parts of the union.

The situation of his country at this time, when contrasted ed with that in 1789, at the commencement of his administration, presented a very striking difference; and this was a subject of congratulation which did not pass unnoticed in these various addresses. In the short period of eight years, all the disputes between the United States and foreign nations had been adjusted, with the exception of those with France, which had arisen during that time, out of the new state of things in Europe.

At home, public and private credit was restored—ample provision made for the security and ultimate payment of the public debt—commerce had experienced unexampled prosperity—American tonnage had nearly doubled—the products of agriculture had found a ready market—the exports had increased from nineteen millions to more than fifty six millions of dollars—the imports in about the same proportion—and the amount of revenues from imports had exceeded the most sanguine calculations. The prosperity of the country had been, indeed, without example, notwithstanding great losses from belligerent depredations.

In announcing his determination to decline another election, president Washington, for the last time, addressed his fellow citizens, on subjects which he deemed highly important and intimately connected with their future political welfare and felicity. Long experience had made him fully acquainted with the evils, to which the people of the United States, from their local situation, the nature of their government, and other causes, were particularly exposed. This experience, and his well known disinterestedness,

gave his sentiments and advice respecting the various subjects
on which he touched, peculiar claims to the attention, and gratitude of his fellow citizens.

Although this address is very generally known, we cannot, in
the conclusion, refrain from recalling to the notice of our rea-
ders, particularly the younger part of them, a small portion of this
inestimable legacy which the father of his country left them.

An inviolable preservation of the great charter, which formed the national union, and made the Americans one people, was
an object very near his heart.

" The unity of government," he said, " which constitutes you
one people, is now dear to you. It is justly so ; for it is a main
pillar in the edifice of your real independence ; the support of
your tranquility at home ; your peace abroad ; of your safety ; of
your prosperity ; of that very liberty which you so highly prize.
But, as it is easy to foresee that, from different causes and from
different quarters, much pains will be taken, many artifices employed, to weaken in your minds the conviction of this truth ; as
this is the point in your political fortress against which the bat-
teries of internal and external enemies will be most constantly
and actively, (though often covertly and insidiously) directed, it
is of infinite moment, that you should properly estimate the immense value of your national union to your collective and individual happiness ; that you should cherish a cordial, habitual, and
immoveable attachment to it ; accustoming yourselves to think
and speak of it, as of the palladium of your political safety and
prosperity ; watching for its preservation with jealous anxiety ;
discountenancing whatever may suggest even a suspicion that it
can, in any event, be abandoned, and indignantly frowning upon
the first dawning of every attempt to alienate any portion of our
country from the rest, or to enfeeble the sacred ties which now
link together the various parts."

He reminded his fellow citizens, that " the very idea of the
power and the right of the people to establish government, pre-
supposes the duty of individuals to obey the established government ;" and that " all obstructions to the execution of the laws,

all combinations and associations under whatever plausible character, with the real design to direct, control, counteract, or awe the regular deliberations and actions of the constituted authorities, are destructive of this fundamental principle." And after warning them "in the most solemn manner against the baneful effects of the spirit of party generally," he particularly cautioned them to avoid "inveterate antipathies against particular nations, and passionate attachments for others," as tending to introduce foreign influence, against which he particularly warned them to be on their guard. "Against the insidious wiles of foreign influence, (I conjure you to believe me fellow citizens,) the jealousy of a free people ought to be constantly awake ; since history and experience prove, that foreign influence is one of the most baneful foes of republican government. But that jealousy to be useful, must be impartial ; else it becomes the instrument of the very influence to be avoided, instead of a defense against it. Excessive partiality for one foreign nation, and excessive dislike for another, cause those whom they actuate, to see danger only on one side, and serve to veil and even second the arts of influence on the other. Real patriots, who may resist the intrigues of the favorite, are liable to become suspected and odious ; while its tools and dupes usurp the applause and confidence of the people, to surrender their interests.

"The great rule of conduct for us, in regard to foreign nations, is, in extending our commercial relations, to have with them as little *political* connection as possible. So far as we have already formed engagements, let them be fulfilled with perfect good faith —Here, let us stop."

But above all, this great and good man reminded his fellow citizens, that without *religion* and *morality*, they would expect political prosperity in vain.

"Of all the dispositions and habits which lead to political prosperity," he observed, "*religion* and *morality* are indispensible supports. In vain would that man claim the tribute of patriotism, who should labor to subvert these great pillars of human happiness, these firmest props of the duties of men and citizens.

The mere politician, equally with the pious man, ought to respect and to cherish them—a volume could not trace all their connections with private and public felicity. Let it simply be asked, where is the security for property, for reputation, for life, if the sense of religious obligations *desert* the oaths which are the instruments of investigation in courts of justice? and let us with caution indulge the supposition that morality can be maintained without religion. Whatever may be conceded to the influence of refined education on minds of peculiar structure, reason and experience both forbid us to expect, that *national morality* can prevail in exclusion of *religious principle*."

APPENDIX—NOTES.

NO. 1, omitted.

NO. 2.

Letter to the President of Congress, from the British Commissioners,
June 10th, 1778.

Gentlemen—With an earnest desire to stop the further effusion of blood and the calamities of war, we communicate to you with the least possible delay, after our arrival in this city, a copy of the commission with which his majesty is pleased to honor us, as also the acts of parliament on which it is founded; and at the same time we assure you of our most earnest desire to re-establish on the basis of equal freedom and mutual safety, the tranquillity of this once happy empire, you will observe that we are vested with powers equal to the purpose, and such as are even unprecedented in the annals of our history.

In the present state of our affairs, though fraught with subjects of mutual regret, all parties may draw some degree of consolation, and even auspicious hope from the recollection that cordial reconciliation and affection have, in our own and other empires, succeeded to contentions and temporary divisions not less violent than those we now experience. We wish not to recal subjects which are now no longer in controversy, and will reserve to a proper time of discussion both the hopes of mutual benefit, and the consideration of evils that may naturally contribute to determine your resolutions as well as our own, on this important occasion. The acts of parliament which we transmit to you, having passed with singular unanimity, will sufficiently evince the disposition of Great Britain, and shew that the terms of agreement in contemplation with his majesty and with parliament, are such as come up to every wish that North America, either in the hour of temperate deliberation, or of the utmost apprehension of danger to liberty, has ever expressed. More effectually to demonstrate our good intentions, we think proper to declare, even in this our first communication, that we are disposed to concur in every satisfactory and just arrangement towards the following, among other purposes:

To consent to a cessation of hostilities both by sea and land.

To restore free intercourse, to revive mutual affection, and renew the common benefits of naturalization through the several parts of this empire.

To extend every freedom of trade that our respective interests can require.

To agree that no military forces shall be kept up in the different states of North America without the consent of the general congress or particular assemblies.

To concur in measures calculated to discharge the debts of America, and to raise the credit and value of the paper circulation.

To perpetuate our union by a reciprocal deputation of an agent or agents from the different states, who shall have the privilege of a seat and voice in the parliament of Great Britain, or if sent from Britain, in that case, to have a seat and voice in the assemblies of the different states to which they may be sent in order to attend to the several interests of those by whom they are deputed.

In short, to establish the power of the respective legislatures in each particular state, to settle its revenues, its civil and military establishments, and to exercise a perfect freedom of legislation and internal government, so that the British states throughout North America, acting with us in peace and war, under one common sovereign, may have the irrevocable enjoyment of every privilege that is short of a total separation of interests, or consistent with that union and force on which the safety of our common religion and liberty depends.

In our anxiety for preserving those sacred and essential interests, we cannot help taking notice of the insidious interposition of a power, which has, from the first settlement of these colonies, been actuated with enmity to us both. And, notwithstanding the pretended date or present form of the French offers to North America, yet it is notorious that these were made in consequence of the plans of accommodations previously concerted in Great Britain, and with a view to prevent our reconciliation, and to prolong this destructive war. But we trust that the inhabitants of North America connected with us by the nearest ties of consanguinity, speaking the same language, interested in the preservation of similar institutions, remembering the former happy intercourse of good offices, and forgetting recent animosities, will shrink from the thought of becoming an accession of force to our late mutual enemies, and will prefer a firm, free, and perpetual coalition with the parent state, to an insincere and unnatural foreign alliance.

This dispatch will be delivered to you by Dr. Ferguson, the secretary to his majesty's commission, and for fuller explanation and discussion of every subject of difference, we desire to meet with you, either collectively, or by deputation, at New York, Philadelphia, Yorktown, or such other place as you may propose; we think it right, however, to apprise you, that his majesty's instructions, as well as our own desire, to remove from the immediate seat of war, in the active operations of which we cannot take any part, may induce us speedily to remove to New York. But the commander in chief of his majesty's land forces (who is joined with us in the commission) will, if it should become necessary, either concur with us in a suspension of hostilities, or will furnish all necessary passports and safe conduct to facilitate our meeting, and we shall of course expect the same of you.

If after the time that may be necessary to consider this communication, and to transmit your answer, the horrors and devastations of war should continue, we call God and the world to witness, that the evils which must follow, are not to be imputed to Great Britain, and we cannot, without the most real sorrow, anticipate the prospect of calamities which we feel the most ardent desire to prevent.

We are, with perfect respect, gentlemen,

Your most obedient, and most humble servants,

CARLISLE,
WILLIAM EDEN,
GEORGE JOHNSTONE.

_____

NO. 3.

Instructions to Dr. Franklin, minister plenipotentiary of the United States, to the court of France, October 22, 1778.

We, the congress of the United States of North America, having thought it proper to appoint you their minister plenipotentiary to the court of his most christian majesty, you shall in all things, according to the best of your knowledge and abilities, promote the interest and honor of the said states at that court, with a particular attention to the following instructions:

1. You are immediately to assure his most christian majesty, that these states entertain the highest sense of his exertions in their favor, particularly by sending the respectable squadron under the count d'Estaing, which would probably have terminated the war in a speedy and honorable manner, if unforeseen and unfortunate circumstances had not intervened. You are further to assure him that they consider this speedy aid, not only as a testimony of his majesty's fidelity to the engagements he hath entered into, but as an earnest of that protection which they hope from his power and magnanimity, and as a bond of gratitude to the union, founded on mutual interest.

2. You shall, by the earliest opportunity, and on every necessary occasion, assure the king and his ministers, that neither the congress nor any of the states they represent, have at all swerved from their determination to be independent in July, 1776. But as the declaration was made in face of the most powerful fleet and army which could have been expected to operate against them, and without any the slightest assurance of foreign aid, so, although in a defenseless situation, and harassed by the secret machinations and designs of intestine foes, they have, under the exertions of that force, during these bloody campaigns, persevered in their determination to be free. And that they have been inflexible in this determination, notwithstanding the interruption of their commerce, the great sufferings they have experienced from the want of those things which it procured, and the unexampled barbarity of their enemies.

3. You are to give the most pointed and positive assurances, that although the congress are earnestly desirous of peace, as well to arrange their finances, and recruit the exhausted state of their country, as to spare the further effusion of blood, yet they will faithfully per-

form their engagements, and afford every assistance in their power to prosecute the war for the great purposes of the alliance.

4. You shall endeavor to obtain the king's consent to expunge from the treaty of commerce the eleventh and twelfth articles, as inconsistent with that equality and reciprocity which form the best security to perpetuate the whole.

5. You are to exert yourself to procure the consent of the court of France, that all American seamen, who may be taken on board of British vessels, may, if they choose, be permitted to enter on board American vessels. In return for which, you are authorized to stipulate, that all Frenchmen who may be taken on board of British vessels, by vessels belonging to the United States, shall be delivered up to persons appointed for that purpose by his most christian majesty.

6. You are to suggest to the ministers of his most christian majesty, the advantages that would result from entering on board the ships of these states, British seamen who may be made prisoners, thereby impairing the force of the enemy, and strengthening the hands of his ally.

7. You are also to suggest the fatal consequences which would follow the commerce of the common enemy, if, by confining the war to the European and Asiatic seas, the coasts of America could be so far freed from the British fleets as to furnish a safe asylum to the frigates and privateers of the allied nations and their prizes.

8. You shall constantly inculcate the certainty of ruining the British fisheries on the banks of Newfoundland, and consequently the British marine, by reducing Halifax and Quebec, since, by that means they would be exposed to alarm and plunder, and deprived of the necessary supplies formerly drawn from America. The plans proposed to Congress for compassing these objects are herewith transmitted for your more particular instruction.

9. You are to lay before the court the deranged state of our finances, together with the causes thereof; and show the necessity of placing them on a more respectable footing, in order to prosecute the war with vigor on the part of America. Observations on that subject are herewith transmitted; and more particular instructions shall be sent whenever the necessary steps previous thereto shall have been taken.

10. You are, by every means in your power, to promote a perfect harmony, concord and good understanding, not only between the allied powers, but also between and among their subjects, that the connexion so favorably begun may be perpetuated.

11. You shall in all things take care not to make any engagements, or stipulations, on the part of America, without the consent of America previously obtained.

We pray God to further you with his goodness in the several objects hereby recommended; and that he will have you in his holy keeping.

Done at Philadelphia, the 26th day of October, 1778.

By the congress.   H. LAURENS, *President.*

Attest, CHARLES THOMSON, *Secretary.*

NO. 4.

Plan for reducing the province of Canada, referred to in the instructions of Hon. B. Franklin, minister to the court of France, October, 1778.

Plan of attack.—That a number of men be assembled at Fort Pitt, from Virginia and Pennsylvania, amounting to one thousand five hundred rank and file; for which purpose three thousand should be called for; and if more than one thousand five hundred appear, the least effective to be dismissed. To these should be added one hundred light cavalry, one half armed with lances. The whole should be ready to march by the first day of June; and for that purpose they should be called together for the 1st of May, so as to be in readiness by the 15th. The real and declared object of the corps should be to attack Detroit, and to destroy the towns on the route thither, of those Indians who are inimical to the United States.

2. That five hundred men be stationed at or near Wyoming this winter, to cover the frontiers of Pennsylvania and New Jersey; to be reinforced by one thousand men from those states early in the spring. For this purpose, two thousand men should be called for, to appear on the first of May, so as to be in readiness by the 15th. They must march on the first of June at farthest, for Oneoquago; to proceed from thence against Niagara. This is also to be declared.

3. That in addition to the garrison at Fort Schuyler or Stanwix, one thousand five hundred men be stationed this winter along the Mohawk river; and preparations of every kind made to build vessels of force on lake Ontario early next spring; and to take post at or near Oswego. A reinforcement of two thousand five hundred men, from the militia of New York and the western parts of Connecticut and Massachusetts Bay, must be added to these early in the spring; for which purpose a demand must be made of five thousand. A party, consisting of five hundred regular troops and one thousand militia, must march from Schenectady; so as to meet those destined to act against Niagara at Oneoquago. They should be joined by about one hundred light dragoons, armed as aforesaid, together with all the warriors which can be collected from the friendly tribes. In their march to Niagara, they should destroy the Senecas and other towns of Indians which are inimical.

4. That two thousand five hundred men be marched from fort Schuyler, as early as possible after the middle of May, to Oswego, and take a post there, or in the neighborhood; to be defended by about five hundred men. That they also be employed in forwarding the vessels to be built for securing the navigation of lake Ontario, and in making excursions towards Niagara; so as to keep the Indian country in alarm, and facilitate the operations in that quarter.

5. That a number of regiments be cantoned along the upper parts of Connecticut river, to be recruited in the winter; so as to form a body of five thousand regular troops, rank and file; and every preparation made to penetrate into Canada by way of the river St. Francis. The time of their departure must depend upon circumstances; and

their object kept as secret as the nature of the thing will permit. When they arrive at the St. Francis, they must take a good post at the mouth of St. Francis, and turn their attention immediately to the reduction of Montreal and St. John's, and the north end of lake Champlain. These operations will be facilitated by the several movements to the westward, drawing the attention of the enemy to that quarter. If successful, so as to secure a passage across the lake, further reinforcements may be thrown in, and an additional retreat secured that way. The next operation will be in concert with the troops who are to gain the navigation of lake Ontario, &c. This operation, however, must be feeble, so long as the necessity exists of securing their rear towards Quebec. Such detachments, however, as can be spared, perhaps two thousand, with as many Canadians as will join them, are to proceed up Cadaraqui, and take a post, defensible by about three hundred men, at or near the mouth of lake Ontario. They will then join themselves to those posted, as aforesaid, at or near Oswego; and, leaving a garrison at that post, proceed together to the party at or near Niagara, at which place they ought, if possible, to arrive by the middle of September. The troops who have marched against Detroit should also, whether successful or not, return to Niagara, if that post is possessed or besieged by the Americans; as a safe retreat can by that means be accomplished for the whole, in case of accident. On the supposition that these operations should succeed, still another campaign must be made to reduce the city of Quebec. The American troops must continue all winter in Canada. To supply them with provisions, clothing, &c. will be difficult, if not impracticable. The expense will be ruinous. The enemy will have time to reinforce. Nothing can be attempted against Halifax. Considering these circumstances, it is perhaps more prudent to make incursions with cavalry, and light infantry, and chasseurs, to harrass and alarm the enemy; and thereby prevent them from desolating our frontiers, which seems to be their object during the next campaign.

But if the reduction of Halifax and Quebec are objects of the highest importance to the allies, they must be attempted.

The importance to France is derived from the following considerations:

1. The fishery of Newfoundland is justly considered as the basis of a good marine.

2. The possession of those two places necessarily secures to the party, and their friends, the island and fisheries.

3. It will strengthen her allies; and guarantee more strongly their freedom and independence.

4. It will have an influence in extending the commerce of France, and restoring her to a share of the fur trade, now monopolized by Great Britain.

The importance to America results from the following considerations:

1. The peace of their frontiers.

2. The arrangement of their finances.

3. The accession of two states to the union.

4. The protection and security of their commerce.

5. That it will enable them to bend their whole attention and resources to the creation of a marine, which will at once serve them and assist their allies.

6. That it will secure the fisheries to the United States, and France their ally, to the total exclusion of Great Britain. Add to these considerations:

1. That Great Britain, by holding these places, will infest the coast of America with small armed vessels to the great injury of the French as well as the American trade.

2. That her possessions in the West Indies materially depend on the possession of posts to supply them with bread and lumber, and to refit their ships, and receive their sick, as well soldiers as seamen. In order then to secure, as far as human wisdom can provide, the reduction of those places, aid must be obtained from France. Suppose a body of four or five thousand French troops sail from Brest, in the beginning of May, under convoy of four ships of the line and four frigates. Their object to be avowed; but their clothing, stores, &c. such as designate them for the West Indies. Each soldier must have a good blanket, of a large size, to be made into a coat when the weather grows cool. Thick clothing for these troops should be sent in August, so as to arrive at such place as circumstances by that time may indicate, by the beginning of October. These troops, by the end of June or beginning of July, might arrive at Quebec, which for the reasons already assigned, they would in all probability find quite defenseless. Possessing themselves of that city, and leaving there the line of battle ships, the marines and a very small garrison, with as many of the Canadians as can readily be assembled, (for which purpose spare arms should be provided, which might be put up in boxes, and marked as for the militia of one of the French islands,) the frigates and transports should proceed up the river St. Lawrence, and a debarkation take place at the mouth of the river St. Francis. If the Americans are already at that place, the troops will co-operate for the purposes abovementioned: if not, a post must be taken there, and expresses sent, &c. In the interim, three of the frigates, with four of the smallest transports, should proceed to Montreal, and if possible possess that city; when the nobles and clergy should be immediately called together by the general, who should, if possible, be well acquainted with the manners both of France and of the United States. The troops should bring with them very ample provisions, especially of salted flesh, as they will come to a country exhausted by the British army. By the latter end of July, or middle of August, the reduction of Canada might be so far completed, that the ships might proceed to the investiture of Halifax, taking on board large supplies of flour. A part of the troops might march, and be followed by the sick, as they recover. A considerable body of American troops might then be spared for that service, which, with the militia of the states of Massachusetts Bay and New Hampshire, might proceed to the attack

of Halifax, so as to arrive at the beginning of September; and if that place should fall by the beginning or middle of October, the troops might either proceed against Newfoundland, or remain in garrison until the spring; at which time that conquest might be completed. If Halifax should not be taken, then the squadron and troops would still be in time to co-operate against the West Indies.

To the Hon. Benjamin Franklin, Esq.

Sir—The above plan, referred to in your instructions, you shall lay substantially before the French minister. You shall consult the marquis de la Fayette on any difficulties which may arise; and refer the ministry to him, as he hath made it his particular study to gain information on these important points.

By order of Congress.
Attest, C. T. *Secretary.*   H. L. *President.*

NO. 5, omitted.

NO. 6.

Extract from a statement made to congress, by the French minister Gerard, concerning negociations for peace, in July, 1779.

That the British ministry seem to be solicitous to be reconciled with France, and to keep up this negociation; that from thence probable hopes may be entertained of their internal disposition to peace; but at the same time, they reject with haughtiness the formal acknowledgment of the independence insisted on by France and Spain. New orders have been given to the Spanish ambassador at London to ascertain, as nearly as possible, those dispositions. In these circumstances the king his master ordered him to communicate this intelligence to the United States, that they may, if they think proper, take under consideration, if it would not be expedient to give their plenipotentiary instructions and full powers founded upon the necessity of the conjuncture and upon the treaty of alliance, the express and formal terms of which are, that peace shall not be made without an express or tacit acknowledgment of the sovereignty, and consequently and *a fortiori*, of the rights inherent in sovereignty as well as of the independence of the United States, in matters of government and of commerce. This substantial alternative in an engagement which is a mere gratuitous gift without any compensation, or stipulation, ought indeed never to be forgot in a negociation for peace. France foresaw the extreme difficulties a formal and explicit acknowledgment might meet with. She knew by her own experience in similar contests in which she.has been deeply concerned, respecting the republics of Holland, Genoa, and the Swiss cantons, how tenacious monarchs are, and how repugnant to pronounce the humiliating *formula*. It was only obtained for Holland tacitly, after a war of thirty years; and explicitly, after a resistance of seventy. To this day Genoa and the Swiss cantons have obtained no renunciation, nor acknowledgment, either tacit, or formal, from their former sovereigns. But they enjoy their sovereignty and independence only under the guarantee of France. His court thought it important to provide, that difficulties of this nature, which reside merely in words, should not delay or prevent America from enjoying the thing itself. From these considerations arose the very important and explicit stipulation in the treaty, which he has just now related, and which has received the sanction of the United States. The circumstances seem already such as call for the application of the alternative of tacit, or explicit acknowledgment. All these considerations therefore are mentioned, that Congress may, if they think proper, consider whether the literal execution of the treaty in this point is not become necessary, and whether the safety and happiness of the American people, as well as the essential principles of the alliance, are not intimately connected with the resolutions that may be taken on this subject. And it remains with the prudence of congress to examine whether instructions upon some particular conditions may not frustrate the salutary purpose of the treaty of alliance relative to a tacit acknowledgment which the situation of affairs may require. In thus executing, continued he, the orders I have received, I cannot omit observing, that these orders were given with the full presumption, that the business which I laid before congress in February last *would have been settled long before these despatches should come to my hands.* However sensibly my court will be disappointed in her expectations, I shall add nothing to the information and observations which with the warmest zeal for the interest and honor of both countries and by the duties of my office and my instructions, I found myself bound to deliver from time to time to congress, in the course of this business. The apprehension of giving new matter to those who endeavor to throw blame upon congress, is a new motive for me to remain silent. I beg only to remind this honorable body of the aforesaid information and reflections, and particularly of those which I had the honor to deliver to an assembly similar to the present. I shall only insist on a single point, which I established then, and since in one of my memorials, namely, the manifest and striking necessity of enabling Spain, by the determination of just and moderate terms, to press upon England with her good offices, and to bring her mediation to an issue, in order that we may know whether we are to expect war or peace. This step is looked upon in Europe as immediately necessary. It was the proper object of the message I delivered in February last. I established then the strong reasons which require, that at the same time and without delay, proper terms should be offered to his catholic majesty, in order to reconcile him perfectly to the American interest. I did not conceal, that it was to be feared, that any condition inconsistent with the established form of the alliance, which is the binding and only law of the allies, and contrary to the line of conduct which Spain pursued in the course of her mediation, would lead her to drop the mediation, and prevent his catholic majesty, by motives of honor and faithfulness, from joining in our common cause, and from completing the intended triumvirate. No loss, no unhappy event could be so heavy on the alliance as this. Indeed although the British forces are already kept in check by the combined efforts of France and America, it is nevertheless evident that the accession of Spain only can give to the alliance a decided superiority adequate to our purposes, and free us from the fatal chance that a single unlucky event may overturn the balance.

NO. 7.

Instructions to Mr. Adams, in negociating a treaty of commerce with Great Britain, August 14th, 1779.

Sir—You will herewith receive a commission, giving you full power to negociate a treaty of commerce with Great Britain in doing which you will consider yourself bound by the following information and instructions:

1. You will govern yourself principally by the treaty of commerce with his most christian majesty; and as, on the one hand, you shall grant no privilege to Great Britain not granted by that treaty to France, so, on the other, you shall not consent to any peculiar restrictions or limitations whatever in favor of Great Britain.

2. In order that you may be the better able to act with propriety on this occasion, it is necessary for you to know, that we have determined, 1st, that the common right of fishing shall in no case be given up; 2d, that it is essential to the welfare of all these United States, that the inhabitants thereof, at the expiration of the war, should continue to enjoy the free and undisturbed exercise of their common right to fish on the banks of Newfoundland, and the other fishing banks and seas of North America, preserving inviolate the treaties between France and the said states; 3d, that application shall be made to his most christian majesty to agree to some article or articles for the better securing to these states a share in the said fisheries; 4th, that if, after a treaty of peace with Great Britain, she shall molest the citizens or inhabitants of any of the United States, in taking fish on the banks and places herein after described, such molestation being in our opinion a direct violation and breach of the peace, shall be a common cause of the said states, and the force of the union be exerted to obtain redress for the parties injured; and 5th, that our faith be pledged to the several states, that, without their unanimous consent, no treaty of commerce shall be entered into, nor any trade or commerce carried on with Great Britain, without the explicit stipulation herein after mentioned. You are therefore not to consent to any treaty of commerce with Great Britain without an explicit stipulation on her part, not to molest or disturb the inhabitants of the United States of America in taking fish on the banks of Newfoundland and other fisheries in the American seas any where, excepting within the distance of three leagues of the shores of the territories remaining to Great Britain at

the close of the war, if a nearer distance cannot be obtained by negociation. And in the negociation you are to exert your most strenuous
endeavors to obtain a nearer distance to the gulf of St. Lawrence, and
particularly along the shores of Nova Scotia, as to which latter we
are desirous that even the shores may be occasionally used for the
purpose of carrying on the fisheries by the inhabitants of these states.

3. In all other matters you are to govern yourself by your own discretion, as shall be most for the interest of these states, taking care
that the said treaty be founded on principles of equality and reciprocity, so as to conduce to the mutual advantage of both nations, but not
to the exclusion of others.

NO. 8.

*Instructions of Mr. Jay, for negociating with the court of Spain, in Sep-
tember, 1779.*

Sir—By the treaties subsisting between his most christian majesty
and the United States of America, a power is reserved to his catholic
majesty to accede to the said treaties, and to participate in their stipulations, at such time as he shall judge proper, it being well understood, nevertheless, that if any of the stipulations of the said treaties
are not agreeable to the court of Spain, his catholic majesty may propose other conditions analogous to the principal aim of the alliance,
and conformable to the rules of equality, reciprocity, and friendship.
Congress is sensible of the friendly regard to these states manifested
by his most christian majesty, in reserving a power to his catholic majesty of acceding to the alliance entered into between his most christian majesty and these United States; and therefore, that nothing may
be wanting on their part to facilitate the views of his most christian
majesty, and to obtain a treaty of alliance and of amity and commerce
with his catholic majesty, have thought proper to anticipate any propositions which his catholic majesty might make on that subject, by
yielding up to him those objects which they conclude he may have
principally in view; and for that purpose have come to the following
resolution:

That if his catholic majesty shall accede to the said treaties, and,
in concurrence with France and the United States of America, continue the present war with Great Britain for the purpose expressed
in the treaties aforesaid, he shall not thereby be precluded from securing to himself the Floridas : on the contrary, if he shall obtain the
Floridas from Great Britain, these United States will guaranty the same
to his catholic majesty : provided always, that the United States shall
enjoy the free navigation of the river Mississippi into and from the
sea.

You are therefore to communicate to his most christian majesty,
the desire of congress to enter into a treaty of alliance and of amity
and commerce with his catholic majesty, and to request his favorable

interposition for that purpose. At the same time, you are to make such proposals to his catholic majesty, as in your judgment, from circumstances, will be proper for obtaining for the United States of America equal advantages with those which are secured to them by the treaties with his most christian majesty ; observing always the resolution aforesaid as the ultimatum of the United States.

You are particularly to endeavor to obtain some convenient port or ports below the thirty-first degree of north latitude, on the river Mississippi, for all merchant vessels, goods, wares, and merchandises belonging to the inhabitants of these states.

The distressed state of our finances and the great depreciation of our paper money inclined congress to hope that his catholic majesty, if he shall conclude a treaty with these states, will be induced to lend them money : you are therefore, to represent to him the great distress of these states on that account, and to solicit a loan of five millions of dollars upon the best terms in your power, not exceeding six per centum per annum, effectually to enable them to co-operate with the allies against the common enemy. But before you make any propositions to his catholic majesty for a loan, you are to endeavor to obtain a subsidy in consideration of the guarantee aforesaid.

NO. 9.

Statement of the claim of the United States to the western country as far as the river Mississippi, as well as their right to the navigation of that river, drawn up by congress, in October, 1780, in answer to the extraordinary claim of the Spanish court ; and transmitted to the American minister at Madrid.

SIR—Congress having in their instructions of the 4th instant, directed you to adhere strictly to their former instructions relating to the boundaries of the United States, to insist on the navigation of the Mississippi for the citizens of the United States in common with the subjects of his catholic majesty, as also on a free port or ports below the northern limit of West Florida, and accessible to merchant ships for the use of the former ; and being sensible of the influence which these claims on the part of the United States may have on your negociations with the court of Madrid, have thought it expedient to explain the reasons and principles on which the same are founded, that you may be enabled to satisfy that court of the equity and justice of their intentions. With respect to the first of these articles, by which the river Mississippi is fixed as the boundary between the Spanish · settlements and the United States, it is unnecessary to take notice of any pretensions founded on a priority of discovery, of occupancy, or on conquest. It is sufficient that by the definitive treaty of Paris, of 1763, article seventh, all the territory now claimed by the United States, was expressly and irrevocably ceded to the king of Great Britain, and that the United States are, in consequence of the revolution in their government, entitled to the benefits of that cession.

The first of these positions is proved by the treaty itself. To prove the last, it must be observed, that it is a fundamental principle in all lawful governments, and particularly in the constitution of the British empire, that all the rights of sovereignty are intended for the benefit of those from whom they are derived, and over whom they are exercised. It is known, also, to have been held for an inviolable principle by the United States, while they remained a part of the British empire, that the sovereignty of the king of England, with all the rights and powers included in it, did not extend to them in virtue of his being acknowledged and obeyed as king by the people of England, or of any other part of the empire, but in virtue of his being acknowledged and obeyed as king of the people of America themselves; and that this principle was the basis, first of their opposition to, and finally of their abolition of his authority over them. From these principles it results, that all the territory lying within the limits of the states, as fixed by the sovereign himself, was held by him for their particular benefits, and must equally with his other rights and claims in quality of their sovereign, be considered as having devolved on them, in consequence of their resumption of the sovereignty to themselves.

In support of this position it may be further observed, that all the territorial rights of the king of Great Britain, within the limits of the United States, accrued to him from the enterprises, the risks, the sacrifices, the expense in blood and treasure of the present inhabitants and their progenitors. If in latter times, expenses and exertions have been borne by any other part of the empire, in their immediate defense, it need only be recollected, that the ultimate object of them was the general security and advantage of the empire ; that a proportional share was borne by the states themselves; and that if this had not been the case, the benefits resulting from an exclusive enjoyment of their trade have been an abundant compensation. Equity and justice, therefore, perfectly coincide in the present instance, with political and constitutional principles. No objection can be pretended against what is here said, except that the king of Great Britain was, at the time of the rupture with his catholic majesty, possessed of certain parts of the territory in question, and consequently that his catholic majesty had and still has a right to regard them as lawful objects of conquest. In answer to this objection, it is to be considered, 1. That these possessions are few in number and confined to small spots. 2. That a right founded on conquest being only coextensive with the objects of conquest, cannot comprehend the circumjacent territory. 3. That if a right to the said territory depended on the conquests of the British posts within it, the United States have already a more extensive claim to it than Spain can acquire, having by the success of their arms obtained possession of all the important posts and settlements on the Illinois and Wabash, rescued the inhabitants from British domination, and established civil government in its proper form over them. They have, moreover, established a post on a strong and commanding situation near the mouth of the Ohio: whereas Spain has a claim by conquest to no post above the northern bounds of West Florida, except that of the Natchez, nor are there any other British posts below the mouth of the Ohio for their arms to be employed against. 4. That whatever extent ought to be ascribed to the right of conquest, it must be admitted to have limitations which in the present case exclude the pretensions of his catholic majesty. If the occupation by the king of Great Britain of posts within the limits of the United States, as defined by charters derived from the said king when constitutionally authorized to grant them, makes them lawful objects of conquest to any other power than the United States, it follows that every other part of the United States that now is, or may hereafter fall into the hands of the enemy, is equally an object of conquest. Not only New York, Long Island, and the other islands in its vicinity, but almost the entire states of South Carolina and Georgia, might, by the interposition of a foreign power at war with their enemy, be forever severed from the American confederacy, and subjected to a foreign yoke. But is such a doctrine consonant to the rights of nations, or the sentiments of humanity? Does it breathe that spirit of concord and amity which is the aim of the proposed alliance with Spain? Would it be admitted by Spain herself, if it affected her own dominions? Were, for example, a British armament by a sudden enterprise to get possession of a seaport, a trading town, or maritime province in Spain, and another power at war with Britain, should, before it could be re-conquered by Spain, wrest it from the hands of Britain, would Spain herself consider it as an extinguishment of her just pretensions? Or would any impartial nation consider it in that light? As to the proclamation of the king of Great Britain of 1763, forbidding his governors in North America to grant lands westward of the sources of the rivers falling into the Atlantic ocean, it can by no rule of construction militate against the present claims of the United States. That proclamation, as is clear both from the title and tenor of it, was intended merely to prevent disputes with the Indians, and an irregular appropriation of vacant land to individuals; and by no means either to renounce any parts of the cessions made in the treaty of Paris, or to affect the boundaries established by ancient charters. On the contrary, it is expressly declared that the lands and territory prohibited to be granted, were within the sovereignty and dominion of that crown, notwithstanding the reservation of them to the use of the Indians.

The right of the United States to western territory as far as the Mississippi, having been shown, there are sufficient reasons for them to insist on that right, as well as for Spain not to wish a relinquishment of it. In the first place, the river Mississippi will be a more natural, more distinguishable, and more precise boundary than any other that can be drawn eastward of it; and consequently will be less liable to become a source of those disputes which too often proceed from un-

Secondly, It ought not to be concealed, that although the vacant territory adjacent to the Mississippi should be relinquished by the United States to Spain, yet the fertility of its soil, and its convenient situation for trade, might be productive of intrusions by the citizens of the former, which their great distance would render it difficult to restrain; and which might lead to an interruption of that harmony which it is so much the interest and wish of both should be perpetual.

Thirdly, As this territory lies within the charter limits of particular states, and is considered by them as no less their property than any other territory within their limits, congress could not relinquish it without exciting discussions between themselves and those states, concerning their respective rights and powers, which might greatly embarrass the public councils of the United States, and give advantage to the common enemy.

Fourthly, The territory in question contains a number of inhabitants, who are at present under the protection of the United States, and have sworn allegiance to them. These could not by voluntary transfer be subjected to a foreign jurisdiction, without manifest violation of the common rights of mankind, and of the genius and principles of the American governments.

Fifthly, In case the obstinacy and pride of Great Britain should for any length of time continue an obstacle to peace, a cession of this territory, rendered of so much value to the United States by its particular situation, would deprive them of one of the material funds on which they rely for pursuing the war against her. On the part of Spain, this territorial fund is not needed for, and perhaps could not be applied to, the purposes of the war; and from its situation, is otherwise of much less value to her than to the United States. Congress have the greater hopes that the pretensions of his catholic majesty on this subject will not be so far urged as to prove an insuperable obstacle to an alliance with the United States, because they conceive such pretensions to be incompatible with the treaties subsisting between France and them, which are to be the basis and substance of it. By article eleventh of the treaty of alliance, eventual and defensive, the possessions of the United States are guarantied to them by his most christian majesty. By article twelfth of the same treaty, intended to fix more precisely the sense and application of the preceding article, it is declared, that this guaranty shall have its full force and effect the moment a rupture shall take place between France and England. All the possessions, therefore, belonging to the United States at the time of that rupture, which being prior to the rupture between Spain and England, must be prior to all claims of conquest by the former, are guarantied to them by his most christian majesty.

Now, that in the possessions thus guarantied, was meant, by the contracting parties, to be included all the territory within the limits assigned to the United States by the treaty of Paris, may be inferred from the fifth article of the treaty abovementioned, which declares, that if the United States should think fit to attempt the reduction of the British power remaining in the northern parts of America, or the islands of Bermudas, &c., those countries shall, in case of success, be confederated with, or dependent upon, the United States. For, if it had been understood by the parties that the western territory in question, known to be of so great importance to the United States, and a reduction of it so likely to be attempted by them, was not included in the general guaranty, can it be supposed that no notice would have 'been taken of it, when the parties extended their views, not only to Canada, but to the remote and unimportant island of Bermudas. It is true that these acts between France and the United States, are in no respects obligatory on his catholic majesty, unless he shall think fit to accede to them. Yet as they show the sense of his most christian majesty on this subject, with whom his catholic majesty is intimately allied; as it is in pursuance of an express reservation to his catholic majesty in a secret act subjoined to the treaties aforesaid of a power to accede to those treaties, that the present overtures are made on the part of the United States; and as it is particularly stated in that act, that any conditions which his catholic majesty shall think fit to add, are to be analogous to the principal aim of the alliance, and conformable to the rules of equality, reciprocity, and friendship, congress entertain too high an opinion of the equity, moderation, and wisdom of his catholic majesty not to suppose, that, when joined to these considerations, they will prevail against any mistaken views of interest that may be suggested to him.

The next object of the instructions is the free navigation of the Mississippi for the citizens of the United States, in common with the subjects of his catholic majesty.

On this subject, the same inference may be made from article seventh of the treaty of Paris, which stipulates this right in the amplest manner to the king of Great Britain; and the devolution of it to the United States, as was applied to the territorial claims of the latter. Nor can congress hesitate to believe, that even if no such right could be inferred from that treaty, that the generosity of his catholic majesty would not suffer the inhabitants of these states to be put into a worse condition, in this respect, by the alliance with him in the character of a sovereign people, than they were in when subjects of a power which was always ready to turn its force against his majesty; especially as one of the great objects of the proposed alliance is to give greater effect to the common exertions for disarming that power of the faculty of disturbing others. Besides, as the United States have an indisputable right to the possession of the east bank of the Mississippi for a very great distance, and the navigation of that river will essentially tend to the prosperity and advantage of the citizens of the United States that may reside on the Mississippi, or the waters running into it, it is conceived that the circumstances of Spain's being in possession of the banks on both sides near its mouth, cannot be deemed a natural or equitable bar to the free use of the river. Such a principle would authorize a nation disposed to take advantage of circumstances, to contravene the clear indications of nature and Providence, and the general good of mankind.

The usage of nations accordingly seems in such cases to have given to those holding the mouth or lower parts of a river no right against those above them, except the right of imposing a moderate toll, and that on the equitable supposition, that such toll is due for the expense and trouble the former may have been put to. " An innocent passage, (says Vattel,) is due to all nations with whom a state is at peace ; and this duty comprehends troops equally with individuals." If a right to a passage by land through other countries may be claimed for troops, which are employed in the destruction of mankind, how much more may a passage by water be claimed for commerce, which is beneficial to all nations.

Here again it ought not to be concealed, that the inconveniences which must be felt by the inhabitants on the waters running westward-ly, under an exclusion from the free use of the Mississippi, would be a constant and increasing source of disquietude on their part, of more vigorous precautions on the part of Spain, and of an irritation on both parts, which it is equally the interest and duty of both to guard against.

But notwithstanding the equitable claim of the United States to the free navigation of the Mississippi, and its great importance to them, congress have so strong a disposition to conform to the desires of his catholic majesty, that they have agreed that such equitable regulations may be entered into as may be a requisite security against contraband ; provided, the point of right be not relinquished, and a free port or ports below the thirty-first degree of north latitude, and accessible to merchant ships, be stipulated to them.

The reason why a port or ports, as thus described, was requested must be obvious. Without such a stipulation, the free use of the Mississippi would in fact amount to no more than a free intercourse with New Orleans and other ports of Louisiana. From the rapid current of this river, it is well known that it must be navigated by vessels of a particular construction, and which will be unfit to go to sea. Unless, therefore, some place be assigned to the United States where the produce carried down the river, and the merchandise ar-riving from abroad, may be deposited till they can be respectively taken away by the proper vessels, there can be no such thing as a foreign trade.

There is a remaining consideration respecting the navigation of the Mississippi which deeply concerns the maritime powers in gene-ral, but more particularly their most christian and catholic majesties. The country watered by the Ohio, with its large branches, having their sources near the lakes on one side, and those running north westward and falling into it on the other side, will appear from a sin-gle glance on a map to be of vast extent. The circumstance of its being so finely watered, added to the singular fertility of its soil, and other advantages presented by a new country, will occasion a rapidity of population not easy to be conceived. The spirit of emigration has already shown itself in a very strong degree, notwithstanding the many impediments which discourage it. The principal of these impediments is the war with Britain, which cannot spare a force sufficient to protect the emigrants against the incursions of the savages. In a very few years after peace shall take place, this country will certainly be overspread with inhabitants. In like manner as in all new settlements, agriculture, not manufactures, will be their employment. They will raise wheat, corn, beef, pork, tobacco, hemp, flax, and in the southern parts, perhaps, rice and indigo, in great quantities. On the other hand, their consumption of foreign manufactures will be in proportion, if they can be exchanged for the produce of their soil. There are but two channels through which such commerce can be carried on; the first is down the river Mississippi; the other is up the rivers having their sources near the lakes, thence by short portages to the lakes, or the rivers falling into them, and thence through the lakes and down the St. Lawrence. The first of these channels is manifestly the most natural, and by far the most advantageous. Should it however be obstructed, the second will be found far from impracticable. If no obstructions should be thrown in its course down the Mississippi, the exports from this immense tract of country will not only supply an abundance of all necessaries for the West India islands, but serve for a valuable basis of general trade, of which the rising spirit of commerce in France and Spain will no doubt particularly avail itself. The imports will be proportionally extensive ; and from the climate, as well as from other causes, will consist of the manufactures of the some countries. On the other hand, should obstructions in the Mississippi force this trade into a contrary direction through Canada; France and Spain, and the other maritime powers will not only lose the immediate benefit of it themselves, but they will also suffer by the advantage it will give to Great Britain. So fair a prospect could not escape the commercial sagacity of this nation. She would embrace it with avidity. She would cherish it with the most studious care. And should she succeed in fixing it in that channel, the loss of her exclusive possession of the trade of the United States might prove a much less decisive blow to her maritime pre-eminence and tyranny than has been calculated.

The last clause of the instructions, respecting the navigation of the waters running out of Georgia through West Florida, not being included in the ultimatum, nor claimed on a footing of right, requires nothing to be added to what it speaks itself.

The utility of the privileges asked to the state of Georgia, and consequently to the union, is apparent from the geographical representation of the country. The motives for Spain to grant it must be found in her equity, generosity, and disposition to cultivate our friendship and intercourse.

These observations you will readily discern are not communicated in order to be urged at all events, and as they here stand in support of the claims to which they relate. They are intended for your private information and use, and are to be urged so far, and in such forms only, as will best suit the temper and sentiments of the court at which you reside, and best fulfil the objects of them.

NO. 10.

Memorial of the French Minister to Congress, concerning the offered mediation of the Empress of Russia and the Emperor of Germany.

Philadelphia, May 28, 1781.

The underwritten minister plenipotentiary of France has received orders to communicate to congress some important details touching the present situation of sundry affairs in which the United States are immediately interested. The most essential respects some overtures which announce, on the part of Great Britain, a desire of peace. The empress of Russia having invited the king and the court of London to take her for mediatrix, the latter court considered this as a formal offer of mediation, and accepted it. It appeared at the same time to desire the emperor to take part therein; and this monarch has in fact proposed his co-mediation to the belligerent powers in Europe. The king could not but congratulate himself on seeing so important a negociation in the hands of two mediators whose understanding and justice are equal. Nevertheless, his majesty actuated by his affection for the United States, returned for answer, that it was not in his power to accept the offers made to him, and that the consent of his allies was necessary. The king wishes to have this consent before he formally accepts the proposed mediation. But it is possible that circumstances joined to the confidence he has in the mediators, and the justice of his cause, and that of the United States his allies, may determine him to enter upon a negociation before the answer of congress can reach him. But in either case, it is of great importance that this assembly should give their plenipotentiary instructions proper to announce their disposition to peace, and their moderation, and to convince the powers of Europe that the independence of the thirteen United States, and the engagements they have contracted with the king, are the sole motives which determine them to continue the war; and that whenever they shall have full and satisfactory assurances on these two capital points, they will be ready to conclude a peace. The manner of conducting the negociation, the extent of the powers of the American plenipotentiary, the use to be made of them, and the confidence that ought to be reposed in the French plenipotentiaries and the king's ministers, are points which should be fully discussed with a committee. And the underwritten minister entreats that congress would be pleased to name a committee, with whom he will have the honor to treat. He thinks that this assembly will be sensible that the king could not give a greater mark of his affection for the thirteen United States, or of his attachment to the principles of the alliance, than by determining not to enter upon a negociation before they were ready to take part therein, although, in other respects, his confidence in the mediators, and the relation he stands in to one of them, were sufficient motives to induce him to accept their offers.   Congress are too sensible of the uncertainty of negociations of this sort not to know, that the moment of opening them is that precisely when the efforts against the enemy ought to be redoubled; and that nothing can facilitate the operation of the negociators so much as the success of the arms of the allies; that a check would be productive of disagreeable consequences to both, and that would rise in their pretensions, their haughtiness and obstinacy, in proportion to the languor and slackness of the confederates.

The undersigned will have the honor to communicate to the committee some circumstances relative to the sending Mr. Cumberland to Madrid; to the use which Mr. Adams thought he was authorized to make of his plenipotentiary powers; to the mission of Mr. Dana; to the association of the neutral powers, and to the present state of affairs in the south.   Congress will find new motives for relying on the good will of the king, and on the interest he takes in favor of the United States in general, and of each one of them in particular.

NO. 11.

Report of a committee appointed by congress to confer with the French minister, on the subject of the mediation offered by the Empress of Russia, and the Emperor of Germany, &c. made in May, 1781.

That the minister communicated some parts of a despatch which he had received from the count de Vergennes, dated the 9th of March, 1781.

That the resolves of congress which had been adopted on the associations of the neutral powers, were found very wise by the council of the king; and that it was thought they might be of service in the course of the negociation.   The French ministry did not doubt but they would be very agreeable to the empress of Russia.   But they were not of the same opinion with respect to the appointment of Mr. Dana, as a minister to the court of Petersburg.   The reason is that Catharine the second has made it a point, until now, to profess the greatest impartiality between the belligerent powers.   The conduct she pursues on this occasion, is a consequence of the expectation she has that peace may be re-established by her mediation; therefore she could by no means take any step which might show on her side the least propension in favor of the Americans, and expose her to the suspicion of partiality towards America, and of course exclude her from the mediation.   The appointment of Mr. Dana, therefore, appears to be at least, premature; and the opinion of the council is, that this deputy ought not to make any use of his powers at this moment.   The case he applies to the count de Vergennes for advice, he shall be desired to delay making any use of his powers. The count observes, it would be disagreeable to congress that their plenipotentiary should meet with a refusal, that their dignity would be offended, and that such a satisfaction ought not to be given to the court of London, especially when negociations of a greater moment, are about to commence. However, the French minister had orders to assure the committee that his court would use all their endeavours in proper time to facilitate the admission of the plenipotentiary of congress.

The minister communicated to the committee several observations respecting the conduct of Mr. Adams; and in doing justice to his patriotic character, he gave notice to the committee of several circumstances which proved it necessary that congress should draw a line of conduct to that minister, of which he might not be allowed to loose sight. The minister dwelt especially on a circumstance already known to congress, namely the use which Mr. Adams thought he had a right to make of his powers, to treat with Great Britain. The minister concluded on this subject, that if congress put any confidence in the king's friendship and benevolence; if they were persuaded of his inviolable attachment to the principle of the alliance, and of his firm resolution constantly to support the cause of the United States, they would be impressed with the necessity of prescribing to their plenipotentiary a perfect and open confidence in the French ministers, and a thorough reliance on the king, and would direct him to take no steps, without the approbation of his majesty; and after giving him, in his instructions, the principal and most important outlines for his conduct, they would order him, with respect to the manner of carrying them into execution, to receive his direction from the count de Vergennes, or from the person who might be charged with the negociation in the name of the king. The minister observed that this matter is the more important, because, being allied with the United States, it is the business of the king to support their cause with those powers with whom congress has no connection, and can have none, until their independence is in a fair train to be acknowledged. That the king would make it a point of prudence and justice to support the minister of Congress; but in case the minister, by aiming at impossible things, forming exorbitant demands, which disinterested mediators might think ill founded, or perhaps by misconstruing his instructions, should put the French negociators under the necessity of proceeding in the course of the negociation without a constant connection with him, this would give rise to an unbecoming contradiction between France and the thirteen United States, which could not but be of very bad effect in the course of the negociations.

In making these observations, the minister remarked, that it was always to be taken for granted, that the most perfect independency is to be the foundation of the instructions, to be given to Mr. Adams, and that without this, there would be no treaty at all. The count de Vergennes observes that it is of great importance that the instructions aforesaid be given as soon as possible to Mr. Adams. And the minister desired the committee to press congress to have this done with all possible despatch. He communicated to the committee the following particulars, as a proof that this matter admits of no delay, and that it is probable the negociation will very soon be opened. He told the committee that the English ministry, in the false supposition that they might prevail on the court of Madrid to sign a separate peace, had begun a secret negociation with that court, by the means of Mr. Cumberland, but without any success. That the court of Spain had constantly founded her answer on her engagements with his most christian majesty. That on the other side, the king of France had declared to the king his cousin, that the independence of the United States, either in fact, or acknowledged by a solemn treaty, should be the only foundation of the negociations of the court of France with that of London. That the British court not seeming to be disposed to grant the independency, it appeared the negociation of Mr. Cumberland was superfluous. However, this English emissary continued and still continues his residence at Madrid, although he cannot have any expectation of obtaining the object of his commission. That this direct negociation, was known to all Europe; and that it seemed to render every mediation useless. That, however, the empress of Russia, excited by motives of friendship, to the belligerent powers, and in consequence of the share which the association of the neutral powers had given her in the general emergency, has invited the king of France and the court of London, to require her mediation. That the court of London has accepted the invitation with a kind of eagerness, and at the same time desired the emperor of Germany to take a part in it. That the answer of the king of France to the overtures of the court of Petersburg was, that he would be glad to restore peace by the mediation of Catharine, but that it was not in his power immediately to accept her offers, as he had allies whose consent was necessary for that purpose. To the same application made by the court of Petersburg to that of Madrid, this court answered, that having entered into a direct negociation with the court of London, by the means of Mr. Cumberland, it thought proper to wait the issue of it before it had recourse to a mediation. The emperor, as has already been observed, having been desired by the court of London to take part in the mediation, immediately informed the king of France, as well as his catholic majesty, of this circumstance. offering his co-mediation to both the allied monarchs. To this the king of France gave the same answer which he had given to the empress of Russia. As to the king of Spain, he again expressed his surprise at the English ministry's requesting a mediation, after having entered into a direct negociation; and he declared that unless this negotiation should be broken off by the English themselves, it would be impossible for him to listen to a mediation which, in any other circumstance, would be infinitely agreeable to him.

These answers, though of a dilatory nature, may be looked upon as an eventual acceptation of the mediation. The minister observed that it will be, in effect, difficult to avoid it. That a refusal will not be consistent with the dignity of the two powers that had offered their interposition. That the king is obliged, from friendship and good policy, to treat them with attention. He further observed, that the demands of the king of France will be so just and so moderate, that they might be proposed to any tribunal whatever. That the only reason the king could have to suspend a formal acceptation is, that at the time the offer was made, he was not acquainted with the intentions of his allies, namely, Spain and the United States.

The minister observed to the committee, that, in his opinion, this conduct must afford congress a new proof of the perseverance of the king in the principle of the alliance, and of his scrupulous attention to observe his obligations; he added that, however, it is not without inconveniency that this dilatory plan has been adopted. The distance between the allied powers of France and the United States has obliged the court of Versailles to adopt that plan, though liable to inconveniences, in order to conform to the engagements made by the treaties to determine nothing into a negociation without the participation of congress. Besides, several states being invaded by the enemy, the French council thought it inconvenient to begin a negociation under these unfavorable circumstances. And being in hopes that the diversions made by the king's arms will prevent the British from making very great exertions against the thirteen United States, the French minister expected that during the course of the present campaign they might be enabled to present the situation of their allies in a more favorable light to the congress that might assemble for peace. These delays, however, cannot with propriety take place for any long time; and it was the opinion of the French ministry that it would be contrary to decency, prudence, and the laws of sound policy again to refuse listening to the propositions of peace made by friendly powers; for which reason the chevalier de la Luzerne was directed to lay all these facts confidentially before congress. The minister informed the committee that it was necessary that the king should know the intentions of the United States with regard to the proposed mediation; and that his majesty should be authorized by congress to give notice of their dispositions to all the powers who would take part in the negociation for a pacification. The minister delivered his own opinion, that he saw no inconveniency arising from the congress imitating the example of the king, by showing themselves disposed to accept peace from the hands of the emperor of Germany and the empress of Russia. He added, that congress should rely on the justice and wisdom of those two sovereigns; and at the same time, he renewed the assurances that his majesty will defend the cause of the United States as zealously as the interests of his own crown. He informed the committee that, according to all accounts, the British ministry were removing as far as possible, in this negociation, every idea of acknowledging the independence of what they call their thirteen colonies; and he said that congress would judge by themselves that the court of London would debate with the greatest energy and obstinacy, the articles relating to America. He availed himself of this reflection to impress the committee with the necessity congress are under of securing in their favor the benevolence and good will of the mediating powers, by presenting their demands with the greatest moderation and reserve, save independence, which will not admit of any modification. He further observed, that it was possible the difficulty of making a definitive peace might engage the mediators to propose a truce; and that it was necessary therefore to authorize eventually the plenipotentiary of the United States to declare their intention thereon.

He further observed that whatever might be the resolution of congress, they would do well to recommend to their plenipotentiary to adopt a line of conduct that would deprive the British of every hope of causing divisions between the allies, and to assume a conciliating character as much as can be consistent with the dignity of his constituents, and to show such a confidence in the plenipotentiary of his most christian majesty as is due to a power so much interested to support the dignity and honor of a nation whose independence they have acknowledged.

The minister told the committee that whatever might be the resolution of congress respecting a peace or a truce, it was necessary to carry on the war with the utmost vigor. He urged reasons too well known to congress to be related.

He desired the committee to inform congress, that in case the offer of mediation from the two imperial courts should become so serious and so pressing as to oblige the king to give a decisive answer, his majesty would accept of it conditionally for himself and the United States. The taking this resolution would have no inconvenience, as the court of France knew no reasons which could prevent them from following the example of the king by trusting their interests into the hands of just and wise mediators, and the refusal being liable to very dangerous concequences. The minister concluded the conference by observing, that a great object was to secure the United States from the proposition of *uti possidetis:* that the surest way to obtain that end was to reduce the English to confess that they are not able to conquer them. That present circumstances require great exertions from the consideration; and that it was plain that every success gained by the army of congress would infinitely facilitate the negociations of their plenipotentiaries.

NO. 12.

A FRAGMENT OF POLYBIUS.

From his treatise on the Athenian government.

This was presented by Sir William Jones, to Dr. Franklin at Paris, about the last of June, 1782. It was, no doubt, drawn by him, and was supposed to be an indirect mode of sounding Dr. Franklin, as to terms of accommodation with Great Britain, short of an express and open acknowledgment of the independence of the United States.

Athens had long been an object of universal admiration, and consequently of envy; her navy was invincible, her commerce extensive; Europe and Asia supplied her with wealth; of her citizens, all were intrepid, many virtuous; but some too much infected with principles unfavorable to freedom. Hence an oligarchy was, in a great measure established; crooked counsels were thought supreme wisdom; and the Athenians, having lost their true relish for their own freedom, began to attack that of their colonies, and of the states which they had before protected! Their arrogant claims of unlimited dominion, had compelled the Chians, Coans, Rhodians, Lesbians, to join with nine other small communities in the *social war*, which they began with inconceivable ardor, and continued with industry surpassing all example, and almost surpassing belief. They were openly assisted by *Mausolus*, king of *Caria*, to whose metropolis the united islands had sent a philosopher, named *Eleutherion*, eminent for the deepest knowledge of nature, the most solid judgment, most approved virtue, and most ardent zeal for the cause of general liberty. The war had been supported for three years with infinite exertions of valor on both sides, with deliberate firmness on the part of the allies, and with unabated violence on the part of the *Athenians;* who had, nevertheless, dispatched commissioners to Rhodes, with intent to propose terms of accommodation; but the states, (perhaps too pertinaciously,) refused to hear any proposal whatever, without a previous recognition of their total independence by the magistrates and people of Athens. It was not long after this, that an Athenian, who had been a pupil of Isæus together with Demosthenes, and began to be known in his country as a pleader of causes, was led by some affair of his clients to the capital of Caria. He was a man, unauthorized, unemployed, unconnected; independent in his circumstances as much as in his principles: admitting no governor, under Providence, but the laws; and no laws but those which justice and virtue had dictated, which wisdom approved, which his country had freely enacted. He had been known at Athens to the sage Eleutherion; and, their acquaintance being renewed, he sometimes took occasion in their conversations to lament the increasing calamities of war, and to express his eager desire of making a general peace on such terms as *would produce the greatest good from the greatest evil;* for "this," said he, "would be a work not unworthy of the divine attributes, and if mortals could effect it, they would act like those beneficent beings, whom *Socrates* believed to be the constant friends and attendants of our species."

He added, " As to the united nations, I applaud, admire, and almost envy them ; I am even tempted to wish that I had been born a Chian or a Rhodian ; but let them be satisfied with the prize of virtue which they have already obtained. I will yield to none of your countrymen, my friend, in my love of *liberty ;* but she seems more lovely to my eyes, when she comes hand in hand with *peace.* From that union we can expect nothing but the highest happiness of which our nature is capable ; and it is an union, which nothing now obstructs but—a mere word.

" Let the confederates be contented with the *substance* of that *independence* which they have asserted, and the *word* will necessarily follow.

" Let them not hurt the natural, and, perhaps, not reprehensible, pride of *Athens,* nor demand any concession, that may sink in the eyes of *Greece,* a nation to whom they are and must be united in language, in blood, in manners, in interest, in principles. Glory is to a nation, what reputation is to an individual ; it is not an empty sound : but important and essential. It will be glorious in Athens to acknowledge her error in attempting to reduce the islands, but an acknowledgment of her inability to reduce them, (if she *be* unable,) will be too public a confession of weakness, and her rank among the states of Greece will instantly be lowered.

" But, whatever I might advise, if my advice had any chance of being taken, this *I know,* and positively pronounce, that while Athens is Athens, her proud but brave citizens will never *expressly* recognize the independence of the islands : their resources are no doubt exhaustible, but will not be exhausted in the lives of us and of our children. In this resolution all parties agree : I, who am of no party, dissent from them ; but what is a single voice in so vast a multitude ? Yet the independence of the United States was tacitly acknowledged by the very offer of terms, and it would result in silence from the natural operation of the treaty. An *express* acknowledgment of it *is* merely *formal* with respect to the allies ; but the prejudices of mankind have made it *substantial* with respect to Athens.

" Let this obstacle be removed : it is slight, but fatal ; and, whilst it lasts, thousands and ten thousands will perish. In war much will always depend upon blind chance, and a storm or sudden fall of snow *may* frustrate all your efforts for liberty ; but let commissioners from both sides meet, and the islanders, by not insisting on a *preliminary* recognition of independence, will *ultimately* establish it forever.

" But *independence* is not *disunion.* Chios, Cos, Lesbos, Rhodes, are *united,* but *independent* on each other : they are connected by a common tie, but have different forms and different constitutions. They are gems of various colors and various properties, strung in one bracelet. Such an *union* can only be made between states, which, how widely soever they differ in form, agree in one common property, *freedom.* Republics may form *alliances,* but not *a federal union,* with arbitrary monarchies. Were *Athens* governed by the *will* of a monarch, she could never be co-ordinate with the free islands; for such an union would not be dissimilarity but dissonance: but she is and shall be ruled by *laws* alone, that is, by the *will of the people,* which is the *only law.* Her Archon, even when he was *perpetual,* had no essential properties of monarchy. The constitution of Athens, if we must define it, was then *a republic with a perpetual administrator of its laws.* Between *Athens,* therefore, and the freest states in the world, an *union* may naturally be formed.

" There is a *natural* union between her and the islands, which the. gods have made, and which the powers of hell cannot dissolve. Men, speaking the same idiom, educated in the same manner, perhaps, in the same place; professing the same principles; sprung from the same ancestors, in no very remote degree; and related to each other in a thousand modes of consanguinity, affinity, and friendship, such men, (whatever they may say through a temporary resentment,) can never in their hearts consider one another as *aliens.*

" Let them meet then with fraternal and pacific dispositions, and let this be the *general* ground-work and plan of the treaty.

· 1. " The *Carians* shall be included in the pacification, and have such advantages as will induce them to consent to the treaty rather than continue a hazardous war.

2. " The archon, senate, and magistrates of Athens shall make a complete *recognition of rights* of all the Athenian citizens of all orders whatever, and all former laws for that purpose shall be combined in one. There shall not be one *slave* in Attica.

NOTE. " [By making this a *preliminary,* the islanders will show their affection for the people of Athens; their friendship will be cemented and fixed on a solid basis; and *the greatest good will be extracted,* as I at first proposed, *from the greatest evil.*]

3. " There shall be a perfect *co-ordination* between Athens and the thirteen united islands, they considering her not as a *parent,* whom they must *obey,* but as an elder *sister,* whom they cannot help *loving,* and to whom they shall give *pre-eminence of honor and co-equality of power.*

4. " The new constitutions of the confederate islands shall remain.

5. " On every occasion requiring *acts* for the *general* good, there shall be an assembly of deputies from the senate of Athens and the congress of the islands, who shall fairly adjust the whole business, and settle the ratio of the contributions on both sides. This committee shall consist of fifty islanders and fifty Athenians, or of a smaller number chosen by them.

6. " If it be thought necessary and found convenient, a proportionable number of Athenian citizens shall have seats, and power of debating and voting on questions of *common* concern, in the great assembly

of the islands, and a proportionable number of islanders shall sit with the like power in the assembly at Athens.

NOTE. "[This *reciprocal representation* will cement the union.]

7. "There shall be no obligation to make war but for the *common* interest.

8. "Commerce shall flow in a free course, for the *general* advantage of the united powers.

9. "An universal unlimited *amnesty* shall be proclaimed in every part of Greece and Asia.

"This," said the *Athenian*, "is the rough sketch of a treaty founded on virtue and liberty. The idea of it still fills and expands my soul; and *if* it cannot be realized, I shall not think it less glorious, but shall only grieve more and more at the perverseness of mankind. May the eternal Being, whom the wise and the virtuous adore, and whose attribute it is to convert into good, that evil which his unsearchable wisdom permits, inspire all ranks of men to promote either this or a similar plan! If this be impracticable, O miserable human nature! But I am fully confident that, if * * * more at large * * happiness of all."

* * * * * *

No more is extant of this interesting piece, upon which the commentary of the sage Polybius would have been particularly valuable in these times.

NO. 13.

Letter of Barbe de Marbois, charge d'affairs in America to count de Vergennes, which was intercepted and placed in the hands of the American negociators at Paris, in September, 1782.

Philadelphia, March 13, 1782.

Sir,—South Carolina again enjoys the benefit of a legislative body, after having been deprived of it for two years; it was summoned together towards the latter end of last January, at Jacksonburg, only ten leagues distant from Charleston; where deliberations are carried on with as much tranquility as if the state was in profound peace. Mr. Rutledge, who was the governor, opened the meeting with a speech greatly applauded, wherein he represents in their full extent, the important services rendered by the king to the United States, expressing their just acknowledgment for the same. This sentiment prevails much, sir; the different states are eager to declare it, in their public acts, and the principal members of government, and the writers employed by them, would forfeit their popularity were they to admit any equivocal remarks respecting the alliance. General Greene affirms that in no one state is attachment to independence carried to a higher pitch; but that this affection is yet exceeded by the hatred borne to England. The assembly of Carolina is going to make levies of men, and has imposed pretty large sums; as there is but little money in the country, the taxes will be gathered in indigo, and what deficiency may then be found, will be supplied by the sale of lands of such Carolinians as joined the enemy while they were in possession of the country. South Carolina was the only state that had not confiscated the property of the disaffected. The step just taken puts her on a footing with the other states in the union. The assembly of this state has passed a resolution, in consequence of which a purchase of land is to be made of the value of two hundred and forty thousand *livres tournois*, which Carolina makes a present to general Greene as the saviour of that province.

Mr. Matthews, a delegate from congress, lately arrived in Carolina, has, it is said, been chosen governor in the room of Mr. Rutledge; he has communicated to persons of the most influence in his state, the ultimatum of the month of * * last, who approved of the clauses in general, and particularly that one which leaves the king master of the terms of the treaty of peace or truce, excepting independence, and treaties of alliance. A delegate from South Carolina told me, that this ultimatum was equally well known by persons of note in this state, and this had given entire satisfaction there; it is the same with regard to several other states; and I believe I may assure you, upon the testimony of several delegates, that this measure is approved by a great majority; but Mr. Samuel Adams is using all his endeavors to raise in the state of Massachusetts a strong opposition to peace, if the eastern states are not thereby admitted to the fisheries, and particularly to that of Newfoundland. Samuel Adams delights in trouble and difficulty, and prides himself on forming an opposition against the government whereof he is himself the president. His aim and intentions are to render the minority of consequence, and at this very moment he is attacking the constitution of Massachusetts, although it is in a great measure his own work; but he had disliked it since the people had shown their uniform attachment to it.

It may be expected that with this disposition, no measure can meet the approval of Mr. Samuel Adams, and if the United States should agree relative to the fisheries, and be certain of partaking therein, all his manoeuvres and intrigues would be directed towards the conquest of Canada and Nova Scotia; but he could not have used a fitter engine than the fisheries, for stirring up the passions of the eastern people. By renewing this question, which had lain dormant during his two years absence from Boston, he has raised the expectation of the people of Massachusetts to an extraordinary pitch. The public prints hold forth the importance of the fisheries; the reigning toast in the east is, *may the United States ever maintain their rights to the fisheries.* It has been often repeated in the deliberations of the general court; *no truce without fisheries.* However clear this principle may be in this matter, it would be needless and even dangerous to attempt informing the people through the public papers, but it appears to me possible to use means for preventing the consequences of success to Mr. S. Adams and his party; and I take the liberty of submitting these to your discernment and indulgence ; one of those means would be for the king to cause it to be intimated to congress or to the ministers, " his surprise that the Newfoundland fisheries have been included in the additional instructions ; that the United States set forth therein pretensions *without paying regard to the king's rights,* and without considering the impossibility they are under of making conquests, and keeping what belongs to Great Britain."

His majesty might at the same time cause a promise to be given to congress, " of his assistance for procuring admission to the other fisheries, and declaring however that he would not be answerable for the success, and that he is bound to nothing as the treaty makes no mention of that article." This declaration being made before the peace, the hopes of the people could not be supported, nor could it one day be said, that we left them in the dark on this point. It were even to be wished that this declaration should be made whilst New York, Charleston, and Penobscot are in the enemy's hands ; our allies will be less tractable than ever upon these points whenever they recover these important posts. There are some judicious persons to whom one may speak of giving up the fisheries, and the*   of the west, for the sake of peace. But there are enthusiasts who fly out at this idea, and their numbers cannot fail increasing when, after the English are expelled from this continent, the burthen of the war will scarce be felt. It is already observable that the advocates for peace are those who lived in the country. The inhabitants of towns whom commerce enriches, mechanics who receive there a higher pay than before war, and five or six times more than in Europe, do not wish for it ; but it is a happy circumstance that this division be nearly equal in the congress and among the states, since our influence can incline the beam either for peace or war, which ever way we choose. Another means of preserving to France so important a branch of her commerce and navigation, is that proposed to you, sir, by M   viz. the conquest of cape Breton ; it seems to me, as it does to that minister, the only sure means of containing within bounds, when peace is made, those swarms of smugglers who, without regard to treaties, will turn all their activity, daring spirit, and means towards the fisheries, whose undertakings congress will not, perhaps, have the power or the will to suppress. If it be apprehended, that the peace which is to put an end to the present war, will prove disagreeable to any of the United States, there appears to me a certain method of guarding against the effects of this discontent, of preventing the declaration of some states, and other resources which turbulent minds might employ for availing themselves of the present juncture. This would be for his majesty to cause a memorial to be delivered to congress, wherein should be stated the use made by his ministers of the powers entrusted to them by that assembly ; and the impediments which may have stood in the way of a fuller satisfaction on every point. This step

* Suppose Lands.

would certainly be pleasing to congress; and should it become necessary to inform the people of this memorial, it could easily be done; they would be flattered by it, and it might probably beget the voice and concurrence of the public. I submit these thoughts to you early, and although peace appears yet to be distant, sir, by reasons of delays and difficulties attending the communication, that period will be a crisis when the partizans of France and England will openly appear, and when that power will employ every means to diminish our influence, and re-establish her own; it is true, the independent party will always stand in great want of our support, that the fears and jealousies which a remembrance of the former government will always produce, must operate as the safeguard to our alliance, and as a security for the attachment of the Americans to us. But it is best to be prepared for any discontents, although it should be but temporary. It is remarked by some, that as England has other fisheries besides Newfoundland, she may perhaps endeavor that the Americans should partake in that of the Great Bank, in order to conciliate their affection, or procure them some compensation, or create a subject of jealousy between them and us; but it does not seem likely that she will act so contrary to their true interest, and were she to do so, it will be for the better to have declared at an early period to the Americans, that their pretension is not founded, *and that his majesty does not mean to support it.*

I here inclose, sir, translations of the speech of the governor of South Carolina to the assembly, and of their answer. These interesting productions convey in a forcible manner the sentiments of the inhabitants of that state, and appeared to me worth communicating to you. I am, &c.

(Signed)   BARBE DE MARBOIS:

NO. 14, omitted.

NO. 15.

Letter and representation of Congress to the King of France, November 22d, 1780.

Great, Faithful and Beloved Friend and Ally,—Persuaded of your majesty's friendship, and of your earnest desire to prosecute the war with glory and advantage to the alliance, we ought not to conceal from your majesty the embarrassments which have attended our national affairs, and rendered the last campaign unsuccessful.

A naval superiority in the American seas having enabled the enemy, in the midst of last winter, to divide their army, and extend the war in the southern states, Charleston was subdued before a sufficient force could be assembled for its relief.

With unabated ardor, and at a vast expense, we prepared for the succeeding campaign; a campaign from which, in a dependence on the co-operation of the squadron and troops generously destined by your majesty for our assistance, we had formed the highest expectations. Again the enemy frustrated our measures. Your majesty's succors were confined within the harbor of Newport, while the main body of the British army took refuge in their fortresses, and under protection of their marine, declining to hazard a battle in the open field; and, regardless of their rank among civilized nations, they descended to wage a predatory war. Britons and savages united in sudden irruptions on our northern and western frontiers, and marked their progress with blood and desolation.

The acquisition of Charleston, with the advantages gained in Georgia, and the defeat of a small army composed chiefly of militia, which had been hastily collected to check their operations, encouraged the British commander in that quarter to penetrate through South Carolina into the interior parts of North Carolina. And the ordinary calamities of war were imbittered by implacable vengeance. They did not, however, long enjoy their triumph. Instead of being depressed, impending danger served only to rouse our citizens to correspondent exertions; and by a series of gallant and successful enterprises they compelled the enemy to retreat with precipitation and disgrace.

They seem however resolved, by all possible efforts, not only to retain their posts in Georgia and South Carolina, but to renew their attempts on North Carolina. To divert the reinforcements destined for those states, they are now executing an enterprise against the seacoast of Virginia; and from their preparations at New York, and intelligence from Europe, it is manifest that the four southern states will now become a principal object of their hostilities.

It is the voice of the people, and the resolution of congress, to prosecute the war with redoubled vigor, and to draw into the field a permanent and well appointed army of thirty five thousand regular troops. By this decisive effort, we trust that we shall be able, under the divine blessing, so effectually to co-operate with your majesty's marine and land forces, as to expel the common enemy from our country, and render the great object of the alliance perpetual. But to accomplish an enterprise of such magnitude, and so interesting to both nations, whatever may be our spirit and our exertions, we know that our internal resources must prove incompetent. The sincerity of this declaration will be manifest from a short review of our circumstances.

Unpracticed in military arts, and unprepared with the means of defense, we were suddenly invaded by a formidable and vindictive nation. We supported the unequal conflict for years with very little foreign aid but what was derived from your majesty's generous friendship. Exertions uncommon, even among the most wealthy and best establishments, necessarily exhausted our finances, plunged us into debt, and anticipated our taxes; while the depredations of an active enemy by sea and land made deep impressions on our commerce and our productions. Thus encompassed with difficulties, in our representation to your majesty of June 15, 1779, we disclosed our wants, and requested your majesty to furnish us with clothing, arms and ammunition for the last campaign, on the credit of the United States. We entertain a lively sense of your majesty's friendly disposition in enabling our ministers to procure a part of those supplies, of which, through unfortunate events, a very small proportion hath arrived. The sufferings of our army, from this disappointment, have been so severe that we must rely on your majesty's attention to our welfare for effectual assistance. The articles of the estimate transmitted to our minister are essential to our army; and we flatter ourselves that, through your majesty's interposition, they will be supplied.

At a time when we feel ourselves strongly impressed by the weight of past obligations, it is with the utmost reluctance that we yield to the emergency of our affairs in requesting additional favors. An unreserved confidence in your majesty, and a well-grounded assurance that we ask no more than is necessary to enable us effectually to co-operate with your majesty in terminating the war with glory and success, must be our justification.

It is well known that when the king of Great Britain found himself unable to subdue the populous states of North America by force, or to seduce them by art to relinquish the alliance with your majesty, he resolved to protract the war, in expectation that the loss of our commerce, and the derangement of our finances, must eventually compel us to submit to his domination. Apprised of the necessity of foreign aids of money to support us in a contest with a nation so rich and powerful, we have long since authorized our minister to borrow a sufficient sum in your majesty's dominions, and in Spain, and in Holland, on the credit of these United States.

We now view the prospect of a disappointment with the deeper concern, as the late misfortunes in the southern states, and the ravages of the northern and western frontiers have, in a very considerable degree, impaired our internal resources. From a full investigation of our circumstances it is manifest, that in aid of our utmost exertions a foreign loan of specie, at least to the amount of twenty five millions of livres, will be indispensably necessary for a vigorous prosecution of the war. On an occasion in which the independence of these United States and your majesty's glory are so intimately connected, we are constrained to request your majesty effectually to support the applications of our ministers for that loan. So essential is it to the common cause, that we shall without it be pressed with wants and distresses, which may render all our efforts languid, precarious, and indecisive. Whether it shall please your majesty to stipulate for this necessary aid as our security, or to advance it from your royal coffers, we do hereby solemnly pledge the faith of these United States to indemnify, or reimburse your majesty, according to the nature of the case, both for principal and interest, in such manner as shall be agreed upon with our minister at your majesty's court.

We beseech the Supreme Disposer of events to keep your majesty in his holy protection, and long to continue to France the blessings arising from the administration of a prince who nobly asserts the rights of mankind.

Done at Philadelphia, the 22d day of November, in the year of our Lord, 1780, by the congress of the United States of North American, and in the fifth year of our independence.

Your faithful friends and allies.

Signed,   SAM'L HUNTINGTON, *President.*

Attest.   CHARLES THOMSON, *Secretary.*

NO. 16, omitted.

NO. 17.

In the formation of treaties of amity and commerce with the different nations of Europe, the ministers plenipotentiary of the United States, in May, 1784, were instructed to procure stipulations to the following effect.

1. That each party shall have a right to carry their own produce, manufactures, and merchandise, in their own bottoms to the ports of the other; and thence to take the produce and merchandise of the other, paying, in both cases, such duties only as are paid by the most favored nation, freely where it is freely granted to such nation, or paying the compensation, where such nation does the same.

2. That with the nations holding territorial possessions in America, a direct and similar intercourse be admitted between the United States and such possessions; or if this cannot be obtained, then a direct and a similar intercourse between the United States and certain free ports within such possessions; that if this neither can be obtained, permission be stipulated to bring from such possessions, in their own bottoms, the produce and merchandize thereof to these states directly; and for these states to carry in their own bottoms their produce and merchandise to such possessions directly.

3. That these United States be considered in all such treaties, and in every case arising under them, as one nation upon the principles of the federal constitution.

4. That it be proposed, though not indispensably required, that if war should hereafter arise between the two contracting parties, the merchants of either country, then residing in the other, shall be allowed to remain nine months to collect their debts and settle their affairs, and may depart freely, carrying off all their effects without molestation or hindrance; and all fishermen, all cultivators of the earth, and all artisans or manufacturers, unarmed and inhabiting unfortified towns, villages or places, who labor for the common subsistence and benefit of mankind, and peaceably following their respective employments, shall be allowed to continue the same, and shall not be molested by the armed force of the enemy, in whose power, by the events of war, they may happen to fall; but if any thing is necessary to be

taken from them for the use of such armed force, the same shall be paid for at a reasonable price; and all merchants and traders exchanging the products of different places, and thereby rendering the necessaries, conveniences, and comforts of human life more easy to obtain and more general, shall be allowed to pass free and unmolested; and neither of the contracting powers shall grant or issue any commission to any private armed vessels empowering them to take or destroy such trading ships, or interrupt such commerce.

5. And in case either of the contracting parties shall happen to be engaged in war with any other nation, it be further agreed, in order to prevent all the difficulties and misunderstandings that usually arise respecting the merchandise heretofore called contraband, such as arms, ammunition, and military stores of all kinds, that no such articles carrying by the ships or subjects of one of the parties to the enemies of the other, shall on any account, be deemed contraband, so as to induce confiscation and a loss of property to individuals. Nevertheless, it shall be lawful to stop such ships, and detain them for such length of time as the captors may think necessary to prevent the inconvenience or damage that might ensue from their proceeding on their voyage, paying, however, a reasonable compensation for the loss such arrest shall occasion to the proprietors; and it shall further be allowed to use, in the service of the captors, the whole or any part of the military stores so detained, paying the owners the full value of the same to be ascertained by the current price at the place of its destination. But if the other contracting party will not consent to discontinue the confiscation of contraband goods, then that it be stipulated, that if the master of the vessel stopped will deliver out the goods charged to be contraband, he shall be admitted to do it, and the vessel shall not in that case be carried into any port, but shall be allowed to proceed on her voyage.

6. That in the same case, where either of the contracting parties shall happen to be engaged in war with any other power, all goods not contraband belonging to the subjects of that other power, and shipped in the bottoms of the party hereto, who is not engaged in the war, shall be entirely free. And that to ascertain what shall constitute the blockade of any place or port, it shall be understood to be in such predicament, when the assailing power shall have taken such a station as to expose to imminent danger any ship or ships that would attempt to sail in or out of the said port; and that no vessel of the party who is not engaged in the said war shall be stopped without a material and well grounded cause; and in such cases justice shall be done, and an indemnification given, without loss of time to the persons aggrieved and thus stopped without sufficient cause.

7. That no rights be stipulated for aliens to hold real property within these states, this being utterly inadmissible by their several laws and policy; but where on the death of any person holding real estate within the territories of one of the contracting parties, such real estate would by their laws descend on a subject or citizen of the

other, were he not disqualified by alienage, there he shall be allowed a reasonable time to dispose of the same, and withdraw the proceeds without molestation.

8. That such treaties be made for a term not exceeding ten years from the exchange of ratifications.

9. That these instructions be considered as supplementary to those of October 29th, 1783; and not as revoking, except where they contradict them. That where, in treaty with a particular nation, they can procure particular advantages, to the specification of which we have been unable to descend, our object in these instructions having been to form outlines only, and general principles of treaty with many nations, it is our expectation they will procure them, though not pointed out in these instructions; and where they may be able to form treaties on principles which in their judgment will be more beneficial to the United States than those herein directed to be made their basis, they are permitted to adopt such principles. That as to the duration of the treaties, though we have proposed to restrain them to the term of ten years, yet they are at liberty to extend the same as far as fifteen years with any nation which may pertinaciously insist thereon. And that it will be agreeable to us to have supplementary treaties with France, the United Netherlands, and Sweden, which may bring the treaties we have entered into with them as nearly as may be to the principles of those now directed; but that this be not pressed, if the proposal should be found disagreeable.

Resolved, That treaties of amity, or of amity and commerce, be entered into with Morocco, and the regencies of Algiers, Tunis, and Tripoli, to continue for the same term of ten years, or for a term as much longer as can be procured.

That our ministers to be commissioned for treating with foreign nations, make known to the emperor of Morocco the great satisfaction which congress feel from the amicable disposition he has shown towards these states, and his readiness to enter into alliance with them. That the occupations of the war and distance of our situation have prevented our meeting his friendship so early as we wished. But the powers are now delegated to them for entering into treaty with him, in the execution of which they are ready to proceed. And that as to the expenses of his minister, they do therein what is for the honor and interest of the United States.

Resolved, That a commission be issued to Mr. J. Adams, Mr. B. Franklin, and Mr. T. Jefferson, giving powers to them, or the greater part of them, to make and receive propositions for such treaties of amity and commerce, and to negotiate and sign the same, transmitting them to congress for their final ratification; and that such commission be in force for a term not exceeding two years.

NO. 18, omitted.

NO. 19.

*ist of the members who attended the General Convention, which form-
ed the new Constitution, in 1787.*

New Hampshire.
JOHN LANGDON,
NICHOLAS GILMAN.
Massachusetts.
ELBRIDGE GERRY,
NATHANIEL GORHAM,
RUFUS KING,
CALEB STRONG.
Connecticut.
WM. SAMUEL JOHNSON,
ROGER SHERMAN,
OLIVER ELLSWORTH.
New York.
ROBERT YATES,
ALEXANDER HAMILTON,
JOHN LANSING, JR.
New Jersey.
WM. LIVINGSTON,
DAVID BREARLEY,
WM. C. HOUSTON,
WM. PATTERSON,
JONATHAN DAYTON.
Pennsylvania.
BENJAMIN FRANKLIN,
THOMAS MIFFLIN,
ROBERT MORRIS,
GEORGE CLYMER,
THOMAS FITZSIMONS,
JARED INGERSOLL,
JAMES WILSON,
GOVERNEUR MORRIS.
Delaware.
GEORGE READ,
GUNNING BEDFORD, JR.

JOHN DICKINSON,
RICHARD BASSET,
JACOB BROOM.
Maryland.
JAMES MCHENRY,
DANIEL OF ST. THOMAS JENIFER,
DANIEL CARROLL,
JOHN FRANCIS MERCER,
LUTHER MARTIN.
Virginia.
GEORGE WASHINGTON,
EDMUND RANDOLPH,
JOHN BLAIR,
JAMES MADISON, JR.
GEORGE MASON,
GEORGE WYTHE,
JAMES MCCLURG.
North Carolina.
ALEXANDER MARTIN,
WM. R. DAVIE,
WM. BLOUNT,
RICHARD D. SPAIGHT.
HUGH WILLIAMSON.
South Carolina.
JOHN RUTLEDGE,
CHARLES C. PINCKNEY,
CHARLES PINCKNEY,
PIERCE BUTLER.
Georgia.
WM. FEW,
ABRAHAM BALDWIN,
WM. PIERCE,
WM. HOUSTON.

NO. 20.

Abstract of the accounts of the respective States, for expenses incurred during the Revolutionary War, as allowed by the Commissioners who finally settled said accounts.

STATES.	Sums allowed for expenditures.	Sums charged for advances by U. States, including the assumption of State debts.	Expenditures excluding all advances	Balances found due from the U. States.	Balances found due to the U. States.
New Hampshire,	$4,278,015 02	$1,082,954 02	$3,195,061	$ 75,055	- -
Massachusetts,	17,964,613 03	6,258,880 03	11,705,733	1,248,801	- -
Rhode Island,	3,782,974 46	1,977,608 46	1,805,366	299,611	- -
Connecticut,	9,285,737 92	3,436,244 92	5,829,493	619,121	- -
New York,	7,179,982 78	1,960,031 78	5,219,951	- -	2,074,846
New Jersey,	5,342,770 52	1,343,321 52	3,999,449	49,030	- -
Pennsylvania,	14,137,076 22	4,690,686 22	9,446,390	- -	76,709
Delaware,	839,319 98	229,898 98	609,421	- -	612,428
Maryland,	7,568,145 38	1,592,631 38	5,975,514	- -	151,640
Virginia,	19,085,981 51	3,803,416 51	15,282,865	- -	100,879
North Carolina,	10,427,586 13	3,151,358 13	7,276,228	- -	501,082
South Carolina,	11,523,299 29	5,780,264 29	5,743,035	1,205,978	- -
Georgia,	2,993,800 86	1,415,328 86	1,578,472	19,988	- -

NO. 21.

Questions proposed by President Washington, for the consideration of the members of the Cabinet, in April, 1793, with the Letter which enclosed them.

Philadelphia, April 18th, 1793.

Sir,—The posture of affairs in Europe, particularly between France and Great Britain, places the United States in a delicate situation, and requires much consideration of the measures which will be proper for them to observe in the war between those powers. With a view to forming a general plan of conduct for the executive, I have stated and enclosed sundry questions to be considered preparatory to a meeting at my house to-morrow, where I shall expect to see you at nine o'clock, and to receive the result of your reflections thereon.

Quest. 1. Shall a proclamation issue for the purpose of preventing interferences of the citizens of the United States in the war between France and Great Britain, &c.? Shall it contain a declaration of neutrality or not? What shall it contain?

2. Shall a minister from the republic of France be received?

3. If received, shall it be absolutely or with qualifications'; and if with qualifications, of what kind?

4. Are the United States obliged by good faith to consider the treaties heretofore made with France as applying to the present situation of the parties? may they either renounce them or hold them suspended until the government of France shall be established?

5. If they have the right, is it expedient to do either ? and which ?

6. If they have an option, would it be a breach of neutrality to consider the treaties in operation ?

7. If the treaties are to be considered as now in operation, is the guaranty in the treaty of alliance applicable to a defensive war only, or to a war, either offensive or defensive ?

8. Does the war in which France is engaged appear to be offensive or defensive on her part ? or of a mixed and equivocal character ?

9. If of a mixed and equivocal character, does the guaranty in any event apply to such a war ?

10. What is the effect of a guaranty, such as that to be found in the treaty of alliance between the United States and France ?

11. Does any article in either of the treaties prevent ships of war, other than privateers, of the powers opposed to France, from coming into the ports of the United States to act as convoys to their own merchantmen ? or does it lay any other restraints upon them more than would apply to the ships of war of France ?

12. Should the future regent of France send a minister to the United States, ought he to be received ?

13. Is it necessary or advisable to call together the two houses of congress with a view to the present posture of European affairs ? if it is, what should be the particular objects of such call ?

FINIS.